Union Power and New York

Union Power and New York

VICTOR GOTBAUM
and
DISTRICT COUNCIL 37

by
Jewel Bellush
and
Bernard Bellush

PRAEGER

PRAEGER SPECIAL STUDIES • PRAEGER SCIENTIFIC

New York • Philadelphia • Eastbourne, UK
Toronto • Hong Kong • Tokyo • Sydney

Library of Congress Cataloging in Publication Data
Bellush, Jewel, 1924–
   Union power and New York.
   Includes index.
   1. AFSCME. District Council 37 (New York, N.Y.)—
History. 2. Gotbaum, Victor. 3. Wurf, Jerry, 1919–
I. Bellush, Bernard, 1917-   . II. Title.
HD8005.2U53N43 1984 331.88′1135′000097471 84-15926
ISBN 0-03-000122-6 (alk. paper)
ISBN 0-03-001322-4 (pbk. : alk. paper)

Photo Credits: Geri Ruth; Bill Schleicher; George Cohen; Michael Rosenbaum; Alan Howard; June Ringel; Walter Balcerak

Cover Photo: Walter Balcerak

Published in 1984 by Praeger Publishers
CBS Educational and Professional Publishing,
a Division of CBS Inc.
521 Fifth Avenue, New York, NY 10175 USA

© 1984 by Praeger Publishers

We dedicate this book to those who built DC 37—
they know who they are.

Foreword *by Seymour Martin Lipset*

The transformation of the U.S. labor force from industrial to service sector employment has been particularly dramatic since World War II. Employment has grown more swiftly in the public service arena than in any major private industry. Compared to the national scene, state and local governments mushroomed at a phenomenal pace between 1947 and 1978, adding some 10 million jobs. Despite earlier pessimistic projections that the public sector was unorganizable, unionism took hold during the 1960s and 1970s. The organizing of public employees gave a staid, declining union movement some much needed resiliency and a new source for militant leadership and innovative programs. Perhaps no regional union better exemplifies the possibilities and hopes for a revitalized labor movement than New York's District Council 37 of the American Federation of State, County and Municipal Employees.

This Council has been a pioneer in exploring new ways of servicing its members—providing career ladders for tens of thousands in traditionally trapped, dead-end jobs and offering a wide range of direct health, educational, and legal benefits. The serious inadequacies of the U.S. welfare state, and various gaps in benefits and social services, have been largely filled by the experimental programs initiated by DC 37.

Under the leadership of Jerry Wurf, Victor Gotbaum, and Lillian Roberts, DC 37 gradually built up its influence through imaginative organizing, skillful collective bargaining, and strategic legislative lobbying in Albany and at City Hall. The fiscal crisis of the mid-1970s served as a litmus test of the union's ability to survive as a viable and influential movement. In cooperation with other municipal labor organizations, Gotbaum and the Council helped fashion a collaborative endeavor with government and financial community representatives that helped save New York City from bankruptcy. While many major unions recently experienced serious setbacks in membership and influence, and were forced to accept drastic cutbacks, DC 37 held firm, maintained its position as an important decision-maker in city affairs, and preserved collective bargaining in municipal planning.

The story of why and how all this was possible is unfolded in a fresh and intriguing manner by an unusual writing duo of Jewel and Bernard Bellush—one, a scholar-practitioner of urban politics and administration, the other a veteran historian of the New Deal and progressive eras. For almost a half century, both have been close observer-participants of the labor and progressive scenes in the nation. In this book, they build up their arguments carefully, tell the story in a straightforward way, and make their points concisely.

In his study of America, de Tocqueville concluded that for democracy to flourish, society required a pluralistic political system. He feared that bureaucratization, nationalism, and the increasing concentration of power in the leviathan-state threatened freedom and individualism. He believed that two institutions that might combat these tendencies were local self-government and voluntary associations. In explaining his views, I have written that, "By disseminating ideas and creating consensus among their members, [associations] become the basis for conflict between one organization and another. And, in the process of doing so, they also limit the central power, create new and autonomous centers of power to compete with it, and help to train potential opposition leaders in political skills." This book amply demonstrates the value of the active organizational life de Tocqueville suggested as necessary to a democratic polity. This union builds consensus among its members, instills in them pride and dignity, educates and trains them for leadership and political action, and, as a result, competes rather effectively with most other constellations of power in the city and state.

To those concerned with the serious decline in voter turn-out at elections and the lack of civic activity among large numbers of the nation's citizenry, the extensive participation program provided its 100,000 members by D 37 serves as a challenging case study of innovative ways to stimulate wider involvement. This union reveals a level of participation significantly higher than that found in most other unions and civic organizations. Many of the strategies described by the authors provide suggestive ideas for those anxious to invigorate America's democratic political institutions.

Over the years, inter-group ethnic tensions have mounted considerably in New York City and elsewhere in the nation. The controversies over school integration, affirmative action, job quotas, and criteria for admission to colleges and professional schools have exposed the delicate character of, and sharp cleavages among, eth-

nic and racial groups. The multi-cultural and multi-ethnic character of DC 37's membership reflects the polyglot makeup of many
of the nation's urban centers. Through the skilled leadership and
commitment of Victor Gotbaum, Lillian Roberts, and the Council
staff, a large portion of New York City's public workers have been
integrated into a cohesive and unified federation that has largely
overcome differences in background and outlook. They have been
unusually successful in urging members to work together, directing their energies toward common economic, social, and political
goals.

DC 37's leaders have been responsible for minimizing the pressures toward bureaucratic inactivity or conservatism by commitment to an activist political ideology that views the labor movement as an instrument for progressive purpose and social change.
Much of the special character of the union may be credited to Victor Gotbaum. While the Bellushes do not suggest a great
man/woman theory of leadership, their work underscores the vital role of leadership as key to the achievements of District Council
37 during its first forty years.

Seymour Martin Lipset
Stanford University
August 1984

Preface

For almost half of its history, we have been interested observers of DC 37, attentive to the union's emergence as a progressive and caring force for social justice and human dignity. As an earlier political colleague of Jerry Wurf, and then as friends of the Gotbaum family, we have shared the joys and sorrows, the problems and crises of this organization. For a short period, one of the authors served on the staff of its Education Department. Concerned that his friend was about to retire from the City College's history department in 1978, Victor Gotbaum, supported by his close associates, suggested that Bernard Bellush write the story of DC 37, with complete freedom. For some 18 months I received a stipend, but with a temporary onset of fiscal difficulties for the union, I decided to pursue the project without further financial assistance from the Council, and was joined by my wife, a political scientist at Hunter College.

This is not an authorized work. No one at DC 37 read the manuscript before it was printed, nor has Gotbaum permitted anyone, including himself, to suggest or direct how this study be conducted. We alone are responsible for the analyses presented and the views expressed. We hope that the readers, but particularly the members and staff of the Council, will find this an objective, carefully researched portrayal of the life and vitality of one of the outstanding unions on the American scene. We will always remember the trust, encouragement, openness, and readiness of those involved to discuss with us events, personalities, and key union decisions. We hope that each local will undertake its own history, supplementing the work of this endeavor.

Earlier versions of the chapter on the fiscal crisis were presented at meetings of the American Political Science Association, the Northeastern Political Science Association, and the American Studies Association in Israel. Carol O'Cleireacain, the union's economist, reviewed parts of the chapter for possible errors in data alone and bears no responsibility for its contents.

Jewel Bellush
Bernard Bellush

Acknowledgments

MERCI

In writing this biography of a union and its leaders, a key source of information has naturally been those who participated in its growth and development, many of whom continue to play important roles. We are deeply grateful to each of them, for they have given us invaluable insights and freely shared their personal experiences, often in lengthy, tape-recorded interviews. Over the years, the following staff members of DC 37 have been particularly helpful and encouraging: Saki Miyashiro, one of the most unwavering union advocates we know; Bernie Stephens and Walter Balcerak, keen observers and reporter-editors for *Public Employee Press* who shared a vital sense of history; Richard Niles, artist–graphic expert extraordinaire, for his creative input; Evelyn Seinfeld, librarian-researcher, who served as sleuth for documents, reports, and all sorts of information; Margaret Pierce, coordinator of an unending interview schedule; Carol Thomas, mastermind and the human element in the intricacies of the word processor machine; Carmen Hayes, who proved that the word processor is more alive than a machine; John Boer, a self-made historian who brought clarity and understanding to the early years of the union; Shaurain Farber, a quiet storehouse of knowledge; Bill Schleicher, staff reporter who made available invaluable documents and insights relating to the welfare strike of 1965; Bart Cohen, activist and union negotiator, who always made time to share his grass-roots perspective of the union's development; James Carossella, typical of those unionists who were always warm, interested, and encouraging; Arthur Tibaldi, always cooperative and immediately responsive to every request for important data; and Victor Gotbaum, whose limitless confidence in us created the climate for open access to all sources.

We also thank Professor Murray Hausknecht, sociologist at Lehman College, a long-time friend who shared his insights in reviewing several of the chapters. At the University of Haifa in Israel, Michael Goodich, chair of the history department, and a former student, made available a quiet office overlooking the Galilee, while the secretarial staff did nobly in making sense of handwritten revisions of the manuscript. Colin Jones, director of

New York University Press, the first to read the manuscript, encouraged us at a critical stage. Michele Julian knows what an important part she plays in our family household, for our children, who press us on, and even for our little grandchildren, who distract us from our work. At Praeger a real team effort enabled smooth sailing and a sharpened product: Betsy Brown, Barbara Leffel, Rachel Burd, and David Stebbing.

Contents

List of Tables

List of Figures

Sources

Interviews: Scores of interviews with Council members, encompassing rank-and-file unionists, staff associates, local and Council leaders, as well as government figures, have been an invaluable source for a living history of DC 37.

Observation: Over the years, the openness of the leadership and staff have enabled us to have a "front row seat" at meetings of locals, the executive board, delegates council, and many of the conferences and activities in education, health, and political affairs.

Written Records: Internal reports, documents, correspondence, and memoranda were made available without reservation or restriction. In a nearby warehouse were found hundreds of unorganized, stacked cartons from a variety of Council departments which go back to the beginnings of the organization. The personal files of Victor Gotbaum and Lillian Roberts, and the records in each department, were also researched. The library of the Research and Negotiations Department, the service arm to the staff and membership, provided us with immediate access to national, state, and local materials pertaining to public service workers, economic trends, and other unions.

Conversations: We have spoken informally with scores of members, staff, and local leaders on buses to Albany for lobbying activity, en route to a demonstration in Washington, and in the hallways of union headquarters. These have been important sources of information and have provided much of the background for this study. These informal settings have also given us insight into the human dimensions of the Council, the problems as well as the critical concerns, and the energetic and progressive spirit of the union and its workers.

Abbreviations

AFDC	Aid to Families with Dependent Children
AFGE	American Federation of Government Employees
AFL	American Federation of Labor
AFSA	American Federation of School Administrators
AFSCME	American Federation of State, County and Municipal Employees
AVC	American Veterans Committee
AWPRA	Association of Workers in Public Relief Agencies
BASR	Bureau of Applied Survey Research (Columbia University)
BLS	Bureau of Labor Statistics
BSEIU	Building Service Employees International Union
CBO	Congressional Budget Office
CETA	Comprehensive Employment and Training Act
CIO	Committee for Industrial Organization (later Congress of Industrial Organizations)
CIR	Committee of Interns and Residents
COLA	Cost of living adjustment
COUR	Committee on Union Responsibility
CP-USA	Communist Party, USA
CSC	Civil Service Commission
CSEA	Civil Service Employees Association
CTLC	Central Trades and Labor Council (AFL)
DC 37	District Council 37
EFCB	Emergency Financial Control Board
GHI	Group Health Insurance
HCI	Hospital Care Investigators
HHC	Health and Hospitals Corporation
HIP	Health Insurance Plan
H/S	Health and Security Plan
HSE	High School Equivalency
IBT	International Brotherhood of Teamsters
IEB	International Executive Board (AFSCME)
ILA	International Longshoremen's Union
ILGWU	International Ladies Garment Workers Union
LPN	Licensed Practical Nurse
MAC	Municipal Assistance Corporation

MELS	Municipal Employees Legal Services (DC 37)
MLC	Municipal Labor Committee
MUFL	Municipal Union/Financial Leaders
MVO	Motor Vehicle Operators
NAACP	National Association for the Advancement of Colored People
NYCHA	New York City Housing Authority
NYCTA	New York City Transit Authority
OCB	Office of Collective Bargaining
OSHA	Occupational Safety and Health Acts
PAC	Political Action Committee
PBA	Police Benevolent Association
PEC	Public Employees Conference
PEOPLE	Public Employees Organized to Promote Legislative Equality
PEP	*Public Employee Press*
PERB	Public Employment Relations Board
PSU	Personal Services Unit (DC 37)
SCMWA	State, County and Municipal Workers of America
SIU	Seafarers International Union
SOS	Save Our Social Security
SP-USA	Socialist Party, USA
SSEU	Social Service Employees Union
SSI	Supplemental Security Income
TWU	Transport Workers Union
UAW	United Auto Workers
UDC	Urban Development Corporation
UFT	United Federation of Teachers
UPW	United Public Workers
USA	Uniformed Sanitationmen's Association
YCL	Young Communist League
YPSL	Young People's Socialist League

1
A Harassed, Coerced, and Dismissed Union

The United States has been, historically, a hostile setting for organized labor. The pages of union history, the decades of struggle for human dignity by working men and women, are filled with violence by the government and private industry. And even when labor finally won its Magna Carta from private industry during the New Deal era, public service workers were not included. Demeaned as servants, they were not afforded the right to organize. And when they did join together successfully, Federal and state laws did not require public management to recognize or bargain with them.

"There is no right to strike against the public safety by anybody, anywhere, anytime," warned Governor Calvin Coolidge of Massachusetts in 1919.[1] This became the rallying cry of those who fought, over the years, to keep the public sector free of unionizing efforts. Prior to 1960, only the state of Wisconsin protected the organizing and bargaining activities of public workers.

Traditional union leaders and labor observers had long considered the public sector unorganizable. The largely craft-dominated union movement proved inhospitable to public workers. At the same time, professionally oriented civil servants tended to be attracted to associations, rather than to trade union strategies and traditions. Even the Wisconsin State Employment Association, the key organization of public workers in that state, sought to achieve its goals through the merit system, the enactment and revision of civil service laws, and legislative lobbying. These associations originally rejected militant demonstrations, strikes, or collective bargaining

An anemic Local 420 begins an organizing drive among lowly paid and demeaned hospital workers shortly after Jerry Wurf took over control of a weak council in 1952. Wurf is adjacent to the curb with upturned collar.

between representatives of management and their members. One early organizer of public workers criticized the associational strategy of the American Federation of State, County, and Muncipal Employees (AFSCME), led by President Arnold Zander, as "hat-in-hand politics, petitions, lobbying and pleading."[2]

The years immediately following World War II found Zander and AFSCME (which he had helped to organize in Wisconsin in 1932) totally unprepared for the unrest among local public employees that swept the country. As the U. S. economy expanded to meet the desires of a consumer society that had been unable to satisfy its material needs during the war years, jobs in private industry became plentiful at wages far higher than those given public employees. This development intensified the feeling of second-class status among public workers and led to a series of strikes among city and local employees that spread across the country. This was a weapon Zander had sought consciously to avoid in the AFSCME constitution.

Public response was swift and legislative reaction repressive. Virginia's employees were forbidden to join a union that claimed the right to strike. New York's Condon–Wadlin Act of 1947 outlawed public employee strikes and set severe penalties for strikers, as did at least seven other states. In 1947, a Republican Congress, supported by many Democrats, passed the Taft–Hartley Act, which was an attempt to curtail many of the rights gained by trade unions during the New Deal. Within a short time some 45 states adopted legislation outlawing strikes by public sector workers.[3]

Despite these general setbacks to organized labor and the bias against public employees in particular, AFSCME managed to increase its membership to 100,000 by the time the American Federation of Labor (AFL) and the Congress for Industrial Organization (CIO) merged in 1955. Changes within as well as external to the organization played a role in this growth and eventually established a semblance of stability. About this time, Jerry Wurf entered the New York public service scene.

Following the merger of the AFL and the CIO, the latter's 30,000-member Government and Civic Employees Organizing Committee fused with AFSCME in 1956. Those locals and councils that began to rely increasingly on collective bargaining rather than paternalistic governments expanded their memberships significantly. By 1958, after 25 years at its helm and one year after he moved AFSCME headquarters to Washington, D.C., Zander seemed to be at the height of his power. But profound changes were taking place in big city locals and councils.

PLAYING THE POLITICAL MACHINE

Prior to the 1930s, the history of public employee organizations in New York City and other urban centers was, with some exceptions, insignificant. Some history textbooks still record the Boston police strike of 1919 as a memorable event in the political career of Calvin Coolidge, but not in the development of public service unions.

Operating in a hostile environment, especially with city administrations which concluded that recognition and bargaining would constitute an improper delegation of their sovereign authority, anemic public employee organizations in New York spent the first three decades of the twentieth century reaching accommodations with the city's dominant political machine, the Democratic party's Tammany Hall. Only in this manner could they survive, by securing incentives and cooperation with reference to appointments, promotions, wages, transfers, and "soft details." Although the Central Trades and Labor Council (CTLC) of the AFL remained closely allied to the Democratic party, through such powerful leaders as Martin Lacey of the Teamsters, new developments were reshaping the restricted confines of organized labor in New York City.

As part of the turbulent changes sweeping the nation during the New Deal, the drive to organize independent trade unions encompassed an increasing number of public service employees; New York City was no exception. In contrast to the Civil Service Forum and other earlier associations of civil servants, these new unions did not generally seek to ally themselves as closely with Tammany Hall in an endeavor to secure a base for influencing City Hall decisions on personnel, wages, and working conditions. After 1935 the fledgling unions affiliated themselves, instead, with either the AFL or CIO and sought to establish a formal mechanism of collective bargaining with which to strengthen their role and effectiveness as representatives of public employees. Competing for the tens of thousands of unorganized city employees were AFSCME; the State, County, and Municipal Workers of America of the CIO; the Transport Workers Union (TWU); the Building Service Employees International Union (BSEIU); and the International Brotherhood of Teamsters (IBT).

THE COMMUNIST INFLUENCE

The initial attempt by AFSCME to secure a base in New York City occurred in 1936, but through no serious efforts on the part of its national leadership. It was largely the result of decisions external to the organization. By the early 1930s, social worker Abram Flaxer and like-minded colleagues began organizing fellow employees in New York City's Emergency Relief Bureau, initially set up in the Department of Public Welfare by the Walker administration in 1931. At its height, the bureau had some 10,000 staff members. While a student at City College, Flaxer had come under the influence of an English tutor, Morris Schappes, and other Marxists on and off the campus. By the time he graduated from college, where he participated in a Marxist study group, he was an active sympathizer of the Communist Party. A brilliant and committed organizer who had been deeply moved by the destructive impact of the Great Depression on relatives, friends, and the community, Flaxer, along with Frank Herbst, Jack Bigel, Ewart Guinier, and others, set about organizing fellow social workers in the Bronx and elsewhere in the city into what became known as the Association of Workers in Public Relief Agencies (AWPRA). Flaxer resigned his job as social worker to become a full-time staff member of the union and assumed the post of executive director for what he claimed was some 10,000 members.

Prior to 1935, the creation of Communist-led dual unions independent of and competitive with the AFL was in accord with the "third period" policies defined earlier by the Third International in Moscow. By 1935, however, finally concluding that Hitler and Nazism were a permanent and distinct threat to the Soviet Union, Premier Stalin and the leadership of the Third International altered the policy of "unity from below" with members of social democratic parties to one of active collaboration with "democratically oriented" bourgeois movements and organizations. This sudden, radical change in policy by the Communist International insured the advent of the popular front era and obliged communist leaders in the United States to drop their support of dual unionism and affiliate themselves with the former "labor fakers" in the AFL. Matters became somewhat complicated, however, with the birth of the CIO, later that same year, which subsequently became the Congress of Industrial Organizations.

Following adoption of the popular front policies in Moscow, Flaxer and the leadership of his union approached conservative, building trades–oriented George Meany for admission into the New York State Federation of Labor. When Meany vetoed the proposal, apparently suspecting the background of Flaxer and his colleagues, the latter turned first to the American Federation of Government Employees (AFGE), and then to Arnold Zander and AFSCME in

Madison, Wisconsin. Between early 1935, when the fledgling AFSCME met in joint convention with the AFGE, and the first regular convention of AFSCME at Detroit's Cadillac Hotel in September 1936, Flaxer and Zander were in periodic negotiations. Finally, an understanding was reached whereby Flaxer would bring the more than 5,000 members of AWPRA into AFSCME at the 1936 convention, in return for the positions of two vice-presidents and International secretary-treasurer. The agreements were kept, and Flaxer and an associate, William Gaulden, were elected as two of nine vice-presidents. Gaulden was one of the first blacks to reach such an elevated union position in the nation. Flaxer's friend and colleague, David Kanes, was elected the first regular secretary-treasurer of AFSCME.[4]

A few months after the September 1936 AFSCME convention, by which time the popular front policies of the Communist International were being implemented throughout the world, the leadership of the U. S. Communist party (CP-USA) directed its members and followers to throw their energies behind the CIO. At about this time, Flaxer received a telegram from a CIO leader, John Brophy, inviting him to establish and head a public worker union within the CIO. After failing to convince Zander to transfer AFSCME to the CIO, Flaxer, Gaulden, and Kanes decided to resign and withdraw the New York local from AFSCME, along with other units in Philadelphia, San Francisco, and elsewhere, totalling some 5,000 claimed members.

Transferring loyalty to the more militant CIO was a comparatively easy decision for Flaxer, who found Zander and AFSCME to be tied too narrowly to voluntarism, associationism, and the civil service merit system. Flaxer and his colleagues took a large sector of the AFSCME membership, certainly its more aggressive segment, into the dynamic, industrially oriented CIO. Thereafter, Flaxer's organization became known as the State, County, and Municipal Workers of America (SCMWA). Initially, some 80 percent of its membership was in New York City, composed primarily of Emergency Relief Bureau employees, although smaller locals around the country managed to give the SCMWA a national base. With the passing months and years, many public workers joined the SCMWA on their own initiative, attracted by the more progressive organization of public service unionism and the dramatic leadership and fervent appeals of CIO leader John L. Lewis. By

1940, with Flaxer as president, the organization claimed a membership of 220,000, far more than AFSCME.[5]

For the decade following secession, the SCMWA, and its successor, the United Public Workers (UPW), supplied aggressive opposition to AFSCME. In addition, the Teamsters, the BSEIU, and other craft unions obstructed the jurisdictional aspirations of Zander, and ensured for him and AFSCME a beleaguered life within the labor movement. Throughout the later 1930s, the lone organizer for AFSCME in New York City did little more than sign up some civilian employees in the Fire Department and retain the supervisors from the Emergency Relief Bureau, who had refused to go along with Flaxer.

AFSCME CHARTERS DC 37

In 1941 Zander must have concluded that his organization was finally starting to move in New York. At that time, some 2,000 sanitation workers, in the Joint Council of Drivers and Sweepers, left the Civil Service Forum to affiliate with AFSCME. To ward off a threatening organizing drive by militant leftist Mike Quill and the TWU, sanitation leader John DeLury cooperated with Mayor LaGuardia and sanitation commissioner William Carey to convince Zander to issue five boroughwide charters to the Joint Council. AFSCME, in New York, finally seemed to be on its way, having secured the support of a citadel union, one that dominated the membership of at least a key city department. But New York AFSCME was growing through absorption of other organizations, not because it was organizing the unorganized.[6]

In the meantime, Henry Feinstein, president of Council 209 of the Civil Service Forum (a small group of Manhattan auto-enginemen), was expelled from the Forum for "flirting with union affiliation." Seeking a haven that would permit him virtual autonomy and enable him to maintain control in the imperious manner to which he had become accustomed, Feinstein eventually transferred his small group to AFSCME. Toward the end of October 1944, at a conference reported to include 20 New York City locals of public workers, AFSCME officially chartered District Council 37 (DC 37), with Feinstein as its first president. The 34 delegates present, which included four women, one of them black, listened to U.S. Senator Robert F. Wagner defend the expansion of social security, as proposed by the Wagner–Murray–Dingell bill. Also in attendance were Vice-President Matthew Woll of the AFL; Arnold Zander; Ellis Ranen, the lone general representative of AFSCME in New York; President Newbold Morris of the New York city council; and a host of officials from the CTLC and politics. It was a memorable start for a new public employee coalition in New York City.

Three years later, Feinstein was joined by fewer than 700 un-skilled workers and maintenance men in the city hospitals, who had transferred from the BSEIU. In 1947 a minor AFL local of transit employees also joined Feinstein's group. Thus, the modest growth of DC 37 in New York City continued to be the result of absorption of a number of unimportant units into an equally unimportant council of affiliated organizations.[7]

Away from the Manhattan borough president's office, or when not observing motor vehicle operators and others repaving the streets and filling potholes, Feinstein could be found in the tiny DC 37 meeting room on Broadway near City Hall. His acquaintance and union colleague, DeLury, remained unaffiliated with DC 37 and was housed near the Sanitation Department in the uniquely designed municipal building. There existed very close, nonconfrontational relationships between these union leaders and the departments from which they had to secure basic concessions for their members.

DC 37 never really grew under Feinstein's leadership, for his primary interests remained those of maintaining control over his fellow auto-enginemen, filling as many potholes as possible, and being chauffeured by a city-paid employee to and from work. Feinstein personified the machine model of the old-fashioned trade unionists who were closely associated with Tammany Hall bosses. It was Feinstein's boss approach to unionism that helped create an undemocratic, business-oriented organization while he was with AFSCME and, subsequently, with the Teamsters. The less effort entailed in expanding the DC 37 membership, the fewer the time-consuming responsibilities.[8]

If AFSCME was ever to grow in New York City, it would have to change leadership and develop a new set of organizational goals. Feinstein would have to be moved out of AFSCME, or at least circumvented. But would the AFSCME president invest the funds necessary behind new leadership in light of an earlier disinterest in urban centers? In addition, would a revitalized and enlarged AFSCME unit in the city pose a possible threat to Zander's policies and leadership, which were based on small, rural locals throughout the country?

IMPOSING OUTSIDE HELP

When Zander finally concluded that he could no longer collaborate with Feinstein, he began to appoint a set of new international representatives to the New York area. He hoped in this way to circumvent the head of a stultified DC 37. The individual first appointed to this position, a former official in the Welfare Department under LaGuardia, soon became ill and died. After some time, the vacancy was filled by Walter Pasnick as general representative. Originally recommended by William Becker, labor secretary of the Socialist party (SP-USA), Pasnick had had extensive union experience with the aluminum workers in Pennsylvania, and had served in a state hospital as a conscientious objector during World War II.

Not long afterwards, in 1947, Pasnick brought John Boer onto his minuscule staff. A young, austere, Swiss-born socialist, Boer was a self-trained intellectual who had worked for some time in New York City hospitals. During the years before World War II, he had been an elected, paid official of Local 171 of the SCMWA (CIO), until the Communist-oriented leadership learned of his socialist affiliation. Working out of the AFSCME office on Broadway, opposite City Hall, Boer quickly learned that the SCMWA, which had merged into the UPW, had a strong foothold, if not a majority of the workers, in the city hospitals. But there was no checkoff of union dues to prove it. The strength of the UPW was centered in the old Metropolitan Hospital on Welfare Island, along with kitchen staffs in other institutions. Some unskilled workers in Fordham Hospital in the Bronx, and the ambulance drivers, known as Motor Vehicle Operators, were in two small hospital locals attached to DC 37 under Henry Feinstein. During the months that followed, Boer was instrumental in expanding the AFSCME units at Bellevue, Morrisania, and Willard Parker hospitals, among others.

By the time Boer left the AFSCME staff in 1949 to assume a

civil service position with the city, there were some 1,200 paying members in AFSCME hospital locals, and another 500 or so who were one to two months behind in dues. Almost half of them were in Bellevue Hospital. And these numbers were achieved in the face of irresponsible racial charges hurled by UPW leaders against Boer and AFSCME, indicting them as "anti-Negro" and "Uncle Toms." During earlier years, similar charges were levelled by "third period" Communists against socialist Norman Thomas, Negro leaders Roy Wilkins and W.E.B. DuBois, and against other socialist unionists. Familiar with these tactics by Communists and their active sympathizers, Boer used a camera to take pictures of AFSCME meetings in city hospitals showing large numbers of blacks in attendance. When these photos were subsequently published in the New York AFSCME newspaper, Bill Lewis and other UPW leaders no longer raised this issue.[9]

In response to prodding from AFL headquarters in Washington, Zander was prevailed upon to appoint a staff member to organize public employees in New York City subway and transit systems. Behind this move was the apparent desire of AFL leaders to curtail the expanding power base of the TWU (CIO) and to clip the wings of its fiery, pro-Communist president, Mike Quill. For years, the anti-Communist AFL leadership had detested "Red Mike" because he was a major force in pushing the CIO Council in New York to oppose U.S. foreign policy in the cold war with the Soviet Union.

ENTER JERRY WURF

At this time, Zander again approached William Becker and asked him to suggest a candidate for the job of organizing the city's public transit employees. Recalling the young, zealous socialist who had fought valiant but losing battles against the benighted leadership of New York's Hotel and Restaurant Workers, Becker recommended 28-year-old Jerry Wurf. Who could possibly visualize that within 16 years after Zander designated Wurf an international representative, this mild-mannered leader, who had virtually created AFSCME, would be challenged by this rough, outspoken New Yorker?

Born in New York City on May 18, 1919, Jerome Wurf was

a son of Sigmund and Frieda Tennenbaum Wurf, first and second generation Americans of Central and Eastern European Jewish ancestry. Jerry was eleven when his father, a textile jobber, died, and fourteen when his mother remarried. A polio attack during childhood had left Jerry with a distorted torso and his left leg thinner and shorter than his right. He could never again run or walk easily without pain. These physical deformities and painful, fruitless operations left deep psychological scars on a youngster restricted for months to a wheelchair.

For the remainder of his childhood, Jerry's forceful mother remained overly protective and anxious about his physical setbacks. This meant that far less attention was devoted to the younger brother, Al, which also apparently left its psychological impact. In contrast to his healthy brother, Jerry was always the last one chosen for stickball or baseball games. For the rest of his life, he fought and scratched his way against most everyone else. In spite of his physical shortcomings, he had a brilliant mind that enabled him to surpass others in organizational knowhow and in battlefield and back-ally tactics. Jerry may have used his leg deformity, in later years, to strengthen his attacks against others. He berated opponents, egged on cops, and launched into tirades against individuals who were far stronger and bigger than he. At the same time, he lacked balance and was frequently a man of extremes in work, dedication, and profanity. Everything he did was in superhuman proportions.

During his formal education at P.S. 100 in the Bronx and at high schools in Brooklyn and Nassau County's Floral Park, he did poorly in the physical sciences, which repelled him, but excelled in history, economics, and political science. While attending Brooklyn's James Madison High School, when the worst effects of the Great Depression were being eased by some enlightened New Deal legislation, Jerry became an activist with Marxist youth organizations in the Jewish Brighton Beach section. To this young, involved idealist, there seemed to be more socialists and Communists per square foot than Republicans and Democrats. There was no family tradition of radicalism to help influence his decision to join Norman Thomas's Young Peoples Socialist League (YPSL), rather than the Young Communist League (YCL). In fact, his mother viewed his subsequent involvement with the labor movement as the work of destructive Bolsheviks. He had not read *Das Kapital* or other

Marxist works. And though he never viewed himself as a theoretician, and professed not to be an intellectual, he carried on the Jewish tradition of profound respect for the written word, and for the individual of letters.

At first he was attracted by the membership of the YCL. It was larger, had many more young girls and decent places in which to meet, and seemed to be involved everywhere in Brighton Beach. Eventually, however, he turned against the Communist party because of the virulent hatred expressed by its leadership, and then dutifully voiced by its membership, against other Marxists, pseudo-Marxists, and radicals who did not accept the "third period" policies of extreme sectarianism and revolutionary fervor. As he subsequently put it, "they hated too many things and too many movements."

The YPSL , on the other hand, turned out to be more attractive to Wurf because its members were not only studious and thoughtful, but committed to defending the rights and liberties of others, including Communists. At the same time, Jerry was repelled by Leon Trotsky's followers, who, at that moment, were running in and out of the Socialist party and the YPSL in an attempt to gain control of another organization or seduce members for their own ends. Wurf was drawn to Norman Thomas whom, he felt, had freed socialism from the harshness of European dogma and had effectively and realistically related it to an ethical and practical philosophy on the American scene. Wurf insisted that except for his second wife, Mildred Kiefer, "Norman Thomas and the Socialist party left the most profound impact upon me. The Socialist movement was the great force which helped me construct a set of ethics and social concerns which enabled me to veer away from the standard goals and practices traditionally orated on July 4."[10]

This sickly son of a textile jobber, who climbed Socialist party soapboxes in all types of weather, soon proved that he could communicate with others. He demonstrated the potential for impassioned, extemporaneous orations that held street-corner audiences spellbound for long periods. And that was an unusual achievement. He hoped to go on to Tufts University, but when his strong, protective mother decided against his leaving town, he entered New York University as an undergraduate. As he once put it, "If it hadn't been for my mother, I'd probably be a Wall Street lawyer today."

By the time he left college in 1940, with the Great Depression still affecting the nation, Wurf was confronted with a key question: where could he be most influential? In order to survive, he became a cafeteria busboy, and then cashier, often working 12-hour days, and sometimes seven-day weeks, for $2 a day. In the process, he started doing what came natural to him—organizing fellow workers into the Food Checkers and Cashiers Local 448 of the Hotel and Restaurant Employees Union. But when that local was absorbed by the Cooks and Countermen, Wurf found himself back at a cafeteria cash register. After many bouts with Communist union leaders and some gangsters, Jerry left the union movement about the time the United States became involved in World War II.

An unhappy first marriage, which began at the age of 21 and ended in divorce ten years later, enabled him to get out of his mother's home and away from her strong influence. The need to sustain a developing family, after the arrival of daughter Linda Susan, impelled him to join his brother, Al, in purchasing a delicatessen on Long Island. Not only did this experiment end in disaster, and come close to destroying the relationship of the brothers, but it also convinced Jerry that he could never cut slices of corned beef and pastrami thin enough to make a business profit. And he also learned that he would never make a success as a private entrepreneur. He would have to look elsewhere for a future.[11]

After World War II, with the Socialist movement no longer affording him an outlet for his energies, Wurf turned to the trade union movement to carry on the work of Norman Thomas, and to bring economic and social justice to the nation's minorities. His experiences also convinced him that, given the American environment and its hostility to socialism, compromise was essential. But the movement also taught him the need to carry on its idealism and preserve its integrity.

In a small room adjoining AFSCME headquarters on lower Broadway, Wurf and others usually found the door to the office of District Council 37 closed. Henry Feinstein rarely held union meetings or open court. And this was especially true for the few members in the Joint Board of Hospitals, which was loosely held together and appeared to have no specific mission. Feinstein issued infrequent union decrees from the office of the borough president of Manhattan, especially under Robert F. Wagner, Jr. Like DeLury, Feinstein retained strong personal connections with his close friends at City Hall. And the latter were still licking their wounds from the destructive impact of the Seabury Investigation of the 1930s and the ensuing political successes of the LaGuardia administration.The reform tradition of FDR, Herbert H. Lehman, and Robert F. Wagner, Sr., had been accepted without fervor by Feinstein, DeLury, and Teamster leader Martin Lacey, who now headed the CTLC. But these traditional union bosses gave no hope or encouragement to any public service leader who yearned for a more aggressive, independent, and socially conscious movement. In 1948, these latter tendencies were still to be found in the increasingly embattled UPW, led by left-wing trade unionists Flaxer, Bigel, Godhoff, Herbst, and others. If it were not for their adherence to Soviet foreign policy and the disastrous fallout from the cold war with the Soviet Union, the future might have been easier for the UPW.

Wurf's first mission with AFSCME in 1948, which was to organize a competitor to the TWU (CIO), was doomed from the start. As he subsequently put it, trying to win Irish-American subway workers away from Mike Quill was "like trying to melt an iceberg with a match." After seven months of dismal failure, Jerry concluded that it was an impossible job. Alerted by Becker that Wurf was about to quit, Zander invited Jerry to Madison, Wisconsin.[12]

ZANDER ENCOURAGES WURF

Moved by the fact that the International president met him at the airport and invited him home for dinner, the youthful Wurf felt beholden to this veteran, Lincolnesque leader. When asked to detail the condition of AFSCME in New York, Wurf's recollection was that he refused to act as an informer and did not detail the endless inadequacies and shortcomings of Pasnick, Feinstein, and DeLury. However, by the following day, when meeting with Secretary-Treasurer Gordon Chapman and Zander, Wurf made it abundantly clear that if AFSCME was to ever grow in New York, organizing campaigns would have to be initiated with specific known targets, in order to strengthen fragmented locals. Furthermore, he insisted, it was senseless to maintain such disjointed groups like hospital and sanitation workers and motor vehicle operators. They had to be brought together into one, effectively functioning organization with a staff leadership committed to aggressive union organization and democratic representation.

By the end of these meetings in Madison, it was clear that Wurf had attacked Henry Feinstein in particular for having prospered from political connections, and for having done nothing to expand a collection of paper locals. According to Wurf, the last thing Feinstein wanted at this stage of his union career was more members. Wurf insisted that Feinstein "was a city chauffeur who had worked out such a great deal that the city sent a car and chauffeur to pick him up at home every morning. Can you imagine that, a chauffeured chauffeur?"[13]

It did not take much pleading by Zander to convince Wurf to return to New York to reorganize and revive AFSCME. The latter had no other job waiting for him and, besides, he wanted to remain in the union movement. Furthermore, Jerry was perceptive enough to realize that the public sector in New York was a comparatively untapped segment of labor, that he might be in a position to play an important role in organizing the civil servants there, and he would be paid for doing work that he enjoyed.

Shortly after Wurf's return to New York, a number of decisions were made by others that were instrumental in shaping the future of AFSCME along lines helpful to him and to the union. In 1949, when it was learned that Pasnick had initiated secret negotiations with the BSEIU, which might have split AFSCME in New York, he was removed as international representative. By this time, Wurf was AFSCME's sole remaining international staffer in New York. John Boer, meanwhile, had accepted a civil service appointment as investigator for the Finance Department, and immediately joined Local 1113 of DC 37. Not only did Local 1113 remain with AFSCME through trying times ahead, but Boer soon climbed the union ladder to become a local official and, eventually, president of a revived DC 37. By 1949 Jerry was virtually alone in the New York office. But this was not much different from the International headquarters in Madison, where the entire staff consisted of some ten employees, sustained by one of the lowest per capita taxes of any union in the nation. Voluntarism remained a motivating force for Zander.

In 1948, DeLury's 2,300 sanitation men made up just under 50 percent of dues-paying AFSCME members in New York. Three years later, the sanitation workers had doubled, while the rest of

AFSCME locals had suffered a slight decline. By the end of 1951, the 12 locals associated with DC 37 under Feinstein numbered less than 800 paying members.

There were sharp ideological and personality contrasts between Feinstein and DeLury, on the one hand, and a newly determined Wurf, on the other. The latter had a clear set of union principles. He was committed to organizing a general, citywide public employee organization in New York, and to substituting a system of collective bargaining in every department for secret negotiations at City Hall. He wanted the same rights for public workers as those accorded private sector employees by the Wagner Labor Relations Act. As a result, he was aware that he would have severe competition from organizations with similar membership goals—the BSEIU and, after 1952, Teamsters Local 237. They, along with other AFL craft unions, exerted significant influence in the CTLC and were, in turn, strengthened by Lacey's autocratic leadership.

Not to be ignored in eventual decisions by DeLury, Feinstein, and others was a personality trait that plagued Wurf his entire life. As an overly aggressive individual, he was unable to work in harmony for long periods of time with even the closest of colleagues and working associates. It was not unusual for him to burst into tirades and to publicly humiliate staff members one moment and then seem to forget the entire incident hours later. Despite the loyalty and abilities of key staff members attracted by Wurf's idealism and dynamic leadership, his personality and intolerance of dissent created serious organizational problems. Working relationships were often so tempestuous that there ensued, in New York and later in Washington, D.C., a significant turnover of able personnel in AFSCME. Jerry realized that his union policies and strategies constituted distinct threats to the private power of Feinstein and DeLury. His original commitment to elements of membership participation in the determination of major policy decisions was distinctly alien to the leaders of the sanitation workers and auto-enginemen.[14]

THE TEAMSTERS' ATTRACTIONS

When Wurf headed the AFSCME office in the late 1940s and 1950s, the economy of New York City was still burgeoning, enabling it to remain the economic capital of the nation. Economic trials would not plague the city until years later. Public sector unions were in a weakened state, while those in private industry had generally become stronger. The most influential labor group was the Teamsters, which could, with the cooperation of the waterfront's International Longshoremens' Association (ILA), shut down most any workplace in the city. But the most powerful individual among labor leaders was Teamster Martin Lacey, who headed CTLC of the AFL. Lacey's power within New York was heightened by his close association with City Hall and the election of Democrat William O'Dwyer as mayor in 1945. O'Dwyer's victory signaled the end of the LaGuardia era, of independent, anti-Tammany leadership, and a return to more traditional labor–management relationships at City Hall. It was then that Lacey became an influential political figure as well.

As long as Mayor LaGuardia dominated New York politics, public sector workers were generally treated as second-class citizens. And this was in spite of his Congressional record of defending the downtrodden and protecting some of the most exploited working men and women in the nation. In 1932, for example, he pushed through enactment of the Norris–LaGuardia Anti-Injunction Act, which forbade injunctions to sustain yellow-dog, or anti-union employment, contracts, or to prevent strikes, boycotts, and picketing. As mayor of New York, however, LaGuardia opposed the endeavors of city employees to organize themselves into viable, independent unions, with the possible exception of DeLury's sanitation workers. And he went further to condone the indiscriminate transfer to distant work sites of some public workers who sought to unionize other civil servants.

Long-time leaders of private sector unions tended not to support the efforts of public workers to create independent unions of their own, or to accord civil servants the right to strike, which they retained for themselves. In fact, most progressive union leaders had come to look upon LaGuardia as their champion and went along with his view that public workers should not be organized. Much of this changed with the election of O'Dwyer in November 1945.

Dominating the various trades in the city, especially in alliance with the ILA, Lacey was now in a position to wield significant influence at City Hall. As a result, he evolved as a forceful magnet for those trade union leaders who sought political clout. One of them was sanitation leader John DeLury, who emerged as an important labor figure when he joined the Teamsters. During 1950–51, he was an unhappy international vice-president of AFSCME who found the organization lacking in vibrancy or influence, particularly in New York.[15]

AFSCME had barely attained a membership of some 68,000, was "nowhere fully organized, rarely recognized," and, as Al Bilik indicated, was "at worst harassed, coerced, dismissed—or entirely ignored." With neither AFSCME nor SCMWA attractive to DeLury or Feinstein, the appeals of Lacey, as the powerhouse of the New York City labor movement, facilitated their move to the Teamsters.

DeLury was a fatherly figure who was committed, in the inimitable manner of a classical trade unionist, to organizing and leading the sanitation workers in the city. It was not difficult for him to perceive that the energy of the labor movement was centered in Martin Lacey and the Teamsters. In addition, he had managed to develop an easy working relationship with Lacey, whose style and philosophy he could readily understand and endorse. By 1951, DeLury concluded that the financial resources and influence he sought for himself and his members could not be attained through an apathetic AFSCME, and thus he responded to Lacey's invitations by transferring to the Teamsters. This meant, among other things, that in negotiations with the mayor, DeLury would have the active support of one of the most powerful union leaders in the city, as well as what remained of the Democratic Party.[16]

Only a few months earlier, Martin Lacey executed a political coup of historic proportions. With the support of a limited number of conservative unions, he was able to overwhelm the united opposition of Mike Quill, the New York City CIO Council, David Dubinsky's International Ladies Garment Workers Union (ILGWU), Jacob Potofsky's Amalgamated Clothing Workers, Joseph Curran's National Maritime Union, his own Joint Teamsters Council, Paul Hall's Seafarers, and Carmine DeSapio's Democratic party organization in New York.

Following the sudden decision of Mayor William O'Dwyer to resign, under a cloud of suspicion, city council president Vincent R. Impellitteri became the acting mayor on September 1, 1950. Shortly thereafter, he decided to run for mayor in November.

Alerted in advance to the possibility of organizational rejection of his candidacy for the Democratic nomination, Impellitteri decided to run as an independent candidate on a newly created Experience Party ticket.

In early October, Lacey had pushed through the CTLC a rare labor endorsement of the Impellitteri candidacy by means of a voice vote, refusing to recognize a motion requesting a hand vote on the endorsement. And at a subsequent executive committee meeting, he pushed postponement of the November delegates meeting until after election day, in order to avoid a request for reconsideration of the earlier endorsement by a number of major affiliates, including the ILGWU. Taking the cue of an anti-bossism, anti-organization wave sweeping the nation, Impellitteri attacked the bosses of the Democratic party. He amazed political experts by overwhelming both major party candidates, with the aid of door-bell ringers and fundraisers supplied by Lacey's members in Teamsters Local 816, and by DeLury's sanitation men.[17]

Out of an alliance that had its roots in the immediate past, and while Lacey was still riding the crest of power, DeLury transferred his sanitation workers from a somnolent AFSCME to a vibrant Teamsters union. At the same time, Henry Feinstein found himself in a similar quandary. As leader of a comparatively small group of auto-enginemen, and a smaller contingent of hospital workers, he lamented his association with an organization that had no political or economic clout in New York City. Zander had neither the funds, the organizational staff, nor the desire to push Feinstein to greater endeavors among public employees. He simply wanted to get rid of him. Unlike Zander and Wurf, Feinstein was much more at home socializing and playing cards with Democratic stalwarts Carmine DeSapio, Robert F. Wagner, Jr., and Abe Beame of Brooklyn.

Like DeLury, Feinstein had few mental reservations about transferring from AFSCME. By tying his fate to that of the Teamsters, he believed that he could become an influential union figure in New York and, with little energy, secure significant gains for his members. Soon thereafter Feinstein received his Teamster charter and managed to transfer about half of DC 37's 800 members to the City Employees Union Local 237. But he failed to take with him the bulk of hospital workers, or the members of Local 1113, the finance employees of the city. DeLury, on the other hand, had transferred all of the sanitation workers to the Teamsters, insuring an immediate loss of two-thirds of the AFSCME membership in New York City. This left Wurf with some 400 members. In four additional AFSCME locals, which had never affiliated with Feinstein's DC 37, there was significantly less than the claimed 1,500 paying members.[18]

WURF AT THE HELM

Wurf was now in complete control of a faltering union with a staff that numbered a mere handful. This depressing situation was in sharp contrast to the rest of the nation, where some of the greatest advances of organized labor were being made among public employees. The civil service in New York was wide open for those with organizing talent. The Civil Service Forum was all but dead, divorced from most of its former membership. The UPW, formerly the State, County, and Municipal Workers of America, had been expelled by the CIO in 1949, and, after losing the bulk of its membership by 1952, was no longer a rival of AFSCME. DeLury, meanwhile, had decided to restrict his organizing endeavors to the sanitation workers. This left Henry Feinstein in a position to do battle with Wurf and DC 37. And he would do so, at times, with the assistance of former UPW leaders. Sustained by Lacey and his brand of Democrats at City Hall, Feinstein decided to devote the remainder of the decade to expanding the membership and influence of Local 237. Until his death in January 1960, he managed to gain control of most of the employees of a burgeoning New York City Housing Authority (NYCHA), and attain a strong foothold in the city's hospital system. Not long afterwards, Local 237 and a newly revived DC 37 were involved in a life-and-death struggle for control of the public hospital workers. The victor would become the flagship of public sector workers in the city.[19]

In 1952 Wurf started virtually from scratch. Not only did none of his struggling locals control a city department, but he was not well known. As a longtime socialist and maverick, he exerted no influence within the Democratic party nor at City Hall. In addition, he and other union leaders were severely constricted by Lacey's authoritarian control of the CTLC. The Teamster's high-handedness had recently been brought to the attention of a special committee of the AFL executive council by the ILGWU. Wurf had to fight for the right to be heard at CTLC meetings and to be permitted to canvass public employees in New York freely. Isolated at first from the rest of organized labor in the city, he was treated with utter contempt by Lacey and his cohorts. Wurf needed every bit of help he could get, and he did, from an unexpected source.

WURF'S PADRONE, PAUL HALL

Paul Hall was a short, husky, fearless leader of sailors. He literally had to fight his way to leadership against industry goons, as an organizer and then New York leader of some of the most exploited workers in the nation. A native of Birmingham, Alabama, Hall joined the Seafarers International Union (SIU) in 1938, and 19 years later became its president. In 1957, as well, he was elected head of the AFL–CIO Maritime Trades Department. During the years that followed, he built up the SIU to 80,000 strong. It was Hall and his sailors who not only contributed to the strike fund of other unions, but were often to be found on the picket lines of AFSCME, the Newspaper Guild, the Meat Cutters, and the ILGWU.

Hall was attracted to Wurf from the moment he first heard Jerry's grating voice and constant appeals to parliamentary rulings of Lacey at meetings of the CTLC. For years Hall had been in conflict with the corrupt waterfront dockers union, which had been sustained by Lacey and the Teamsters. As a result, anyone who irritated and challenged the authoritarian leadership of Lacey and who might be able to help him augment his own influence on the city's docks was attractive to Hall. It was the SIU leader who became the most powerful voice in defense of Wurf's right to be heard at CTLC meetings and to organize the unorganized among public workers.

During these early organizing days, it was Hall who supplied his AFSCME friend with strong-arm men to protect him from physical threats by Teamster goons or underworld elements. And it was Hall who helped subsidize many of Jerry's organizing drives with significant funds and other forms of vital assistance. Without the constant cooperation of the SIU leader, Wurf might have made little progress in the city. At least it would have been far more difficult. Thus, Hall turned out to be the most vital source of support for Wurf, and his strongest protective element against hostile moves by the Democratic leadership at City Hall, or by Lacey at the CTLC.[20]

TRADE UNION STRATEGY

Designated general representative of AFSCME in New York, Jerry set about reorganizing and reviving the nearly defunct DC 37. He was a workaholic, often to be found in the office at 7 a.m. and usually the last to leave in the evening. It was not unusual, throughout his years in New York, for him suddenly to convene a general staff meeting for late Friday afternoon, when most individuals were anxious to get home. By mid-April 1952, he convened representatives of some 26 locals, some of them mere paper organizations, in what was hailed by an overly optimistic union observer as a "historic step" in the drive to organize all city workers under the AFSCME banner. For too many years, insisted a new officer of the Council, city workers had been preyed upon or misled by a variety of so-called employee unions or associations, which were either too fearful to stand up and be counted when the chips were down, or else served no other purpose than to elevate its leaders to higher positions.

This time, however, it was going to be different. Wurf was spearheading all of AFSCME in the city, assisted by a core of dedicated rank-and-file members who were committed to some of the more responsible traditions of trade unionism. They were willing to give freely of their time, energy, and personal funds to sustain this struggling organization, alongside a handful of poorly paid organizers. Within two months, as a result of careful planning by Jerry, newly selected officers representing a variety of ethnic and religious backgrounds (in other words, a balanced ticket) took over the reins of what remained of the AFSCME Council. The president was Nicholas DeProspo of Finance Local 1113; executive vice president Ralph Chernack was from the comptroller's office, Local 1407; treasurer Julian Mandle represented Sanitation Local 1010; recording secretary George Foley was associated with Housing Local 824; and corresponding secretary Leah Hurwitz was from Welfare Local 1193. The executive board consisted of the officers of the Council and the president of each local. Twenty-seven members were assigned to six standing committees, the most important being the organizing committee. This was the first group to help Wurf organize a campaign for wages, grievances, and working conditions among clerical workers in particular and city employees in general.

By the September meeting of the Council, the situation had stabilized sufficiently to enable the officers to host International president Zander and Secretary-treasurer Gordon Chapman. Zander commended the new leadership of DC 37 on the unity that they had established, noting that all of them were now able to work effectively through one central organization. This was an overly optimistic appraisal of a still tenuous situation. Nevertheless, Wurf was encouraged by the personal plaudits of the International leaders. Chapman went on to laud the new spirit that characterized the organizing staff of AFSCME in New York and the dedication of the new rank-and-file officers and local representatives. This, he felt, augured well for expanding the membership.[21]

Wurf's small staff afforded him the ongoing assistance he badly needed to enlarge the remnants of the Council. But one of the most important keys to his future in labor was a young graduate student who subsequently played a major role in his private life as well. A native of California and an undergraduate at Berkeley, Mildred Kiefer began her graduate work in sociology in 1951 at Columbia University. A soft-spoken, warm, and independent individual with a unique memory for names, Kiefer had been employed at all sorts of part-time jobs since the age of 16. More recently, before coming to New York, she had done administrative and managerial work for the National Student Association. When she learned that a part-time job was available with AFSCME in New York, she sought out Wurf in his lower Broadway office. Although she suspected, like many knowledgeable, politically left graduate students, that AFL unions tended to be traditionally staid (in contrast to the militant and progressive CIO), a quick survey of newspaper articles convinced her that there was still some hope for this struggling public employee union.

Kiefer met Jerry on the day that the city paid homage to General Douglas MacArthur with a parade on lower Broadway. MacArthur had been discharged as head of the Allied forces in Korea by President Truman in April 1951. After being interviewed by AFSCME staffer Eric Schmertz, Kiefer adjourned to the roof with Wurf, where they observed the usual ticker-tape parade to City Hall and the welcome by Mayor Impellitteri. Jerry was sufficiently impressed by the strength and determination of Kiefer to offer her a part-time job preparing the script for a weekly radio program on a local FM station. In the process he made clear that MacArthur was a "son of a bitch," a man on a white horse who was a serious threat to American democracy. While Kiefer wasn't enamored by Wurf's profanity, she was attracted by his clear-cut ideological positions and denunciation of the reactionaries associated with MacArthur. From that moment she became instrumental in sustaining Wurf's drive to organize the public employees of New York and in strengthening his determination to evolve as a national labor leader.

In the process of preparing scripts for these weekly radio talks, Kiefer discovered that there was no available list of officers and members of locals, and no files of correspondence. In fact, there was no administrative system for most anything. Before Wurf concluded his radio series, Kiefer had developed membership lists, a recognizable filing system of correspondence, and an office that began to function with some degree of effectiveness. She soon made herself indispensable. Although never acting in the capacity of a secretary, many early male members of the Council still insist that that was her original job. She placed no limit on the hours or energy she expended as evolving office manager, even though she earned less than the male organizers.

Jerry's small office, which also served Schmertz, Kiefer, and any other staff member, was always open to everyone. When Seymour Schneider wanted to bring the health sanitarians into AFSCME, he was initially shunted aside by Feinstein, before the latter transferred to the Teamsters. Feinstein felt he had enough work servicing his own auto-enginemen. But Schneider was welcomed with open arms when he crossed over into Jerry's office, and within a short period, AFSCME had a new local and one of the more committed public employee units in the city.[22]

CITY–LABOR RELATIONS

When Wurf assumed sole responsibility for directing New York's AFSCME in the early 1950's, the city government had no consistent pattern of organized labor relations for its employees. Prior to introduction of a uniform approach to collective bargaining, organizations of civil servants resorted to a variety of informal approaches to supplement, if not circumvent, outdated methods of negotiations. As urban specialist Raymond Horton has indicated, during the early 1950s neither the municipal public workers nor Mayor Impellitteri (1950–53) exerted much influence on New York's personnel system. What did exist was an assortment of political and administrative influences over municipal labor relations and the rules of the personnel system. By the time Robert F. Wagner, Jr., was elected mayor in November 1953, the bulk of more than 200,000 public employees in the city were not yet members of unions. And overlapping authority to decide labor questions was dispersed among many officials. Unable to exert any significant impact on Impellitteri, some unions resorted to an end run around the mayor, lobbying the state legislature for salary increases, fringe benefits, and a form of recognition.

Those having a hand in various stages of the city's labor relations and personnel systems, with varying degrees of influence, included the Board of Estimate, the mayor, the Bureau of the Budget, the city council, the Municipal Civil Service Commission, the comptroller, and more than 100 departments, agencies, and authorities. As a result of formal powers derived from the city charter, the Board of Estimate retained greatest influence on matters of interest to city employees, through control and domination over the administration of expense and capital budgets.

It was the Board of Estimate that was assigned the constitutional responsibility for final determination of the salaries of public employees. Each year, a cacophony of testimony was presented to the board by representatives of assorted public employee groups for wage increases and improved working conditions. Finally, after everyone had been heard, the board acted on the recommendations of the mayor. This antiquated procedure did not make for an efficient or enlightened approach to labor–management relations in a large city.[23]

Far more important for the viable municipal unions, or those allied with Teamster Martin Lacey, were such informal approaches as direct negotiations with the mayor. Prior to presenting his wage settlement recommendations to the Board of Estimate, the mayor met quietly with a limited number of union representatives in an endeavor to reach acceptable compromises. Lacey's allies were assured easy access to the mayor's office, in contrast to the leader of DC 37.

Despite an outstanding ability to marshal figures and to argue persuasively before the budget director and the Board of Estimate, the leader of DC 37 remained handicapped as long as he was denied the opportunity to negotiate privately at City Hall. Thus he felt obliged to resort to militant measures that would attract newspaper, radio, and television coverage, like demonstrations in front of key city agencies, picket lines around City Hall, and mass meetings to pressure lawmakers, the Budget director, and members of the Board of Estimate. Not until he had won recognition as a labor leader in his own right and gained the support of an expanded membership was Wurf welcome in the mayor's office. It took years of tireless effort organizing the unorganized and overcoming the hostility and isolation created by Lacey and his followers in the CTLC and in the Democratic party.[24]

Another strategy of labor leaders utilized effectively by Henry Feinstein was dealing directly with independent administrative agencies. Feinstein's Local 237 had its major strength in the NYCHA, which operated independently of the mayor. Prior to the determination of new wage scales, Feinstein met secretly with the Housing Authority chairman. At that time, they both discussed what the Teamster leader was going to demand publicly, and what the Housing Authority felt it could ultimately afford in the way of wage increases and improvements in pensions, work conditions, and related issues. Finally, they reached an understanding as to the public compromise they could both accept. For show, each played his respective role—Feinstein made public demands on behalf of his members, entered into "public negotiations" with the Housing Authority chairman, and the two sides then compromised along previously agreed lines.

As far as the hospital workers (the second largest group in Teamsters Local 237) were concerned, Feinstein's close relations with Robert Wagner, Jr., when borough president of Manhattan, and his card-playing nights with Tammany Hall leader DeSapio, Abe Beame, and others, enabled him to conduct private negotiations with Mayor Wagner between 1953 and his death in 1960. Even though Feinstein had some discussion, as well as public disputes, with the city's budget director, the real deals were made in private meetings in the mayor's office.[25]

ORGANIZE! FOR POWER

Through these early years, Wurf was strengthened by a small coterie of organizers who had the imposing task of convincing the unorganized to join a comparatively unknown and uninfluential AFSCME. They could promise changes in the future, but only infrequently in the immediate present. DC 37 was in no position to distribute patronage or allocate favors such as individual transfers, promotions, or temporary appointments. Wurf and his colleagues rejected that type of "crony unionism," organizing and agitating instead for a collective bargaining process through which wage increases, pensions, and better working conditions could be negotiated. DC 37 organizers struggled to convince workers that by organizing they, too, would soon get "pie in the sky."

The handful of professional DC 37 staff were strengthened by idealistic rank-and-file organizers who, because of their daily, intimate association with fellow workers, helped AFSCME locals grow slowly but steadily. The Great Depression had obliged many bright, intelligent, and progressive men and women to forego professional or business careers for the availability and security of civil service positions. Among them the union found the bulk of its leadership cadre.

If some rank-and-file leaders were not as idealistic as others in their commitment to the cause of unionism, at least DC 37 afforded them status and social rewards associated with such posts as shop steward or local officer. Between 1952 and 1957, DC 37 developed 55 locals or organizing committees, thus providing opportunities for talented members to assume leadership and responsibility. Without an automatic checkoff system, union dues had to be collected laboriously by hand, by shop stewards or organizers, at the workplace or at union meetings. The shop stewards were the key individuals in any union; their jobs usually the first step in a career of service to fellow union members. In most locals, those who attended meetings were the board members and the stewards. A few faithful might also attend, and sometimes a handful of others because they had a special axe to grind at a specific meeting. But they might not come to another meeting for a year or more. During the early days of DC 37, the average attendance at most membership meetings rarely went beyond ten percent of the total membership.

WURF'S ADMINISTRATIVE STYLE

Close observers viewed Wurf as a poor administrator, his active mind rushing from one organizing idea to another as, from early morning to late at night, he raced from one workplace to the next. Uneasy in sharing power with associates, he shaped the Council into a highly centralized structure. Throughout his years with AFSCME in New York, and later in Washington, Jerry sought to be the center of all decision making, severely limiting the freedom and scope of his closest and most competent staff.

He often appointed individuals as special representatives, without clearly defined areas of delegated authority. Because of the great diversity among unorganized public workers, he gave a variety of assignments to the same staff member, thus preventing, with rare exception, a situation in which his underlings assumed exclusive, ongoing responsibility for a specific aspect of organizing or administering. For example, during the few years he worked for Wurf, William Casamo was assigned, at various times, to service the Laborers in Local 924, the Motor Vehicle Operators (MVOs) in most every city department, Parks Department employees, white-collar workers in the Board of Higher Education, five or six titles in the Tax Department, the hospital employees in Local 420, and the technical and professional public employees associated with Local 375. Stability and continuity within the Council was not part of the picture for Casamo and many of his colleagues.

Wurf sought to instill in staff members his compulsive drive to organize. Some of them turned out to be among the brightest and best educated in the trade union field, but a number of them left the Council when they could no longer take his authoritarianism and neurotic behavior. At times, even Wurf lost the ability to sustain the intensity of his organizing drive, and on such occasions the Council would be in trouble. He never permitted second-level staff members to assume responsibility in decision making. There were many difficulties when he decided to seek the International presidency of AFSCME in the early 1960s, for the race took him away from his New York base for weeks on end, leaving the Council somewhat rudderless at critical junctures.

The organization and staff learned much from their hard-driving leader. As one council organizer (who subsequently became a vice-president of another international union) put it, Wurf was a "hard son of a bitch to work with," but he "learned more from him than anyone else," in his entire union career. He was the best teacher of the history of the U.S. labor movement any staff member had ever had. He drove himself, as did other staff members, with one objective in mind—the uninterrupted growth of DC 37. He rarely socialized, went to the movies, or discussed theater. His whole life was the union, and that eventually became too overbearing for a number of those who worked closely with him.[26]

At the same time, Wurf's militant tactics and unceasing activism enabled the Council to be viewed increasingly among public employees as more committed to pressing grievances with departmental administrators and to a variety of collective actions than were other civil service unions. Although the pay for staff members remained low, and the work was ceaseless, Jerry's vigorous and exciting leadership, compassion for workers, and devotion to progressive unionism constantly attracted talented and socially conscious individuals. They came, spent a few years organizing, and then used DC 37 as a stepping-stone for professional careers, or better-paying jobs in the union movement. In the interim, they served the Council well before making their marks elsewhere; they included lawyer–arbitrator Eric Schmertz, civil rights pioneer James Farmer and union leaders Bill Evans, Jean Couturier, Bill Casamo, Bert Rose, Ted Bleecker, Hyman Peck, and many others.

Jerry was far happier devoting his energies and talents to the larger organizing endeavors out in the field than he was to supervising the daily administrative responsibilities associated with an expanding headquarters. Fortunately for the organization, an exception occurred when Wurf permitted a considerable portion of this task to be assumed, gradually, by Mildred Kiefer. Wisely, he granted her an increasing share of administrative initiative. While coordinating the endeavors of staff and rank-and-file members, Kiefer met shop stewards as they came into the Council's small office with their dues collections, and listened to their woes and tribulations. She came to know each one by name, and they soon realized that they had an interested friend in headquarters.

Not only did Kiefer become a prime resource for an expanding Council and the contact person for many active members who walked into union headquarters, but she gradually assumed the task of cajoling and gently pushing Wurf back on the track when necessary. With great discipline and tact, she managed to overlook Jerry's emotional eruptions. She helped keep him on an even keel for considerable periods. But she did far more than that. As a result of her common sense, strong character, and ability to listen, she became knowledgeable about developments in bargaining and mediation in the locals. Given that rare leeway by the AFSCME leader in New York, she conceived, and gradually put into operation, a varied program of training classes for stewards, devoted to parliamentary procedure, civil service, and grievance rules, and courses for promotional examinations. During these early years, Kiefer exhibited one of the cooler and sounder minds in the Council office, and, eventually, as education director, was invited to participate in policy discussions.[27]

An encouraging sign for Council growth was the realization that its headquarters had become too confining for the expanding membership and staff. So Jerry decided to move to 321 Broadway, just up the street from their cramped office. It seemed like a gigantic step forward, especially after partitions were built by staff members providing them, for the first time, something akin to individual offices. At the same time, Kiefer hired a bookkeeper to develop an accounting system for the money that had started to trickle in steadily from members of various locals.

SUMMARY

Public service unionism had difficult beginnings, for the idea of belonging to a union, let alone striking, was not deemed appropriate for government employees. In New York City, most organizations representing public workers, such as firefighters, police, and sanitation workers, were led by men with personal political influence, who made their deals in the back rooms of politicians, with the mayor or with a particular administrative chief.

Henry Feinstein, who received the first charter for DC 37, kept the Council small and ineffective, arranging with his political cronies at City Hall whatever wage increases he could get for his members. When the young, idealistic Wurf took over the reins of the union in 1952, he inherited a weak, failing organization with less than 1,000 members. By dint of endless organizing, he and a group of dedicated local leaders and staff began building the Council. He was not far from the mark, in 1957, when he claimed 25,000 members in 33 departments and agencies.

NOTES

1. Claude M. Feuss, *Calvin Coolidge: The Man From Vermont,* Hamden, CT: Archon Books, 1965, p. 226.

2. Fred C. Shapiro, "How Jerry Wurf Walks on Water," *New York Times Magazine,* April 11, 1976, p. 78. Interviews with Al Bilik, October 21, 1981; and Leo Kramer, September 8 and October 1, 1982.

3. Richard N. Billings and John Greenya, *Power to the Public Worker,* New York and Washington, D.C.: Robert B. Luce, Inc., 1974, pp. 37-39. For a brief history of AFSCME through 1960 that is sympathetic to Arnold Zander, see Leo Kramer, *Labor's Paradox—The American Federation of State, County and Municipal Employees, AFL–CIO,* New York: John Wiley & Sons, 1962.

4. Interview with Abram Flaxer, October 4, 1981; Joseph Ames, *Annotated Constitution of AFSCME,* pp. VI-1, VII-1. This constitutional history of AFSCME was completed in February 1978.

5. *New York Times,* July 13, 1937, p. 1; July 14, 1937, p. 8; John Boer tape recording, August 21, 1980; interview with Abram Flaxer October 4, 1981.

6. Sterling D. Spero and John M. Capozzola, *The Urban Community and its Unionized Bureaucracies,* New York: Dunellen Publishing, 1973, pp. 212-216; *Proceedings,* AFSCME Convention, Chicago, 1946, pp. 101-102.

7. *New York Times,* October 29, 1944, p. 45; October 30, 1944, p. 20; *Proceedings,* AFSCME Convention, Chicago, 1946, pp. 101-102; *Proceedings,* AFSCME Convention, Boston, 1948, pp. 127-130; Ralph T. Jones, *City Employee Unions, Labor and Politics in New York and Chicago,* unpublished document, 1975, pp. 156-157. Also, John Boer tape recordings, August 21, 1980 and June 16, 1981.

8. Tape recordings of John Boer, August 20, 1980 and June 16, 1981; interview with Bert Rose, September 16, 1981; interview with Louis Yavner, April 8, 1982. Rose was a key staff member, first of DC 37 and then of Teamsters Local 237, which was subsequently headed by Henry Feinstein. Yavner, a prominent city figure during and after the LaGuardia administration, was for many years legal counsel to Feinstein and Teamsters Local 237.

9. Tape recordings of John Boer, August 21, 1980 and June 16, 1981.

10. Interviews with Jerry Wurf, August 20 and 21, 1979.

11. Fred C. Shapiro, "How Jerry Wurf Walks on Water," *New York Times Magazine,* April 11, 1976, p. 74; interviews with Jerry Wurf, August 20 and 21, 1979; tape recording of John Boer, August 21, 1980.

12. Shapiro, "Wurf Walks on Water," p. 74.

13. Interviews with Jerry Wurf, August 20 and 21, 1979.

14. Tape recordings of John Boer, August 21, 1980 and June 16, 1981; interviews with Bernard Stephens, February 2, 1981; Bert Rose, September 16, 1981; Al Bilik, October 21, 1981; and Joseph Ames, October 26, 1981.

15. Interviews with Jerry Wurf, August 20 and 21, 1979; Barry Feinstein,

April 22, 1981; Jack Bigel, February 18, 1982; Louis Yavner, April 8, 1982.

16. Spero and Capozzola, *The Urban Community,* p. 18; interview with Jack Bigel, February 18, 1982.

17. *New York Times,* August 16, 1950, p. 1; September 5, 1950, p. 2; September 13, 1950, p. 1; September 14, 1950, p. 1; September 15, 1950, p. 21; October 6, 1950, p. 21; October 19, 1950, p. 36; October 23, 1950, p. 16; October 25, 1950, p. 40; October 29, 1950, p. 64; November 8, 1950, p. 1; September 17, 1953, p. 1; November 20, 1957, p. 27.

18. Jones, *City Employee Unions,* pp. 157–158; 163–165. In addition to 550 laborers in Local 924, there were the Playground Directors (Local 149) with 359 members, the Municipal Transit Workers (Local 380) with 278 members, and the Sanitation Department Officers (Local 750) with 359 members. Interviews with Jerry Wurf, August 20 and 21, 1979; tape recording of John Boer, August 21, 1980; and Jack Bigel, February 18, 1982.

19. Interviews with Barry Feinstein, April 22, 1981; Bert Rose, September 16, 1981; Jack Bigel, February 18, 1982; Louis Yavner, April 8, 1982.

20. *New York Times,* December 21, 1950, p. 32; *Spotlight,* July 1, 1953, p. 1; interviews with Jerry Wurf, August 20 and 21, 1979; and Philip Ross, September 16, 1982. Ross is currently writing a biography of Hall.

21. *Spotlight,* August 1952, p. 3; October 1952, p. 3.

22. Interviews with Jerry Wurf, August 20 and 21, 1979; Mildred Kiefer Wurf, August 21, 1979; John Boer tape recording, August 21, 1980.

23. Raymond D. Horton, *Municipal Labor Relations in New York City, Lessons of the Lindsay-Wagner Years,* New York: Praeger, 1972, pp. 16–19; interview with Solomon Hoberman, February 16, 1984. The Board of Estimate was composed of the mayor, the comptroller, the president of the city council, and the presidents of the five counties.

24. Interviews with Jerry Wurf, August 20 and 21, 1979; William Casamo, October 17, 1979; John Boer, September 22, 1981.

25. Interview with Louis Yavner, April 8, 1982. Yavner was legal counsel to Feinstein and Local 237 from 1954 to 1975.

26. Interviews with William Casamo, October 17, 1979; Victor Gotbaum, May 11, 1981; Dena Schur Geschwind, December 15, 1982 (secretary to Wurf, 1955–1957); John Boer tape recording, July 16, 1981.

27. Jerry Wurf to New York State School of Industrial and Labor Relations, October 7, 1957; interviews with Jerry Wurf, August 20 and 21, 1979; Mildred Kiefer Wurf, August 21, 1979; William Casamo, October 17, 1979; Bernard Stephens, February 2, 1981; and Victor Gotbaum, April 30, 1982; John Boer tape recording of July 16, 1981.

2
Jerry Wurf
Creates A Power Base

Assigned by the International office to build AFSCME in New York City, Wurf set to work constructing a solid foundation for DC 37 and a power base for his leadership. He skillfully utilized the prevailing rate issue, enhanced the role of Local 924, battled Henry Feinstein of the Teamsters for membership, and transformed the Council into an around-the-clock operation.

THE "PREVAILING RATE" BATTLE

Wurf's involvement with the prevailing rate issue, in 1952, was a turning point in his relationship with those city laborers affiliated with Local 924, and a major factor in the renaissance of DC 37. Skilled craftsmen or maintenance employees, working for the city, came within a state statute that, when successfully applied, required that they be paid a wage equivalent "to that prevailing in the private sector for the same work."

Section 220 of the New York State Labor Law, adopted in 1921, provided that the wages of employees in these categories were to be unilaterally fixed by the city comptroller. The law stated that their wages "shall be not less than the prevailing rate...in the same trade or occupation in the locality within the state...." Testimony was presented by unions, and other interested organizations and individuals, at public hearings to assist the city comptroller in determining the prevailing rate for a given job classification, and his decision was final and binding. The role of the union in those

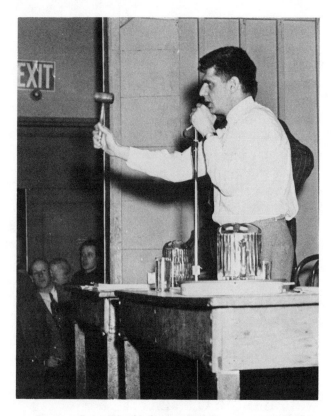

A young Jerry Wurf informs city laborers at an overflow
meeting of Local 924 in 1952 that he has just reached an
agreement with the city comptroller concerning their prevailing rate claims, a turning point in DC 37's development.

areas was limited to negotiation of noneconomic matters. Since
1948 it had been the practice of the comptroller's office to equate
the prevailing rates of the five craft titles involved with union scales
in the construction trades. As a result, there was a comparability
of hourly rates between these crafts and those of the organized
building trades. The workers affected involved less than one percent of the city's workforce.[1]

Since private industry tended to pay its skilled laborers more
than New York City did, an imaginative and aggressive use of Section 220 could readily insure increased wages for hundreds of
members of a key local, and favorably influence the thinking and
attitude of unorganized public laborers toward DC 37. However,

these laborers had to file annual applications with the city, requesting the differential in wages, in the form of timely "labor-law complaints," contending that they were not being paid the prevailing rate.

Lawyers had made a racket of aiding workers filing claims. Since the wage differential to be paid laborers eventually depended on the date on which the labor law complaint was filed, "prevailing rate" lawyers sought to drag out negotiations with the city, since the larger the final wage settlement, the larger the lawyer's fee. Some of these lawyers were found to be "working" on unsettled "prevailing rate" claims for almost a decade, in cooperation with some self-styled employee representatives whose actual function seemed to be ambulance chasing for certain law offices.[2]

Early in 1952 Wurf was alerted to these prevailing rate claims, the contingency-fee racket, and the potential for increased membership. His decision was that DC 37 should respond positively to this problem in the form of a service to members and nonmembers alike. He went directly to the city comptroller's office, the source of funds, where he found Lazarus Joseph to be a sympathetic and understanding individual. Because the cultural backgrounds of the two were similar, they were soon at ease, and before long reached an agreement. Not only would the comptroller facilitate a speedy settlement of existing prevailing rate cases but, in the future, after periodic determination of wage rates, involved laborers would be required merely to submit simple request forms. Traditional red tape was slashed drastically. Shortly thereafter, on June 30, 1952, the comptroller pushed through the city's Board of Estimate settlements of an overall $5,000,000 in claims, covering up to nine years back pay. At the same time, the board approved new pay scales ranging from $2,485 to $3,495 annually, the highest ever received by laborers.[3]

Wurf had accomplished, in one meeting, what involved lawyers with contingency-fee retainers had avoided for a decade or more. Seeking maximum advantage of this fortuitous development, he realized the potential of this major breakthrough with blue-collar workers. These were workers AFSCME had neglected to organize in the past under Zander, but who were soon to become the cornerstone of a new organization in New York. Planning strategy with Kiefer and other staff members, Jerry arranged to have these laborers sign a simple form designed by the city, had them notarized by an AFSCME lawyer, and then submitted them to the comptroller's office. In the process, many nonunion laborers came into contact with the Council's staff, who urged them to sign membership cards. It was Jerry's hope that, thereafter, contingency-fee lawyers would become increasingly isolated from this formerly lucrative trade.

Laborers could secure the official form from the comptroller's office in the municipal building, but Joseph's busy staff was not anxious to confront any such deluge. Furthermore, how was the money to be distributed—as lump sum payments to individual laborers; as contributions assigned to their pension funds; in the form of reduced work hours in the future; or a combination of these?

By the time a Local 924 meeting was convened at Werdermann's Hall on a broiling hot night in July, word was out that the AFSCME leader had found a speedy solution to their prevailing rate claims. Many of them now knew that they would shortly be compensated with large sums of money. Although Fire Department regulations set a maximum of 400 individuals for this meeting place, that number was easily surpassed before the start of the meeting. Scores were forced to stand in aisles, and overflow spilled into an outer room in the rear.

At this mass meeting of laborers, Wurf sought to explain the various alternatives available to them for disposition of the settlement. But there evolved no speedy resolution from the floor. Finally, one laborer arose and indicated that he and his fellow workers could not possibly make a decision concerning such complex alternatives. However, he felt he spoke for the others when he suggested that Wurf make that decision, for "we have faith in you." They could not possibly retain all the information that Jerry sought to share with them. They needed someone to make the final determination. And since they appreciated what he had already done, they wanted him to make the ultimate move and they would abide by it. The majority of the assembled laborers endorsed this suggestion. Not only did they line up to complete the application forms for their respective shares of back pay, but scores signed up as new members of Local 924, and paid their dues.

The hundreds of laborers who signed up with Local 924 that night insured a turning point for Jerry and for the Council. These blue-collar workers, primarily from the Parks Department, demonstrated in subsequent years a commitment to union solidarity and a loyalty to Wurf's leadership. They became a cornerstone of the Council, sustaining it at critical junctures and supporting the militant, socially conscious unionism exemplified by Wurf, and later by Victor Gotbaum.[4]

Jerry had come to be viewed as a labor leader not to be ignored. But in order to strengthen his personal base, he hit upon a tactic that brought him some criticism from within the Council. After assuming the stewardship of New York AFSCME, Wurf was in constant search of a strong, independent base of support within DC 37. Appointed special representative by the International office, and on seemingly friendly terms with Zander, Jerry realized that he could readily be removed from his position, at the whim of the president. For protective purposes, he sought to develop his own power base within one of the Council's locals. Following his success in the prevailing rate case, Jerry turned to the AFSCME unit that had benefited most.

He first worked for one day as a laborer at the Willard Parker Hospital and immediately joined Local 924. Not long afterward, he convinced enough members of 924 to avoid possible dissension within the local by electing him as their next president. Thereafter, the laborers local afforded him a power base that made him independent of the International office. At the same time, it was a move that was resented, although quietly, by a number of activists and local leaders within the Council. They felt that as the leader of DC 37, he should not hold the office of president of an affiliated local.[5]

Local 924 became the largest and most influential local. The great majority were, at that time, either immigrants from southern Italy or their descendants. For them, the *padrone* or godfather tradition was an important way of life. And they came to view Jerry in that image, as a result of his unique success with the prevailing rate issue. Although most members of the local knew he was Jewish, they were moved by a deep sense of gratitude for his early endeavors. .

Within a year of the prevailing rate victory, membership in Local 924 trebled, representing 45 percent of the Council's dues-paying members. When the Sanitation Officers (Local 750) left AFSCME in 1954 to join the BSEIU, Local 924's share of the membership increased to 57 percent. During the last three months of

1952 these developing locals of DC 37 were starting to make their voices heard among various agency offices and at City Hall. And they were beginning to make a difference in the work conditions and the status of some city employees. Students of New York might not view these developments as significant, but they were in the eyes of public workers who viewed themselves as second-class citizens. Before the end of 1952, increasing activism enabled Wurf and the staff to win some important gains for different workers in various agencies—wage differentials, a right to a hearing, fairer civil service test procedures, additional paid holidays, compensatory time off, improved safety precautions, and elimination of unnecessary night-duty requirements.

FEINSTEIN AND THE "RED MENACE"

During the months that followed reorganization of DC 37 under Wurf, Feinstein and DeLury were busy going their separate ways. DeLury was successful in building his sanitation workers into one of the more influential unions in the city. As for Feinstein, as a result of the personal animosity that had developed between Wurf and himself, he was determined to overwhelm DC 37 in numbers and influence. Teamsters Local 237 remained undemocratic, with virtually no membership involvement in decision making. Nevertheless, Feinstein made steady inroads among exploited hospital workers and Housing Authority employees. In the process, he and Wurf became involved in an endless series of costly, debilitating jurisdictional disputes as they sought to organize clerks, accountants, investigators, laborers, lawyers, and others in various city departments.[6]

The leader of DC 37 never shied away from a fight. In fact, he was most anxious to attack Feinstein at every opportunity, for he viewed him as the greatest threat to the growth of the Council. Within the year after he took over stewardship of the Council, Jerry publicly denounced Teamster Feinstein for appointing to his staff former officials, as he put it, of the "communist-dominated United Public Workers." He insisted that under cover of jurisdictional wrangles, "this hard core of communists and/or fellow travellers—expelled by the CIO and now shunned by their former members" were endeavoring to use Teamster Local 237 as a "Trojan horse in order to gain access to the House of Labor." In March 1953, in the midst of cold war reaction trampling civil liberties throughout the nation, Wurf threw more fuel onto the fire.

Fully aware of the outstanding organizing and administrative talents of former UPW leaders Jack Rigel, Elliot Godhoff and Frank Herbst, Feinstein cared little about the political ideology of his union organizers. He was simply anxious to use their talents to help him expand his membership and overwhelm AFSCME in New York. At the same time, Wurf knew that the creative power behind the organizing endeavors of Local 237 was now at the disposal of these former UPW advocates. If he could destroy or neutralize them, he could frustrate the competition from 237. Wurf went on the attack, resorting to back-alley tactics and infighting, as had former UPW leaders. Wurf was determined that neither "Stalinists" nor "fellow travelers" would destroy his plans for DC 37. In a highly publicized letter, which he addressed to the leadership of the International Brotherhood of Teamsters (IBT), Wurf wrote, "... granting asylum to communists not only affronts the high principles and great tradition" of the AFL but belied the "exemplary role of the International Brotherhood of Teamsters in rooting them out of the labor movement."[7]

Feinstein and his Teamster colleagues at first ignored this initial broadside. Wurf, however, returned to the issue again and again. With the nation engaged in a cold war against communism, he persisted in his public attacks against Communists in Feinstein's Local 237. Before a hearing at City Hall, Wurf let loose a sweeping indictment of Communists in the trade union movement, urging the city to exclude from collective bargaining rights those organizations that admitted Communists into key positions. He went on to name individuals and submitted a series of documents he claimed described the cloaked maneuvers and methods used by the Communist party and its followers to assume policy positions in public employee unions. These documents, he felt, demonstrated the subversive character of the defunct UPW, which had been ousted by the CIO in 1949. He then branded as Communists those former UPW leaders who, at that very moment, were paid organizers for Teamsters Local 237.[8]

Wurf's steady barrage against Communists proved effective, as hundreds refused to renew their membership, or signed up with AFSCME locals. Responding to pressure from within the

Democratic party and observing a steady decline of membership in his local, Feinstein finally fired the former UPW leaders from his staff. AFSCME's leader had achieved his primary goal.[9]

WURF'S MILITANCY

In his tireless efforts to expand Council membership, Wurf was demonstrating that he was a conscientious, committed labor organizer and a stimulating and challenging teacher who was clever at the use of media to influence public opinion and potential members. He felt it was necessary to constantly agitate, educate and organize. When he couldn't get into the columns of local newspapers or be heard on daily news broadcasts of New York's radio or television stations, he would use the issues of his union newspaper— at first the *Spotlight*, and then the *Public Employee Press* (PEP)—to harangue elected officials, indict legislative bodies, criticize commissioners and deputy commissioners, and attack division heads. All this was done to insure maximum publicity for AFSCME, to push aggressively for improvements in working conditions and pay scales, and to hasten adoption of a collective bargaining procedure for the city.

When Jerry could not achieve any significant breakthrough for his expanding Council, when he found himself boxed in by some of the stultifying and depressing civil service regulations, and when officialdom persisted in opposing a collective bargaining system, he knew he had to resort to more militant tactics. On such occasions, he would galvanize his organizers around a specific activity, seeking to give civil service workers a sense of the union's caring and dynamic behavior and put administrators on the defensive.

He would undertake a series of publicized conferences on labor relations with department heads or their immediate subordinates. Present at these meetings were always the AFSCME leader, a delegation of chief stewards of the department involved, and a photographer–reporter for the newspaper. The stated purpose of most meetings was to reach a better understanding of the problems affecting public employees, and how they could best handle immediate grievances. The unstated reasons were to impress civil servants with the ceaseless activities of DC 37 representatives, and to convey to elected officials and adminstrative bureaucrats an impression of steady growth, along with dynamic, influential leadership.

At every opportunity, the Council's leader appeared before the city's Board of Estimate where, with his mastery of figures and blaring voice, he testified on matters relating to public employees, particularly the determination of wages and hours. On such occasions, he harangued board members with statements that reporters always found colorful, thereby "making them newsworthy and assuring wider coverage of his statements in the civil service press." At these annual hearings, Wurf arranged for hundreds of AFSCME members to crowd the attractive chambers of the Board of Estimate and applaud his remarks and those of local presidents, conveying a feeling of overwhelming support by public employees. And if that was insufficient, Jerry would ring City Hall with a picket line.[10]

Since the newly revived DC 37 could not, at first, afford a newspaper of its own, Wurf arranged (with a controversial publisher, Ernest High) to issue a monthly 16-page paper, *Spotlight*, at no expense to the Council, with the cost to be absorbed by advertisements. However, following a series of disputes with the publisher, the council began issuing its own *Public Employee Press* in June 1959, another landmark for DC 37 and Wurf's stewardship. Just eight years earlier, less than a handful of organizers worked out of a barren, miniscule office. The membership was so small that AFSCME was ignored by other unions and City Hall. By 1959, the Council claimed 30,000 members, although 20,000 would have been closer to the mark. In the meantime, there had been pioneering developments in labor–management relations—increasing numbers of public agencies were sitting down and negotiating with unions of their employees. The leader of DC 37 was steadily building an organization.

BUILDING COUNCIL POWER

In 1955, aware of the imminent amalgamation of the AFL and CIO, and the complex merger negotiations which lay ahead for AFSCME in New York and their CIO counterparts, the Government Employees and Civic Organizing Committee, Wurf realized that an experienced and forceful president was needed to represent the Council and protect its dominant role in any coalition with the CIO. Wurf decided on John Boer, former staff member of his early AFSCME days, one-time comrade in the Socialist party, a self-made student of history, and an immovable defender of the Council. An active leader of Finance Local 1113, as well as within the Council itself, Boer was elected president of DC 37 in 1955. From that moment, the new president was instrumental in seeking to alter the role and shape of the Council. From a "more or less social get-together" of a couple of dozen members, the delegates council became an instrument that successfully hurdled merger negotiations and assumed, on occasion, some independence in decision making. No longer were all proposals by the AFSCME leader automatically rubber-stamped. The delegates council gradually emerged as an internal check to Wurf.

The responsibilities of executive leadership of the Council remained in the hands of regional director Wurf, who was appointed and paid by the International union. With the adoption of a new Council constitution in 1959, written largely under the direction of John Boer and a new core of local leaders, DC 37 provided for an executive director of its own. This further liberated Wurf from dependency on the International office. Initially, the director was appointed by the Council's executive board, with the approval of the delegates council. The latter body was made up of representatives from each local and was, supposedly, the highest constitutional authority of DC 37. The delegates council members selected an executive board that, between Council meetings, made decisions and implemented policy. (The new constitution also dispensed with a number of archaic forms, going back to pre-Wurf days, such as trustees, and provided for an executive board composed of a president, secretary, treasurer, and ten vice-presidents. In 1964, when it was expected that Wurf would be elected International president, the constitution was further amended to provide for the direct election of the executive director by the delegates council. Five members of the board, including the president and the executive director, constitute the finance committee, which deals with all financial matters.)

The executive director was, and is, the day-to-day administrator of the Council's business. He carries on negotiations, heads organizing drives, and handles union publicity with the assistance of Council staff and employees. The director appoints and supervises the staff but is, constitutionally, responsible to the executive board for its actions.

As John Boer and other union veterans recall, the Council became a "round-the-clock-union." Most locals, expecially the smaller ones, tended to exist from meeting to meeting and from grievance to grievance, with respites in between. But at the Council, the problems were endless and had to be dealt with day and night. Each hour might bring a new crisis confronting one or more locals that had to be responded to immediately. And the crisis and campaign of the next day or week had to be planned for.

No local, even the biggest, could afford or provide overall services at the cost of what it paid the Council in per capita dues. Being vested with a charter, a jurisdiction, and autonomy, the more than 50 locals that made up the Council had far-reaching responsibilities. If they were to progress under Wurf's stewardship, these locals had to organize constantly, process grievances, develop and carry out plans for improvements in pay and working conditions, establish a collective bargaining relationship, and carry on educational, legislative, and welfare activities. These were overwhelming tasks for small locals, and challenging for the large ones. Increasingly, it became clear that these locals could do far better working within the framework of a Council, for mutual protection and establishment of uniform policies. In addition, Wurf needed a Council-level organization as a power base for his own independence from the International office. Less than a decade after taking over the stewardship of DC 37, Wurf could point to a series of Council victories, the work of an expanding Council staff, local officers, volunteer activists, and the hard-hitting columns of the Council newspaper.[11]

SUMMARY

As AFSCME became known for its aggressive challenge to city authorities, scores of public workers began visiting the Council office for advice on social security, pension payments, vacation rights, sick leave, mistakes on paychecks, and problems involving the city's health plans. Council telephones seldom stopped ringing with members calling in every conceivable grievance. Staff members were assigned to answer telephones during evening hours, attended dozens of classification hearings, testified at salary appeals board meetings, wrote briefs, gathered comparative wage data, made surveys on prevailing rates, conducted shop steward, grievance, and promotions study classes, and kept members informed of their rights. Key AFSCME leaders began to be invited to meetings with the mayor, the budget director, the comptroller, and commissioners of departments.

Signaling the steady increase in Council membership, Irene Scott, a practical nurse at Kings County Hospital, became the 25,000th member of DC 37 in 1957 when she joined Local 420 of the Hospital Employees. Her membership card was given to her by a smiling Wurf, in the presence of Mayor Robert F. Wagner, Jr., and 250 leading city officials and labor, community, and civic leaders. The next goal was 50,000 members.[12]

NOTES

1. Arvid Anderson to Herbert Bienstock, November 9, 1972. Anderson was chairman of the Office of Collective Bargaining while Bienstock was head of the U.S. Department of Labor's Bureau of Labor Statistics for the New York metropolitan area.

2. Ralph T. Jones, *City Employee Unions, Labor and Politics in New York and Chicago,* unpublished document, 1975, p. 169; interview with Jerry Wurf, August 20, 1979; John Boer tape recording, August 21, 1980.

3. *Spotlight,* October 1952, p. 3; interview with Wurf, August 21, 1979.

4. *Spotlight,* August 1952, p. 1; interview with Mildred Kiefer Wurf, August 21, 1979.

5. Interviews with John Boer, December 7, 1978; January 29, 1979; February 15, 1979; John Boer tape recording, July 16, 1981; interview with Bert Rose, September 16, 1981.

6. Interview with Bert Rose, September 16, 1981.

7. *Spotlight,* April 1, 1953, p. 3; interviews with Jerry Wurf, August 20, 1979; Barry Feinstein, April 22, 1981; Bert Rose, September 16, 1981; John Boer, September 22, 1981.

8. *Spotlight,* May 1, 1955, p. 4; August 1956, p. 1; *New York Times,* September 22, 1955, p. 22.

9. Interviews with Jerry Wurf, August 20, 1979; and Barry Feinstein, April 22, 1981.

10. Jones, *City Employee Unions,* p. 169; Mark H. Maier, ''The City and the Unions, Collective Bargaining in New York City: 1954–1973,'' Ph.D. dissertation, New School for Social Research, 1980, p. 77.

11. The bulk of information about the internal structure of DC 37 was gleaned from many interviews with John Boer, Eliot Reif, Jerry Wurf, Bill

Casamo, and other early staff members. In addition, there were extremely perceptive articles written by John Boer for the *Public Employee Press* over a number of years.

12. *Spotlight,* November 1, 1957, pp. 1, 12.

3
Who Built This Union?
Robert Moses!

Wurf decided in the mid-1950s, in his determination to extend true collective bargaining to public workers, that the Parks Department afforded him the best opportunity for a major organizing endeavor and struggle with the city. However, the young leader had to confront Robert Moses, one of the most powerful, imperious, anti-labor administrators. In the course of this engagement, Wurf was severely constrained by legal limitations as to the strategies he could pursue, and so he was compelled to search for the most innovative and imaginative schemes to attract attention and gain public sympathy.

The labor policies of New York City's government took a step forward on July 21, 1954. Some seven months after taking office, Mayor Robert F. Wagner, Jr., sought to emulate his progressive father (author of the famed National Labor Relations Act), when he issued his "Preliminary Report on Labor Relations in the Municipal Service." In it, a New York mayor recognized, for the first time, some of the modern responsibilities of city government toward its public employees and proposed what Wurf and others hailed as a sane and humane labor relations policy. Wagner insisted that it was to be the basic policy of the city to assure its employees full freedom of association as well as designation of bona fide and responsible representatives of their own choosing, for the orderly presentation and adjustment of their grievances.

Directing department heads to establish a system of grievance machinery, Wagner decreed the creation of union–management committees, which would assist in formulating policies concern-

Jerry Wurf's resort to a dramatic technique in his successful campaign in 1955 to secure union recognition and collective bargaining rights from the powerful anti-union figure, Parks Commissioner Robert Moses.

ing wages, hours, and working conditions. Responding to the cold war tidal wave sweeping the nation, and to incitement by Wurf and others, the mayor's directive also barred Communist or fascist unions from recognition by any city department or agency. Since there were no fascist unions in existence (although some labor leaders pursued authoritarian if not totalitarian behavior patterns), this part of the executive order was directed, in particular, to the former officers of the defunct UPW, who had become associated with DeLury's sanitation workers and Feinstein's Local 237.[1]

The leader of AFSCME seemed overjoyed with the mayor's executive order, feeling that New York had finally come of age. He expressed the hope that municipal employees would soon enjoy parity with workers in private industry in terms of collective bargaining, voluntary dues deduction, and grievance machinery. But would city administrators implement the recommendations of the mayor, especially after he twice extended the deadline for departmental compliance? Delighted with the proposals to screen out "subversives," the head of DC 37 urged that responsible bureaucrats eliminate those splinter outfits and paper unions whose sole mission was "ambulance chasing." He noted, however, that the interim order had several serious omissions regarding collective bargaining rights and dues checkoff. Voluntary dues checkoff, he insisted, would solve the problem of determining who represented what in the city, while collective bargaining could facilitate negotiated agreements on wages, hours, and grievances between city and union representatives, instead of unilateral declarations by administrators.[2]

Eight months after Wagner issued his interim order, and even after the extended deadline, too many city administrators continued to drag their feet. The leader of DC 37 called for an end to the existing "jungle of labor relations." While hailing Wagner for contributing more to orderly labor relations than any administration in the previous 20 years, he contended that numbers of public officials were still ignoring the mayor's directive. Wurf insisted that the labor code had to apply across the board, in every city department, covering every city employee, including uniformed personnel. Only those in policy-making positions should be excluded from joining a labor union and bargaining collectively. A contract had to be signed between the city and the labor organization representing a majority of the employees in an agency, giving it exclusive bargaining rights and voluntary dues deduction. The circus atmosphere that had hitherto surrounded parleys on wages and work conditions and testimony before the Board of Estimate had to be replaced with serious negotiations and contracts. Only bona fide labor unions should participate in such bargaining, which meant exclusion of "bowling clubs, bird watchers, and chowder societies," which represented few municipal workers and fostered irresponsible negotiations.[3]

Implementation of Executive Order 49 awaited strong, effective organizing by imaginative union leaders to win the promises projected. During the months that followed, Wurf threw the energies of his small staff into an intensive organizing drive among Parks Department employees. He had come to the conclusion that this department was likely to become his greatest source of strength and that he could build the Council around its membership, particularly the laborers. Aided by activists from ten locals in the city's parks, Wurf crisscrossed the city's parks and playgrounds from early morning until nightfall, signing up new members by the score. However, they were up against the toughest administrator in the city.[4]

INTRODUCING ROBERT MOSES

Within a year after he was brought into the administration of a reform mayor, John Purroy Mitchel of New York, in 1914, Robert Moses devised a system that made every aspect of a public worker's performance subject to a numerical grade; personality traits were also judged this way. Those employees who did not score high enough on his tests, he felt, should be demoted and given pay cuts. Thus, seniority was to be thrown out the window.

In January 1934, after Governor Herbert H. Lehman signed legislation creating a unified, citywide Parks Department, Mayor LaGuardia appointed Moses as its commissioner. Shortly thereafter, Moses began to circumvent civil service regulations at whim, firing Parks Department employees when he wished, or impelling them to resign after assorted forms of harassment and disagreeable assignments. As a recent biographer has indicated, he resented organized labor and told Frances Perkins, when she was state industrial commissioner under Governor Franklin D. Roosevelt, that he would never permit a union bricklayer to work at Jones Beach, which he also supervised. Through subordinates he made it clear that if civil service workers joined a union, he would not only view it as little short of open rebellion, but would feel free to resort to "the remorseless exercise of the executive power of suppression and dismissal to solve this question." It was not unusual, therefore, for Moses's administrators to assign suspected union activists who lived in the Bronx to work in Staten Island, while those who lived in Staten Island might be detailed to the Bronx. Whenever it rained, Moses sent his parks workers home, without pay for the day, and forced them to work 12-hour days the rest of the time.[5]

Over the years, Moses built a fabulous network of bridges, roads, parks, playgrounds, and beaches. Although never elected to public office, he tangled with governors, mayors, and the press and invariably came out on top. The Triborough Bridge and Tunnel Authority, which became his great power base, was so surrounded by legal protections that he could, and did, normally defy chief executives of the city and state. He was a unique public entrepreneur who piled up extraordinary influence and control through the creation of public authorities.[6] Those who succeeded LaGuardia as mayor of New York continued to reappoint Moses as parks commissioner. Wagner was no different when he took over City Hall in January 1954. As his predecessors, the new mayor not only respected the manifold legendary contributions of Moses, but was deeply appreciative of the fact that the latter was perceived as the most powerful individual in the city. Wagner was determined to avoid any confrontations with him, even at the expense of other elements in the community, including organized labor.

Moses was still being hailed by good government leaders as the individual who had bulldozed out of sight numerous offending slums throughout the city. Few were aware of the feudal principality he had developed, and of his exploitation of thousands of city workers in the Parks Department. Moses achieved many of his miracles, including the development of vest-pocket parks, by imposing a six-day, 72-hour week among his city laborers, instead of the 36 to 48 hours normally associated with other public employees. His administrators sometimes explained that there was a shortage of relief men and that parks had to be kept open and maintained from 8 a.m. until 9 p.m. A refusal to work overtime often led to disciplinary proceedings on charges of leaving the assigned work location without being properly relieved.

No matter what work they performed, all Parks Department

employees had to be in proper uniform. This meant wearing a green, six-point, visored cap; a green, longsleeve shirt; black tie; green "Eisenhower" jacket with maple leaf patch and maple leaf pins on the lapels; and green socks and brown shoes. And what were many of these Parks Department laborers doing in this dress uniform? They were lugging bags stuffed with paper, bottles, hubcaps, and other refuse across parks and along the lawns of busy parkways. It was not unusual for a bright, shiny car to suddenly stop alongside one of these Parks employees, and discharge an assistant borough director of the department who would inquire of the worker: "Let me see your socks." If he decided that they were not of the correct hue, then disciplinary proceedings might follow. The formal charge would be "out of uniform."

Another factor that facilitated Moses's miracle was inclement weather. A rainy day meant that Parks Department employees working outdoors would be sent home without pay. If anyone complained against this or other administrative decisions, the ensuing charge might be "insubordination." Workers then had the choice of defending themselves or hiring a lawyer. The latter decision meant a cost of from $50 to $150. Department administrators usually advised the worker involved that if he pleaded guilty, all he would receive was a fine that ranged from $10 to $100, depending on the infraction and the hearing officer. Losing that amount of money was a considerable sacrifice to Department employees, who earned $2,600 a year or less.

Robert Moses ran a quasi-military operation, with an internal spy system. There were, for example, periodic uniform inspections to oblige workers to replace worn-out uniforms at their expense. It was not unusual for supervisors to intimidate workers by having them do jobs that were out-of-title, unsafe, or both. The method of harassment was usually in the form of threats of disciplinary action, delinquency reports, and below-standard ratings.[7]

The situation had worsened to such an extent that in 1950, recreation people on Staten Island sent out an appeal to colleagues in the other four counties to convene a secret meeting in mid-Manhattan. At that time, those who assembled listened to a young organizer from AFSCME, Jerry Wurf. As a follow-up, two representatives from each county met with the AFSCME leader. Everything had to be done surreptitiously to avoid discovery by Moses's spies, and to prevent acts of recrimination, such as transfer to distant work sites.

Strengthened by the knowledge that increasing numbers of laborers in the Parks Department were joining an expanding Local 924, another organizing meeting was planned for recreation employees. When over 50 percent of the department's 400 recreation people appeared, it was clear that the yearning for dignity and first-class citizenship was strong, and that Moses was in trouble. It was not long thereafter that Local 299—New York City Recreational Employees—was in full bloom with a charter of its own. Membership increased steadily as Wurf and his staff journeyed from park to park and playground to playground. No meeting was too small, too distant, too early or too late in the day, for the DC 37 leader.

The group of Career and Salary employees that evolved as the most militant and that soon comprised a large proportion of DC 37 membership was the laborers. With large numbers in the city's Department of Parks, they aimed their greatest barbs at Robert Moses and his Byzantine methods of controlling workers. Wurf rallied this discontent by frequent resort to protests that were successful in gaining media attention. The laborers also found DC 37 attractive because of Wurf's increasing effectiveness in representing union members before the Salary Appeals Board. Wurf soon enabled these employees to gain entrance to the city's Department of Personnel, where he helped voice their bitter complaints against demeaning, out-of-title, assignments. Even though they initially gained little recognition from this city agency, AFSCME urged recreation employees to reject all laborer's work assigned to them. And if they needed lawyers to defend them in disciplinary cases, Wurf would make them available. The Parks Department bureaucracy soon realized that a vibrant union was developing in their midst and that protest and challenges would be made on a regular, organized basis.

TAKING ON MOSES

Beginning in 1955, however, New York AFSCME began to change its organizing strategy. Instead of relying on appeals, the union used its new solid base to call for direct negotiations. The first target was the employer of many Local 924 workers, Robert Moses. The most independent of all department heads, Moses was not only well known for his iron-fisted enforcement of department rules, but he had no grievance procedures and no collective negotiations. Moses seemed to be at the zenith of his power. In addition to being city parks commissioner, he was state parks commissioner, Long Island park commissioner, state power authority chairperson, Triborough Bridge and Tunnel Authority chairperson, city construction coordinator, member of the City Planning Commission, city representative on arterial highways, and slum clearance chairperson.

As Nelson Seitel, city commissioner of labor, subsequently conceded, there was no endeavor by Moses or his administrators to develop a more enlightened labor–management policy. Nor did they seek to implement Mayor Wagner's 1954 edict. Until Wurf appeared on the scene and insisted on change, workers were not allowed to have representatives of their own choosing present at departmental trials, or at what was purported to be grievance hearings. Commissioner Moses remained unavailable to union representatives who wished to discuss the mayor's interim order on labor relations.[8]

Besides organizing the unorganized and issuing statements supportive of Wagner's labor relations policy, there were few alternatives available to Wurf, and many limitations as to what he might do to the various units of the Parks Department. He could attempt to use the media to educate the public and put increasing pressure on City Hall and, eventually, on Moses. He might resort to some type of job action, as long as it did not fall within the provisions of the state's Condon–Wadlin Act, which prohibited public employee strikes and made it obligatory to fire striking employees. But, whatever he did, it would not really affect a vital service. The grass might grow a little taller. Someone would see that the animals were fed. There might not be a recreation leader present at playground sites, and the swimming pools might not have enough chemicals.

Yet, Parks was the city department where DC 37 was best organized, claiming a majority of its workers. If the Council could pull off a successful job action against this department and against the most powerful figure in New York, and at the same time avoid Condon–Wadlin penalties, then AFSCME would have a citadel local, and be recognized as an influential public employee group.

Having mastered the use of the press, Wurf used it to ventilate the many grievances and indignities inflicted on municipal workers. Public response seemed positive and encouraging. Thus, when confronted with the ultimate power figure in New York and the imperious behavior of Parks Department administrators, Wurf finally resolved to publicize in dramatic fashion, the feudal behavior and the inhumanity of this commissioner who was perverting the labor policy set down by the mayor.

A NOVEL JOB ACTION

In collaboration with the presidents of the locals involved in the Parks Department, the Council leader recommended a number of job-related actions. To avoid violation of the Condon–Wadlin law, the director of DC 37 suggested, and local officers agreed to, a novel tactic. On the day of the job action, those who did not report for their usual assignment would, instead, assemble at department headquarters in Central Park's Arsenal Building and file leave-of-absence request forms for the day.

The final decision on the job action, however, was to be made by the members involved, for they would bear the brunt of any penalties, including possible job loss. Most of them were new to the union movement and, therefore, untried as to strike actions and picket lines. At local meetings, the DC 37 leader cautioned that if only a few hundred left their work sites, they might well lose their jobs. On the other hand, if thousands joined, then the city would not dare discharge that number. The recommendation for job action was overwhelmingly approved.

On November 3, 1955, over 2,000 park employees did not report to their work sites throughout the city. Instead, they assembled in front of the Parks Department headquarters at the Arsenal in Central Park, just off Fifth Avenue. That day, most of them spent some eight hours on picket lines, first at the Arsenal and then at City Hall, demonstrating against "flagrant union-busting" and carrying signs accusing Moses of flouting the labor relations code issued by Wagner, 16 months earlier. These picketing workers blocked all traffic that sought to cross the park at that point, and soon began to ruffle the composure of administrators inside the building. Wurf was unaware, at first, that Moses did not use the Arsenal as his personal headquarters and that, at that moment, he was miles away at the offices of the Triborough Bridge and Tunnel Authority on Randalls Island.

The workers continued to picket in front of the dismal Arsenal with simulated battle turrets. To point up the inhumane treatment accorded park employees, Mildred Kiefer had rented a large steel cage that was placed on the base of a flat truck. Occupied by uniformed parks personnel, the cage displayed, in typical zoo fashion, two huge signs. The top one advised passersby that this was "Bob Moses' Zoo." A lower identification poster contained the following description of the caged inhabitants:

SPECIES: Park Worker
HABITAT: New York City Parks
CHARACTERISTICS: Resembles Normal American Worker BUT
                      Has No Collective Bargaining
                      Has No Grievance Machinery
                      Has No Dignity On The Job
                      Works for Absentee Owner[9]

While observing the pickets marching up and down in front of the Arsenal, busy newsmen and photographers were gathering material for the afternoon or the next day's editions of newspapers. There was ample copy and pictures, especially of the caged Parks Department employees, and the thousands carrying placards urging Moses to stop stalling. Wurf found himself in a quandary when he learned that Moses was on Randalls Island. One message, Wurf recalled later, informed him: "We don't care if you wear out the pavement. We can take the strike forever." That last communiqué troubled the AFSCME leader, for he knew it came from Moses and his command post, from which safety point the parks commissioner was directing the battle of his administrators. How could he affect a distant, powerful commissioner? For want of a better tactic, at the moment, the thousands continued to picket the Arsenal. Wurf, meanwhile, grasped for alternatives as he sought to keep the job action alive and to influence the public and the mayor through newspapers, radio, and television. After hours of picketing, Wurf grasped at a suggestion that he transfer the scene of the battle to the mayor's front yard. If one of AFSCME's objectives was to force Moses to sit down at the same table with their representatives, in the absence of the parks commissioner, Wagner alone could ensure that outcome. Wurf directed picketers to City Hall. The New York Times labor reporter, Abraham Raskin, wagered that these workers would disappear on the way down and wander back to their homes. But he lost the bet. Within the hour some 2,000 council members regrouped with their placards in a long picket line, which wound slowly around the park, in front of the venerable City Hall.[10]

Indifferent journalists who covered events at City Hall from room 9 did not stop their marathon card game until they heard a deafening roar outside: "Which Bob is Boss?" Some picketer had started the slogan and it was repeated endlessly by the marching union members. When the reporters ventured out, they not only observed thousands of placard-carrying picketers but spotted the labor reporters of their own newspapers who had traveled downtown with Wurf. Disturbed by the possibility that other reporters might end up writing the story about workers in their territory, they hastened to the AFSCME commander to get the facts. Wurf was about to be given all the publicity he wanted. And it would not necessarily be hostile.

The continued roar of the pickets also infiltrated the mayor's office. Within a brief period Wagner's executive secretary, William Peer, ventured out to the steps of City Hall and beckoned to Wurf. Towering over the labor leader by a full head, Peer's well-tailored clothes, with white handkerchief sticking out of the breast pocket of his neatly pressed jacket, contrasted sharply with the rumpled, baggy outfit of the labor spokesperson.

Peer reminded Wurf that it was the mayor who had given him and other public employee unionists one of the most enlightened labor policy statements in the nation. Wurf's gripe, insisted Wagner's assistant, was with Moses, and he suggested that the union leader go fight him. "You're a nice guy," Wurf was purported to have replied. "I love you like a brother. But tell the mayor we want to meet with him." When Peer insisted that the mayor would not do so, Wurf suggested that if the mayor did not meet with a union delegation then they would be back the next day, and the day after, picketing City Hall until they sat down and talked. Confronted with this threat, Peer retreated to confer with Wagner. Afternoon deadlines of newspapers were passing, and reporters were unable to telephone any conclusive developments. For the DC 37 leader, this was Armageddon, and there was no turning back. It was to be either a signal victory or a resounding defeat.

Eventually, the mayor's secretary returned and informed Wurf that the mayor would see him. Jerry then led a delegation of local officers and activists into the beautiful rotunda, past iron gates and a small army of the mayor's staff before they entered the historic office of the city's chief magistrate. A short, friendly Wagner welcomed the group and then started offering all sorts of explanations as to why they had come to the wrong man, and why he could do nothing about their dispute with Bob Moses. At this point, Wurf resorted to his typical exchange with city officials who sought to avoid a decision that was within their purview. As Wurf recalled the encounter, he informed the mayor that he did not wish to be malicious, tactless, or discourteous. But the point was that Wagner had issued an executive order and had assured Wurf, privately and publicly, that this directive would be carried out. Neglecting to insist on Moses's adherence to his labor policy, the mayor had demonstrated a lack of commitment to the issue. Furthermore, by permitting the Parks Department to be the worst violator, he had facilitated this inevitable confrontation. Expecting the ultimate defeat of these "leave of absence" workers by the "lord of the manor," Wagner knew that it would then be easier to remain master of other sectors of public employment. Wurf expressed the feeling that he had been set up for a downfall by a liberal Democratic mayor, the son of the famed New Deal senator.

When the Mayor proceeded to underscore his difficulties in dealing with Moses, Wurf interrupted with a voice that was now a few decibels louder. The order, he contended, was meaningless, and he threatened to inform the newsmen outside that the mayor was playing games and that the mayor and the labor commissioner had deliberately set up this confrontation with Moses. Finally, he insisted that the mayor tell Moses, on the telephone, to meet with a union delegation and implement his executive order.[11]

THE MAYOR MAKES A PHONE CALL

At that very moment, Wagner was in one of his periodic crises with Democratic Party leaders, and had been publicly rebuffed, only two weeks previously, by his police commissioner in a matter that involved labor relations. He could not readily afford to have his liberal, pro-union image tarnished further by thousands of public employees protesting his lack of courage and leadership through daily picketing and slogan shouting around City Hall. New York was a city of strong labor traditions and young Wagner sought to carry the mantle of his famed father, friend of unions. It was the elder Wagner who had given birth to labor's Magna Carta in 1935.

In response to Wurf's repeated insistence that he arrange a conference with Moses and union representatives, the mayor telephoned the commissioner. The mayor sought to make clear that his labor code was intended to cover all agencies, including parks. He also relayed the comments of his labor commissioner, who agreed with the union that the Parks Department was violating key provisions of his labor relations code, such as refusing to allow workers to express their view through chosen union representatives, or to set up joint labor–management committees for the discussion of employee problems. Robert Moses, while still powerful in the 1950s, was becoming increasingly vulnerable. No longer did he carry the "white knight" image in the New York press. Using this well-publicized demonstration, Wurf and the Council locals were able to point out how Moses had flagrantly flaunted Wagner's directive by refusing to meet with union representatives. Visualizing continued harassment by newspaper, radio, and television coverage, and pressured by a troubled mayor, Moses reluctantly agreed to meet with an AFSCME delegation.

To his assembled members outside, Wurf's foghorn voice roared out the good news. The mayor, he insisted, had "ordered" Moses to go to a Monday morning meeting at the arsenal, and "His imperial majesty, Robert Moses, is going to have to come, whether he wants to or not. The Stars and Bars have been removed from the Parks Department, and it's now on the same basis as any other." They were to return to their jobs. The victory roar that followed sent City Hall pigeons scurrying into the skies.[12]

IN THE BIG TIME

A few days later, in front of reporters and photographers, a jocular Moses greeted Wurf as if he were a long-lost brother. Pictures were taken of the two smiling and shaking hands. Moses spoke of his friend, Jerry Wurf, who did things in a dramatic fashion. He assured the journalists that they would sit down and work things out, for they had one thing in common, and that was a concern for the well-being of the workers. These were strange and unfamiliar sentiments from Bob Moses. As soon as the two walked alone into a private office, however, the parks commissioner let loose with a blast of profanities that momentarily set Wurf back on his heels. After regaining his composure, the union leader replied in kind. When the tirades stopped, Moses called in members of his own staff and the rest of the union delegation, and insisted that DC 37 would first have to prove that it represented a majority of the workers involved. Wurf's immediate rejoinder was, "Do you want me to bring them back in front of the arsenal?" The Parks commissioner didn't want it done by mob rule, but agreed to hold an election in a few weeks, for which the workers would have time off. The department's employees would then vote for union representatives to participate in joint labor–management committees on personnel problems. Despite the insistence of the department's executive officer, Stuart Constable, that other unions would be on the ballot, local leaders affiliated with DC 37 contended that there were no other unions with membership among the department's attendants, gardeners, laborers, and other classes of blue-collar workers. The voting results would prove them correct.

During the 75-minute meeting, which turned into something of a love-fest, at least on the surface, the union delegation came away with other significant assurances. Annual service ratings, which controlled a worker's right to periodic pay raises, would not be used for "coercive purposes." Workers would be allowed to designate a union representative to speak on their behalf at grievance sessions relating to such matters as transfers, vacation rights, promotions, and rates of pay. And, finally, all employees would thereafter have the right to be represented by union counsel at disciplinary hearings.

The AFSCME delegation avoided any appearance, before the waiting newsmen, of crowing over the outcome of the meeting. "Nobody claims a victory," Wurf said. "We have a working relationship with the department for the first time and we are very happy about it. We think the agreement to hold an election sets a healthy precedent for other municipal agencies." A.H. Raskin observed that in sharp contrast, Moses had nothing to say after the meeting. He merely picked up his hat and coat and walked toward the elevator without a word for reporters.

The Parks Department workers had achieved a remarkable victory for themselves and for public workers throughout the city. One of the most powerful individuals in New York had conceded the initial DC 37 demands—a representation election and, for the victor, exclusive voice at the bargaining table. This concession gave the Council the glory and the clout of a citadel union among public employees. From this moment, Wurf's stature increased dramatically, along with that of the Council. The editors of the *New York Times* deemed this an unusual if not historic event, according the story front-page billing, near the top, alongside a picture of Moses and Wurf shaking hands and smiling.[13]

In little over two months, elections were held among the employees of the Parks Department. Traveling considerable distances to polling sites, over 95 percent of the workers voted, with 4,117 casting their ballots for DC 37 locals, 85 for the Teamsters, and 88 for no union. Rarely had such an impressive turnout been recorded for one organization in a representation election in city history.[14]

SUMMARY

The one-day job action against Robert Moses was a historic event in municipal labor relations. It reaffirmed the premise for a new set of labor–management relationships, and became a turning point for Wurf and DC 37. The mayor's interim order, which Parks Department employees helped make meaningful, eventually became a basis for President Kennedy's Executive Order 10988, which provided a similar program for Federal employees. From this point on, representation elections and collective bargaining became the focus of the struggle for public employees across the country. This victory also helped change the thinking and behavior of increasing numbers of public workers. From long-time commitment to a civil servant, false merit orientation, they began to support a trade union approach. By adopting the new strategy, public workers had to build a bold political thrust to enhance collective bargaining. The scope of negotiations would be shaped by union power and skilled leadership. During the months that followed the victory over Moses, DC 37 became recognized, increasingly, as a militant, fast-growing public employee union. But the organization would have to continue its struggles with mayors and municipal agencies every step of the way.

NOTES

1. *New York Times,* July 22, 1954, p. 25; *Spotlight,* August 1954, p. 1; September 6, 1954, p. 2.

2. *New York Times,* October 3, 1954, p. 28; December 1, 1954, p. 12.

3. *New York Times,* March 26, 1955, p. 8; April 19, 1956, p. 22; *Spotlight,* April 1, 1955, pp. 1, 11.

4. Eliot Reif to author, August 7, 1981; interview with Bert Rose, September 16, 1981. Staff members included Bill Evans, Ted Bleecker, Jean Couturier, Eugene Schwartz, and Mildred Kiefer. Among the leading activists were Hymie Greenberg, Johnny Hauson, Tommy Hart, Irving Baron, Eliot Reif, John Byrne, Elizabeth Jesinkey, and Cornelia McCarthy.

5. Robert A. Caro, *The Power Broker,* New York: Alfred A. Knopf, 1974, pp. 74-76, 78-81, 276, 360-362, 368, 735. Also, interviews with Eliot Reif, November 27, 1978; Bert Rose, September 16, 1981. Reif was first appointed playground director in 1931 and served as president of Local 299 from 1968 to 1978.

6. Jewel Bellush and Murray Hausknecht, "Entrepreneurs and Urban Renewal: The New Men of Power," in Bellush and Hausknecht, eds., *Urban Renewal: People, Politics and Planning,* Garden City, NY: Doubleday Anchor, 1967, pp. 209-224.

7. Nick Cifuni to Morris Riger, April 1, 1963; Nick Cifuni, "Who Built This Union? Robert Moses!" *Public Employee Press,* December 12, 1969, p. 14; Burney Rydzeski to author, December 4, 1978; Fred Szabo to author, December 26, 1978. Also, interviews with Eliot Reif, November 27, 1978; and Bert Rose, September 16, 1981.

8. *New York Times,* November 4, 1955, p. 60; November 8, 1955, p. 1. Also, see Mark H. Maier, "The City and the Unions, Collective Bargaining in New York City: 1954-1973," Ph.D. dissertation, New School for Social Research, 1980, pp. 75-77.

9. *New York Times,* November 4, 1955, p. 60; *Public Employee Press,* December 12, 1969, p. 15.

10. Fred Shapiro, "How Jerry Wurf Walks on Water," *New York Times Magazine,* April 11, 1976, p. 76; interviews with Eliot Reif, January 15 and March 7, 1979; and Jerry Wurf, August 20 and 21, 1979.

11. *Ibid.* It was the elder Wagner who had been the keynote speaker at the ceremonies marking the issuance of an AFSCME charter to DC 37 in 1944.

12. *New York Times,* November 4, 1955, p. 60; Caro, *The Power Broker,* Part VII; interviews with Elliot Reif, December 18 and 28, 1978; and Jerry Wurf, August 20, 1979. See also, Maier, "The City and the Unions," p. 77.

13. *New York Times,* November 8, 1955, p. 1; interview with William Casamo, October 17, 1979.

14. *Spotlight,* February 1, 1956, p. 1; February 15, 1956, p. 1.

4
Collective Bargaining—
Not Collective Begging

Jerry Wurf sought to have the city adopt, for its public workers, the bilateral collective bargaining process won by organized labor in the private sector some two decades previously. Despite the growth of public worker unions, the civil service approach and mentality continued to dominate labor relations. Even in New York, widely known as a labor town, public employee unions confronted a highly fragmented political system in which power over personnel and budget matters was scattered over a large number of municipal agencies. Although he professed to be determined to carry on the progressive traditions of his father, particularly those relating to organized labor, Mayor Robert F. Wagner, Jr. (1954–1965) did not enable Wurf to achieve his major goal easily. Instead, the labor leader was obliged to resort to a combination of painstaking organizing endeavors, lobbying City Hall and administrative agencies, as well as to an assortment of militant job actions or threats.

FRAGMENTED POWER IN LABOR RELATIONS

In the early 1950s, neither the city's public workers nor the mayor exerted much influence over New York's personnel system. What existed was fragmentation of political influence over municipal labor relations and the rules of the personnel system. During his 1953 election campaign, Wagner ensured the vital support of most public employees when he promised to reorganize the Mu-

Throughout the 1950s a militant DC 37 frequently demonstrated before City Hall to call attention to the need for establishing a modern collective bargaining process and more humane personnel practices.

nicipal Civil Service Commission, revise the city's classification and pay plan and, without going into details, endorsed the concept of a "genuine pattern of collective bargaining" for city workers. During his subsequent years in City Hall, Mayor Wagner succeeded in overhauling the process, enabling him to move closer to the center of political power in the municipal personnel system.

The formal structure of the city's labor relations system was chaotic. Those having a hand in various segments of the city's personnel system (with varying degrees of influence) included the Board of Estimate, the mayor, the Bureau of the Budget, the city council, the Municipal Civil Service Commission, the comptroller, and more than 100 departments, agencies, and authorities. To all this must be added a variety of interventions by the state legislature and the state Civil Service Commission.

The greatest measure of control was exercised by the Board of Estimate, due to its influence over compensation and the city's expense and capital budgets. The Bureau of the Budget had a significant impact on the personnel system because of its mastery of information, administration of the budget, and access to departmental operations.[1]

The mayor, as chief executive, had the power to appoint and remove the directors of Budget and Personnel, as well as virtually all of the city's line agency heads. While influential, his role as a member of the Board of Estimate was not always controlling in the determination of capital and expense budgetary items. Although the most powerful city official, his ability to affect the salaries of public employees was limited, at times, by board members who could muster political influence to resist the mayor. The Bureau of the Budget could, on occasion, challenge mayoral authority.

The Municipal Civil Service Commission, which administered the merit system in hiring, promotion, discipline, and classification, was intent on perpetuating its existence and resisted intrusions into its jurisdiction, precisely the subjects spotlighted by Wurf for collective bargaining. It was at the departmental level, however, that key decisions were constantly made concerning work conditions, workloads, job assignments, scheduling, and other elements of the personnel system. Increasingly, over the years, frustrated union leaders began journeying to Albany to seek from state officials what they were denied by the fragmented personnel system of the city. It was not easy for union officials, who were pressured by members to gain significant improvements in wages, hours, work conditions, and fringe benefits.[2]

Most public employee unions were comfortable with what Wurf described as, the "public fix." Government representatives, from the mayor on down, were accustomed to elaborate civil service laws, regulations, and procedures and continued to resist what appeared as intrusions into their managerial prerogatives.

Wurf realized that whereas it was easy to know and involve the principals in the private sector in direct bargaining, it was frequently difficult to identify, let alone bring to a bargaining table, the key managers responsible in the public sector. Even though the AFSCME leader might negotiate with the commissioner of a major department, he soon realized that administrators often had to operate in severely circumscribed settings. Consultation, for example, was frequently required with directors of Personnel and

Budget, and any commitments made usually affected other city agencies. From Wurf's perspective, bargaining in such circumstances was destined to be a bewildering, protracted, and frustrating experience.[3]

DISAPPOINTED WITH CAMPAIGN PROMISES

To fulfill some of his campaign promises, Wagner created four new overhead agencies, established a Career and Salary Plan, and eventually issued the interim order on the conduct of relations between the city and its public employees. A Department of Labor, at first invested with substantial independence from the Board of Estimate and the Bureau of the Budget, was assigned major responsibilities for developing and supervising the city's labor-management program. Wagner's influence over this department, however, remained strong throughout his 12 years as mayor.

Following severe criticisms of the old Civil Service Commission, a Department of Personnel and a new City Civil Service Commission (CSC) were created, headed by one individual who was made directly responsible to the mayor. Both agencies were involved in setting salary levels and scheduling civil service examinations. The new CSC was circumscribed by the persistent intervention of the Board of Estimate and the Bureau of the Budget.

As far as Wurf was concerned, when the new administration was confronted with one of its first important tests on employee relations, it failed miserably. All of Wagner's glowing promises to establish something akin to collective bargaining went out the window when he and his departmental heads refused to negotiate with accredited union representatives on the crucial matters of minimum wages, pay raises, and overtime. Instead, public employee unions were notified after the fact that the budget had been agreed to by the city administrators and they could, if they wished, argue it before the Board of Estimate. Since Wurf insisted that he would not seek any backdoor agreements with the mayor and his subordinates, he viewed the immediate results as a fiasco.[4]

THE CAREER AND SALARY PLAN

In July 1954, the mayor created his Career and Salary Plan. This was an endeavor to revise the city's outdated personnel system, whereby public workers were classified into more sensible categories, salary levels were upgraded, and out-of-title work was eliminated. Hopefully, this was to be the beginning of better things for public workers. The new Personnel Department, the CSC, and the Budget Bureau were directed to develop a comprehensive system classifying public employees into specific titles and broad occupational groups to facilitate such decisions as determining salaries, examinations, appointments, and promotions. While the Board of Estimate retained the final say over decisions reached under this new plan, the Personnel Department and the city CSC made the initial classification and salary decisions. And since the mayor had significant influence over the personnel director, he was in a position to be involved in important personnel decisions on salaries and job classification.

To enable civil servants to appeal these decisions, the Board of Estimate created two appeals boards—the Classification Appeals Board and the Career and Salary Appeals Board—with duplicate membership: the directors of Budget and Personnel, the labor commissioner, who served as chairperson, and two employee representatives. Since the labor commissioner and the personnel director always supported the mayor, and usually the budget director, appeals decisions rarely favored city workers. As decisions of the appeals boards were subject to final approval by the body that created them, the Board of Estimate, this generally insured that they would rarely be upset.[5]

The Career and Salary Plan applied to most white-collar positions in the city's civil service under the jurisdiction of the mayor. Under it, the city proceeded to establish uniform policies for pensions, health plans, pay practices, the workweek, overtime, shift differentials, time and leave (including vacations), personnel practices, transfers, and retraining reassignment. This plan, however, was jeopardized from the start by a contradiction in Wagner's policy on reclassification. It relegated employee groups like DC 37 to the role of supplicants, instead of allowing them to participate as equals on levels of planning and negotiation. During the years that followed, the plan tended to turn many civil service jobs into dead ends by ending differential pay for experience. A second consequence of the plan was to reduce the scope and limits of collective bargaining for any single union that did not have "fifty plus one percent," for it could only bargain within the framework of the plan.

Confronted with the proposed executive budget for 1955–56, Wurf complained about the omission of the 40-hour workweek and a minimum raise of at least $500 for all city employees. Over the years, these budget hearings developed a character more in keeping with a three-ring circus, a poor substitute for collective bargaining. Wurf underscored the increasing difficulties in the Career and Salary Plan. He insisted that reorganization of the social service structure in the Department of Hospitals was causing a mass exodus of psychiatric and medical social workers, who were forced to resign to safeguard their professional standing. In the face of a growing juvenile delinquency problem, the city's low salaries discouraged recruitment and training of quality personnel. Despite the critical shortage of nurses and other personnel in the municipal hospital system, the city offered salaries so low that it accelerated turnover.

Wagner, meanwhile, had assured public employee unions that reclassification within the Career and Salary Plan was not a rigid, fixed formula but an elastic process, subject to modification and improvement. Through the medium of the job audit and appeals machinery, inequities not resolved by the career plan would still be corrected. Local AFSCME leaders, however, sought to remind city administrators that there were important human elements involved, which could not be ignored. Management had to recognize the full scope of existing services, standards, and goals of professional employees, as well as the need to stimulate the aspirations of all municipal workers, especially those in the lowest categories. Too many bureaucrats, from commissioners on down, tended to have a low esteem of the public servants they were assigned to supervise.

WAGNER NEEDS PRODDING

Throughout the 12 years of the Wagner administration, Wurf and his colleagues constantly had to threaten and plead to win any concessions in labor–management relations. Wurf would often have to surround City Hall with his chanting picketers until the mayor, anxious to preserve his pro-labor image, would invite them in for discussion and some compensation.[6]

Not until 18 months after taking office did Wagner fulfill one of his campaign pledges when he convinced the Board of Estimate to provide for the voluntary checkoff of union dues. This act insured a steady, increasing income into the coffers of AFSCME locals. It also helped bring order out of the chaos due to irresponsible actions and claims of small splinter groups. That same year, the mayor pushed through the 40-hour workweek for municipal employees not yet covered, finally bringing city policy in line with the private sector.

By 1957, another mayoral election, AFSCME claimed 25,000 members, the largest single union of public employees in the city. It had signed up individuals in every department and agency, in cultural institutions, and in various authorities. But DC 37 was not yet permitted to bargain collectively. City administrators were not of uniform mind—some officials opposed collective bargaining while others, especially in the Labor Department, urged building a bargaining machinery that would serve as a prototype for the city and state. In the meantime, leaders of public service employees were still placed in the position of supplicants, pleading, often ineffectually, before the Board of Estimate for alterations in annual budgetary decisions decided unilaterally, without union consultation. Most city officials continued, in autocratic fashion, to decide when they would follow a consultative strategy and when to go it alone. This contrasted sharply with the situation in Philadelphia, where municipal officials had recently signed an exclusive bargaining contract with a sister council of AFSCME.

As far as DC 37 was concerned, the grievance machinery had become an excuse for paper work, and the labor–management committees, established at the behest of the mayor, evolved primarily as opportunities for "sterile, academic studies" by the Department of Labor. The many purported "accomplishments" of the Wagner administration were viewed by AFSCME as "rituals without meaning." The author of the Executive Order of 1954 had not fundamentally altered the situation of the average public employee. Despite creation of the Department of Labor and issuance of the order, city employees remained without a genuine labor code administered by impartial individuals.[7]

LABOR'S MAGNA CARTA, EXECUTIVE ORDER 49

The local leadership of DC 37 continued to press for genuine collective bargaining. It was affronted by the need to fight for every request for its workers among the far-flung bureaucratic maze of agencies headed by individuals whose attitudes towards labor usually ranged from indifferent to hostile. Word began to circulate of a new plan, written by Ida Klaus, which would rationalize the highly fragmented process in labor relationships. The District Council, meanwhile, continued its pressure group tactics, taking its criticisms to the public through television and a rally that overflowed the old St. Nicholas Arena. Finally, the famous "Magna Carta" surfaced in March 1958.

Executive Order 49 formally recognized the organization and bargaining rights of city employees, codified grievance procedures, established joint labor relations committees, and conferred on the Department of Labor authority to resolve representation issues, determine appropriate bargaining units, and intervene in bargaining impasses between the city and its organized employees. Wagner had extended private-sector-type bargaining to the city, and centralized municipal labor relations. As a result, his control over city management substantially increased and strengthened his political power. He became, in effect, the municipality's chief labor negotiator, setting the terms and conditions of employment.

The order was intentionally vague, giving Wagner maximum managerial authority and control over its decision making. It related to workers in mayoral agencies, which encompassed about one-half of the city's public employees. While many civil service leaders viewed the order as their "Magna Carta," others, especially in DC 37, remained critical. While providing for the exclusive recognition of those who won a majority of workers in an appropriate unit, it did not spell out the scope of bargaining for such important benefits as welfare plans, promotion, time and leave rules, and pay plans and regulations.[8]

A major hurdle for public employee unions remained—to win certification as the exclusive representative of a specific employee group. The labor commissioner was given major responsibility for deciding the appropriateness of a bargaining unit and for certifying an organization as a public employee union for that unit. This proved to be a key phase for union recognition because, when certified, a union had the theoretical right to process grievances, represent employees on departmental labor relations commissions, and bargain collectively. The commissioner also determined that an organization could be certified, following an election, to act as the collective bargaining representative. The election could be dispensed with if more than 50 percent of the workers in that unit authorized a specific union to receive the checkoff of union dues. Once a union was certified by the Labor Department no other organization could process grievances.

As a consequence, the number and scope of grievances filed increased significantly, and bargaining certificates granted by the Labor Department proliferated. The result, as Horton put it, was "a crazy patchwork of bargaining units, excessive in number and highly complicated." However, the new executive order improved on the Interim Order of 1954 by requiring that only certified unions could represent employees on labor relations committees, thus substantially reducing the number of organizations. Unfortunately, many administrators simply postponed meetings in which there was endless discussion and little action. Wagner did not rush his subordinates into any collective bargaining negotiations with public employee unions, making it clear that the scope of bargaining would be limited. DC 37 officers, as a result, became increasingly frustrated by his failure to spell out his new labor policy.[9]

INCH BY INCH, TITLE BY TITLE

Through the months that followed, Council members were obliged to resort periodically to demonstrations, mass meetings, full-page newspaper ads, radio announcements, and even job actions, at almost every important point of negotiations. Refreshed by a Bermuda vacation, Wagner returned to his office on the first anniversary of Executive Order 49. Welcoming him back to City Hall were thousands of AFSCME members who circled the building for hours with placards that urged him to get the collective bargaining process off the ground—"We don't want a vacation in Bermuda . . . We just want a living wage!"; "Mayor Wagner Keep your Pledge"; "No Career, No Salary, in Career and Salary Plan." Old-timers in the union recall it as their "Easter Rebellion."[10]

Disturbed by the size of the demonstration, and annoyed that it made front-page news, Wagner pushed city officials toward a modified form of collective bargaining for a number of categories of career and salary workers. The Board of Estimate ratified the results by voting salary raises of from one to three grades for over

DC 37 members welcoming Mayor Robert F. Wagner, Jr., back to City Hall from one of his vacations in Bermuda.

33 titles, mostly from the Parks and Traffic Departments and cultural and quasi-public institutions. As news of the Council's militancy and claims of victory spread, hundreds of public workers in other titles and departments signed the DC 37 green membership card.

Where the majority of employees in a particular title were employed in one department, collective bargaining rights were won comparatively early. They included gardeners, climbers, and pruners in the Parks Department, the public health sanitarians in the Health Department, social workers in the Department of Hospitals, and social service titles in the Welfare Department. However, where employees in a title were dispersed throughout the city, such as MVO's, or in unusually large bargaining units like clericals, organizing took much longer.[11]

Finally, in May 1960, the directors of Budget and Personnel spelled out the procedures for joint collective bargaining they would follow under Executive Order 49. The city would bargain only with those unions that represented a citywide majority of all employees in a specific class of work, such as clericals or laborers, who were located in more than one department. Those unions that were certified by the Labor Department were not automatically admitted to collective bargaining because certificates were granted on a departmental, rather than a citywide basis, whereas many important titles, like MVOs, clerks, or laborers, cut across departments. And until a citywide majority was attained by DC 37, or by any other public worker union, the benefits accruing to those certified under Executive Order 49 were comparatively minor, such as processing grievances and representing employees in an endless series of frustrating experiences in departmental labor relations committees.[12]

It was during these developments that the management of cultural and quasi-public institutions, whose workers' salaries were paid primarily by the city, added to the sense of frustration that enveloped Council leaders. In the process of halting negotiations with DC 37 representatives, these administrators ensured interminable delays in the settlement of wage and other disputes. It was again largely through strikes and job actions at the Youth House, the Brooklyn Botanical Garden, the Bronx Zoo, and the Coney Island Aquarium that administrators were brought to the bargaining table. Significant strides were made on many issues, including modification of salary scales, expecially at the lowest levels, and the institution of a voluntary dues checkoff.[13]

The Council achieved a major breakthrough in 1960 when, as a result of collective bargaining negotiations for Department of Parks employees, it won an across-the-board wage increase. The victory was unprecedented because it was the first time that such increases had been won over the modest incremental policies of the City's Career and Salary Plan. For Parks Department workers it meant that they would receive cash-in-pocket increases over and above any annual increments due them. It seemed to mark the beginning of a new era in collective bargaining for New York City's public employees, for DC 37 had started to weaken the barriers of the Career and Salary Plan. Thereafter, AFSCME members in other departments and agencies would benefit whenever they gained a majority of the employees in a specific job category.

In the absence, however, of a genuine collective bargaining system, Council negotiators felt frustrated in securing benefits for their other members. Despite its sharp indictments of the Wagner administration, the Council and its locals managed, by the end of 1960, to win certification of exclusive bargaining status for thousands of workers embracing dozens of titles in a variety of departments and cultural and quasi-public institutions.

City Hall acknowledged the growing importance of AFSCME and its leadership; the Department of Personnel announced that when bargaining began after May 1, 1961 for some 43 different classifications, DC 37 would bargain for 29, more than 60 percent of the total. In addition, the Council held bargaining talks for some dozen titles in the cultural institutions and a large number of Parks Department titles. With a claimed membership of some 30,000, Wurf spoke for the strongest union of public workers in New York. And yet, representatives of various locals continued to appear before the Salary Appeals Board, negotiating for additional wage increases. Strengthened by the Council's research staff and negotiators, several groups won a number of upgradings for hospital workers, clericals, public health assistants, and cashiers.[14]

DC 37 JOINS THE "BOSSES"

By the time Wagner decided to run for a third term in 1961, he was viewed as too independent by City Hall, the Bronx Democratic leader, and by those controlling the remnants of decaying party organizations throughout the city. A slate headed by state controller Arthur Levitt was put together to challenge Wagner. Paul Hall, Wurf's mentor and important supporter, went along with the "boss-led" Democratic organization and Levitt, as did Wurf. Over the years, the Council leadership had been frustrated by the slow, difficult struggle to attain genuine collective bargaining rights under the Wagner administration. As a result of Wurf's urging, the Council supported Levitt who subsequently was soundly defeated in the primaries. Remaining neutral in the general elections, which Wagner won handily, Wurf soon found that City Hall doors were not readily opened for him during the remaining Wagner years.

The Council, meanwhile, continued to grow. By 1962 it claimed some 36,000 members and a substantial dues income, which enabled it to move to larger offices and hire additional staff for organizing work.

MVOS MILITANT ACTION

A key event for 1962, in emotional impact and organizational significance, was the strike of some 2,000 MVOs. These blue-collar workers, overwhelmingly white ethnics, were rough-and-tumble individuals who had a long history of loyal commitment to their union. They were among the first to resort to job actions, or even strikes, when necessary. And they were usually to be found on the picket lines or public demonstrations of other locals. After an intense organizing drive in ten departments and a key election in the city hospitals, MVO Local 983 attained a citywide majority. Although the MVOs had finally won the right to collective bargaining representation in July, not until the end of October was the first negotiating session held between city administrators and union representatives. When the local's membership was alerted that Wagner's negotiators had refused to budge from an offer of one grade increase in wages, it voted to strike within two weeks unless the city increased the proposed raise. In response, the mayor's office halted further negotiations until the union called off its scheduled walkout and renounced its right to strike.

Insistent on retaining the right to strike, and aware of the possible penalties awaiting them if the Condon–Wadlin Act was invoked, they refused to be overawed by threats from City Hall. On a November morning, some 2,000 MVOs exchanged their trucks, limousines, and ambulances for picket signs, and immediately curtailed important operations in most city departments and agencies. Every facet of government was affected—commissioners were forced to use taxis or the subway system to get around to meetings and offices. This work stoppage hurt both sides, for it tarnished the pro-labor image of Mayor Wagner, and brought into question the sense of responsibility of a union that would pull ambulance drivers off their jobs.

Policemen manned ambulances as the mayor spurned an offer by the Council's executive director and President Joseph Passarella of Local 983 to cooperate in maintaining these and other vital services. Although the MVOs were ordered back to work and threatened with firings if they refused, the only act of reprisal was taken by the police commissioner, Michael J. Murphy. Without apparent consultation with the mayor, he invoked the Condon–Wadlin Law and suspended a total of 16 striking drivers in his department.

For 48 hours thereafter, Wurf telephoned other labor leaders, alerting them to the anti-union implications of the suspensions. In his resort to the much-hated Condon–Wadlin Law, Murphy's action sent a warning and a direct challenge to the labor movement of this "union town." These first Condon–Wadlin dismissals in New York City were viewed by many labor leaders as a hasty, negative response to an unfortunate labor–management dispute. If permitted to remain unchallenged, it might become a precedent for similar moves by city administrators in the future.

Condon–Wadlin had been used as a forceful weapon only in those areas of the state where organized labor was generally weak and ineffective. In large union centers, however, most public officials had been pressured by labor leaders to avoid its use because of its stress on automatic retribution against striking unions rather than recalcitrant administrators. Union leaders had urged more positive alternatives such as mediation and arbitration. President Paul Hall of the SIU charged the police commissioner with gestapo tactics. A troubled mayor, who appeared not to have been consulted in advance by his police head, gingerly supported Murphy's moves while insisting that the police drivers had not been dismissed but merely suspended. Within hours, the police commissioner reiterated his earlier contention that, in accord with the Condon–Wadlin Act, the striking MVOs in his department had been "effectively dismissed." The mayor and the police chief were now in conflict.

Two days after the start of the strike, and in response to pleas from Wurf, the top leadership of some 200 international, state, and local labor organizations convened in an emergency meeting, which was rare in the annals of New York's labor history. Momentarily circumventing the Central Labor Council, headed by Wagner's friend, Harry Van Arsdale, these labor leaders expressed support for the suspended MVOs. They hastily made plans for a demonstration and mass picketing. Within days, thousands of rank-and-file hospital and restaurant workers, longshoremen, sailors, firemen, carpenters, department store employees, and teachers joined DC 37 members in front of City Hall. While the police estimated a crowd of 3,000, labor leaders claimed close to 12,000. Wurf demanded that the ousted police drivers be reinstated as a condition for ending the strike.

In a highly publicized maneuver, 16 Democratic and Republican state lawmakers reminded the mayor of his earlier condemnation of Condon–Wadlin as a bad law, and appealed for a "fair and equitable" settlement of the strike. Wurf saw to it that the pressure on Wagner remained unyielding. AFSCME members from many locals helped sustain the strike through extensive personal involvement. After picketing hospital MVOs had maintained 24-hour vigils at 16 facilities for almost a week, Parks Department MVOs replaced their striking brethren on the picket line for an entire weekend. Although covered by a separate contract, these parks employees demonstrated a union consciousness that paid dividends for the MVOs in Local 983. Together, they helped make the Council the largest and most effective public workers' union in New York.

With the strike well into its second week and the bulk of the union movement firmly behind it, Harry Van Arsdale entered the picture. As president of New York City's Central Labor Council, the electrical union leader had often been called on by Wagner to restrain Jerry Wurf. At this stage of the strike, Van Arsdale invited Wurf to discuss a way out of the impasse. After much heated discussion, the two finally agreed on a proposal for creation of an impartial three-person board to arbitrate the issues. Anxious to bring a halt to the debilitating strike, which was damaging to the city and to his reputation as a friend of labor, Wagner readily agreed to Van Arsdale's proposal.

Ten days after the strike began, it suddenly ended. Wagner immediately appointed the panel, which consisted of Reverend Father Philip A. Carey, S.J., director of the Xavier Institute of Industrial Relations, a long-time friend and supporter of organized labor in New York; Charles H. Tenney, city administrator; and Harry Van Arsdale. The striking MVOs had two very sympathetic and understanding friends on the committee.[15]

THE MVO SETTLEMENT AND ITS IMPACT

The MVOs were awarded a wage and fringe benefit package that was two and one-half times the size of the city's "final" offer. The suspended 16 were reprimanded and then transferred to other city departments for re-employment, a face-saving device for Murphy. This settlement also provided for city contributions to the first union welfare fund for non-uniformed public employees, thus setting the groundwork for innovative DC 37 education, health, and security plans.

The MVO strike had a significance far beyond the settlement of wage demands. As far as DC 37 leaders were concerned, it spotlighted some of the glaring defects of the city's labor relations procedures, whereby the labor commissioner sought to represent the mayor as an employer antagonist and, at the same time, the public as an "impartial mediator." Wurf viewed this as an impossible task that discriminated against unions. In labor disputes in private industry, the state or federal government might step in as a third-party mediator or referee, to keep things reasonable and fair. A similar approach, he felt, had to be instituted in order to settle disputes in a responsible and equitable fashion between public worker unions and the city government.

The strike also brought into sharp focus the inadequacies of the Condon–Wadlin Law. As most public union leaders saw it, the 1947 law provided no useful machinery for solving labor disputes. It offered harsh penalties to striking public employees as the only alternative to accepting, at times, arbitrary and unfair decisions by the city or other public employers. Wurf urged development of some form of agency that would focus on employee problems in an informed, efficient, and expeditious manner.

At the same time, the strike sparked a heightened sense of dignity for MVOs and other members of the Council and illustrated the potential strength of a unified labor movement. This was a major turning point for DC 37 and its director, who won important recognition as a prominent labor leader.[16]

SUMMARY

By the end of 1962, Wurf, his colleagues in the Council, and local leaders could look back on some unusual achievements. Well over 17,000 members had been added to the 54 locals that comprised DC 37. There had been slow but steady progress in wages and grievance procedures, and improvement in health and hospitalization benefits and working conditions. And a new relationship seemed in the making between union and city representatives, which tended toward greater equality at the bargaining table. But none of this came easily. Wurf and his staff had to constantly organize, agitate, and educate the unorganized and provide new benefits and improvements for the members. To attain their ultimate goals, the Council resorted to militant strategies through job actions and strikes.

NOTES

1. Raymond D. Horton, *Municipal Labor Relations in New York City, Lessons of the Lindsay-Wagner Years,* New York: Praeger, 1973, pp. 24–28.

2. *Ibid.,* pp. 19–20.

3. *Spotlight,* October 1952, p. 1; February 1, 1953, p. 1; March 1, 1953, p. 1.

4. *Spotlight,* March 20, 1954, p. 1; April 7, 1954, p. 2; *New York Times,* February 9, 1954, p. 27; March 21, 1954, p. 1; June 17, 1954, p. 34.

5. Horton, *Municipal Labor Relations,* p. 25. The police, firefighters, sanitationmen, and correction officers, with separate appeals boards, were called "uniform personnel," while the remaining public workers were identified as "career and salary employees."

6. *New York Times,* May 27, 1955, p. 24; June 1, 1955, p. 1; June 2, 1955, p. 60.

7. *Spotlight,* June 1, 1957, p. 2.

8. *Executive Order 49,* New York City, Office of the Mayor, March 31, 1958; *New York Times,* April 1, 1958, p. 1; Horton, *Municipal Labor Relations,* pp. 30–35; David Lewin, "Mayoral Power and Municipal Labor Relations: A Three City Study," unpublished paper, June 1980, p. 6. Excluded from the provisions of this Executive Order were employees in the Board of Education, the City University, Housing, Transit, cultural institutions, judicial agencies, the Triborough Bridge and Tunnel Authority, and some other offices. Four years later, the Board of Estimate afforded them admission on a full or limited basis by expanding the coverage of Executive Order 49.

9. New York City Department of Labor, *Procedures for Joint Collective Bargaining with the Director of the Budget and the Personnel Director Under Executive Order 49,* May 28, 1960; Horton, *Municipal Labor Relations,* pp. 32–34.

10. *New York Times,* February 5, 1958, p. 26; April 1, 1958, p. 1; April 15, 1958, p. 1; June 10, 1958, p. 35; October 11, 1958, p. 46; March 8, 1959, p. 43; March 22, 1959, p. 1; April 1, 1959, p. 1; June 25, 1959, p. 1. Interview with John Boer, September 22, 1981.

11. June Ringel, "A Short History of DC 37," *Public Employee Press,* December 12, 1969, p. 14.

12. New York City Department of Labor, *Procedures for Joint Collective Bargaining.*

13. *New York Times,* June 10, 1958, p. 35; June 11, 1958, p. 37; June 12, 1958, p. 23; October 11, 1958, p. 46; Thomas F. Cohalan to AFSCME, March 6, 1957; Jerry Wurf to Mrs. Alfred Landau, June 10, 1958 and August 4, 1958; Bernice

Fisher and James Corcoran to John Poe, June 30, 1958; Bernice Fisher to John Poe, August 7, 1958; Wurf telegram to New York newspapers, September 30, 1958; Francis J. Petrocelli to Robert F. Wagner, Jr., October 1, 1958; Samuel H. Friedman to James Corcoran, October 2, 1958.

14. *Public Employee Press*, September 4, 1959, p. 6; November 13, 1959, p. 3; December 24, 1959, p. 3; January 8, 1960, p. 3; June 23, 1961, p. 7.

15. *New York Times*, November 27, 1962, p. 1; November 28, 1962, p. 1; November 29, 1962, p. 1; November 30, 1962, p. 1; December 4, 1962, p. 1; December 6, 1962, p. 47; December 8, 1962, p. 33. Interview with William Casamo, October 17, 1979. Casamo was present at the meeting between Wurf and Van Arsdale.

16. *New York Times*, December 22, 1962, p. 4; *Public Employee Press*, February 1, 1963, pp. 8-9; also, interviews with John Toto, May 29, 1979; John Boer, September 22, 1981.

5
Victor Gotbaum in Daley's City

Since the inception of AFSCME, its leadership and that of the AFL–CIO viewed the attainment of collective bargaining for public workers as a virtual impossibility, a "slogan for a few crackpots." President George Meany wrote in 1955, "It is impossible to bargain collectively with the government." Although the AFL–CIO executive council conceded, in February 1959, that "in terms of accepted collective bargaining procedures, government workers have no right beyond the authority to petition Congress...," nevertheless the AFL–CIO convention, later that same year, adopted a resolution supporting collective bargaining legislation for public employees.

Some scholars insisted that public employee unions would have great difficulty attaining collective bargaining as long as the doctrine of state sovereignty held sway. State legislatures were dominated by rural and antilabor interests, there was unqualified acceptance of the prohibition against strikes by public employees, and public employee unions remained weak. Until some of these obstacles were overcome, these developing unions were expected to concentrate their endeavors on civil service rulings and political lobbying.[1]

Developments in the 1950s, however, insured dramatic changes in the U. S. labor movement. Among them were general prosperity, a vast suburban sprawl, and explosive expansion of the welfare state in response to demands for increased public services such as highways, schools, police, and fire departments. The dramatic increase in public employee jobs, however, did not insure automatic affiliation with unions. Many of those who sought the

Discovered by Gotbaum in a Chicago hospital, former nurse's aide Lillian Roberts became one of the most effective organizers of hospital workers and a symbol for black workers first in Mayor Daley's city and then in New York.

security of civil service lacked an understanding of the history, traditions, and overall objectives of unionism, and were often limited by a constricted civil service mentality. An additional obstacle to union organizing was the spillover from the negative attitude of much of the public toward what they saw as lazy, incompetent, and inhumane civil servants, and toward the organizations that represented them.

UNION MILITANCY AMONG PUBLIC WORKERS

Yet there were major factors in fighting quiescence among public workers. One of them was their perception of a large gap in wages between the private and public sectors. Government pay scales in the postwar United States were usually well below those paid by private industry. AFSCME leaders like Wurf insisted that public workers frequently earned 10 to 30 percent less than their counterparts in private industry, which amounted to a subsidy of the mounting cost of government through low wages. In Detroit, unions cited a median private hourly wage of $2.04 in 1955, as against $1.79 for government workers. Twelve years later, the gap had widened with private industry employees receiving $3.49, as opposed to $3.09 for civil servants. The appeal of job security in civil service had lessened considerably, in light of an expanding industrial and service economy where the demand for labor often outstripped the supply, and facilitated a widening gap in wages. As a result, more and more public workers came to view unions as a major solution to their economic problems and joined them in a steady stream. Traditionally docile, public servants were now resorting to unionization, and even strikes, to resolve complaints not only about lagging wages, but unsafe working conditions and indignities inflicted upon them by arbitrary and insensitive administrators.[2]

Another important factor that strengthened public employee unionism was President Kennedy's executive order in 1962 that provided for collective bargaining in the Federal service. That presidential directive established a more favorable environment for public worker unions and set the tone for similar developments in states, counties, and cities across the nation. Not only were scores of cities bargaining with unions for the first time, but 11 states enacted various forms of collective bargaining laws. Federal managers, in the interim, signed about 600 union contracts covering just under 1 million workers. After 1964, some of this growth of public unionism would stem from increasingly imaginative organizing efforts by the new leader of AFSCME, Jerry Wurf, as well as by those of other public employee unions.

In the eyes of many, the 1960s came to be viewed as the decade of the public employee. The rise of public sector unions during this decade became the most significant development in the industrial relations field since the birth of the CIO in 1935. Across the country, tremendous interest developed among public employees in union organizing and in establishing their right to collective bargaining.

While these developments meant an endless series of new challenges to public managers, it offered fresh hope to a stalemated labor movement that had lost the momentum and idealism of the 1930s. During the decade of the 1950s, union membership among public workers increased some 60 percent to about 1.5 million. This was due partly to the fact that public employment was the fastest-growing segment of the labor force. In the ten years following 1955, AFSCME grew from 99,000 to some 350,000, the American Federation of Teachers climbed from 46,500 to 135,000 while the AFGE rose from 51,600 to 234,000. In less than a decade, union membership tripled among federal, state, and local employees. This growth was crucial for the merged labor movement, whose share of the non-farm labor force declined from 28.9 percent, in 1953, to some 22 percent by 1966. Here was a tremendous, only partially tapped area.

By the middle of the 1960s some 12 million people, one-sixth of the national labor force, worked in the public sector. These public employees had doubled in little more than 15 years, and would increase dramatically through the next decade. It was only a short time since the general public believed that government workers had no right to organize, let alone strike. In 1937, Franklin D. Roosevelt called public strikes "unthinkable and intolerable." Some three decades later, President Walter Reuther of the UAW held that society could not tolerate strikes that endangered "the very survival of society." Although viewed as a militant labor leader, he sought to find a new "mechanism by which workers in public service can secure their equity without the need of resorting to strike action."[3]

Half the states had laws prohibiting strikes by government workers. Yet public employees, like many students on college and university campuses across the country, were restless and unhappy. While vast numbers of students demonstrated against the inequities of the "impersonal multiversity," or the war in Vietnam, public workers continued to stream into unions and resorted to sit-ins and walkouts. Antistrike laws, directed against state and local employees, just weren't working. It may have been that many public workers, like civil rights activists and student demonstrators, were convinced that unorthodox tactics, such as walkouts, brought them gains they could not otherwise attain. Instead of preventing strikes, punitive laws seemed to provoke them; during the late 1960s strikes and sit-ins spread across the country like a prairie fire.

The vast majority of states, however, had no negotiating procedures, but even those with laws relating to labor–management disputes continued to have serious difficulties. Michigan, for example, with a labor law modernized in 1965, had at least 23 work stoppages the following year, mostly in education. Although traditionally illegal—by statute, court decision, or common law—walkouts rose dramatically from 28 in 1962 to 150 in 1966. The 1960s were to public employees what the 1930s had been to workers in private industry. These developments led one of the authorities on industrial relations, Professor George W. Taylor of the University of Pennsylvania, to conclude, "It's going to be a mess for generations."

As a result of increasing militancy by AFSCME and other public employee unions, and successful dramatization of demands for better contracts, taxpayer organizations in New York were beginning to protest against what they saw as a revolution in public employment. They were concerned about a dramatic expansion in public employment rolls, increasing strikes by civil service unions, and the resultant economic pressures on state and city governments, which many were beginning to view as onerous.[4]

Although New York City's population remained at 8 million for almost a decade, demands for increased municipal services added thousands to the city payroll. There was a two-thirds growth in the city's work force from 247,000 in 1958 to some 400,000 by 1968. Between 1964 and 1968, for example, the city's budget nearly doubled (reaching $6.1 billion), with welfare and labor costs leading the way. This "revolution" in civil service also manifested itself in a dramatic increase in AFSCME membership nationally as well as locally. Within four years after Wurf took over the international organization, it grew from 250,000 to almost 400,000, amidst a turbulence that had been associated with the early CIO organizing drives in the mid-1930s. The 1968 sanitationmen's strike in Memphis, Tennessee, in which civil rights leader Dr. Martin Luther King was assassinated, gave Wurf his first major victory in the South.

With a black membership approaching 30 percent, AFSCME was increasingly in a position to improve the economic and social status of some of the most exploited workers below the Mason–Dixon line.

Not averse to selected strikes by most civil servants, Wurf was at odds with the traditional governmental policy, believing that the strike was a right that could not be denied to public workers, except police, firefighters, and prison guards. Wurf insisted that the traditional demarcation between public and private sectors had steadily been vanishing. He pointed to a double standard that allowed private industry bus drivers in the nation's capitol to strike while denying this same right to the drivers of city-owned buses in New York.

Most public employers, including New York City, continued to find it difficult to deal with the concept of unions. Too many public managers failed to adjust honest worker grievances simply because they felt they could fall back on a law like Condon–Wadlin, which prohibited strikes by public employees. And there were those officials, throughout the country, who lacked the courage to seek higher taxes to enable them to pay adequate wages to workers.

VICTOR GOTBAUM

In the midst of these revolutionary currents in public unionism, DC 37 underwent a dramatic change in leadership. In his second try for the International presidency in 1964, Jerry Wurf successfully challenged Arnold Zander in a uniquely democratic insurgency. As his replacement in New York he eventually appointed Victor Gotbaum. The latter had been assigned, in October 1957, to what turned out to be a hopeless task as AFSCME director of the Chicago–Cook County area. Richard Daley ran his town with an iron hand, keeping unions at bay and controlling labor leaders with his limitless patronage system. As a young, struggling labor leader in Chicago, Gotbaum had been one of the strategists in Wurf's two presidential campaigns, which were spearheaded by the Committee on Union Responsibility (COUR). His preparation for this new assignment was, in many ways, not very different from Wurf's.

Victor was born in the predominantly Jewish East Flatbush section of Brooklyn on September 5, 1921, one of five children of Harry and Mollie Gotbaum. He inherited a sense of restlessness and repressed rebellion from his father, who was an unfulfilled and unhappy printing salesman. Harry was never the respected leader of the household. Victor's maternal grandmother, who lived with them, and his mother's brother, Jack, made the vital decisions for the Gotbaum family.

The Great Depression threw Harry Gotbaum into the ranks of the unemployed, and the family, along with millions of others, into a state of poverty. Victor was obliged to start work at the age of 13, as a dishwasher and short-order cook in a luncheonette, laboring 50 hours a week for $6, and then as a feeder to a printing press in his Uncle Jack's shop at $15 per week. In the process he accumulated a record-breaking number of absences from Samuel J. Tilden High School, along with poor grades. He developed an easy rapport with exploited black workers in his uncle's shop and helped them win wages equivalent to those of their white counterparts.

Mollie Gotbaum bore the brunt of the shame associated with the family's dependence on welfare, causing her to fight frequently with the landlord when she didn't have money for the rent. There were no books in this household, and little stimulating discussion with a defeated father who was seldom at home. Victor had a "black market" bar mitzvah on a weekday morning, at age 13, simply repeating the prayers after the rabbi. All this left a permanent scar on young Victor, for he hated poverty and the long hours of labor that kept him away from school, books, and close association with his father. Not until the age of 19, when he met vivacious Sarah Cohen and her politically sophisticated sister did he become involved in discussions concerning Roosevelt's New Deal, Hitler's nazism, Stalin's communism, and Leon Trotsky's Marxism. By that time, his father had died.

All along it was taken for granted that Victor could not go on to college, for the family's energies and meager resources were devoted to getting his older brother, Irving, into an institution of higher learning. Even then the family had to borrow $100 for Irving's tuition in 1938. After Victor managed to graduate from high school on the eve of World War II, it was his uncle Jack who rationalized, for a distraught nephew, that he wasn't cut out for college and that he should work in his printing plant. Not until after the war could Victor return to school, thanks to the GI Bill of Rights, the determination of his wife, Sarah, whom he married in August 1943, and his own desire for more formal education.

As a soldier, Victor was among the more fortunate in his outfit. In the face of an 85 percent casualty figure, he survived three turbulent years as a machine gunner and radio operator with mechanized cavalry reconnaissance. But, for the first time, he experienced considerable anti-Semitism, from which he had been protected while living in a Jewish neighborhood in Brooklyn. After landing on Omaha Beach in Normandy two weeks after D-Day in June 1944, he and his fellow GIs went deeper into the heartland of Europe, observing some of the worst scourges of the Nazi holocaust. Reconnoitering the French town of Robert d'Espagne, he encountered hysterical women and old men who informed him that retreating German SS troops had just shot and then burned the bodies of the younger men of the village. Gotbaum was not prepared for that type of inhumanity, or for what he observed when he helped liberate the starving, skeletal remnants of European Jewry at Buchenwald concentration camp. These experiences made a deep impact on Gotbaum. He later described his encounter with a beautiful, young Jewish concentration camp refugee at Yom Kippur services in occupied Germany. When asked, "Where do you want to go?" she replied to Victor, "Wherever I can be a Jew."

A whole new world was opened to him in faraway places like France, Germany, Austria, and Czechoslovakia. As a survivor of World War II battles, Gotbaum savored each additional day as an unexpected gift. He became far more conscious of his historic association with the Jewish secular community, and was totally committed to the state of Israel after its birth in 1948. And he was more determined than ever to attain a formal education that would prepare him for that world beyond East Flatbush.

With the war over on the European continent, and after accumulating six battle stars, Victor returned to the United States and Sarah. He was discharged from the armed services in October 1945, with the prior understanding that he and Sarah would return to school immediately. Despite high grades on an entrance examination for Tufts College and applications to a number of mid-Western colleges, he was rejected by all of them because of his poor high school records. Only Brooklyn College was willing to overlook his grades and respond favorably to his deep hunger for knowledge. Sarah and he were admitted as full-time freshmen to the Brooklyn campus of the City University of New York. During their two and a half years on the campus of this urban institution, they received superior educations inside and outside the classroom. Throughout, Victor was sustained by his restless, inquisitive wife, who had been a member of the YPSL.[5]

Every morning they would be greeted on the campus by an assortment of leaflets from socialists, Communists, Trotskyists, and the Schachtmanites who had split off from Leon Trotsky's organization. During these years, when a cold war broke out between Washington and Moscow, Gotbaum learned about what he called the duplicity practiced by Stalinists and their fanatical support of Soviet policy. By 1948 he deemed himself sophisticated enough not to be taken in by Henry A. Wallace and the Progressive party. Instead, he voted for Socialist Norman Thomas during his last of six presidential campaigns.

Sarah was president of the college chapter of the Intercollegiate Zionist Federation, while Victor majored in political science and soon headed the Brooklyn College unit of the American Veterans Committee (AVC). AVC was a young, intellectually boisterous, and progressive World War II veterans organization that contained many of the nation's bright young minds committed to a more democratic and egalitarian society. Within the AVC chapter at Brooklyn College, 6-foot, 2½-inch Victor Gotbaum quickly stood out as a handsome, rugged spokesperson for those who rejected the extremes of the Communists on the one hand and of the rabid anti-Communists on the other. His warm personality was complemented by a logical, no-nonsense mind and booming voice.

Staking out the middle ground as a national leader of a small "Build AVC" caucus during a bitter cold-war struggle within the organization, Victor rejected the appeals of the Stalinists and their sympathizers in the larger "Progressive" caucus. At the same time, he avoided those who followed, equally blindly, U. S. foreign policy under the Truman administration, and who found themselves at home in the "Independent Progressive" caucus, the largest of the three. At the height of this internecine conflict, the Independent Progressives were led by a bright, articulate veteran of the pre–World War II Socialist party, and a masterful field tactician, Gus Tyler. Developing into one of the outstanding pamphleteers of his day, Tyler broadened his horizons while working for the ILGWU under David Dubinsky. Originally viewed by Gotbaum as a maker of men and ideas, Tyler eventually became the union's political and educational director.

In the 1950s Gotbaum was caught in the uncomfortable position between the attacking front lines of the two major cold war forces within AVC. Yet it was as an embattled leader within AVC that Victor first learned that he enjoyed political infighting of a high intensity, and could master leadership techniques and parliamentary procedure. And it was here as well that he was educated to the "anti-democratic tactics" of "Stalinists," as well as those by the virulent anti-Communists, who sought to beat the "Stalinists with Stalinist methods." For the remainder of his union career in Washington, Turkey, Chicago, and New York, Victor would build on his experiences in AVC, adhering to democratic, independent, progressive traditions which, at times, seemed confounding and confusing to more simplistic friends and foes alike.[6]

In 1950, two years after they graduated from Brooklyn College, Sarah received her M. A. degree from the Columbia University School of Social Work, while Victor acquired a master's degree in international affairs from the same institution. During this time, Sarah and her husband sustained themselves and their small apartment in a public housing project in Brooklyn with educational subsidies from the GI Bill of Rights, tuition fellowships, part-time jobs, and tips from summers waiting on dining tables at the ILGWU Unity House in the Pocono Mountains in Pennsylvania. Victor's awkwardness around tables was overlooked because of Sarah's masterly handling of trays and clients.

It was during these summers at the Unity House that Victor and Sarah enlarged their horizons and gained some strong personal insights into labor unions and labor leadership. They observed President George Meany of the AFL, the former Bronx plumber, being educated at dining tables on the complexities of national issues by a knowledgeable and experienced David Dubinsky. It was this same Dubinsky who had been active among Jewish socialists, first in Eastern Europe and then on New York's Lower East Side. And it was he who had matured among U. S. socialists who revered the courage and integrity of Eugene V. Debs and Norman Thomas. With this background, Dubinsky went on to become head of the ILGWU and a political force on the New York and national scenes.

The Unity House had a unique cultural program featuring daily lectures and discussions by a variety of talented individuals from the political, economic, and cultural fields. Rare was the day, during these three summers, when Victor and Sarah were not attending lectures and acquiring knowledge that challenged and stimulated their interests, particularly in labor movements at home and abroad. In fact, Victor's decision to research and write his master's thesis on the French labor movement came from one of these lectures.

In the process they were exposed to all sorts of individuals within the labor movement, including ILGWU vice-presidents who had little interest in young people. An exception was Sasha Zimmerman and his wife, Rose. She was a forceful ally of the Unity House waiters and waitresses who, one summer, threatened to strike against an autocratic, demeaning headwaiter and a sweetheart contract that had been signed by management without prior consultation of the workers involved. Embarrassed by the possibility of a strike, the ILGWU quickly reached a resolution of the disputes.

A semester as a political science lecturer at Brooklyn College convinced the department and Victor that the "publish or perish" syndrome of academia was not for him. Although he had an easy rapport with students, a restless and gregarious Gotbaum could not abide the sedentary, monkish life of the serious scholar. He could, painfully, devote himself to research and scholarly writing, but college teaching was not sufficiently active for Victor. Upon receiving his master's degree, he applied to the State Department and was given an assignment with its Office of International Education. After a few unhappy months he accepted an invitation to become a program officer with the Labor Department's Office of International Labor Affairs. His primary task was to facilitate and schedule the visits of foreign trade unionists and to accompany some of them as they traveled within the United States. In his spare time he was active in organizing and leading a unit of the federal workers union.

Frustrated by an unimaginative and fearful superior, by the slow pace of the office, and by unusual control exerted by the State Department, Victor decided to go abroad for more varied and challenging experiences. In May 1954, shortly before their second son was born, Victor inveigled an assignment to the U.S. embassy in Ankara, Turkey as part of a team of labor education specialists. They found themselves hamstrung by embassy directives that seriously restricted free communications and social engagements with Turkish labor.

Realizing that this job was not for him, Victor managed to be present at an international labor conference in Vienna that he knew would be attended by a number of representatives of AFL–CIO unions. By that time he concluded that if he was ever to play an important role in organized labor, to which he and Sarah were committed, then he had to return to the United States. Helmuth Kern, one-time German social democrat but now education director at the Chicago headquarters of the Amalgamated Meat Cutters and Butcher Workmen, met Victor at the Vienna Conference and offered him a job as assistant director, which he eagerly accepted. He returned with Sarah and the children to the United States in 1955, little more than a year after they had left Washington.

Kern had an excellent reputation as a labor educator, technician, and hard-working bureaucrat. But he turned out to be rigid and insecure in the face of an energetic and imaginative assistant. Working seven days a week, Victor sought to make the union's education program more meaningful and acceptable to the rank-and-file membership. He instituted weekend educational conferences for different locals and, with the cooperation of faculty from Roosevelt University, developed one-week regional institutes for members and union bureaucrats. He created workshops and seminars dealing with their day-to-day organizing and servicing problems, relationships with the local communities and governmental agencies, and plans for local leadership to facilitate membership participation in decision making and union activities. Young Victor's personality attracted members across the country, but Kern, who had become increasingly nervous about the endless stream of innovative proposals from his assistant, fired him claiming personal incompatibility.

Before he was discharged, however, Gotbaum had carefully observed the leadership offered by the union's president, Patrick Gorman. The latter preferred that Victor remain with the union, but did nothing about it except to carry him on the union payroll until he found another job. Gotbaum observed that in general, Gorman was an outstanding leader but a poor one when he became emotionally involved in decision making. He appointed excellent leadership in the field, through which he maintained ongoing communication with rank-and-file members.

Gotbaum renewed the negotiations that he had begun with Arnold Zander before he left for Turkey in May 1954. It was at this early stage that Sarah asked Victor why he would want to work for an individual who was magnificent on international affairs, but sadly lacking in trade union knowhow and commitment to the day-to-day struggles associated with organizing, representing, and servicing public workers. But Victor needed a job. Finally, after a series of communications and meetings with Zander, Gotbaum was appointed, in October 1957, as AFSCME director of the Chicago–Cook County area. Although the salary was far below that which he had received with the Meatcutters, Sarah nevertheless remained supportive of Victor's move to AFSCME. Despite new economic stringencies, she continued to manage a growing and exciting household.

AFSCME IN DALEY'S NET

At this time, AFSCME had one viable hospital unit (Local 1657) of 600 members in Chicago, encompassing the nonprofessional staff at the University of Illinois and the University of Chicago hospitals. The BSEIU, headed by William McFettridge, controlled large segments of the city's public workers, in virtual partnership with Mayor Richard Daley and his boss-ridden Democratic party. Throughout the seven years in which Gotbaum labored against the antilabor machine in Chicago, Daley worked with wondrous efficiency. It was Daley who directed one of the largest patronage programs in the nation, involving tens of thousands of personal appointees, closed shops, and sweetheart contracts to powerful cooperating labor leaders like McFettridge. In return, most labor leaders supplied Daley with votes on election day, campaign funds and workers, and lobbying support in the state legislature.

In contrast to New York City, Chicago's Daley maintained an informal, undeveloped system of public sector labor relations—"managerial autocracy, centralized negotiations, an absence of statutory guidelines, private sector-oriented labor organizations, substantial patronage employment, and a close, even familial relationship between organized labor and the Democratic party." During the period from 1955 to 1976, Daley dominated labor relations and the municipal government to a degree unmatched by the mayors of other large U.S. cities.

As urban specialist David Lewin and others have pointed out, labor relations in Chicago were not governed by local statute or ordinance. There were "no written contracts, no certified bargaining units, no labor relations staff in the city government and . . . no formal collective bargaining between municipal employees and city management" throughout the six terms of the Daley administration. Each year, Mayor Daley met with representatives of the major unions in the city and on the basis of the "highest, most recently bargained rates" in private industry, decreed "prevailing" wages for the primarily patronage-appointed public employees. In this manner, Daley kept collective bargaining out of city government.[7] Unlike New York, few jobs in Daley's Chicago were filled through civil service channels. City employees were expected to be members of the Democratic party and to join whatever union the mayor favored. Thus, Daley insured the total allegiance and political support of municipal workers and their leaders to his political organization.

During the months and years that followed, the new AFSCME leader in Chicago became somewhat of a public nuisance to the mayor, receiving newspaper and radio publicity far beyond what his small membership merited. And that was because much of the time he was the only labor leader to speak out against the mayor. He was almost alone among hundreds in the Chicago Federation of Labor in voting against Daley measures.

Since Daley seemed to have more patronage jobs to dispense in one Chicago precinct than Mayor John Lindsay would subsequently have in the entire city of New York, and since most city employees felt personally beholden to Daley, or to the union he suggested they join, Gotbaum was faced with a superhuman task. After months of lonely campaigning, he barely managed to increase AFSCME membership in Chicago to some 1700, and finally brought six anemic locals under the umbrella of District Council 19.

Victor learned that his appointment to the Chicago post was not for the exclusive purpose of standing up to Daley and the city administration, but primarily as a symbol of AFSCME's continued existence in that city, and as a form of opposition to Zander's competitor, Bill McFettridge. It was a partial replay of David and Goliath, with some crucial assistance from his growing family.

Sarah hung drapes in the tiny AFSCME office and supplemented the family income with part-time work. Although seldom at home, Victor loved and had pride in his family. In the process of attempting to build AFSCME in Chicago, Victor found it increasingly time consuming, requiring much of the burdens of family direction and responsibility to be assumed by Sarah. Infrequently, eight-year-old Joshua would drive into the big city with his father and help Sakiko Miyashiro, the lone secretary, arrange leaflets and tidy up the office. From the start, he knew his father as a hard-working union organizer and as a leader of strikes.

If Gotbaum was ever to justify the existence of AFSCME in Chicago and grow within the national organization, he would have to expand his base of membership and influence. It was then that he turned to a potentially lucrative field, and his last great hope in Chicago, the voluntary, nonprofit hospitals. Its nonmedical workers, primarily black, were generally unorganized, paid miserable wages, and denied any sense of human dignity. Since these institutions were not owned by the city government, but controlled by charitable boards, Gotbaum thought he would not have to contend with the Daley machine, at least not directly. But he soon learned that Daley had his tentacles everywhere, and that even leaders of the Jewish community, who were traditionally liberal and sympathetic toward organized labor, could not readily tolerate a direct, militant challenge to "their" hospital and charitable leadership.

Complicating the situation for a number of competing unions was the fact that not-for-profit hospitals were not covered by any federal law requiring them to recognize a union. Existing law, however, was interpreted to permit a state to encompass nonprofit hospitals in labor–management legislation, if they so chose. Wisconsin and California did include hospitals in their enactments, but they were the exceptions. In Illinois there had been no legislation requiring hospitals to bargain collectively, although during the 1959 session of the state legislature, state representative Abner Mikva did introduce a labor–management relations bill prohibiting strikes against hospitals and providing for compulsory arbitration. The hospitals would have been required to bargain collectively with unions elected by a majority of the employees. Mikva's proposal, however, was not enacted. Hospital workers were also exempted from unemployment insurance protection and, if discharged for any reason, could not draw unemployment compensation.[8]

Immediately prior to Gotbaum's decision in 1959 to begin an

organizing drive among nonprofessional employees, the Retail Drug Employees Union ended a 45-day strike against several private non-profit hospitals in New York City. The settlement of the strike, in which Mayor Wagner played an instrumental role, consisted of the acceptance of a hospital association policy statement offering to establish a one dollar minimum wage, a 40-hour work week, time and a half for overtime, and the establishment of an administrative committee for each member hospital to deal with wage and employment conditions.

After considerable research into working conditions at various Chicago hospitals, which involved visiting the homes of workers and spending time in hospital cafeterias, Gotbaum decided to organize Mt. Sinai Hospital and the Chicago Home for the Incurables. Mt. Sinai was classed as a large hospital, with some 400 beds, a nursing school, and a medical research department. Severe complaints about work conditions made his subsequent organizing campaign a comparatively easy task. Workers conveyed a sense of wanting to do something decisive about their depressing working conditions, an attitude which Gotbaum associated with a cultural solidarity, for about 80 percent of them were black.[9]

The Chicago Home for the Incurables was located in the multi-racial neighborhood of Hyde Park, which included intellectuals from the nearby University of Chicago. Many of these individuals were generally vocal about political and social issues. With approximately 210 patients, the nonprofessional work force was composed of 130 individuals, mostly blacks. AFSCME was the bargaining agent for the nonprofessional employees at the nearby University of Chicago clinics and represented some of the residence halls and housekeeping employees in other areas of the university. The home was scheduled to cease operations shortly and to merge with the university. For some time Gotbaum sought contact with hospital directors to discuss unionization and negotiations, but they refused to respond, ignoring him completely.

LILLIAN ROBERTS

Concluding that his organizing endeavors would be strengthened by a black colleague, Victor invited Lillian Roberts, a nurse's aide, to join the union staff. As secretary of the University of Chicago Hospital local, she had demonstrated unusual courage with administrators, a keen sense of humanity toward fellow workers, and a potential for union organizing. A product of the impoverished ghetto of Chicago, Roberts had dropped out of college during her first year of studies.

Since Arnold Zander and Leo Kramer, his assistant in Washington, were opposed to subsidizing organizing endeavors in Chicago, let alone a strike, which they felt were doomed to failure, Gotbaum turned to Jerry Wurf in New York for assistance. Having served a brief apprenticeship with the head of DC 37 immediately after his appointment to AFSCME, Gotbaum was able to appeal to the New York leader for vital financial and staff aid. It was then that he set out to organize the hospital workers.

The union began its organizing drive in late June 1959. Within three weeks, AFSCME signed up 73 percent of the 400 nonprofessionals at Mt. Sinai and claimed 85 percent of those at the home. Gotbaum sought "recognition, bargaining and grievance machinery rights," and a $1.00 minimum per hour. But neither the hospital directors nor the board of trustees would sit down with Gotbaum, or even with the Illinois state labor director. They stressed the need to protect their independence and underscored their exemption from labor–management legislation. Eventually, they were joined by representatives from 70 Chicago hospitals, all of whom pledged not to bargain with any union official. An official from another union appealed to Mayor Daley to avert the threatened strikes by appointing a mediation committee, especially in light of the willingness of the hospital workers' union to accept such a commission's findings. The hospitals refused such efforts and Mayor Daley never made a public reply to this initiative.[10]

Within days after the workers at Mt. Sinai and the home voted to strike, the powerful City Federation of Labor refused to back them, but the CIO council announced its support. The strike at both hospitals was comparatively effective for the first few days, with the picket lines joined by volunteers from United Packinghouse Workers, the United Steelworkers, the United Auto Workers (UAW), the Communication Workers, and the Jewelry Workers unions.

A number of student groups and professors from the University of Chicago contributed money and picket time to support the strikers, while the Hyde Park Cooperative gave funds, food, and moral support. The National Association for the Advancement of Colored People (NAACP), and other civic and religious groups, also offered support in the way of resolutions and joining the picket lines. After mid-September, however, with hospital management refusing to budge an inch, news about the strike disappeared from much of the daily press.

When the strike began, Mayor Daley and many community leaders viewed it as a personal affront, and the trustees at Mt. Sinai were outraged. They were particularly upset that a union, headed by a Jew, had struck "their" hospital. The confrontation became a tense, emotional battle with community pressure mounting steadily against those who had walked out, and personal attacks against the Gotbaum family. As the strike lengthened into weeks, and then months, emotions approached the breaking point.[11] Poison-pen letters and vituperative telephone calls were directed to the Gotbaum household. In Evanston's elementary school, eight-year-old Joshua was insulted by classmates. At the North Shore Congregation of Israel, where she worked part-time as its youth director, Sarah felt an uncomfortable pressure from adults, some of whom were trustees at Mt. Sinai. Even the family doctor felt obliged to inform her, in her ninth month of pregnancy, that he didn't know if any hospital would readily admit her. But it was five-year-old Irving who brought the family some much-needed humor and encouragement. When it finally came his turn to answer the question posed by his kindergarden teacher, "What does your father do?" Irving replied, with apparent pride, "My father is a striker."

There were some encouraging aspects to what was often a lonely and discouraging struggle. Every week, during this drawn-out conflict, a Teamster union leader would covertly drop a cash-laden envelope at an adjacent union office, destined for the striking hospital workers. Victor also received unpublicized help from some minor unions, as well as weekly funds and temporary staff from DC 37 in New York.

Lillian Roberts gradually learned to trust Gotbaum. She began to acknowledge his commitment and integrity when he showed up at 4 a.m. to walk the picket line, or slept in a station wagon adjacent to Mt. Sinai. He wanted to be on constant call to prevent violence on picket lines. Pickets were directed not to stop doctors and nurses, nor to halt the delivery of food or needed medical supplies. He hoped, in vain, that the Teamsters driving laundry trucks and other nonessential service vehicles would honor the picket lines.

Mt. Sinai was located in a section of Chicago where considerable unemployment existed and replacements were easily recruited. Surprisingly, some of those who replaced striking porters were themselves striking steel workers who had been involved in a nationwide steel shutdown for over a month. Day and night, for the first few weeks, rank-and-file hospital workers walked the picket lines, despite economic sacrifices and psychological trauma. The strike had become a symbol for many of the fight against black exploitation by the Daley machine and by business leaders who viewed themselves as liberals. Time and again, their flagging spirits were lifted, and their morale sustained by the charismatic appeals of union leader Gotbaum.

As the hospitals continued to hold firm, with volunteers and strikebreakers, those on the picket lines began to trickle back to work, or found jobs elsewhere. By the first week in January, there were no more than one or two strikers picketing. By January 31, 1960, even this token picketing was brought to a halt. Gotbaum had lost his first strike. One striker, about 70 years old, insisted, however, that they hadn't lost. As the strike leader recalled her remarks, more than a decade later, she maintained that it was Gotbaum who had helped the hospital workers find themselves. "Nobody knew we were alive until you came.... you made us proud of ourselves."[12]

Although this organizing campaign failed, members of the union did achieve some significant changes. They won reluctant recognition from newspaper reporters and civic leaders, of the exploitative wages paid them, and the indignities inflicted upon them by administrators. Even hospital managers came to concede the legitimacy of union grievances. Mt. Sinai decreed a general wage increase, established a grievance procedure, reduced the workweek to 40 hours with time and a half for overtime, and increased the maximum vacation from one to two weeks. The home reduced its workweek from 44 to 40 hours weekly, with no reduction in pay.[13]

After his traumatic experience with Chicago's hospitals, Gotbaum knew that he and Lillian Roberts had to look elsewhere. He sought the advice of Carl Scheer, a UAW leader who knew the public hospitals outside of Cook County, and whose socialist background and commitment to social justice made him a natural ally. The result was a decision to organize hospital workers in downstate Illinois. During the months that followed, this duo was far more successful downstate than they had ever been in Chicago, in spite of the rampant racism traditionally associated with southern Illinois.

After leading the unsuccessful hospital strike, Gotbaum was elected Democratic alderman from the Eighth Ward of Evanston. With less than 40 percent of the voters registered Democrats, he concluded that his election was some sort of public vindication of his type of union leadership and opposition to Daley bossism.

YOU'RE FIRED!

While attending the 1960 Democratic national convention in Los Angeles as president of the Evanston Democratic reform organization, Gotbaum received an urgent telephone call—Arnold Zander had fired him. After Victor consulted with union colleagues, executive board members of the Chicago Council agreed to hire him as executive director, but at a greatly reduced salary. During the four years that followed, DC 37 sent funds to help pay Roberts's salary, and assigned staff members to supplement AFSCME organizing endeavors in Illinois. Outside of Chicago, Gotbaum and Roberts continued to make significant progress. The idealism that swept the nation in the 1960s, which was catalyzed by the civil rights revolution in the South, influenced changes in attitudes among white hospital workers, enabling many to respond positively to a black union organizer, and a woman at that.

Zander's action was precipitated by Gotbaum's decision to strike the hospitals, in the first place, and by the latter's association with Jerry Wurf as a developing insurgent candidate for the International presidency. Increasingly disenchanted by the lack of militant leadership from the Washington office, and the absence of any support from Zander during the hospital strike, Gotbaum became infuriated when Leo Kramer sent International organizers into downstate Illinois to decertify locals that he and Roberts had struggled to create, and to replace them with "paper locals" loyal to the International office. Those that could not be easily decertified were put into "trusteeships," under the supervision of International representatives.

By this time, a hint of grey appeared in Gotbaum's closely cropped black hair, offset by keen blue eyes under thick brows and a determined set to his squarish jaw. The family, meanwhile, had grown by three bumptious sons and an energetic daughter. After seven tough years in the Chicago area, Gotbaum had learned some lessons that shaped his subsequent role and leadership in New York.

LESSONS DALEY TAUGHT HIM

In the absence of promised support of the hospital strike by a key Teamster leader, it was evident that Gotbaum had been unrealistic in taking on the hospitals and Daley. Even the AFSCME leadership in Washington opposed his strategy and undermined his efforts. Without wider community cooperation he never had a chance. Virtually all of Chicago's political figures and civic communities opposed the walkout, leaving less than a handful of progressive lawmakers like Abner Mikva and Leon Despres to stand by the black hospital employees. Even the black leadership of the city and the leading black newspaper did not speak out in support of exploited black workers. Gotbaum learned that Daley's control over organized labor was so pervasive that it made any independent challenge an impossible task. Obviously, the struggle for democratic, egalitarian goals and for an independent labor movement required more time, greater effort, and limitless courage.

The belief that he had led the "good fight" against overwhelming odds helped carry Gotbaum through his unsuccessful battles with Daley. He appreciated how challenging and exhilarating it could be to take on the mighty forces of the community. This became evident when he found surprising support for the strikers among idealistic and socially conscious men and women from all walks of life. For the first time, he and Sarah felt that they were part of a living movement committed to social justice for exploited blacks in this racist city. And this strengthened Victor in the belief that his cause was just. The strikers had tolerated great hardships in the process of becoming part of the struggle against anti-black attitudes in Chicago. Although he did not attain his goal of a union contract with the struck hospitals, Gotbaum was confident that he had placed this question on the agenda for a future decision.

For the first time in his union career, Victor observed the associated suffering close up. He could never dismiss the thought that, while he had been instrumental in organizing these workers, he had also played a major role in the decision to strike and in the hardships associated with failure. From that moment, he learned to discipline himself against indiscriminate strike calls. Thereafter, when debating the possibility of resorting to the strike weapon, he had to know, in advance, that the prospects for success were good.

Gotbaum learned that he had the skill for union leadership and knew, despite the awesomeness of Daley's power, that one had to make the fight. Laboring in Daley's harsh, unfriendly city had enlarged his horizons and expanded his view of people. His ability to identify outstanding union talent like Lillian Roberts enhanced his confidence in being able to select, educate, and work with people from varied backgrounds.

During these seven years in Illinois, Victor grew perceptibly. He learned that people who differed with him were not necessarily his enemy. When he first took on the leadership of the reform Democrats in Evanston, many members of the organization found him much too aggressive, much too confrontational, and lacking in patience. Under the tutelage of his wife and some close friends like Abner Mikva, he became more understanding of others, especially those of differing viewpoints. Gradually, he mastered many of the skills of media attention, learning how to handle probing, not always friendly, newspaper and television reporters. Before scheduled public addresses, Sarah helped him tone down their shrill qualities and sensitized him to possible audience reactions and public rebuttals. Overall, he responded favorably to advice and criticism, when he felt them pertinent and helpful. By 1964, he was ready for other responsibilities.

NOTES

1. Proceedings of the Third Constitutional Convention of the AFL–CIO, 1959, pp. 191–197; Proceedings of the International Convention of the American Federation of State, County and Municipal Employees, AF of L (AFSCME Proceedings), 1966, p. 13; Leo Kramer, *Labor's Paradox—The American Federation of State,*

County and Municipal Employees, AFL-CIO, New York: John Wiley & Sons, 1962, p. 41; Jack Steiber, *Public Employee Unionism: Structure, Growth, Policy,* Brookings Institution, 1973, pp. 114–115.

2. David R. Jones, "Union Militancy of Nation's Public Employees Is Found Increasing," *New York Times,* April 2, 1967, p. 79.

3. U.S. Department of Labor, Manpower Administration, *Manpower Report of the President,* April 1974, Washington, D.C.: U.S. Government Printing Office, 1974, p. 312; U.S. Department of Labor, Bureau of Labor Statistics, *Monthly Labor Review,* January 1968; p. 94; *Time,* March 1, 1968, p. 34.

4. Jones, "Union Militancy," p. 79; *Time,* March 1, 1968, p. 35; *New York Daily News,* September 10, 1968, p. 38.

5. The bulk of information concerning Gotbaum's early years was secured through many interviews with Victor Gotbaum and Sarah Gotbaum. See also, Bernard Rosenberg and Ernest Goldstein, *Creators and Disturbers, Reminiscences by Jewish Intellectuals of New York,* New York: Columbia University Press, 1982, pp. 246–251.

6. Interview with Victor Gotbaum, January 21 and 28, 1970; Rosenberg and Goldstein, *Creators and Disturbers,* p. 252. One of the authors of the current work was a long-time member of the AVC National Board and, while associated with the Independent Progressive Caucus, observed Gotbaum in action.

7. David Lewin, "Mayoral Power and Municipal Labor Relations: A Three City Study," unpublished paper, June 1980, pp. 27–29; David Lewin, Raymond D. Horton, and James W. Kuhn, *Collective Bargaining and Manpower Utilization in Big City Governments,* Montclair, NJ: Allanheld Osmun, 1979, Chapter 3; Ralph T. Jones, "City Employee Unions in New York and Chicago," Ph.D. dissertation, Harvard University, 1972; A.H. Raskin, "Politics Up-Ends the Bargaining Table," in Sam Zagoria, ed., *Public Workers and Public Unions,* Englewood Cliffs, NJ: Prentice-Hall, 1972, pp. 123–124.

8. Considerable material for the background of the 1959 strike against two Chicago hospitals, led by Gotbaum, was secured from an unpublished and undated case study by Montague Brown, "A Campaign to Organize Hospital Employees." This was written for Professor Robert F. McKersie of the Graduate School of Business, University of Chicago, between 1960 and 1963. Professor McKersie was kind enough to supply the authors with a copy of the case study.

9. *Ibid.,* p. 7. Worker's grievances stressed the extremely low wages; assignments to a variety of jobs and transfers from one floor to another the same day; no time-and-a-half for overtime work; changes in shifts made without notice; there were six holidays, but no extra pay if they worked on the holiday; different allowances for sick leave while dietary employees received no sick leave; one week vacation after a year's employment; no seniority rights; no job security; and no notice when fired. See organizing leaflet issued by Gotbaum for AFSCME Local 1657 in Chicago, otherwise known as the Hospital Workers Union, in Robert B. McKersie and Montague Brown, "Nonprofessional Hospital Workers and a Union Organizing Drive," *Quarterly Journal of Economics,* 77 (August 1963): 375.

10. *Chicago Tribune,* August 14, 1959, Part I, p. 10; August 27, 1959, Part I, p. 14; Brown, "A Campaign to Organize Hospital Employees," pp. 11–17; McKersie and Brown, "Nonprofessional Hospital Workers and a Union Organizing Drive," pp. 374–376. Also, interview with Abner Mikva, September 24, 1983.

11. Brown, "A Campaign to Organize Hospital Employees," pp. 25-26. After the first few days of the strike, the *Chicago Tribune* did not refer to it, while the leading voice of the black community, the *Chicago Defender,* carried nothing in its columns about the dispute.

12. McKersie and Brown, "Nonprofessional Hospital Workers and a Union Organizing Drive," pp. 376-380, 391; Brown, "A Campaign to Organize Hospital Employees," pp. 27-29; Ron Hollander, "Drawstrings vs. Purse Strings," *New York Post,* June 12, 1971, p. 23.

13. McKersie and Brown, "Nonprofessional Hospital Workers and A Union Organizing Drive," p. 375.

6
Transitions in Leadership

Transitions in union leadership have not always been easy or helpful to democratic traditions. Like others in business and government, labor leaders are often skilled at building political machines and adapting democratic structures to their personal advantage. In this chapter, we appraise Wurf's contributions as executive director of DC 37, the impact on Council leadership of his insurgent campaigns and move to Washington, and of a jurisdictional challenge by militant social workers. The changes of leadership in Washington as well as New York illustrate some of the difficulties involved in making union transitions smooth and constructive.

WURF'S LEGACY

In the decade and a half that he was the steward of AFSCME in New York, Wurf built the foundation of an organization, and created a staff for internal management and administration. Responding to a diverse membership spread throughout the five counties, and aware of the need for clout at City Hall and the state capitol to preserve negotiated gains and to protect Council members against hostile legislation and lawmakers, he gave birth to a political action arm of union outreach for electioneering and lobbying.

To educate the membership, to strengthen their sense of dignity and economic well-being, and to foster local leadership, he

The team of Gotbaum and Roberts are brought to New York City from Chicago in late 1964 to strengthen a faltering DC 37 leadership after Wurf is elected International president of AFSCME.

helped design courses for stewards, sponsored Councilwide educational conferences for rank-and-file representatives, and developed promotional classes which signaled the beginnings of a career development program. Alert to the need for direct and intelligible communication with Council members, who ranged from semiliterates to holders of Ph.D. degrees, he directed publication of a Council newspaper.

Wurf helped build a multi-ethnic union reflective of the city's population and representative of many of the titles and agencies of the municipal government. With modest help, at first, from the International office, Wurf and his staff gradually brought increasing dues into the Council treasury. These funds enabled him to appoint additional organizers, improve the union's negotiating skills and service to members, and initiate lobbying endeavors from the grassroots level to the uppermost sources of lawmaking and political power. And when Mayor Wagner and the Board of Estimate responded affirmatively to pressure from DC 37 and other municipal unions for a dues checkoff system, income to the Council's coffers became steady and reliable.

Determined to attain a collective bargaining system for public employees akin to that achieved by private sector unions since the 1930s, Wurf was committed to militant tactics and weapons. Fortunately, he was able to ride a wave of recognition among public sector workers that dependence on the usual forms of political action were no longer productive. This was especially true in light of rising public criticism of civil servants, and their increasing assumption of a defensive role as the "underdog." In response, Wurf sought to instill in city workers an awareness that the union had to become a more important mechanism than their earlier sense of attachment to administrative agencies and supervisory personnel. He helped build among city employees a sense of "we and they," a key element in separating public sector workers from the intimacy and "family" relationships, actual or perceived, that had formerly characterized the work place.

Wurf's dynamism, dedication, and ideological commitment to progressive unionism was particularly attractive to young, idealistic individuals who believed in the union movement and who joined the Council staff at low wages to be on the frontier of organizing civil servants. They soon realized that Wurf had mastered many of the details of a complicated city budget, and willingly faced up to the jungle of complex and difficult procedures for negotiating grievances and fringe benefits. In the process, he developed unusual expertise in collective bargaining and insured increasing visibility for himself and for the Council in New York's highly competitive press.

All this Jerry Wurf achieved within the context of a tough, challenging, and not always friendly environment. During this period, he had to confront a general increase in antagonism toward public service unionism, and contend with private sector labor leaders who showed him and municipal unions either indifference or outright hostility. Craft union leaders were generally supportive of Martin Lacey's endeavors to isolate and sabotage Wurf in the CTLC, as well as in his organizing endeavors among city workers. In addition he encountered competition from other municipal union leaders. With rare exception, city administrators were critical of Wurf's bluster and militant tactics, which threatened their traditional domination of exploited and demeaned public employees. Finally, the media were not friendly to Wurf's aggressiveness in organizing the unorganized.

At the same time, he revealed himself to be irascible and unstable. He was prone to public tirades and demeaning attacks against his own staff, insuring a turnover of Council employees and internal disruption. Holding firmly to the reins of power, he was unable to delegate authority and tended to impede lines of responsibility. He had a neurotic drive that impelled him to do too much. These characteristics created troublesome developments during his long absences while campaigning for the international presidency between 1960 and 1964. By 1960, Wurf headed the largest AFSCME unit in the country, was a labor leader to be reckoned with in the city, and was becoming increasingly familiar to those on the national labor scene. It was time to move on.

THE INTERNATIONAL PRESIDENCY

Ambitious, determined, possessing tremendous energy and drive, and stimulated by his successes, the DC 37 leader turned his attention to the International presidency. Wurf believed that he possessed the superior skills and aggressive style required to make of AFSCME a far more powerful and effective national organization. He viewed Arnold Zander as too weak and lacking the boldness and militancy required of imaginative trade union leadership. Instead, the incumbent president clung to an outmoded civil service mentality and tactics. Zander had brought Wurf into the organization and had been helpful to his New York organizing drive with at least half a million dollars over a two-year period. At International conventions, prior to 1960, Wurf had been instrumental in manipulating parliamentary rules and organizing sessions to protect Zander's leadership.

Not until after the 1960 convention did Wurf ally himself with a group of dissident reformers who eventually called themselves the Committee on Union Responsibility (COUR). This group included, among others, Al Bilik and Robert Hastings of Ohio, Joe Ames of Missouri, and Victor Gotbaum of Chicago. In one of the most carefully constructed grass-roots campaigns, these COUR strategists built an organization that spread its roots throughout the entire country. Wurf's mentor, Paul Hall of the Seafarers, served as an important source of funds and rallied support. Despite the determination of Zander and his colleagues to contain the COUR challenge through trusteeships, special arrangements, and direct International control over certain locals and councils, they failed to stop the widely organized forces developed by this national insurgency.

The power of the International organization was substantial: superior finances, organizational machinery, a paid staff, the union's press, and a nationwide system of communications. And yet, rank-and-file members, sustained by COUR's leadership, outmaneuvered Zander and his associates in one of those rare educational endeavors to displace democratically an incumbent union president. Although COUR began its grass-roots insurgency in 1960, and gained a respectable 40 percent of the convention vote for Wurf two years later, not until 1964 did it reap the full rewards of its dramatic campaign when it barely defeated Zander but gained overwhelming command of the International executive board (IEB).

IT'S HARD TO LET GO

It was somewhat ironic that while Wurf campaigned for four years to attain the pinnacle of power in AFSCME, he found it excrutiatingly difficult, thereafter, to give up control of his home base, DC 37. During his insurgency, he was away from New York for long periods, and yet he was unable to assign full responsibility for the organization to any one individual. Despite pleas by Council president John Boer that assistant director Calogero "Charlie" Taibi be designated acting executive director in Wurf's absence, Wurf avoided granting undue power to a staff member for fear he might suddenly find his leadership challenged. He always reminded Taibi that he was only second in command.

Taibi was a tall, husky, mild-mannered New Yorker who had graduated from Harvard University in 1949, and received a master's degree in economics from Columbia University. After research and administrative work with the Furniture Workers' union and involvement with the remnants of the Socialist movement, he was employed by Wurf in 1959. During the years that followed, this new recruit served successively as a special representative, assistant editor of PEP, political action director, education director and then assistant director in January 1962. He impressed Council leaders with his mastery of figures, his ability to work with others, and his excellent command of language. But he lacked the charisma and the toughness sometimes required of leaders. Before long, he was heading most of the Council's negotiating teams in collective bargaining with the city's Budget and Personnel directors.[1]

Taibi fit Wurf's pattern of a number two man. He was very bright and decent, a good professional, but not tough enough to stand up to a raucous, intervening and authoritarian personality. Between the start of the COUR campaign in 1960, and the election of the Council's executive director in 1964, Taibi "minded the store." And even though he wasn't anxious to become the number-one man, he nevertheless coordinated complex Council activities. With the rapid, uninterrupted growth of union membership and the merger with former CIO units, a number of strong, autonomy-minded leaders emerged who had to be reminded, periodically, of their affiliation with DC 37. The professionals in Technical Guild Local 375, the social workers in Local 371, the school employees in Local 372, and others, over the years had frequently flexed their muscles and sought to go off on their own in organizing, public relations, and bargaining negotiations. A strong, tough hand like Jerry Wurf was constantly necessary to insure unity and build cohesion around the long-range goals of the Council.

Taibi was too gentle to tell a group of determined members not to strike, or to catalyze apathetic unionists to "hit the bricks." There are former staff members who insist that Jerry Wurf built a union on "invectives and hate," while Taibi sought to build it on "love." In his mild-mannered way, he attempted to make the staff more cohesive and strengthened its loyalty to the Council instead of to a single individual. During this period, Taibi pushed educational conferences and staff and shop steward training courses. With Wurf away, the situation around Council headquarters was infinitely calmer, but missing were dynamic leadership, militancy, and a strong voice to foster unity over competing factions.

After being rejected by Joe Ames and Morris Riger, Wurf finally decided that Taibi would succeed him as executive director, but he made it quite clear that he intended to control New York from Washington. Eventually, these plans went awry. Under normal circumstances, Taibi might have headed another, more traditional type of union. But DC 37 was not a typical union, nor were the situations that generally engulfed it. Taibi was not the man for wheeling and dealing, and Wurf knew it when he pushed through his election by the executive board in May 1964 to fill out his unexpired term. As one of the local presidents put it, almost two decades later, Taibi was "too soft a gentleman, too professorial," to head DC 37. What was needed then, and subsequently, was a rough-and-tumble guy who could keep the Council together and who could stand up to the domineering and irascible personality of the new International president.[2]

From the moment Taibi took over, Wurf was constantly second-guessing his decisions. These repeated interventions made it virtually impossible for the new executive to grow into the job or feel that he was its actual director. Sensitive and too gentle to fight Wurf, he was unable to exert the ongoing leadership and discipline necessary. Even though Wurf insisted all along that DC 37 presented a "healthy growth," some of the problems confronting the Council were serious. Two organizational challenges tested DC 37's power and influence—a splinter group of social workers, and the Teamster's competition for hospital and other public employees. The Council was not yet a cohesive organization.

With a potential of some 16,000 members, including practical nurses, Hospital Local 420 had earlier organized a little over 5,000 workers, fragmented among 21 units. By 1964, however, AFSCME was losing members to Local 237 of the Teamsters, which had surpassed them in numbers, under the leadership of Bill Lewis. To compound Council difficulties, the special representative charged with supervising DC 37 staff and shop stewards in hospitals neglected his responsibilities for weeks at a time.

Complicating matters still further, Council leadership had permitted some locals such extreme autonomy as to isolate themselves from the ongoing work of DC 37, and from close cooperation with those staff members who could make significant contributions in furthering membership drives and strengthening their respective organizations. This was particularly evident in the Welfare Department, where Local 371 had fallen far short of the objective of attaining a majority of the membership, let alone effectively organizing the agency. Even in titles that the Council thought were traditional centers of strength, AFSCME had not "attained satisfactory percentages of membership." Wurf and his associates had been remiss in obliging the leadership of Local 371 to plan and carry out a membership drive in the department, expecially with reference to the needs of each title. For example, from among 17 titles, with a potential of 6,370 members in the Welfare Department, Local 371 after eight years had managed to recruit only 2,470 into AFSCME. This was far from a healthy situation and the Council would soon pay a costly price for its neglect.[3]

PROBLEMS INSIDE LOCAL 371

After the UPW was expelled by the CIO in 1949 on grounds that it was dominated by communists, the UPW gradually disappeared. Eventually, it was replaced by the Social Investigators Local 1193 (AFSCME), and by Welfare Local 371, chartered by the CIO. Following the AFL–CIO merger, both locals were combined into Welfare Employees Local 371 of DC 37. From the start, Clericals and Supervisors dominated and Social Investigators, or case workers, played a secondary and often unhappy role. Among rank-and-file professionals during the years that followed, increasing numbers of young ideological militants, idealistic followers, and survivors of the communist-dominated UPW became alienated from what they viewed as an outdated, unimaginative, and opportunistic leadership in Local 371, charging it with "undemocratic procedures" and "nuzzling" too closely to management.[4]

The newly recruited social investigators, primarily young college graduates of the 1950s and 1960s, were sensitive, concerned and often the most vocal members of the Welfare Department. They reflected important changes in the social work field in New York. With advanced academic training, and degrees in social work, these case workers demanded treatment with dignity. An idealistic corps of enthusiastic, budding professionals in their twenties, many were in the process of finding themselves. Concerned with the product of their work, they opposed frequent checkups and home visits to welfare recipients, and believed that their clients' difficulties were rooted in societal problems of poverty, inequality, racism, and war. A number of them were influenced by some socialist or Communist background at college or at home. More militant than the traditional public service worker, many were veterans of sit-ins at college and the civil rights movement. Inspired by President Kennedy's example to the young, they sought to use government and their union as instruments for change—"Change the job and you change the agency. Change the agency and you get a shot at the system."[5]

Welfare rolls expanded dramatically, with the city caring for over a half million, at a cost of $1 million each day, with help from the federal and state governments. Almost equal to the population of Denver, they included homeless children, helpless aged, and mothers of large families without fathers. Despite signs of a healthy economy, the welfare cases continued to grow by 200 daily.

Administering money and a variety of social remedies to poor families was a massive, complex, and thankless task for the 6,000 social workers who handled a minimum of 60 cases and as many as 100 each. As one investigator put it, "If you try to be conscientious you go crazy." Each caseworker was expected to process a never-ending mass of forms and applications, interview families about their situations and backgrounds, locate missing husbands, head off trouble-bound youngsters, find new housing for those evicted by landlords or as a result of tenement house fires, and worry over late or stolen relief checks.

The pay for social workers was poor; the top salary for an investigator with nine years of experience was $7,190 a year—a little more than a city laborer earned after only one year, and only $1,000 more than some welfare clients received. Caseworkers were packed into condemned schools, converted factories, and dilapidated buildings where the air was poor and accommodations totally inadequate. Intake facilities designed for 20 individuals frequently housed as many as 200. Many found it impossible to deal humanely and responsibly with their clients, while key administrators in welfare centers had little interest in the way they were treated. A subsequent slogan on organizing leaflets and picket line placards underscored this dilemma: "Less Paperwork—More Social Work."[6]

Knowledgeable Council staff knew that the leadership of Local 371 remained a poor and inadequate representative of its constituency, tended to avoid confrontations with management, and adopted a smug, self-righteous attitude of isolation from DC 37. The fear of Wurf and Council leadership to "trample on local autonomy" insured, in this instance, poor collective bargaining, an absence of militant organizing, and increasing frustration among staff who had to work with the local's shortsighted officers. Formal negotiations with the city did not result in a contract but a "memorandum of understanding," consisting mainly of vague promises. This led Wallace Sayre and Herbert Kaufman to conclude, in their pioneering work, that:

> The SCME leaders use the demand for the collective bargaining contract more as an evocative symbol than as rigid doctrine. They accept the symbol, if signed and sealed, as a memorandum of understanding, as a substitute for the fine print and precise words of a contract. Recognition and assured access is their first aim: the full panoply of conventional collective bargaining is a goal deferred.[7]

The result was that a newly organized Social Service Employees Union (SSEU) found increasing support among disenchanted social investigators, home economists, homemakers and children's counselors. The leaders of the SSEU underscored their charges of "company unionism" by pointing to a succession of former presidents of Local 371 who later received important jobs in the city government or in the administration of the Welfare Department.

Subsequent to a harsh, repressive campaign against UPW officers and members, an unhealthy atmosphere pervaded many of the city's welfare centers. Individuals suspected of active affiliation with the former UPW or with the SSEU might be called to the central office to answer a variety of charges, including failure to dress properly. Since recognizable grievance procedures did not exist, or were so complex that they could not be carried out, "the helplessness of the workers was almost complete." The life of social investigators was a miserable, exploited, and unhappy one.

In light of the fact that the executive board of Local 371 was dominated by Supervisors and Clerical representatives who lacked militant, traditional trade union commitments, the professional workers felt ignored. Even the leaders of Local 371 conceded their inability to influence the Department of Welfare to improve miserable working conditions, and to call a halt to the shabby treatment accorded welfare workers. As a consequence, professional turnover was rampant, often reaching 40 percent annually. The charges of "company unionism" hurled against Local 371 persisted with telling effect. In spite of warnings from Council staff, Wurf did nothing in response to the organizing drives of the newly formed SSEU.[8]

SSEU'S IDEALISTIC CADRE

Taking advantage of the voluntary dues checkoff system, a former UPW member had attained recognition, in 1961, for fewer than 30 employees in the Brownsville Welfare Center of Brooklyn. The group became the nucleus of the SSEU, which spread to other boroughs. The diversity of the SSEU leadership was typified by two individuals who played important roles—Joseph Tepedino and Judith Mage. Tepedino, who had migrated from Italy some years earlier, was a rank-and-file leader who understood the need for a pragmatic approach to help build an honest trade union, but who had divorced himself from the opportunistic compromises he and his colleagues associated with Local 371 and other old-line unions. He was far more practical in educating and organizing members than he was in negotiating a contract.

Judith Mage was a product of New York City's radical politics, the middle-class Jewish intelligentsia, and an experimental education at Antioch College. A committed activist and political ideologue, she believed that Leon Trotsky had been the brightest of all twentieth century Marxists and that the capitalist system had to be changed in order to fundamentally benefit her welfare clients. After Tepedino's fiery orations, a calm, collected Mage would usually clarify them for their audiences.

The fusion of these streams of thought made for the uniqueness of SSEU. These idealistic leaders, who thought nothing of spending every free moment planning organizing campaigns, writing leaflets, pumping mimeograph machines, and distributing tracts, before and after work hours, became role models for recently appointed caseworkers who flocked into the SSEU.

In September 1964, the SSEU executive board challenged 371 for exclusive representation of the social service titles. During the weeks leading up to the election, every welfare center was snowed under by competing leaflets. Besides indicting the working conditions, the SSEU presented its plans in carefully developed pamphlets, at boroughwide meetings and in individual solicitations. SSEU viewed this as an ethical, moral, and revolutionary crusade.

The campaign of Local 371, on the other hand, was primarily defensive and outdated. Its leadership remained oblivious to the changes that had occurred in the work place, did not respond forcefully to the unbearable work loads, did not involve members in union activities, and shrugged off the opposition as mere malcontents. The basic appeal of Local 371 was its influence and skill in negotiating demands and providing services and benefits.

In October, the SSEU won the representation elections decisively, 2,642 to 1,411, capturing 21 of 22 welfare centers. Within three years, and without adequate funds, staff, or experience, a young group of dedicated activists had defeated Local 371 by appropriating some of the original commitment, idealism, and tactics of an earlier DC 37. If Local 371 was to retain any hope for the future, it needed new leadership.

GOTBAUM BROUGHT TO NEW YORK

Confronted with the defeat of Local 371 by the SSEU, along with heightened frustration, suspicion, and dissatisfaction among some rank-and-file members, Wurf concluded that Taibi was unable to provide the leadership needed. It had likewise become clear to Taibi that he did not have the toughness or the stamina to stand up to an overbearing individual like Jerry Wurf. Taibi had also taken ill, afflicted with the debilitating Hodgkin's disease, which often sapped his physical strength and required frequent visits to the hospital. As one of the few who became privy to Taibi's illness, Wurf took steps to eventually replace his ailing colleague. He convinced Taibi to prevail upon the executive board of DC 37 to request the International president to assign, from outside the Council, someone to assume responsibility for coordinating the field staff.[9]

After being rejected by others, Wurf turned, with some misgivings, to Victor Gotbaum. Recently designated midwestern regional director and general trouble-shooter for AFSCME's new president, Gotbaum was emerging on the AFSCME scene. Called upon to strengthen Taibi, the president promised Gotbaum that, as field staff coordinator, he would "really be number one, because Charlie can't handle it." Gotbaum eagerly agreed to take the assignment in November 1964.[10]

The Chicago leader soon learned that this new task was all but overwhelming. Unknown to Council staff and rank-and-file leaders, the sudden involvement of a stranger as second in command engendered suspicion, bitterness, and hostility. Nor did he enjoy being caught between autonomous locals, independent staffers, and an ailing, insecure director. Having demonstrated his capacity as an organizer and leader for AFSCME, Gotbaum was not prepared to play second fiddle in a situation warranting his total commitment. At the same time, he was excited with the prospects of returning home and the unlimited horizons of the DC 37 challenge.

Wurf's hesitancy about Gotbaum was evoked by the latter's strong character and independent stance, not only in Chicago but throughout the COUR campaign. During strategy planning sessions, there had been frequent head-to-head encounters between the two. Thus, the new president realized that with Gotbaum eventually heading DC 37, he could not readily dominate New York as he had done with Taibi. But developments in the Welfare Department and decisions by the SSEU solved the leadership problem for the Council sooner than Wurf had expected or Gotbaum had contemplated.

SUMMARY

In 1964 there were two major turning points for AFSCME: Wurf defeated Arnold Zander, moved onto the national scene and sought, at the same time, to retain control over his original base of power by designating a gentle, loving soul as his successor. When the latter failed to take the tough stances necessary to maintain a cohesive Council and to respond aggressively to the challenge of SSEU to Local 371, Wurf decided to anoint a new disciple. But the president was aware that this heir apparent from Chicago was far more independent and might indeed alter his historic relationships with the Council.

NOTES

1. DC 37 executive board minutes, November 9, 1960; December 14, 1961; January 17, 1962; February 13, 1963; April 10, 1963; January 8, 1964; and February 13, 1964. DC 37 finance committee minutes, January 17, 1962. *Public Employee Press*, May 15, 1964, p. 1. Interviews with Bert Rose, September 16, 1981; John Boer, September 22, 1981.

2. Minutes of special meeting, DC 37 executive board, May 7, 1964. *Public Employee Press*, May 15, 1964, p. 1. Also interviews with Thomas Hagan, June 9, 1980; Bert Rose, September 16, 1981; John Boer, September 22, 1981; Morris Riger, October 2, 1982; Arthur Tibaldi, December 6, 1982.

3. Minutes of delegates council meetings, May 22 and October 23, 1962; Charles Taibi memorandum to Jerry Wurf, August 2, 1962; memorandum on "Organizational Opportunities of Existing Staff and other Existing Resources of the District," April 1963. The language and perception of this unsigned memo indicates that it was probably written by Morris Riger, who remained for a comparatively brief period on the Council staff as director of organization in 1963. Also, Nick Cifuni to Morris Riger, April 1, 1963; Lenny Seelig to Riger, April 14, 1963. Interview with Morris Riger, October 2, 1982.

4. Bert Cochran, *Labor and Communism,* Princeton, NJ: Princeton University, 1977, pp. 304–313. Also, interviews with Bart Cohen, December 19, 1980; Victor Gotbaum, May 11, 1981; Bert Rose, September 16, 1981; John Boer, September 22, 1981; Abram Flaxer, October 4, 1981; William Schleicher, November 30, 1981; and Alan Viani, February 26, 1982. Also affiliating with DC 37, at this same time, were the CIO School Employee Local 372, Board of Higher Education Employees Local 374, and the Civil Service Technical Guild, Local 375. By 1965, Welfare Department employees included approximately 7,500 caseworkers, 2,400 supervisors, 7,000 in clerical titles, and about 1,000 in miscellaneous titles.

5. Richard H.P. Mendes, "The Professional Union: A Study of the Social Service Employees Union of the New York City Department of Social Services," Ph.D. dissertation, Columbia University, 1974, pp. 29–35, 42–45. Also, interviews with Bart Cohen, December 19, 1980; Bill Schleicher, November 30, 1981; and Alan Viani, February 26, 1982.

6. *Time,* January 22, 1965, p. 20; Mendes, "The Professional Union," p. 40; interviews with Mae Feinstein, May 7, 1979; Michael Rappaport, May 15, 1979; Bart Cohen, September 22, 1981; William Schleicher, November 30, 1981; Alan Viani, February 26, 1982.

7. DC 37 executive board minutes, April 13, 1960; Wallace S. Sayre and Herbert Kaufman, *Governing New York City: Politics in the Metropolis,* New York: W.W. Norton, 1965, p. 409; Monroe S. Walsh, "Welfare Unionism in N.Y.C.," p. 1. This report by the assistant education director of DC 37 was submitted in late 1966.

8. DC 37 delegates council minutes, May 22, 1962, p. 2; interviews with William Ross, February 15, 1979; Mae Feinstein, May 7, 1979; John Boer, September 22, 1981.

9. DC 37 executive board minutes, November 12 and December 9, 1964. Also, interviews with Jerry Wurf, August 20 and 21, 1979; Victor Gotbaum, May 11, 1981; Bert Rose, September 16, 1981; and Joe Ames, September 26, 1981.

10. Interviews with Victor Gotbaum, May 11, 1981; Joe Ames, September 26, 1981; Morris Riger, October 2, 1982.

7
You Can Fight City Hall

The one welfare center that had not been captured by the SSEU was Manhattan's East End. There, a new team of equally dedicated unionists decided to remain with DC 37 but fight for the leadership of Local 371. In this chapter we examine the internal challenge for control of the local and the welfare strike of January 1965 and its impact on the Council's top leadership. In the course of the struggle with City Hall, Wurf again demonstrated his skill as a strategist and his determination to maintain a presence in New York. Gotbaum, newly assigned, was often tempted to leave the scene, but would remain in response to encouragement by rank-and-file leaders, and in recognition of the high stakes involved.

THE FIGHT FROM WITHIN

In the welfare center on E. 108th Street in Manhattan, a young, ascetic-looking Alan Viani had been convinced by Nat Lindenthal to succeed him as shop steward for Local 371. A soft-spoken, serious graduate of Oklahoma University, Viani was not a product of any of the radical subcultures, and was comparatively unsophisticated in the ways of political and union organizing. But he readily displayed a native talent for expressing the dissatisfactions and unhappiness of his co-workers.

Confronted with the serious challenge from the SSEU for representational rights, Viani refused to adhere to the shortsighted, outdated reactions of his local's leadership. Instead, he, Jim

Welfare workers vote for a job action which becomes the longest municipal strike in New York City history. The successful welfare strike of January 1965 profoundly altered the parameters of negotiations for public workers throughout the nation.

McKeon, Nat Lindenthal, and clerical worker Patricia Caldwell secured the assistance of a number of radical colleagues to work with them. They convinced many of the young staff at their center that there were AFSCME members who were committed to responsible trade unionism and who were equally appalled by the insensitive, unimaginative leadership of their local. Viani's approach was positive and respectful of the opposition. He did not wave them off as mere "malcontents," nor did he ignore the legitimacy of their grievances. Consequently, his welfare center narrowly voted to remain with Local 371. Hurrying to headquarters with news of his victory, he was appalled to learn that SSEU had captured every other center. During a postmortem that same night, he was revolted by the remarks of the local's leadership, which questioned the loyalty of those who had defected. Unable to contain himself, Viani warned that if the policies were not altered immediately, the SSEU would soon control the Supervisors and Clericals as well. Before he sat down, he brashly asked the officers to resign.[1]

The response of other shop stewards was more disheartening. Without exception, they publicly berated Viani for his "disloyal" behavior, but as he left the meeting, a number of them came over to quietly assure him that he had done a courageous thing, and agreed that the local's leadership should be replaced. During the days that followed, others contacted him, urging creation of a reform group. Finally, in response to a call from Viani, a dozen shop stewards, including Pat Caldwell, showed up at his apartment to organize an opposition caucus which soon had the support of most shop stewards throughout the city. Shortly after this ground swell of opposition came to the attention of Charlie Taibi, the executive board of Local 371 resigned, facilitating a special election in late November.

The dissident group set up its own slate of candidates for the executive board, with Alan Viani for president and Pat Caldwell for vice-president. Although the old-line leadership put up its ticket, there was really no contest; the Viani–Caldwell slate was swept into office by a 9-to-1 vote.

CONTRACT TIME

Toward the end of 1964, New York City's Department of Welfare employed approximately 12,500 individuals, in an assortment of titles. Local 371 remained the recognized bargaining agent for 1,500 supervisory social service workers and 5,000 clerical and related titles. Since contractual agreements for both unions were to expire on December 31, 1964, preliminary negotiations began in late October, but without material progress.

The collective bargaining objectives of SSEU included the full complement of bread-and-butter items, such as repeal of the Career and Salary Plan, more liberal leaves, health and life insurance, paid overtime, and the use of department premises for union meetings. Moving into areas considered administrative, SSEU asked for the elimination of the Social Investigator Trainee title, a longer training period, free tuition for training courses at the City University, and an increase in the number of scholarships for full-time graduate social work. Of great importance to the SSEU, and most threatening to city officials, was the demand that a maximum caseload of 50 be established, with 25–35 for "problem caseloads."

Offering these "minimum demands" the untried union negotiators were not prepared for the traditional give-and-take of the collective bargaining process.[2] One month after receiving the SSEU recommendations for a new contract, the Department of Personnel finally advised the union that virtually all of their demands were non-negotiable since they were outside the traditional collective bargaining process and the Career and Salary Plan. Only salary changes were deemed legitimate. Caseloads might be discussed but only through separate meetings with the Civil Service Commission, the Department of Personnel, and the Department of Welfare. Outraged SSEU members directed their officers to inform the city that if no agreement was reached by midnight, December 31, they would strike.

SSEU had earlier demanded an increase of $950 in starting salaries for social investigators, in an endeavor to bring degree-holding employees up to a level with some city laborers. The city made a final offer that varied from $240 to $300 per year for a two-year contract, and a welfare fund payment of $60 per worker, should the contract be extended to two and a half years.

In the meantime, the new Viani–Caldwell team, with one eye on the SSEU and another on the bargaining table, established cooperative relationships with DC 37 and worked closely with its negotiating staff. Taibi also became involved when he realized that a strike was imminent. Although the leaders of 371 agreed with the SSEU on wages and health and welfare benefits, they viewed many of the other demands as beyond the scope of bargaining, e.g., the rights of welfare clients. But they rejected efforts by the city to play them off against the SSEU. Special inducements were offered Taibi, along with assurances that the mayor would "take care of you," if only Local 371 would not join the strike. With tremendous pressure from their own membership, and the constant threat of the SSEU to take over exclusive leadership of welfare workers, Viani and Caldwell refused to make a separate deal to abort a walkout.

Three days before the start of the strike, Viani and Victor Gotbaum, who had joined the DC 37 staff little more than a month previously, met with SSEU representatives in an endeavor to make joint plans for the walkout. But the latter were too nervous about being subverted by "old-line" union leaders. Thus, two strikes would develop at the same time.[3]

THE WELFARE STRIKE

Despite a restraining court order, and aware of the automatic penalties of the Condon–Wadlin Act, the membership of both unions voted overwhelmingly to strike. On the first workday of 1965, they began the longest public employee strike in the history of the city. Over 8,000 professional, supervisory, and clerical employees "hit the bricks" for bread-and-butter issues and to extend the scope of bargaining. Strikers refused to believe that "you can't fight City Hall."

The department was obliged to close many of the centers, while the remaining ones were jammed with needy people seeking emergency assistance. Responding to the immediate request of the welfare commissioner, James Dumpson, city comptroller Abraham Beame removed the names of 5,398 social investigators and clerical workers from the payroll for violating the Condon–Wadlin Act, the first time in 17 years that the city enforced the dismissal penalties of the state law. Within a few days of the strike, two leaders from each of the unions were found guilty of defying the court order. A temporary injunction was granted, but action against strikers and union leaders was delayed.

Throughout the month-long strike, the New York press vigorously denounced the unions' leadership and supported application of the Condon–Wadlin Act. According to the *New York Times*, for example, the real target of the strike was "not the city but its most helpless and disestablished citizens." This stoppage, "the largest, longest and most shameful strike of all," was a "rebellion against government, law, court, and the city's unfortunate poor." The city had a clear obligation under the Condon–Wadlin Act to replace the strikers.[4]

Support for the strikers came from a variety of sources. Most important was the solidarity engendered among organized labor in New York. The militants and ideologues who led SSEU had looked disparagingly on the established trade union movement. And yet, it was these "old-line" union leaders who rallied behind the striking welfare workers and helped insure their ultimate success. Jerry Wurf rushed to New York to take command and with Paul Hall played the major role in sustaining the strikers and in facilitating a face-saving settlement. Conscious of the growth and increasing importance of public employee unionism and white-collar workers, traditional union leaders realized the dangers for them if the mayor and his administrators were permitted to break this strike—their strength and organizing endeavors would suffer. They contributed money to the strike funds, maintained mobile canteens, and provided thousands of members for picket lines at welfare centers and around City Hall in the frigid January weather.[5]

Also helpful was encouragement from civil rights leaders Martin Luther King, Jr., A. Philip Randolph, James Farmer, and local chapters of the NAACP. Lawmakers Percy Sutton, Albert H. Blumenthal, and Seymour Posner were joined in their support of the strike by a majority of the staff of the Community Council of Greater New York, the Council of Psychiatric Social Workers in the city schools, the Citizen's Committee for Children, and many local community groups that included welfare clients. By the fourth day Harry Van Arsdale, Paul Hall, and Wurf worked out a face-saving formula for Wagner which was strikingly similar to the final settlement. It provided for a board of five which would consider the negotiable issues and make recommendations within or outside of the Career and Salary Plan. The city was agreeable to let all matters "be considered" by a fact-finding group. Still exhilarated by glorious, dramatic days of militancy on mass picket lines, both unions voted unanimously to reject the proposal when they learned that Wagner was reserving the right to negotiate some, but not all, of the recommendations that might be made by the arbitration panel. The strike continued for three more weeks in frigid, cutting weather before Wagner reconsidered and accepted the basic thrust of this original proposal, although in a new format.[6]

The mayor then asked the deans of six professional schools of social work in New York to initiate covert talks between the city and the unions. They added an atmosphere of trust and respect, but despite a week of tough, drawn-out negotiations, their work foundered on the issue of the scope of bargaining. A suggested approach provided for a fact-finding panel along the model previously presented by the labor leaders: unrestricted bargaining of issues and no reprisals against strikers. The mayor felt bound to reject the agreement. However, the deans had been successful in establishing a basis for trust, and their work, like that of the labor leaders, eventually proved fruitful.

Union leaders Tepedino, Viani, and 16 colleagues were found guilty of contempt of court for continuing the strike, sentenced to

30 days in jail, and fined. The negotiations were momentarily stalled. Having failed to prevent the strike, the Condon–Wadlin Act now became the major obstacle to settling it. Some acceptable and face-saving settlement had to be devised. It was then that Mayor Wagner was visited by President George Meany of the AFL–CIO, Central Labor Council head Harry Van Arsdale and President David Dubinsky of the ILGWU, who urged him to settle immediately. Wagner responded quickly by creating a citizen's task force to reopen direct negotiations.[7] The mayor's group submitted its report within two days, recommending overall acceptance of the agreement worked out by the deans.

All issues raised by the unions, including those declared not negotiable by the city, were to be submitted to a fact-finding panel. The city would agree to cooperate with the unions in seeking release of the antistrike injunction while the unions would apply for a stay on Condon–Wadlin penalties against strikers and, subsequently, contest the constitutionality of amendments approved in 1963. The following day, the mayor accepted the recommendations, Local 371 voted unanimously to return to work, and the SSEU joined them.[8]

A STUNNING VICTORY

The fact-finding panel created by the mayor was composed of Tepedino for the SSEU, Paul Hall for Local 371 (replaced later by Wurf), the directors of Budget and Personnel, and Dr. Charles I. Schottland, Dean of the Graduate School for Advanced Studies in Social Welfare at Brandeis University, who served as chair. Schottland had become familiar with important aspects of the strike in his capacity as consultant to the six New York deans originally involved.

After accumulating some 13 volumes and 2,500 pages of testimony, the chair and the two city representatives, a bare majority, approved a report which recommended most of what the unions wanted and at the same time heralded a revolution in the city's collective bargaining process. The problems of rising caseloads, inadequate staff, high turnover, overemphasis on eligibility, and underemphasis on services were now deemed a legitimate part of the background against which to assess the controversies facing the

Welfare Department. It was suggested that the salaries of most titles be increased by two grades, with a percentage to be determined in subsequent contract talks. A welfare fund was created for educational purposes, and the number of caseloads was reduced to a maximum of 60 per worker. City Hall was to review the entire status of collective bargaining through a committee of city officials, union representatives, and "impartial public representatives."[9]

There then followed three months of intense, often bitter and frustrating negotiations which eventually resulted in new city contracts with SSEU and Local 371. In addition to substantial material gains, the city agreed to ongoing negotiations between union representatives and administrators over policy issues and opened new areas of decision making to worker participation. The contracts gave legitimacy to joint consideration of "workload, working conditions, changes of titles, personnel practices pertaining to the titles in this Contract."[10]

AFTERMATH

In spite of the appointment of Mitchell Ginsberg as commissioner of welfare by Mayor Lindsay, the following two years were almost a continual battle between the city and the unions over contracts and the new issues raised as a result of changing work procedures in the Department of Welfare. As a former dean of the Columbia School of Social Work, Ginsberg was viewed as an ally by SSEU leaders because he had advised the union in the past and had served as one of the negotiators during the welfare strike. One of Ginsberg's first acts was to end investigatory "midnight raids" on welfare clients. But as disputes raged anew, he was soon viewed as a hard-liner by the SSEU.

As far as wages and benefits were concerned, the major problem remained the Career and Salary Plan. The city had so hardened its commitment to it that it found itself unable to extricate itself, making modifications difficult and complex. Serious shortcomings in the grievance procedures also continued to upset workers. In his letter implementing the city–welfare Local 371 contract, Mayor Wagner laid the groundwork for creation of a tripartite committee to "review the entire status of collective bargaining with the city." In it, he referred to his Interim Order of July 21, 1954, and his Executive Order of March 31, 1958, and observed:

When these policies were enunciated, a transitional period of testing and experimentation was contemplated to determine the effectiveness of the new collective bargaining procedures in disposing of the substantive terms and conditions of employment of city employees. It was then recognized that at a future date, review of the city's experience would be essential. That time has come.[11]

A Brookings Institution study underscored the radical nature of the new contracts. It concluded that the work load and staffing provisions represented deep penetrations into what was usually considered management's territory. It was only a matter of time before the scope of bargaining would be changed dramatically throughout the country as public administration theorists and bureaucrats were forced to reexamine their old, traditional assumptions. Urban specialist Raymond Horton, disturbed by the results, voiced the sentiments of those who adhered to a more circumscribed scope of public sector collective bargaining. Both the Schottland Report and the final settlements were viewed as serious setbacks for the city and major victories for the unions. The city's control over the scope of bargaining was broken, and the creation of impasse panels shifted power away from public control. To strike participants, social work had become a recognized profession and, galvanized by organized power, was changing the scope of collective bargaining.[12]

THE STRIKE'S IMPACT ON THE DC 37 LEADERSHIP

Within weeks of assuming the post of field staff coordinator for DC 37 in November, and in the process of working out a very difficult relationship with the Council's executive director, Victor Gotbaum was suddenly confronted with the "Welfare Strike." Friction became inevitable when Wurf decided to assume personal charge of the strike. While the AFSCME national chief disliked the SSEU and its ideological leadership, he saw in their demands an opportunity to shoot down a "blatantly phony system of collective bargaining which the mayor had perpetrated upon the city." He also felt that this strike might serve to enhance his own reputation and afford him an opportunity to make a tremendous breakthrough in state sector unionism on the national scene. With the aid of the striking workers, Paul Hall, George Meany, Harry Van Arsdale and other unions, Wurf succeeded beyond his wildest dreams.

From the start of the strike, Wurf was worried that without his direction, the mayor might be successful through resort to the Condon–Wadlin Act. The rank-and-file and skilled leaders gave the strike its fervor and walked the picket lines, but it was Wurf and Hall who served as the guiding commanders. They were instrumental in convincing other unions to contribute strike funds, sustain the picket lines, and focus unyielding pressure on City Hall.[13]

At one of the weekly rallies of SSEU and Local 371, held simultaneously but separately at the same location, Wurf displayed his skill to excellent effect. After he, Hall, Van Arsdale and other union leaders made ringing speeches of support to the DC 37 picketers in the meeting room upstairs, Wurf and Hall stole downstairs to the SSEU meeting in the main ballroom. Despite some boos and catcalls, they were invited onto the stage to address the assembly. They captivated the large audience, assuring financial and human support from the labor movement. Paul Hall's lengthier address came across with impelling effect upon the SSEU leadership. Indirectly, he made clear that they could not possibly win this, or similar strikes in the future, without organized labor's help and the power to influence lawmakers and political leaders. He urged them to return to the house of labor, or be isolated in the future.

By assuming leadership of the strike, Wurf destroyed Taibi, his crown prince, and anointed a successor. Not only was the International president extremely critical of Taibi, but he all but made him a mere messenger between his luxurious suite at the Commodore Hotel and the Council's offices and strike activities. The debilitating impact of this forceful interposition was devastating to the sensitive executive director. Taibi could no longer escape the realization that he lacked the strength and ability to stand up to Wurf's continuing interventions. The other local chieftains soon knew it, too. To retain his self-esteem and dignity, Taibi resigned in the midst of the strike. The reason given and subsequently propagated was ill health.

From the moment the walkout began, but especially after Wurf took command of the strike, Gotbaum channeled his major energies through the picket lines of Local 371 and cooperated with the local's executive board. He was instrumental in strengthening the morale of picketing unionists, and in fortifying Viani, Caldwell, and their executive board members, who began to view him as a forceful and vibrant leader. He seemed to understand their problems, was committed to their goals, and appeared more open and stable than their International president. As a result, the leaders of 371 came to trust Gotbaum and appreciated his ability to hold the strikers firm for a full month.[14]

Often a calming influence on his International president, Gotbaum nevertheless got into frequent shouting matches with him. Even though he knew that ultimately he would become executive director, Gotbaum's ego and strong, independent strains convinced him that he eventually would have to challenge Wurf's hold on New York. Emotionally more secure than Taibi, Gotbaum was determined to be his own director. On several occasions, he was so infuriated by Wurf's insensitivity and authoritarianism that he submitted his resignation as council staff coordinator. Viani and Caldwell urged him to remain. Lillian Roberts, who had recently been brought onto the Council staff from Illinois on Gotbaum's suggestion, likewise advised Wurf that she would be leaving the New York scene as soon as the strike was concluded. She, too, could not accept his intervention in a local strike, for she had fought this style of leadership under the Zander administration.

Two individuals helped influence Gotbaum to stay—Eric Polisar and Joe Ames. A blossoming professor at Cornell University's School of Industrial and Labor Relations, and a close consultant to Wurf, young Polisar pleaded that Gotbaum remain in New York. The future of the Council was at stake, and with Taibi out of the picture, Gotbaum's strong style and extensive experience could be of inestimable help. Polisar felt confident that he could stand up to the pressures and outbursts of the AFSCME president. On one of the occasions when Gotbaum threatened to resign, Ames, who was visiting from St. Louis, also encouraged him to stay on. Given Wurf's proclivity to intervene in the affairs of DC 37, Ames did not know of anyone else who could check him. Ames reminded Gotbaum of the dead end he confronted in Daley's Chicago, whereas New York afforded him tremendous potential. Gotbaum decided to remain in New York.

Immediately following the conclusion of the strike, the Council's executive board met to accept Taibi's resignation and then selected Wurf's predetermined nominee, Victor Gotbaum, as acting executive director.

INTERNAL LOCAL DISORDER

Approximately a year and a half after the historic strike and victory, Local 371 had serious problems. The collective bargaining situation remained unsatisfactory and its contract with the city was unevenly and inadequately enforced. On the eve of the start of new negotiations in late 1966, the original welfare fund clause had not yet been put into operation. Measures designed to secure implementation, however energetically pursued, had been insufficient. Within Local 371, there was an absence of planning and orderly action. Records could not be located, and intra-office communications were easily lost under the pressure of ongoing crises, weakening the union for future negotiations. Local 371 also suffered a desperate shortage of active volunteers. The unending pressures from the city, the membership, the SSEU, and the District Council were hardly conducive to reflective thought.

Consultant Eric Polisar insisted that the local had to devote itself to contract enforcement, organizing in all welfare titles, a clear approach to the SSEU, and formulation of a union program for all welfare titles. But none of these could be achieved without an administrative structure, a systematic approach to work, proper assignment of responsibility, and a training program which would involve shop stewards and additional union members. The local had to become entrenched in the welfare centers through vigorous but carefully planned field activities.[15]

In general agreement with this indictment, the local's leadership sought to pursue the objectives and strategies laid down by Polisar. Grievance records were to be reconstituted, a filing system was devised to maintain a current record with all relevant information, "ticklers" or reminders were established so that grievances that were filed but not acted upon promptly by the city were not lost but became the subject of persistent reminders and additional pressures. The local's executive board and appropriate Council personnel were informed of the state of contract compliance, stewards at the various centers were trained in grievance procedures and worked with closely, and finally, reports of grievance settlement were filtered back to the membership.[16]

Gotbaum, Polisar, and Viani were fully aware that the SSEU had performed a useful function in bringing new vitality to Local 371. By 1966, however, they came to view the militancy of the often irresponsible SSEU as bordering on hysteria. In the process of responding to SSEU militancy, Local 371 continued to suffer from the image of company unionism. Most of the 371 membership was generally older and in supervisory positions, overburdened with job responsibilities, leaving little time or energy for union work. Many were married, with family responsibilities, making it impossible for them to resort to the intense activity characteristic of SSEU's recent college graduates. Polisar and Gotbaum, however, were convinced that the company union image would be obliterated once the local vigorously confronted the city. Polisar urged that 371 avoid doing battle with SSEU, but to try, through specific accomplishments, to win welfare employees over to its side.

SSEU leaders remained disinterested in a merger. Judith Mage, a devoted and talented leader of the strong, ideological school, who took over the reins of the organization in 1966, expressed vigorous antagonism toward the Council as the "big daddy" of civil service unionism. Mage and her colleagues also recoiled at the financial obligations associated with possible affiliation, and saw no benefit from being allied with "zookeepers, accountants and clerks."[17]

The SSEU leadership resolved to capture the welfare supervisors from 371, but in vain. The Viani–Caldwell team was rebuilding the grievance and service structure of their local, and recreating an effective shop steward structure at the grass-roots level. A number of those involved with the founding of the SSEU, but subsequently promoted to supervisors, joined Local 371 and helped establish its supervisor chapter. Their energy, organizing endeavors, and imaginative spirit helped produce a superior collective bargaining program for the contract agreed to in late 1966.

Local 371 sought to demonstrate that it was no longer a company union when, in October 1966, it called out some 1,000 employees in the Bureau of Hospital Care Service for a two-day strike. The objective was to insure implementation of an agreement reached earlier that year concerning back pay, a new title, and health, welfare and dental coverage. The department had also neglected to live up to its promises to create provisional promotions and to provide sufficient space, equipment, and telephones. Not only did the union win, but equally important, this walkout demonstrated that an industrial-type strike was possible as both clerical and service staff joined professionals and shared in the settlement. Toward the end of 1966, Gotbaum, Viani, and the new head of the Council's research department, Dan Nelson, secured a contract with important gains for Local 371 members.[18]

THE DECLINE OF SSEU

The contract provided, among other things, for Local 371 representation of a new title—Hospital Care Investigators (HCI)—which was specifically identified as equivalent in work responsibilities and wages to the caseworkers represented by the SSEU. As a result of a blunder, the independent union had neglected to organize the hospital investigators, deeming them inadequately trained from a professional point of view, even though the HCIs were college graduates and career-oriented individuals. "Stealing" them away from the SSEU meant that 371 now had its own caseworker component. The city, meanwhile, undertook tortuous negotiations with the SSEU, which did not end until the summer of 1967. The contract offered the independent union was basically similar to that agreed to by the AFSCME welfare employees local. In essence, the SSEU leadership was told that this was the settlement it would have to accept. Mage and her co-leaders were not only confronted with something akin to a coup, but were also aware that a new concept of citywide negotiations was about to become a reality.

In 1966, Mayor John Lindsay created the Office of Labor Relations to represent the city government in collective bargaining, replacing the city's budget director as top negotiator. In April 1967, in the midst of continued unsatisfactory negotiation with the SSEU, Lindsay signed Executive Order No. 40, awarding the majority union authority in citywide bargaining; it would become the sole and exclusive representative in every respect. In addition to negotiating citywide contracts, the majority union would process grievances in all departments where its employees worked, and that union would be their sole representative in setting working conditions. This meant that the SSEU, representing a segment of only one city agency, would soon lose its ability to negotiate contracts because DC 37 was on its way to becoming the majority representative of mayoral agency employees. At the same time, the city made clear that the SSEU had, in effect, lost its right to negotiate independently for its caseworkers' salaries. Local 371 had already reached a wage settlement for the growing number of hospital care investigators, and the city was determined to offer no more to the caseworkers.

When negotiations seemed to be getting nowhere in mid-January, the SSEU struck, in the first of a number of work stoppages in 1967. After three days, a proposal by Gotbaum for fact finding was accepted by city representatives and Judith Mage. Despite his coolness toward the SSEU, the DC 37 executive director did not want it destroyed by the city. Five months later, when confronted with a labor commissioner who refused to bargain on a number of major issues or to grant caseworkers a higher salary scale than that accorded AFSCME, a beleaguered Judith Mage gave in to demands by militants for a "work-in," which was just short of a sit-in. When city officials refused to alter their posture and locked-out SSEU members, the work-in turned into a disastrous six-week strike.[19]

Since its creation, and following the 1965 strike, SSEU leaders persisted in baiting and attacking the organized labor movement in general, and Gotbaum and DC 37 in particular. As Gotbaum put it, on the one hand they "criticize the hell out of us—on the other hand, they ask for our support." The Council adopted a resolution characterizing the SSEU as an association, not a union, and rejecting support of its actions. The rest of organized labor followed suit, severing relations with the SSEU.[20]

THE WRONG KIND OF STRIKE

Many veteran, career-oriented caseworkers were affronted by younger colleagues who, while overly eager to strike, expressed little worry about its possible negative results, for they were prepared, if necessary, to move on to other locales, and different jobs. Leaders of SSEU were no longer in complete control of their own organization. A minority of more extreme "leftists" managed to have enough of their followers elected as union delegates to the executive board, "which they could all but dominate by their caucuses, tight discipline, frequent disruption and sheer weight of their activism." It was this minority that successfully pushed for work-ins and strikes, and helped insure the isolation of the SSEU from organized labor.[21]

Local 371 negotiators had earlier agreed on what could be referred to the fact-finding process. By virtue of its contract and a reliance on the clauses of the new Office of Collective Bargaining (OCB), which DC 37 had helped draft, 371 was enabled to secure a fair and impartial hearing on issues between the union and the city. Council leaders viewed this as the difference between militancy and irresponsibility. Although the OCB offered a useful mechanism for resolving the type of dispute that confronted the caseworkers at that moment, the values of its new bargaining mechanism had not been presented objectively to them by their leadership. Thus, the SSEU resorted to a work-in and then a strike, neglecting to ask the OCB for fair and impartial hearings and recommendations.

The Viani-Caldwell team made clear to the city that while DC members would not honor the picket lines in front of welfare centers, they would not perform out-of-title work. Gotbaum, meanwhile, insisted that Mage and her colleagues were a "willful, peripatetic leadership" that had taken the rank-and-file caseworkers "down a blind alley." The January strike he viewed as a "debacle," and the six-week walkout, in midsummer, a "disaster." Although he expressed distress at their suffering, he indicated that there was a place for caseworkers in the trade union movement, but under "proper leadership." They had a "worthwhile contribution" to make to the labor movement, and they, in turn, had much to gain from organized labor.

The strike was broken before it ended. The SSEU was beaten. It lost its collective bargaining clause, the experimental programs clause was severely weakened, and it gave up the automatic clothing grant to welfare clients. Union leaders had to demean themselves by signing a no-strike clause and enduring reprisals against the most active local union leaders, who were transferred to other welfare centers. SSEU members had not only lost six weeks pay, but in the eyes of their idealistic members, they had lost "a union with a dream." They had surrendered the "dignity of participating in the decisions governing their world of work."[22]

Within days Gotbaum began to receive feelers for merger from the SSEU. Marty Morgenstern, Stanley Hill, Bart Cohen, Bill Schleicher, and even Mage were aware that there was no longer a future for an independent public employee union in New York City outside of the AFL–CIO. While Mage wanted a merger, she could never bring it about. She was always demanding a little more than was possible. She was a masterful organizer and leaflet writer who had been instrumental in the early success of the organization. But she lacked an understanding of the art of the possible, the ability to compromise on vital issues. As a result, during her term as president she failed as a negotiator, both with the city and with Gotbaum.

Serious progress was not made until Mage was replaced by Marty Morgenstern as president in 1968 and negotiations failed with John DeLury of the Sanitationmen, Harold Gibbons of the Teamsters, and Henry Foner of the Fur and Leather Workers. Those who proposed merger with DC 37 contended that there was no future for an independent public employee union, even if it fused with another union outside of AFSCME. DC 37 controlled much of the public work scene in New York and, with the advent of tripartite bargaining under the OCB, would become the dominant public employee union. If SSEU was to exert any significant influence in the future and preserve its gains, it needed Local 371. Equally important, a merger with AFSCME would finally put an end to the interminable waste of funds for duplicating staff, headquarters, leaflets, newspapers, and human resources, which were consumed in perpetuating inter-union rivalry and jurisdictional disputes.

In January 1969, after months of raging debates, which found many of the original militants opposing a merger, the SSEU memberhip cast more than the required two-thirds vote for approval on the second ballot. The following month, the membership of Local 371 did likewise, and by May of that year the merger became a reality. Since the Clericals in Local 371 had previously transferred to Local 1549, the SSEU greatly outnumbered the remaining AFSCME members. As a result, the SSEU was enabled to transfer its name and independent economic and political behavior patterns to Local 371. Marty Morgenstern became the president of the merged local, and Joe Rogoff, who had succeeded Viani as local head, became its executive director. Viani, meanwhile, moved on to Council headquarters as assistant director of research and negotiations under Dan Nelson.[23]

SUMMARY

Jerry Wurf was more than successful in shooting down the "phony" labor–management bargaining system that Mayor Wagner had instituted for public workers. And he did it with the help of the SSEU, traditional trade unions, and leaders like George Meany, Harry Van Arsdale, and David Dubinsky. Wurf took advantage of every opportunity to demonstrate his talents as a brilliant strategist, alongside Seafarer Paul Hall. Catalyzed by the initial moves of a militant, socially conscious SSEU, and by thousands of social service workers who "hit the bricks" for an entire month, Wurf brought into sharp focus the need for a new, unique collective bargaining approach.

Wurf and Hall also implanted in the minds of key SSEU leaders an increasing awareness that their historic strike and any future ones could be sustained only by the resources, power, and publicity at the command of such "old-line" unions as AFSCME and the SIU. It was the beginning of the end for the SSEU, for eventually it would have to merge with DC 37, the dominant public workers union in the city. It was during this historic strike as well that Victor Gotbaum helped soften some of the sharp edges of Wurf and offer a leadership that helped maintain a high morale on the picket lines. And all this was in the face of a cold reception from a hostile media.

After the merger, the militant, independent strains of the SSEU were brought into Local 371. The result was often a smug, self-righteous local leadership offering, until recently, a negative if not hostile relationship with the Council. Nevertheless, a number of Local 371 and SSEU graduates have since advanced to key roles on the Council staff, facilitating the rise of DC 37 as a vital force on the New York metropolitan scene.

NOTES

1. DC 37 executive board minutes, October 14, 1964; interview with Alan Viani, February 26, 1982.

2. *New York Times,* January 2, 1965; Richard H.P. Mendes, "The Professional Union: A Study of the Social Service Employees Union of the New York City Department of Social Services," Ph.D. dissertation, Columbia University, 1974, pp. 71-74.

3. Calogero "Charles" Taibi to Joseph Tepedino, October 22, November 6, December 7 and 8, 1964; Tepedino to Taibi, October 29, November 25, December 4, 7 and 9, 1964; Alan Viani to SSEU executive board, December 30, 1964. Also, interviews with Bart Cohen, December 19, 1980 and September 22, 1981; Bill Schleicher, November 30, 1981; and Alan Viani, February 26, 1982.

4. James R. Dumpson memorandum to the staff, December 4, 1964; *New York Times,* January 1, 1965, p. 20; January 2, 1965, p. 20; January 4, 1965, p. 1; January 5, 1965, p. 1; January 6, 1965, p. 1; January 7, 1965, p. 1; January 22, 1965, p. 42.

5. Paul Hall to Al Shanker, January 14, 1965. Playing helpful roles in this strike were the ILGWU's David Dubinsky, the Seafarer's Paul Hall and Earl Shepard, the Teachers' Charles Cogen and Albert Shanker, District 65's David Livingston, the voluntary hospital's Leon Davis, the Jewish Labor Committee's Emanuel Muravchik, and Harry Van Arsdale.

6. *New York Times,* January 8, 1965, p. 1; January 11, 1965, p. 1; Mendes, "The Professional Union," pp. 92, 113-121; interview with Bart Cohen, December 9, 1980.

7. *New York Times,* January 15, 1965, p. 18; January 18, 1965, p. 1; January 19, 1965, p. 1; January 21, 1965, p. 1; January 22, 1965, p. 17; January 28, 1965, p. 15. Also, Wurf and Viani to state legislators, January 18, 1965.

8. Report of the mayor's task force, January 31, 1965, pp. 1-3. Early in 1966, as a result of an intensive lobbying campaign among Albany lawmakers and Governor Nelson Rockefeller, spearheaded by Gotbaum, DC 37, Local 371, the Central Labor Council, and the New York State AFL-CIO, the state legislature voted to exempt from the penalties of the Condon-Wadlin act those welfare workers who had struck. The legislature had done the same, only days before, for the New York City Transit workers. The governor agreed not to veto it. Victor Gotbaum to Nelson Rockefeller and Earl W. Brydges, February 14, 1966; Gotbaum to John V. Lindsay, William T. Conklin, Edward J. Speno, Thomas Laverne, Martin J. Knorr, John J. Marchi, Harry Van Arsdale, Raymond R. Corbett, and Matthew Guinan, February 18, 1966; Raymond R. Corbett to John V. Lindsay, Nelson Rockefeller, Earl W. Brydges, Joseph Zaretzki, Anthony J. Travia, and Moses M. Weinstein, February 22, 1966; Local 371 "News Roundup," February 24, 1966; Gotbaum to Anthony Travia, March 2, 1966.

9. *New York Times,* March 5, 1965; Summary of Settlement in Welfare Department Dispute, pp. 8-9; Victor Gotbaum to William F. Shea and Theodore H. Lang, March 11, 1965. Also included in the settlements was provision for establishment of a caseload committee to review work loads; a series of recommen-

dations by the chairman which would materially improve working conditions; decentralization of authority for client approvals; new workers were to be given genuine training for periods of six months with a reduced caseload; the city was to accelerate its expansion of welfare centers, properly arranged for the transaction of business and with adequate equipment such as telephones and dictating machines; there was to be third-party "mediation" of grievances, which excluded the city's Department of Labor. The report also recommended that the new title of Caseworker replace Social Investigator, that the number of available scholarships be expanded, and that the full cost of the premiums for HIP-Blue Cross coverage be absorbed by 1966.

10. First Bargaining Contract Between the City of New York and the Social Service Employees Union, June 7, 1965, pp. 17-18. This 19-page pamphlet was distributed by the SSEU in August 1965. Contract between the City of New York and Welfare Local 371 affiliated with District Council 37, June 4, 1965, pp. 2, 5, 7, 9, 11, 13. Also, New York Times, June 5, 1965, p. 32; June 8, 1965, p. 15.

11. Wagner to Jesse Simons, director, Labor Management Institute of the American Arbitration Association, July 26, 1965; as noted in Eric Polisar, "Collective Bargaining in the Private and Public Sectors," p. 25. Polisar's was an in-house document for Gotbaum.

12. David T. Stanley, Managing Local Government Under Union Pressure, Washington, DC: The Brookings Institution, 1972, pp. 93-96, 146-147; Raymond D. Horton, Municipal Labor Relations in New York City, Lessons of the Lindsay-Wagner Years, New York: Praeger, 1972, p. 69.

13. V. Gotbaum to C. Taibi, November 24, 1964. Also, interview with Alan Viani, February 26, 1982. Strike leaders included SSEU's Tepedino, Mage, Bart Cohen, Marty Morgenstern, and Stan Hill, and Local 371's Viani, Lindenthal, Jim McKeon, and Pat Caldwell, among others.

14. Interviews with Jerry Wurf, August 20 and 21, 1979; Bart Cohen, December 19, 1980 and September 22, 1981; John Boer, September 22, 1981; and Alan Viani, February 26, 1982. Taibi left the Council an embittered individual, having given some of the best years of his life to this institution. Less than three years later, he succumbed to Hodgkin's disease.

15. Many of these details were secured from a 16-page memorandum from Eric Polisar to Alan Viani and Victor Gotbaum, dated May 8, 1966.

16. Eric Polisar to Al Viani and Victor Gotbaum, May 8, 1966; Polisar to Viani, Gotbaum and Al Weil, May 17, 1966.

17. Eric Polisar to Viani, Weil, and Gotbaum, June 16, 1966; summary of minutes, Monday, June 27, 1966, of meeting involving Al Weil, Jan Goodman, Nat Lindenthal, Vic Gotbaum and Eric Polisar; Monroe S. Walsh, "Welfare Unionism in New York City," p. 4. Interviews with Patricia Caldwell, April 20, 1981; Bill Schleicher, November 30, 1981; and Alan Viani, February 26, 1982. Walsh's was a DC 37 in-house document.

18. Eric Polisar to Victor Gotbaum, June 28, 1966; Gotbaum to Pat Caldwell, July 27, 1966; interview with Alan Viani, February 26, 1982.

19. New York Times, January 14, 1967, p. 17; January 15, 1967, p. 70; January 17, 1967, p. 1; January 20, 1967, p. 34; February 8, 1967, p. 16; February 9, 1967, p. 19; February 10, 1967, p. 40; Victor Gotbaum to Local 371 executive

board, June 6, 1967; Herbert L. Haber to Judith Mage, June 9, 1967; Mitchell Ginsberg, commissioner of welfare, to staff, June 12, 1967. Joyce L. Miller, "Constraints on Collective Bargaining in the Public Sector: A Case Study," *Urban Analysis,* 1 (1978): 100. Mark H. Maier, "The City and the Unions, Collective Bargaining in New York City: 1954-1973," Ph.D. dissertation, New School for Social Research, 1980, pp. 182-183.

20. Victor Gotbaum to David Livingston, April 14, 1966; Gotbaum to Local 371 executive board, June 6, 1967; Gotbaum to Al Shanker, Leon Davis, Sam Myers, Harry Van Arsdale, Ray Corbett, David Livingston, Israel Kugler, and Douglas McMahon, June 12, 1967; Gotbaum to Henry Foner, June 19, 1967; Harry Van Arsdale and Morris Iushewitz to Judith Mage, June 20, 1967; Morris Iushewitz to Victor Gotbaum, June 20, 1967. Also, interviews with Bart Cohen, December 9, 1980 and September 22, 1981; Bill Schleicher, November 30, 1981.

21. Mendes, "The Professional Union," p. 301. Interviews with Bart Cohen, December 9, 1980 and September 22, 1981.

22. *New York Times,* June 25, 1967, p. 1; July 31, 1967, p. 1; September 22, 1967, p. 3; *Public Employee Press,* July 12, 1967, p. 2; Mendes, "The Professional Union," pp. 298, 299, 301, 303, 307, 308, 323, 324. Also, interviews with Bart Cohen, December 19, 1980 and September 22, 1981; Bill Schleicher, November 30, 1981.

23. *New York Times,* January 12, 1969, p. 29; February 2, 1969, p. 54; February 7, 1969, p. 47; *Public Employee Press,* January 17, 1969, p. 4; merger agreement between Local 371, DC 37, and the Social Service Employees Union, June 1, 1969.

8
I Am Somebody

For decades, one of the most exploited groups in public service had been the nonprofessionals who worked in the city's hospitals. The majority of these workers remained outside the organized labor movement through the 1950s, receiving virtually the lowest pay among public employees. Attempting to fill the breach resulting from the lack of qualified doctors and registered nurses, the city became, in the process, an instrument of economic segregation. It offered low-paying jobs to blacks, Hispanics, and other minority workers, taking advantage of the fact that the private sector avoided hiring them when possible. The city's Department of Hospitals employed them, but at wages far below the standard for the work performed.

In this chapter we review the bitter struggle between DC 37 and the Teamsters for the support of municipal hospital workers. The outcome of this battle provided the key to the future leadership of Victor Gotbaum, as he sought to direct the organizing campaign, while keeping Jerry Wurf from intervening.

WORK WITHOUT DIGNITY

The work environments in kitchens, laundries or large hospital wards were physically unpleasant—hot, crowded, and often unsanitary. Relationships with highly professional, educated people with years of post-graduate training—doctors, nurses, and a variety of technicians—were often strained. The latter treated hospi-

Hospital workers voting in the largest representation election in city history in December 1965. Victory for DC 37 insured its emergence as the leading public worker union and the Gotbaum-Roberts team as key union leaders.

tal aides and orderlies as inferiors who were expected to carry out menial assignments, and whose tasks were viewed as of little importance. They were rarely addressed with respect and were often called by their first names, or were simply referred to as "Hey, you!" Many of the hospital workers were recent immigrants from the South and were looking for any kind of job. They were expected by employers to have a poor attendance record and work performance. With little education or training, they constituted one of the city's underclasses.

Hospital employees like dietary aides, laundry and linen workers, butchers, clerical assistants, watchmen, and truck drivers were not generally noticed by patients or their visitors. Those upon whom the sick depended most for personal attention included the registered nurses, practical nurses, nurses aides and operating room staff. And then there were the housekeeping and maintenance laborers, the elevator and switchboard operators, the ambulance attendants, the social workers, and the psychologists. Many worked under conditions that were difficult and often dangerous. The nurse's aides were assigned a great variety of responsibilities that called for training, skill, and commitment. Perhaps more than any other hospital worker, it was the nurse's aide to whom the patient turned for the many personal services necessary for care and recovery, including food service, taking temperatures, sterilizing operating room equipment, and making emergency packets for ambulance and operating rooms. The practical nurse, who had to be licensed by the state after taking a special training course and passing an examination, assisted the doctors and the professional nurses with examinations and diagnostic tests, and administered medications and treatments.

As James Farmer, civil rights leader and former organizer for Local 420, put it, above and beyond the issue of wages, these hospital workers wanted decency and dignity. They wanted to feel that they were "somebody of importance." There was rampant favoritism among many supervisors in the treatment of work crews, pitting one individual or group against another for special treatment, like extra time off, a desirable vacation schedule, or a preferred work assignment. Firings or transfers to less desirable jobs were achieved by simple administrative fiat, done without concern for due process or for the human element involved.[1]

Despite these depressing conditions, there were serious obstacles to labor organizers. In the first place, both the administrative staff and professionals, who constituted the core of the hospital organization, maintained autocratic control over the health facility. Their training and social background tended to influence the work force to do their bidding, and to bear responsibilities without question, challenge or discussion. With rare exception, where a supervisor, nurse or doctor showed caring sensitivity, administrators tended to rule their agencies like fiefdoms, expecting total and automatic obedience. Part of the difficulty arose from the nature of the work force itself. While their situations may often have been desperate, these employees were generally from inadequate educational backgrounds, and were often dropouts from elementary school. Their morale was so low, and they worked such long hours in dreary, debilitating jobs, that most did not have the time, energy, or interest, at the end of a grueling work day, to consider union activity or sign a membership card. They lacked experience and background in organizational work, and were generally stripped of aspirations and expectations.

Another factor making union work difficult was the physical

layout of city hospitals. The municipal system constituted a network of 21 hospitals spread through each of the five boroughs. And within each of several of the major hospitals, such as Kings County and Bellevue, there were vast complexes of wards and far-flung buildings, which separated departments, agencies, and units. Many of these hospitals were often isolated from surrounding communities, making it difficult for union organizers to find decent meeting places. If these obstacles were ever to be surmounted, a union would have to develop a leadership with special skills and a dedication that could mobilize resources and survive long, difficult periods of organizing endeavors. Many of the officers and shop stewards of individual hospital chapters held other jobs in order to supplement their meager incomes, and thus were frequently unable to attend their own meetings or devote additional time to organizing activities.

When Jean Couturier was first assigned the task of organizing for Local 420 in 1955, there were approximately 480 members in this AFSCME unit, with no apparent growth, no staff, and very few shop stewards. At the immense Lincoln Hospital there were possibly 20 or 30 members. Once every week or two, some Council staff member came to collect dues or held a secretive meeting in a backroom or basement. Hospital workers were afraid to "talk union," for fear they might lose their jobs if it came to the attention of some nurses or supervisors. It was at this time that Wurf consolidated the fragmented units of the old Joint Board of Hospitals into Local 420, and ventured upon an organizing drive of hospital workers. Someday he hoped to displace Teamster Local 237 as the single most influential union in the hospital system. With the intermittent help of Couturier and a few key staff members, Local 420 started organizing in earnest. The initial goals set for the group were humane and decent treatment of workers; a 40-hour, 5-day week; job security and the elimination of arbitrary dismissals of noncompetitive employees; a wage differential for night duty and for work on contagious wards; and promotional opportunities.[2]

ORGANIZING DIFFICULTIES

It was a slow and tortuous task to collect dues by hand. Establishing union awareness and faith in the organization was largely limited to handling grievances—a far cry from a collective bargaining process. Grievances thus constituted a main focus of union activity in which organizers tried to convey the local's concern with their personal and immediate needs. Thus, daily union work consisted of small victories—a free weekend; a few hours off for an appointment with a doctor; an emergency visit with a distant, ill mother on one's own accumulated vacation time; or a discharge or an unwelcome assignment to night duty.

Another problem was continuing administrative harassment of union organizers and shop stewards as they pursued their lonely tasks. Despite Wagner's policies, which established the right to organize and to negotiate grievances, administrators had yet to be convinced of the legitimacy of union activities. And this was especially true of the lower levels of hospital bureaucracy which had to deal with workers on a daily basis. They held firm to the concept of exclusive managerial prerogative over conditions of work and activities within their units, and viewed those who dared challenge their judgment and professional views as intruders on their turf. With rare exceptions, there was ongoing hostility between administrative officials and union representatives. Historically, city hospitals were run as part of a caste system, conveying a feeling to employees that they had to adjust to existing conditions or get out. The mere fact that union staff walked into the offices of management and sought to discuss a change in schedule, or asked to get someone a weekend off, caused concern to many of the supervisory staff.[3]

Many hospital superintendents and their administrative subordinates did not think that Local 420 had the right to exist! Most of them could not conceive of sitting in the same room with union representatives and bargaining with them as equals. Time and again, Wurf brought this predicament to the attention of key hospital administrators, insisting that this treatment caused general hostility. And segregated dining rooms divided nursing aides from nurses and service personnel from the professional.[4]

As the union expanded its organizing endeavors, along with a notable increase in militancy, tension between labor and management escalated. Harold Staley, a key organizer, was barred from the hospital system by the commissioner because of purported violations of unapproved leaflet distribution and aggressive behavior toward administrators. Still lacking majority support among hospital workers despite a dramatic increase in membership, Wurf felt obliged to avoid the strike weapon and resorted to appeals for arbitration of the dispute.

The most difficult problem facing Wurf in the hospitals, however, remained competition with Teamsters Local 237, which had a much larger foothold among service employees. Nevertheless, by 1960 Local 420 had become one of the largest AFSCME units in the nation and in the process had won some improvements. More nonprofessional employees were being addressed with respect, paychecks were being distributed on time, and numbers of hospital workers were being assigned permanent shifts. The more enlightened administrators agreed to abolish their secret files providing that, in the future, no charges, accusations, or statements of alleged wrong doings were to be put in a worker's file without the affected employee having the opportunity to see them. These administrators also agreed that a worker brought up on indictments that might result in discharge, transfer, resignation, or loss of pay had the right to receive written charges in advance, obtain independent counsel, and secure a fair hearing with the aid of the individual's union. But many major problems continued to plague hospital workers.

World War II created a serious gap in nursing personnel in the city's hospitals. After the war, when the city did not pay salaries high enough to compete with private hospitals, the situation worsened. By the mid-1950s, nurse's aides were filling the jobs of registered nurses, without an upgrading of salaries or other forms of recognition. Following the creation of the Career and Salary Plan, Wurf and representatives of Local 420 made annual appearances before the Salary Appeals Board to literally beg for increases in the wages of low-level hospital workers. But the decisions were rarely favorable.[5]

After 1960, workers continued to sign up, but in smaller numbers. Wurf was increasingly distracted by his aspirations for the International presidency. Without direction and sustained leadership, the hospital campaign faltered. By March 1963, DC 37 had organized 4,530 of the 16,000 aides in the city hospital system, while the Teamsters claimed 6,500. The Council had a monumental task if it was to become the majority organization.

The Teamsters had a number of distinct advantages over the Council—an attractive insurance system, its shop stewards and local officers received cash payments, and its nonthreatening representatives appeared to secure far greater cooperation from supervisory personnel than did DC 37 staff members. In addition, not having resorted to strikes or any other form of militant action, the Teamsters local had not exhausted its staff or treasury. By 1964 the fervor of the marching days of the civil rights movement was disappearing, and the situation in Local 420 had begun to deteriorate. Membership was starting to decline, while that of the Teamsters remained stable or increased.[6]

GOTBAUM'S FIRST TEST

Immediately after Wurf was elected International president in April 1964, he transferred his energies to Washington headquarters. He left New York in the hands of Charlie Taibi, who in a short while was replaced by Gotbaum. The new leader found the Council machinery in need of emergency aid, as a result of the tremendous expenditure of the treasury and the exhaustion of staff members who had worked around the clock for four weeks during the Welfare Strike. He quickly discovered that the staff member heading the hospital organizing drive, plagued with personal and psychological problems, had disappeared, and that many of the shop stewards were simply not functioning. The union's bureaucratic problems confronting hospital organizers were extremely frustrating. Some of the staff at Council headquarters had to be pressured to respond quickly when organizing leaflets were ordered. Before the Council could gain majority control in the hospitals, Local 420 would need an overall organizing strategy. The staff members assigned to the hospitals had to learn to operate as a team, instead of using a hit-and-miss approach, and shop stewards had to be trained to improve their organizing skills.[7]

Prior to the Welfare Strike, the membership drives of Local 420 and the Teamsters 237 together succeeded in organizing little more than 60 percent of the aides. Until then, both unions had been fearful that they might kill each other off in the process of seeking a majority in a representation election; but immediately after the strike, with DC 37 in a depleted state, the Teamsters concluded that the time was ripe. Local 420 was losing membership while the Teamsters were adding to their rolls.

Another element in the decision was the new inexperienced

leader at DC 37. Bill Lewis had headed the Teamsters' hospitals division for years and knew many of the workers intimately. Upon the death of Henry Feinstein he had succeeded to the presidency of Local 237. All Lewis had to do to insure the scheduling of representation elections was file dues checkoff cards with the Department of Hospitals for 30 percent of the eligible workers. That meant approximately 5,000 signed-up members, and Lewis claimed he had that number. An experienced and popular black union leader and former hospital employee, Bill Lewis was confident that he could defeat the harried novices, Gotbaum and Roberts. Besides, Henry Feinstein and Lewis had been close political allies of Mayor Wagner and could expect cooperation from City Hall, so Lewis thought. Lastly, unscarred by any strike, Teamsters 237 started its drive with a larger membership and a treasury which, at times, seemed limitless. How could he possibly lose?[8]

CONFRONTING THE TEAMSTERS

Gotbaum and the Council staff had little time to enjoy the victory of the welfare workers, for they knew that Lewis was about to petition for representation elections. Within days, they were obliged to jump from a long, debilitating strike to campaigning throughout the nation's biggest hospital complex for the largest representation election in the city's history. The struggle came at a critical juncture in the history of DC 37, as well as for its new leadership. At stake were over 16,000 hospital aides and some 3,300 clerical–administrative employees.

Victory would make the Council the majority representative for all employees under the Career and Salary Plan, and thus the chief bargaining agent for city employees. When added to the Council's clerical bargaining certificates in other large agencies, the hospitals would put DC 37 locals well over the top of the citywide majority representation rights needed for exclusive bargaining rights for approximately 17,000 nonsupervisory clerical workers. And victory for the Council would mean an end to its most potent opposition. For Gotbaum, it was that rare opportunity to prove himself and to establish his independence from Wurf.

DC 37 entered the contest as a decided underdog, with the

odds against Local 420. But the Council had some decided advantages. It had a far better trained and committed staff, some of unusual calibre and experience, supplemented by a number of rank-and-file activists and leaders, with an ideological commitment to egalitarianism and democratic unionism. They found distasteful the record of company unionism and lack of militancy that had characterized the Teamsters over the years. It was difficult to recall the last time that 237 had staged a demonstration; it had never struck the city or taken on the Wagner administration in any significant way. Henry Feinstein had conducted negotiations with the mayor on a private, personal basis, for Teamster members were never really involved in planning or negotiations.

The Council also had a skilled leadership team of Victor Gotbaum and Lillian Roberts, who successfully catalyzed into action a hospital organizing staff and a membership that had been declining in numbers and influence. They received important moral and, at times, crucial financial support from the International office and from a number of AFL–CIO unions in New York and Washington that were repelled by the corruption of the Teamsters under President Jimmy Hoffa. But it was Bill Lewis who innocently insured victory for DC 37. He was so confident that "my hospital workers" would stick with him that he did not conduct a vigorous campaign until it was too late. Soft-spoken, Lewis proved a most effective public speaker. From a background of discrimination, he was amazed at his own rise in the labor movement. An outstanding football player in a small southern black college, he remained sensitive about its poor academic standards and the inadequacy of his formal education. In contrast to Henry Feinstein, Lewis was a genuine trade unionist with a social conscience, but he was severely limited by the Teamster environment. Normally a tough, careful fighter, he had become overly confident, and as a result made a series of tactical blunders.

Some months before Wurf's election to the International presidency and prior to the decision to hold representation elections, Paul Hall, who had known Henry Feinstein well, sought to call a halt to the internecine struggle over the hospital workers. He convened a meeting involving Wurf, Bill Lewis, union leader Charlie Feinstein (a brother of Henry), and himself. Aware that 420 had a minority of the organized hospital workers, Jerry was willing to accept a compromise offered by Hall, whereby the city hospitals would be split into individual units, on an industrial basis, with control of the respective units going to those unions with a majority of the workers involved. If followed, this proposal would have given the Teamsters the greater number of hospitals. When in the midst of negotiations, Lewis unexpectedly turned down the offer, Charlie Feinstein almost went through the roof, for he wanted to avoid an inevitable, vicious struggle. The Teamster leader felt that he had the votes and the momentum, and saw no need for such a deal.[9]

The new head of the District Council acted quickly. With the aid of Lillian Roberts and other key staffers, they executed an unusual campaign. The strategy and tactics of the hospital battle was a model of any tough, well-planned election campaign, and included doorbell and house-call canvassers, fund raising for the union's war chest, hiring personnel skilled in public relations, buying spot radio announcement time, and issuing leaflets to constituents. Gotbaum secured a loan of some $300,000 from the Amalgamated Bank, in addition to funds contributed by the International office of AFSCME.

During this period, the Council was still controlled by the AFSCME president, who was calling the shots through the executive board and direct dealings with the mayor. To complicate matters, Gotbaum realized that he knew very little about the New York to which he had recently returned. He went through the worst period of his life as he speedily sought to master the political, economic, and social intricacies of the city, and at the same time, galvanize disparate locals, restless chieftains, and veteran staff members, all of them Wurf appointees or followers. He would rise early and work until midnight, often later. When exhausted, he often prowled the historic Lower East Side of Manhattan for relaxation and release from heightened tensions. Accentuating the difficulties of this early period was the decision of his wife to remain in Evanston, requiring frequent weekend shuttling by plane.[10]

ROBERTS COMMANDS THE FIELD

To direct hospital field operations, Gotbaum designated Lillian Roberts, his longtime associate in the struggle against Mayor Daley. Roberts, who first joined the union as an 18-year-old nurse's aide in 1946, was bright, tough, and charming. She had moved up the career ladder to union organizer and eventually International vice-president of AFSCME developing a deep understanding of the needs and difficulties of hospital workers. During her childhood years, she had experienced many tragedies and grew up on welfare, as had many of the workers in the city hospitals. Totally dedicated to the union movement, she was an ideal person to implement the new director's plans and work with other staff members.

She quickly won the respect and confidence of most of her associates and the hospital workers. With only months to carry the challenge to the Teamsters, she spent endless hours roaming through hospital corridors, locker rooms, cafeterias, and wards, supplementing the work of veteran Council staff, and catalyzing shop stewards and rank-and-file activists into greater endeavors. In command of worker sensibilities, she became a symbol for minority employees, but in particular for the many black women in the city's hospitals.

She could walk into any hospital situation and talk to black and Hispanic workers easily and with deep empathy. She knew how to appeal to people spotlighting their exploitation and then inspiring many of them to join the union. Like Martin Luther King, she was a rare personality. With the aid of her mentor, Gotbaum, and the timeliness of the civil rights crusade, Roberts demonstrated profound commitment to the struggle for black equality and an awareness that one of the battles for civil rights in New York had to be made through the union, whites and blacks working together. As she would say again and again, "I have always seen the union as a protector of the working class rights that transcends all the other things." In one of the memos that streamed from the Gotbaum office, it was made clear that Roberts was to present the public image of Local 420 and the Council "on any issues brought up throughout the campaign."[11]

The campaign had a tight organization, with Gotbaum at headquarters and Roberts in the field. The campaign themes underscored the fact that DC 37 was part of the house of labor, with a bigger and more important organizational thrust than the Teamsters. Promises included higher wages, improved working conditions, on-the-job training programs, promotions to better and higher-paying jobs, decent treatment from supervisors, and fair grievance hearings. And should DC 37 win, it would be in a position to get honest collective bargaining.

Above all, the union promised a career training program. Concerned that "her people" had been neglected much too long by an indifferent society, Roberts promised to develop training programs to help them out of boring, dead-end jobs. She lobbied the Federal government for assignment of manpower programs to city hospitals and, assisted by Education Director Sumner Rosen, outlined a step-by-step promotional program. Her public commitment to these efforts spread among hospital employees and facilitated a steady flow of renewed membership into Local 420.

A constant barrage of clear, earthy leaflets, special brochures and biweekly bulletins were produced at Council headquarters and then distributed broadside throughout the hospital complex. Literature focused on militant Local 420 as an "honest, fighting" trade union, with its participation in the civil rights struggle and its refusal to make deals with the city bosses. To insure that these messages got through to the workers, the Council used direct mailings to employees and, for maximum effect, made house calls. A campaign kit was distributed that included a welcoming letter, local insurance benefits, developing Council welfare plans, the educational program for 420, and a booklet on the local's plans for the future. Individual palm cards were handed out with the names of union representatives to be contacted with grievances and for all forms of assistance. The paraphernalia of campaigning included 420 buttons, lollypops, stickers, shopping bags, and radio spots beamed to the black and Hispanic communities. A fact sheet on how to approach employees during weekend visits was distributed at orientation meetings for volunteers from other locals.[12]

For ten months, the total energies of the Council were geared toward the one objective of winning the hospital elections. Virtually all 60 staff members and activists temporarily released from their hospital work were thrown into the battle, each unit covered by at least two staff members and sometimes four. DC 37 sought to show workers its ability to insure improvements even while the contest raged, compelling city officials to fix leaky pipes, falling plaster, and faulty dishwashing machines and ameliorate unsafe and unsanitary work conditions. Some of management agreed to make serious efforts to keep workers on permanent shifts, to facilitate regularly assigned days off and to handle personnel with greater dignity and consideration. More provisionals were appointed, promotional exams given, and eligible lists provided through the insistence of Council staff. Most important of all, however, was the daily work of volunteers and shop stewards who canvassed workers constantly and dealt with grievances of paramount importance to members.[13]

DIFFICULT TURF

It was not an easy campaign in the field, nor was it always safe. This was especially true after Paul Hall decided, unexpectedly, to pull his husky Seafarers out of the battle. Members of the Teamsters staff fought back, harassing Roberts, disrupting meetings at hospitals by turning out lights and initiating fights, interfering with leaflet distribution, and even knifing some Council organizers. Many workers were afraid to come to night meetings, because the Teamsters often made it rough for them. The hospital setting provided other difficulties for organizers not found in the typical industrial situation. In one or more of the hospitals, for example, Local 420 organizers and activists had to contend with employees who were numbers runners, bookies, organized pilferers, or solicitors for prostitutes. Organizers might endanger their lives if they stepped on the toes of such individuals.

Gotbaum met with veteran black leaders Bayard Rustin and A. Philip Randolph, winning their unqualified support for his endeavors to demonstrate to minority employees the Council's close alliance with the civil rights crusade. Through Paul Hall and David Dubinsky, Gotbaum reached out to other labor leaders. On the fiscal front, he appealed everywhere—to the national AFL-CIO, Wurf's International treasury, other unions, and each of the Council's locals. Gotbaum was committed, if necessary, to put the Council "into hock up to its eyeballs...." And he did. Every resource had to be brought into play "so we will win this election."[14]

The Teamsters' campaign was basically negative and hit at individuals, disparaging Roberts and Gotbaum as "outsiders." On one Teamster leaflet Gotbaum was identified as "No. 1's flunky and bosses stooge," who hid "behind his office girl's skirts." In another leaflet, he was a "woman hater" who "attacks girl on Teamster picket line."[15] Lewis's bludgeoning campaign enabled Lillian Roberts to look saintly, a role model for the great numbers of black women. The Teamster leader was so overconfident, and his campaign so counterproductive, that Gotbaum felt he was doing everything possible to hand victory to the Council. As a result of polls taken at various periods of the campaign, the DC 37 leader learned that AFSCME was making significant headway.

In spite of Council efforts, the elections might still have been lost to the Teamsters had they not been delayed until the end of 1965. Barry Feinstein recalled that he learned, years later, that Jerry Wurf had gone to AFL–CIO head George Meany to pressure Mayor Wagner for a postponement, which proved successful. Gotbaum acknowledged that his strategy was to delay, resorting even to costly hearings and "strong legal action" to hold off as long as possible to enable more recruitment of workers. At Labor Department hearings, for example, the final decisions concerning the appropriateness or delineation of the bargaining units was delayed for months by the fancy footwork of attorney Bertram Perkel, who represented the Council and Local 420. Every technical objection conceivable was raised, and an endless array of questions and challenges was made.[16]

Before he died, Henry Feinstein had brought his son, Barry, a recent college graduate onto the staff. In his spare time he completed law school, feeling that this training would better prepare him for lobbying and eventual leadership. After his father died and Bill Lewis took over, the young Feinstein was assigned responsibility for the hospitals. As an unsophisticated staff member, he accepted the election delays as normal operating procedure. Bill Lewis, who thought he was still close to Robert Wagner, could not conceive that these endless hearings might be the result of the mayor's intervention and Gotbaum's machinations.

Council staff generally avoided the negative campaign of the Teamsters and thus projected a more positive image. By September 1965, little more than two months before the elections, Local 420 regained its 4,500 members claimed two years earlier, while the Teamsters recorded a membership of 6,783.[17]

CAMPAIGN CLIMAX

By mid-October, there was a perceptible change in the "it's all sewed up" attitude of the Teamsters. Alerted by Barry Feinstein and others as to the growing effectiveness of the Council campaign, Bill Lewis belatedly threw his full resources into the contest. By this time, however, Local 420 stewards and activists had made a marked impact, helped by the response to the Council's extensive newspaper advertising and hundreds of spot radio announcements in English and in Spanish, over many small stations. On the eve of elections, personal letters were sent to every hospital employee by AFL–CIO President George Meany and by A. Philip Randolph, the venerable black leader of the Sleeping Car Porters and dean of the civil rights movement. During the final hectic days, there was a concerted effort on housecalls by over 130 volunteers and some 50 staff members. Gotbaum was very specific about the monitoring needed during the wrap-up period, when he insisted that:

> By November 10, at a staff meeting called for this purpose, I want a full and accurate appraisal of the situation for cooks and the final week's activities planned out. . . . I want to know which non-members or Teamsters are leaning toward us so a concentrated telephone call campaign can be made just prior to the election.[18]

Helping influence the final outcome was a variety of assistance given DC 37 by a host of unions in the metropolitan area. Driving cars, supplying equipment, getting voters to the polls, and much vital moral support were contributed by members of Anthony Scotto's Longshoremen, Albert Shanker's Teachers, the Amalgamated Clothing Workers, David Dubinsky, Charles Zimmerman and the International Ladies Garment Workers, Leon Davis and the Drug and Hospital Employee Local 1199, the Bakery Workers, the Taxi Drivers Organizing Committee, and the Central Labor Council under Harry Van Arsdale. During this period Gotbaum also came to know and appreciate Sanitation head John DeLury, and his consultant and former UPW leader, Jack Bigel. At the start of the campaign, Bigel sought out the DC 37 executive director with an important message. If Gotbaum did not play a destructive role, nor resort to the name-calling and "red-baiting" of Jerry Wurf's earlier campaigns against Henry Feinstein and DeLury, then the Sanitation leader would stay out of the contest even though both were affiliated with the Teamsters. The result was that DeLury remained neutral, which was of inestimable aid to DC 37.

Of 73 percent of the eligible aides who turned out at the polling places, 5,071 cast their ballots for the Teamsters and 5,903 for the AFSCME local. From Washington, D. C., the International executive board wired Gotbaum:

You won it in a landslide in the voting by the clerks
Messengers said Hoffa's gang are all a bunch of jerks,
The aides made two three seven's crowd look like a gang of
  schnooks.
But let us ask you cousin Vic, what happened to them cooks?[19]

For Bill Lewis, the vote was unexpected and crushing. He never recovered from this blow and shortly thereafter died a broken man. His successor was Barry Feinstein. Teamster Local 237 would never again be a major force on the New York labor scene without the cooperation and sustenance of Gotbaum and DC 37, for AFSCME now represented some 60 percent of all city employees under the Career and Salary Plan.

The City's Department of Labor had to certify the results of the December 3 elections, which took another eight months. Bill Lewis challenged the final election results, except for the cooks. When confronted with the threat of a DC 37 strike against the hospitals on Labor Day 1966, unless the election victories were affirmed, the Labor Department handed down its decision. After seven months of hearings, a 60-page document by the Labor Department disposed of the objections raised by Local 237, and confirmed the AFSCME victory.

The Union's 86-person bargaining team, headed by Dan Nelson, Victor Gotbaum, Lillian Roberts, Local 420 President John Coleman, and the city's representatives, were soon engaged in marathon bargaining. Negotiations were often rough, with emotions running high and Gotbaum's angry voice booming out frequently. Eventually, an agreement was reached. The contract took the aide titles out of the Career and Salary Pay rules and provided for cash raises of $900, and a $60 welfare fund contribution per annum the first year for each employee, rising to $85 a year later. One of the major innovations in city policy was the recognition that, as the exclusive bargaining representative, Local 420 was to have a dues checkoff.[20]

SUMMARY

The successful outcome of the elections gave the Council a majority both in the hospitals as well as citywide among nonuniformed workers. For Gotbaum, the tedious organizational work paid handsome dividends for it assured him a solid base for leadership in the Council. It won him support from large numbers of Wurf adherents who previously had difficulty in switching loyalty. At the same time, the new director attracted important labor leaders who closely watched his campaign. For the first time since his return to New York, Gotbaum became his own person. Along with profound respect for Wurf as a bright, tough, hard-working leader, union staff and local activists experienced serious anxiety over his irascible, short-tempered, and frequently insulting behavior. Until the results of the hospital elections, Gotbaum was viewed as "Jerry's guy," for his designation had been pushed through by the president.

The hospital campaign enabled the new director to make his own way. When Wurf tried to assume leadership of the hospital contest, as he had done during the Welfare Strike, he was warned to stay away. "If you come in," Gotbaum cautioned him, "I'm leaving. And Lil is leaving, too." Displeased and frustrated, the International president remained on the sidelines, except when invited to address some mass rallies. Almost everyone in the Council took note. Many on the outside were well aware that DC 37 started as "impossible underdogs," and yet went on to win.[21]

During the weeks and months that followed, Gotbaum turned his attention to solidifying the disparate locals, gathered together his own professional staff, and pushed on toward the long-range goals he had set for hospital workers. The Council's organizing drives were accelerated as he pushed the field staff into new fronts among public workers. Exclusive bargaining rights were won for the Board of Education's school lunch workers, and Local 372 and DC 37 became the exclusive negotiators for 6,500 school aides. Coming within less than a month after the hospital elections, these gains increased the momentum for further expansion.

By January 1966, the Council was designated exclusive bargaining representative for over 70,000 city workers. Another 12,000 were added before the end of the year, encompassing cleaners, chemists, librarians, actuaries, institutional barbers, exterminators, lifeguards, court reporters, block workers, and service coordinators. New areas for further growth were developed in the public library systems and the antipoverty program. Gotbaum, however, lamented the fact that "jungle relationships among the unions which deal with the city" continued to present a serious problem. Costly organization drives constantly taxed a depleted union treasury, and only amity within the labor movement and exclusive bargaining could possibly end the debilitating warfare. And so he and the Council pressed on.

NOTES

1. *Spotlight*, August 1954, p. 1; Labor Day 1956, p. 7; February 15, 1957, p. 5; March 1, 1957, p. 3; March 15, 1957, p. 2; Jerry Wurf to Morris A. Jacobs, May 8, 1957; James Farmer to Robert J. Mangum, May 26, 1959; "Local 420, 22 Years," p. 4, a DC 37 pamphlet.

2. *Spotlight*, August 1954, p. 1; November 30, 1954, p. 1; Wurf to Randolph A. Wyman, January 23, 1956. Key staff members included Al Weil, James Farmer, and Bill Evans, and chapter leaders Harold Staley, Thomas Tucker, and Rudy Mitaritonna.

3. *Spotlight*, November 15, 1955, p. 3; May 1956, p. 1; August 1956, p. 1; Jean J. Couturier to Chrisman J. Scherf, February 4, 1957; Harold E. Staley to Robert J. Mangum, April 19, 1961; minutes, Local 420 membership meeting, September 4, 1963, p. 4; New York City Department of Labor. In the Matter of New York City Department of Hospitals and Local 420, District Council 37, American Federation of State, County and Municipal Employees, AFL–CIO, before J. Kenneth O'Connor, hearing officer, May 21, 1964, pp. 182–185, hereafter cited as In the Matter of N.Y.C. Department of Hospitals and Local 420, May 21, 1964.

4. Jerry Wurf to Randolph A. Wyman, January 23, 1956; Bert Rose to Evelyn Brand, March 8, 1963; Bernice Fisher to Morris A. Jacobs, undated; Harold E. Staley to George H. Fowler, April 23, 1963; Staley to Robert J. Mangum, May 3, 1963. In the Matter of NYC, Department of Hospitals and Local 420, May 21, 1964, pp. 187, 193, 198, 200. It was estimated that blacks and Hispanics made up some 85 percent of the nonprofessional employees.

5. *Spotlight*, March 1, 1957, p. 4; March 15, 1957, p. 2; Robert J. Mangum to Wurf, October 24, 1962; Wurf to James McFadden, October 21, 1963; Wurf telegram to Robert F. Wagner, Jr., November 6, 1963; In the Matter of NYC, Department of Hospitals and Local 420, May 21, 1964, pp. 184, 185, 187; *New York Times*, June 16, 1965, p. 42; October 15, 1965, p. 29; October 20, 1965, p. 46; November 9, 1965, p. 42; "Local 420, 22 Years," p. 9.

6. Harold Staley memorandum to Morris Riger, April 4, 1963. This 15-page document details AFSCME membership, according to hospital titles. Also, interviews with Barry Feinstein, April 22, 1981; Bert Rose, September 16, 1981.

7. Harold Staley to Morris Riger, April 4, 1963; Ken Wilder to Harry Gray, April 9, 1964; Larry Seelig to Morris Riger, April 14, 1963.

8. Interviews with Barry Feinstein, April 22, 1981; Victor Gotbaum, May 11, 1981; Bert Rose, September 16, 1981; Louis Yavner, April 8, 1982.

9. Interviews with Barry Feinstein, April 22, 1981; Victor Gotbaum, May 11, 1981; Louis Yavner, April 8, 1982. Yavner was legal counsel to Local 237.

The Hospital campaign eventually cost DC 37 and the International union at least $750,000, an immense amount at that time.

10. Interviews with Victor Gotbaum, May 11, 1981; Bert Rose, September 16, 1981. Playing vital roles in the hospital campaign were staffers Al Weil, Bert Rose, Stanley Propper, and Max Dombrow, among others. Amalgamated Clothing Workers unionist Tom Flavell was instrumental in securing the loan.

11. Memo, Hospital Workers Campaign, undated, Gotbaum files; Susan Reverby, "From Aide to Organizer: The Oral History of Lillian Roberts," in Rosalyn Baxandall, Linda Gordon and Susan Reverby, eds., *America's Working Women*, New York: Vintage Books, c. 1976, pp. 303–305; interview with Lillian Roberts, September 28, 1982.

12. *Public Employee Press,* February 12, 1965, p. 8; February 26, 1965, p. 1; March 26, 1965, p. 1; May 7, 1965, pp. 3, 5; June 18, 1965, p. 8; July 1965, p. 5; November 12, 1965, p. 1; November 26, 1965, Election Special, pp. 5, 7. "Election Planning Table," undated but issued by Gotbaum's office prior to August 1, 1965; memo, Hospital Workers Campaign, undated; Victor Gotbaum memorandum to special representatives and field staff, September 15, 1965.

13. Typical of weekly reports by these 60 staff members were those of Vera Simmons, Ella Rose E. Woodley, and Lester Wright, in addition to "Hospital Breakdown" reports for weeks ending June 11, 18, 25, and July 2, 1965. Key to the eventual outcome was the daily activity of hospital aides Adele Nobles, Clyde Goins, John Staten, Lester Wright, James Butler, Miguel Morales, Ella Woodley, Annie Norris, Jim Taylor, Iantha Floyd, and other rank-and-file activists.

14. *Public Employees Press,* April 19, 1965, p. 4; minutes, Local 924 general membership meeting, May 24, 1965; Gotbaum to Wurf, June 7, 1965. Also, interview with Bert Rose, September 16, 1981.

15. Undated leaflets issued by Local 237 Teamsters, 100 Gold Street, NYC; *Public Employee Press,* November 23, 1966, p. 4. Interviews with Barry Feinstein, April 22, 1981; Victor Gotbaum, May 11, 1981.

16. Victor Gotbaum to Jerry Wurf, June 7, 1966; Gotbaum to Gordon Chapman and Wurf, June 30, 1965; *Public Employee Press,* June 18, 1965, pp. 3, 8; September 17, 1965, p. 7; October 1, 1965, p. 3; November 12, 1965, p. 1; *New York Times,* December 4, 1965, p. 17. Also, interviews with Barry Feinstein, April 22, 1981; Victor Gotbaum, May 11, 1981; Bert Rose, September 16, 1981; Bertram Perkel, December 27, 1982.

17. *New York Times,* December 4, 1965, p. 17.

18. "Local 420 Radio Schedule—3-Week Campaign—November 13 through December 3," pp. 1–6, undated report by Furman, Feiner and Company, Inc. of New York. Also, Victor Gotbaum memorandum to Lillian Roberts, Al Weil, Harry Gray, Ed Maher, and Chuck Svenson, re: pending elections, undated, but in all likelihood issued in early November 1965.

19. *New York Times,* December 4, 1965, p. 17; *Public Employee Press,* December 10, 1965, pp. 1–3; interviews with Victor Gotbaum, May 11, 1981; Jack Bigel, February 18, 1982. DC 37 also won the balloting for the messengers and the non-supervisory clerks, but lost the vote of the cooks.

20. *Public Employee Press,* July 1, 1966, pp. 1, 12; August 1966, p. 3. *New York Times,* August 31, 1966, p. 34; November 15, 1966, p. 61.

21. Interview with Victor Gotbaum, May 11, 1981.

9
Collective Bargaining: The Seat of Power

Public unions became a phenomenon during the 1960s and, as labor writer Sam Zagoria noted, burst upon public employers and a general public "less prepared for them than an invasion from outer space." Their rapid growth was unique, attracting a larger proportion of the work force in one decade than industrial unions had achieved in three. In this period, New York became a leader in the development of labor relations programs and the institution-alization of collective bargaining. Union recognition, however, did not come easily nor automatically, requiring persistent organizing, worker militancy, and skilled leadership.[1]

By 1965, city employment reached approximately 260,000 with a wide range of occupations and in a variety of agencies. The complex terms and conditions of employment and the procedures by which they were determined baffled employees. Many workers were in civil service categories governed by the career and salary plan. The uniformed services were treated separately, as were the public school teachers. The proliferation of quasi–labor law estab-lished groups of employees whose compensation was governed by prevailing rates for comparable titles in private industry.

This chapter explores the basic changes in labor relations in New York, from the mayor's domination of negotiations under Wagner to the emergence, under Lindsay, of an impartial process and a more professionalized staff under the OCB. This transforma-tion had important consequences for DC 37 and for the leadership of Victor Gotbaum.

Facilitating the attainment of genuine collective bargaining for New York's public workers, Mayor John V. Lindsay assigned Herbert L. Haber, director of labor relations, to negotiate a new contract with a union team headed by Gotbaum, Dan Nelson and Alan Viani. This session is surrounded by longtime DC 37 activists Joe Zurlo, Victor Honig, Eliot Reif, Mike Gentile, John Boer, Tom Hagan, Fannie Fine, Helen Smith, Joe Spinnachia, and other local leaders.

CONDON-WADLIN

From the start, the new executive director of DC 37 realized that control over collective bargaining was essential, for:

The collective bargaining table is the union leader's seat of power. This is where he makes or breaks it. This can give him the opportunity to politically wheel and deal, and to try to implement his social visions.[2]

By the time Gotbaum took over the leadership of DC 37, he felt there was too much focus on the legality of strikes and not enough on developing machinery to prevent them. Adopted in 1947, the Condon-Wadlin Act made public employee strikes illegal and provided for dismissal or prohibited wage increases for three years for any public striker. Because of their harshness, Condon-Wadlin provisions were often ignored or evaded by mutual agreement. The determining factors appeared less in the critical nature of the service interrupted than in the strength of the union, the climate of the area, or the political ramifications. As a result, the act was utilized almost entirely in upstate New York, where the organized labor movement was not politically influential.

The one clear impact of the strike prohibition, according to most public employee leaders, was that it exerted pressure on union members, in the form of threatened court injunctions and jail sentences, removed pressure from employers, and inhibited genuine collective bargaining. Gotbaum, Dan Nelson, and Eric Polisar insisted on an alternative of impartial arbitration of grievances, impartial mediation of contract impasses, and honest collective bargaining.[3]

A WAGNER LEGACY

Following the Welfare strike of January 1965, a Tripartite Panel of city officials, union spokespersons, and public representatives was established as part of the contract between the city and the unions involved, to review the entire status of collective bargaining. Although this contract was executed in June, it took six months to create the committee and establish its procedures.

The mayor appointed the public members as the first group of the panel who, in October, recommended the structure of the labor contingent and the ground rules for meetings. On the eve of his departure from office, Wagner invited Gotbaum to chair the labor committee of the Tripartite Panel, and Local President Alan Viani to serve as a member of the career and salary section. In response to Wagner's invitation, Gotbaum accepted after the mayor agreed that the proposed career and salary panel was meaningless and deleted it from the Triparitite group.[4]

LINDSAY AND LABOR RELATIONS

City-labor relations changed dramatically with the election of John V. Lindsay as a reform mayor in November 1965, and the fallout of the welfare and transit strikes. In his campaign speeches, which were viewed as antilabor by Quill and others, Lindsay was determined to circumvent the traditional "power brokers" in New York's labor disputes by proposing appointment of impartial fact finders to make recommendations in deadlocks between public unions and city management. Mike Quill responded to the failure to conclude new contract negotiations, started under Wagner, by pulling his TWU members off the subways and buses within hours after Lindsay took the oath of office on January 1, 1966. Before the strike was settled, 12 days later, it was the rough-and-tumble union leader who won a new two-year contract that almost doubled the previous transit agreement. This settlement insured the doom of Condon–Wadlin, for it violated the prohibition on giving public strikers any pay increase for three years. When faced with a court decision against the pact, Governor Rockefeller cooperated with his political ally, Van Arsdale, in pushing through the legislature a bill giving retroactive forgiveness to the transit strikers.[5]

Lindsay enunciated his support of Wagner's Executive Order 49, until such time as the Tripartite Panel completed its study. Rebounding from his severe setback with Mike Quill's TWU, Lindsay made clear his determination to carry out his campaign pledges to create more enlightened and responsible collective bargaining procedures, and to insure peaceful resolution of disputes. He accepted most of the DC 37 proposals, including impartial binding arbitration of grievances by an outside, independent agency, impartial fact finding and mediation of deadlocks in negotiation of new agreements, and establishment of a neutral agency to make the determination of appropriate bargaining units and to conduct bargaining elections. Thus, he was committed to removing one of the primary defects of Wagner's labor relations policy, the city acting both as employer and referee in labor–management relations.

The 23-page Memorandum of Agreement that was finally submitted by the Tripartite Panel was approved unanimously by city and labor representatives. The public members insisted that the recommendations were designed to remove the causes of conflict between the city and its employees, as well as the disorder that had plagued relationships between City Hall and municipal unions. Additionally, implementation of the collective bargaining policy would have to be pursued faithfully by the mayor and his department and agency heads, and would have to establish a process for coping with deadlocks and clarify the scope of collective bargaining.

This was a historic document for municipal labor relations, for it offered city workers, for the first time, the same collective bargaining rights enjoyed by many in private industry. The essential principles included impartiality, tripartism, and proceduralism. It recommended that the city and certified employee organizations engage in collective bargaining on wages, pension, health and welfare benefits, uniform allowances and shift personnel, hours, and working conditions. Further, standards for selecting employees, determination of service and efficiency, and the content of job classifications came within the scope of bargaining. The city was to bargain on overtime, time and leave rules, and pensions only with a union that represented more than 50 percent of all Career and Salary Plan employees. Obviously, DC 37 was the only organization that fell within this category.

The panel also recommended creation of an independent Office of Collective Bargaining (OCB) to oversee bargaining procedures (including impasses), determine bargaining units, and certify bargaining agents. The OCB was to be administered by a seven-member board: two appointed by the mayor, two by a municipal labor committee (MLC), and three impartial members unanimously elected by the four appointees. One of the impartial members was to be designated as chairperson.

Either party could file a bargaining notice with reference to negotiations at least 90 days prior to the expiration of a contract. The parties were obligated to commence negotiations within ten days. On the initiative of the OCB, or at the request of either party, the chair could appoint an impartial mediator to assist the parties in arriving at an agreement. At the request of both parties, or on recommendation of the OCB chair, a dispute panel would be established if a majority of the OCB board determined that a bargaining impasse had been reached. The panel would be made up from a register of impartial persons approved by a majority of the OCB. An impartial disputes panel was to have the power to mediate, hold hearings, and subpoena witnesses and data, although its recommendations were not binding on either party. Finally, collective bargaining agreements between the city and the unions were to contain grievance procedures in steps that terminated in impartial binding arbitration.

Although the new procedures did not include a blanket no-strike pledge from the unions, they did provide a no-strike clause during the terms of contract, negotiations, and the 30-day period following the report of the fact-finding panel. These no-strike clauses were similar to most collective bargaining agreements in private industry. The recommended procedures were also unique in that they provided for centralized bargaining on all matters affecting wages and working conditions, and for written contracts which were enforceable in the courts. Provisions were made for final and binding arbitration of all disputes arising out of the interpretation of a contract, or of a policy rule or regulation. The city would not, thereafter, turn down an award simply because the mayor or his subordinates didn't like it.

The "managerial rights" clause in the procedures were based upon President Kennedy's Executive Order 10988. However, unlike the federal order, the Tripartite Panel recommended that no managerial right that affected employees could be implemented without negotiation of its impact on public workers. For the first time, city employees were afforded the right to negotiate on all working conditions—a right that no federal employee and few state and local employees had achieved.[6]

GOTBAUM'S BABY

Mayor Lindsay, several editorial writers, and a number of civic groups viewed the new proposal as a rational approach to "depoliticize" municipal labor relations and to insure labor peace. Despite certain defects, Nelson, Polisar, and Gotbaum believed that City workers were being offered first-class citizenship, and an effective means to avoid strikes.

A.H. Raskin and others viewed the OCB as "Gotbaum's baby." Judith Mage and her associates feared that creation of the OCB would enhance DC 37 while Bill Lewis, Barry Feinstein, and DeLury, concluded that a labor agency independent of City Hall and the city's Democratic machine would dilute their role and weaken their influence. DeLury dubbed the OCB proposal "gimmickry" and insisted that it would "torpedo" collective bargaining.[7]

Still smarting from their disastrous setback in the hospital elections, Lewis and Feinstein denounced the recommendations as a "betrayal" and Gotbaum as a "labor parasite" who had sold out the city employees. For months thereafter, an unlikely coalition of Mage, Lewis, Feinstein, and DeLury resorted to every means possible to obstruct the recommendations of the Tripartite Panel.

In June 1966, the mayor announced that the Career and Salary Plan would no longer be used as basis for wage negotiations in collective bargaining. This signaled a historic breakthrough for low-level city employees and forecasted major advances in wages for municipal employees. Lindsay then appointed Herbert L. Haber, an experienced, sensitive, and deeply committed labor–management consultant, as director of labor relations. In this newly created full-time post, Haber was given authority to conduct contract negotiations with all city employees covered by collective bargaining agreements and to administer contracts and the grievance process. He was not interested in playing divide-and-conquer games but sought direct negotiations.[8]

In the months following his appointment, Haber settled several contracts fairly quickly, while others were delayed interminably. DC 37 leaders felt that the city was dragging its feet, complaining about Haber's indecisiveness. Nelson and Gotbaum insisted on the implementation of the Tripartite recommendations to prod the disparate elements of city government. The Council director also hoped that creation of the OCB would blunt the drive for punitive, antistrike legislation in Albany generally supported by the public. As an impartial body stressing peaceful resolution of disputes, the city's new approach might yet show the way as a workable alternative to fines and jail sentences in public employee relations.

ROCKEFELLER RESPONDS TO LABOR

In mid-January 1966, in response to the New York City transit strike, Governor Rockefeller conceded the failure of the Condon-Wadlin Act. It was then that he appointed five prestigious experts in labor-management relations, headed by Professor George W. Taylor of the Wharton School at the University of Pennsylvania, to recommend legislation to protect the public against disruption of vital government services by "illegal strikes," while at the same time "protecting" the rights of public employees. There were no representatives of public worker unions. The governor's committee sought greater emphasis on peaceful procedures, but its conclusions were at variance with those of the city's Tripartite group. The Rockefeller panel urged a new law against strikes, changing the emphasis from punishment to improved bargaining machinery. It granted public employee unions organizing and bargaining rights throughout the state and authorized state and local governments to bargain with them. The proposals included a ban on strikes but milder penalties under a more flexible system than that under Condon-Wadlin. A three-member Public Employment Relations Board (PERB) was to oversee mediation, fact finding, and deadlocked talks by the state legislature or local legislative bodies in the event that either management or labor rejected fact-finding proposals. These recommendations were seen as tantamount to ensuring binding settlement of disputes, although the panel rejected the concept of compulsory arbitration. PERB was authorized to rescind official recognition of those unions that resorted to strikes and raised the fines against unions defying court injunctions.

In contrast to New York City's Tripartite group, which proposed an impartial OCB to administer collective bargaining procedures, the state panel authorized the governor to pick the three members of PERB, with the consent of the senate. No one on the board was to represent organized labor. An option clause permitted localities like New York City to develop their own labor-management schemes, as long as they fell within the context of the state's legal framework.

Rockefeller and other proponents of the Taylor proposals defended them as "neutral," "fair to the workers," and "protecting the public." Over the years, as labor reporter and then editorial writer for the *New York Times*, A.H. Raskin was a severe critic of use of strikes by public employee unions, insisting that:

a strike against government becomes an interference with the political process, an attempt by one segment of the people to exert its control over a specific service as a weapon to coerce the whole community into submission on its own terms. And the more vital the service, the greater the chance that the community will have to capitulate.

The *Times* endorsed the Taylor recommendations because they pointed the way toward "effective enforcement of the indispensable principle that there is no right to strike against the government." The newspaper warned the Democratic majority in the assembly not to bow "to insistent pressure from the labor lobby" without a substitute for the "virtually worthless" Condon–Wadlin Act, for it would then leave the city doubly vulnerable in ongoing contract negotiations. Raskin and his colleagues insisted that, under these circumstances, Gotbaum would have a greater chance of "extorting an overgenerous settlement." And this would inevitably require the city to make deep cuts in schools, antipoverty projects, and other underfinanced services.[9]

Raskin and the *Times* infuriated the leaders of DC 37. They insisted that the *Times* refused to recognize the right of public workers "to membership in the human race," and wrongly said that Raskin had been the "chief mouthpiece," for Condon-Wadlin. He did support the Taylor proposals. Gotbaum viewed the efforts of the *Times* as attempts to emasculate the unions of public workers. He insisted that whether or not an industry was privately owned was less important than whether it was responsibly operated. The pressure of a strike—the workers' only weapon of last resort—was as relevant, as persuasive, and as legitimate in the one case as in the other. To deny this was to assign to public employees permanent "second-class citizenship," and to their unions the status of pleaders dependent on the good will of employers. He insisted that unions could only act maturely when they bore real responsibility for the welfare of their exploited members.

Shortly after the governor's committee submitted its recommendations, and the governor requested the state legislature to enact them into law, DC 37 launched a major campaign against the proposed bill. It called on Paul Hall, affiliates of the city's Central Labor Council, and the state AFL–CIO, encouraging them to support Democratic Assembly Speaker Anthony Travia in "his excellent stand" against the bill. Gotbaum claimed the bill would be unworkable and lead to chaos. Although the report mentioned mediation and fact finding, the foundation of true mediation of disputes was still the impartiality of the mediator. Since the governor selected the board that picked the mediators, they could not possibly be impartial.[10]

For the remainder of the 1966 legislative session, Travia and the Democratic majority in the assembly managed to bottle up the recommendations of the Taylor group. Rockefeller, however, demonstrated that he was a master tactician and was extremely effective in undercutting labor's support for the Democratic party. He flattered labor leaders like Harry Van Arsdale, appointed others to honorific positions, secured passage of labor bills and initiated massive state-sponsored construction programs. The governor successfully liberalized the state's minimum wages, enlarged workmen's compensation benefits, augmented the pensions of New York City's firefighters and police officers, and increased unemployment benefits. Van Arsdale and the construction union leaders were enthralled by Rockefeller. One result was the governor's impressive reelection to a third term in November 1966. Another was his increasingly effective pressure on labor and the Democratic leadership in the assembly for enactment of the Taylor proposals.[11] It soon became apparent that Speaker Travia was willing to accept a compromise, and that other Democrats were wavering as a result of public and conservative labor support for Rockefeller and the Taylor recommendations.

As the state legislative session drew to a close in early April, Travia disclosed that with certain new amendments, he would be voting for the bill, and that Democratic assemblymen would be "free" to vote as they wished. Virtually no one knew the exact text of the bill, for it had not yet been printed. Rockefeller, meanwhile, was strengthened by a rash of highly publicized threats of New York City's police and firefighters to resort to strikes and work slowdowns in support of their demands for increased wages.

During the early hours of April 2, the Republican-controlled senate, with the support of six Democrats, approved a revised version of the Taylor proposal. Within the hour, the proposed bill was finally distributed among members of the assembly, only a few moments before it was debated. As pages were turned, fundamental questions rarely received adequate answers. In a move that some political analysts regarded as repayment for Rockefeller's support in his bid for the speaker's post, Travia secured the votes of 26 Democrats for successful passage.[12]

The Taylor Law, like the OCB proposals, recognized the importance of impartial third parties to assist in the collective bargaining process. The significant difference, however, was that under the proposed OCB the panels of mediators and fact finders would be chosen by an impartial board, whereas under the state law the governor would select each of the panels.

The immediate reaction of leaders of firefighters, teachers, and many other public workers was expressed by Sanitation head John DeLury when he insisted that this "infamous bill" would stiffen the posture of local governments across the state. He predicted that the Taylor Law would bring no more peace than had Condon–Wadlin. DC 37 responded with a giant protest rally, accumulation of a strike fund, and a declaration of war on Travia.[13]

Despite the passage of the Taylor Law in 1967, the following year there was a rash of public employee strikes statewide (at least 41 under PERB jurisdiction, as contrasted with 7 under OCB) involving teachers, hospital employees, and others.[14] In response, Governor Rockefeller pushed through bills in 1969 providing for stiffer penalties. The reaction of public workers to the heightened punitive measures in the revised Taylor Law was to resort to 41 work stoppages in 1970, far more than in any other year between 1967 and 1978. During this 12-year period, public employees under PERB jurisdiction were involved in 249 work stoppages or strikes, of varying duration. Those under the OCB, in New York City, resorted to a total of 23 strikes for the same period, which ranged annually from none to a maximum of five.[15]

LINDSAY'S ON-THE-JOB TRAINING

John Lindsay was of a younger, profoundly different generation than many of the veteran union leaders. He did not understand at first the organized labor movement and its historic role in a union town like New York. His predecessor's political style, labor philosophy, and back room bargaining was distasteful to him. When the new mayor moved from Congress to City Hall in Janu-

In protest against Governor Nelson Rockefeller's replacement of the much hated Condon-Wadlin antistrike law with the Taylor enactment in 1967, tens of thousands of members from DC 37, the Transport Workers Union, and the United Federation of Teachers overflowed Madison Square Garden into surrounding streets. Joining teacher leader Albert Shanker in proclaiming the declaration of rights of public employees are Gotbaum, Wurf, Matthew Guinan, Charles Cogen, and Douglas MacMahon.

ary 1966, he had few contacts within the organized labor movement, except for David Dubinsky of the ILGWU and Alex Rose of the Capmakers union, who were leaders of the Liberal Party.

Within days after the state legislature enacted the Taylor Law, Lindsay signed Executive Order 40, which proved to be another important advance in rationalizing the highly balkanized labor situation in the city's bureaucracy. It provided that any union that could muster a majority for a title or group of titles would become the sole representative for bargaining, grievance, and other relationships with management. DC 37 was the primary beneficiary of this latest order. In late June, following a request by the mayor, and despite Barry Feinstein's intense opposition, the city council adopted proposals for creation of the OCB. It was to take effect, along with the Taylor Law, the first of September.[16]

SUMMARY

John Lindsay began his first term as mayor without adequate understanding of the role and importance of organized labor in the city. Talking of key labor leaders as "czars" did not endear him to the public unions. At the outset, Gotbaum characterized him as "an upper-middle-class guy who doesn't really understand unions."

The intensity of the conflict that developed between the municipal unions and Lindsay during his early years as mayor contrasted sharply with the comparative tranquility and inexpensive contracts that had characterized labor–management relations under much of Wagner's three terms in office. Union leaders tended to recall that it was Wagner's "palship" tactics with municipal labor that had been able to buy far greater cooperation with far less investment of public funds during the peaceful 1950s. Van Arsdale, Quill, and others viewed Lindsay as out to bust municipal unions. He was portrayed as a moral reformer prepared to treat unions with contempt. However, during the months that followed his humbling experience with the transit strike, Lindsay became increasingly aware of his basic unfamiliarity with labor–management relations and drew back from his confrontational style. Picking up where Wagner left off, Lindsay retained the Tripartite group appointed by his predecessor, and sought to implement its recommendations. He created the OCB as a pioneering landmark in labor–management relations and gave public workers impartial grievance procedures and genuine collective bargaining, as well as providing more professional, skilled experts at the negotiations table. And he did this without resorting to Wagner's highly politicized game of playing off one union against another.

In the meantime, Governor Rockefeller displayed his masterful talents by securing enactment of the Taylor Law. The thrust of this act was twofold: to establish the right of public employees in New York State to bargain collectively and to prohibit strikes. The act did provide for elaborate dispute settlement mechanisms. DC 37 and a number of other municipal unions vehemently opposed the new law, but to little avail. Nor did the legislature stop all strikes around the state.

NOTES

1. Sam Zagoria, ed., *Public Workers and Public Unions*, Englewood Cliffs, NJ: Prentice-Hall, 1972, p. 1.

2. Victor Gotbaum, "Collective Bargaining and the Union Leader," in Zagoria, ed., *Public Workers and Public Unions*, p. 78.

3. Victor Gotbaum to the *New York Times*, June 11, 1965; *Public Employee Press*, February 18, 1966.

4. Victor Gotbaum to Robert F. Wagner, December 13, 1965; Alan Viani to Wagner, December 17, 1965. On the day of Gotbaum's appointment by the mayor, DC 37 won the critical election in the city's hospitals, enabling the Council to bargain for over 62 percent of all employees covered under the Career and Salary Plan. Time and again, city representatives informed Gotbaum that changes in the plan could only occur when a union represented a majority of the municipality's employees. That time had come; DC 37 was determined to negotiate fundamental changes in the plan and would not share that duty with any group or committee of the Tripartite Panel.

5. *New York Times*, January 12, 1966, p. 17; Raskin, "Politics Up-Ends the Bargaining Table," in Zagoria, ed., *Public Workers and Public Unions*, p. 131.

6. Jesse Simons to John V. Lindsay, March 31, 1966; Memorandum of Agreement, March 31, 1966, pp. 1–23; *New York Times*, March 31, 1966, p. 1. The Labor Committee of the Tripartite Panel drafted rules governing membership eligibility of the MLC and the method of selecting two labor members for the OCB.

The MLC, comprising all city employee unions that agreed to participate, offered public workers, for the first time, a unified voice in dealing with their employer, and possessed the potential for significant economic gain and political influence. The MLC assumed some of the cost of administering the new procedures, insuring a greater sense of impartiality for the OCB.

7. *New York Times*, April 1, 1966, p. 23; September 29, 1966, p. 57. Raskin, "Politics Up-Ends the Bargaining Table," p. 132; Gotbaum, "Collective Bargaining and the Union Leader," p. 82.

8. Leaflet distributed by Teamsters Local 237 shortly after issuance of the report of the Tripartite Panel. A framed copy of the leaflet, which shows Lindsay and Gotbaum shaking hands, hangs outside of Gotbaum's office at DC 37 headquarters. *New York Times*, April 11, 1966, p. 25; May 21, 1966, p. 21; June 2, 1966, p. 24; June 3, 1966, p. 24; June 4, 1966, p. 28; July 19, 1966, p. 15. *Public Employee Press*, October 31, 1966, p. 8.

9. A. H. Raskin, "Strikes By Public Employees," *Atlantic Monthly*, January 1968, p. 48. *New York Times*, April 8, 1966, p. 30; April 17, 1966, sec. 4, p. 3; June 16, 1966, p. 46; June 23, 1966, p. 38.

10. Gotbaum to Anthony Travia, April 12, 1966; Gotbaum to Raymond Corbett, Travia, Harry Van Arsdale, May 6, 1966; Paul Hall to Gotbaum, May 11, 1966; Gotbaum to John DeLury, May 27, 1966.

11. James E. Underwood and William J. Daniels, *Governor Rockefeller in New York: The Apex of Pragmatic Liberalism in the United States*. Westport, CT: Greenwood Press, 1982, p. 63. See also Richard L. Rubin, *Party Dynamics: The Democratic Coalition and the Politics of Change*, New York: Oxford University Press, 1976, p. 76; Michael Kramer and Sam Roberts, *I Never Wanted to be 'Vice' President of 'Anything': An Investigative Biography*, New York: Basic Books, 1976, pp. 346–350; Richard L. Rubin, *Party Dynamics: The Democratic Coalition and the Politics of Change*, New York: Oxford University Press, 1976, p. 76.

12. *New York Times*, March 6, 1967, p. 37; April 1, 1967; p. 1; April 2, 1967, p. 33; April 3, 1967, p. 1. Also, transcript, WINS radio news conference, May 21, 1967, interview with Victor Gotbaum, pp. 4–5.

13. *New York Times*, April 4, 1967, p. 28; April 22, 1967, p. 19; May 10, 1967, p. 1. *Public Employee Press*, April 19, 1967, p. 1A.

The PERB was created to oversee the Taylor Law activities and assist in the mediation and resolution of disputes, including the determination of penalties. It permitted a striker to be fined, at the discretion of his department head, and to be fined and possibly jailed, at the discretion of a court. A striking union was liable to fines of one week's income for the striking group each day of the strike, or $10,000 per day, whichever was less. A union could lose its dues checkoff for 18 months, a severe penalty. These provisions could be set aside, however, if the court found that management and local government officials had exhibited "extreme provocation," thus making the strike inevitable. The court could also reduce or remove the penalties.

14. Joel M. Douglas, "The Labor Injunction: Enjoining Public Section Strikes in New York," *Labor Law Journal*, June 1980, pp. 345, 349. From the enactment of the OCB law to the end of 1970, there were more than 40 impasse panel recommendations under OCB. In every instance, the recommendations were ultimately accepted by both parties. In contrast, a very substantial percentage of PERB factfinder recommendations were rejected by either or both parties.

15. *Public Employee Press*, February 28, 1969. John Corcoran to V. Gotbaum, May 16, 1969; V. Gotbaum to Nelson A. Rockefeller, May 15, 1970. Douglas, "The Labor Injunction;" p. 345. Some of the amendments allowed unlimited fines on public employee unions resorting to work stoppages, mandated the loss of two days pay for each day the striking worker was off the job, and provided for unlimited suspension of dues checkoff. DC 37 was virtually alone in vigorously protesting the amendments and lobbying against them by every possible means.

16. *Public Employee Press*, May 10, 1967, p. 2; *New York Times*, June 23, 1967, p. 42; July 15, 1967, p. 21.

On the day that the OCB law went into effect, Arvid Anderson was named chairperson of the Board of Collective Bargaining and director of the OCB.

10
Gotbaum Takes Command

The tasks confronting Gotbaum as leader of the Council were substantial. In the first place, he had to cut away from the interventions of Wurf and create his own base of power and support. Second, the jurisdictional disputes with Teamsters Local 237 were taxing Council resources and had to be resolved. Third, the membership had to be won over to his leadership and galvanized into a cohesive and formidable force. Finally, a bureaucratic structure had to be put in place and a service arm extended and professionalized. In this chapter we will discuss the first three problems that constituted distinct challenges and confrontations for Gotbaum, requiring a considerable investment of effort, skill, and staff support.

THE FIRST CONFRONTATION: JERRY WURF

These early years were critical in the transition from Wurf to Gotbaum. Within months after replacing Taibi, the International president began looking on the Council's new executive director as a troublesome, nonconforming offspring. Gotbaum refused to follow Wurf's dictates automatically or facilitate the president's involvement in city developments. As tactfully as possible, but less so with the passing years, the DC 37 director sought to make clear that Wurf's uninvited incursions into New York were disruptive and divisive.

Far from being in comfortable command of its loose organization and independent locals which sought to go their own ways,

Having won the crucial hospitals elections and established his independence, an increasingly confident Gotbaum assumed control of the Council's bureaucracy and recruited a staff of experts dedicated to progressive unionism.

the new leader walked a thin line trying to limit communications with Washington. To secure his independence, he pushed on ceaselessly with fruitful organizing campaigns. Less than a month after the monumental victories of DC 37 over the Teamsters, in December 1965, Local 372 (New York City Board of Education) was certified as the exclusive bargaining representative for 6,500 school aides. Since the union already held bargaining rights for workers other than teachers in the Board of Education, this new development meant that within one month the Council had gained negotiating privileges for some 40,000 employees. During its 21st anniversary year, the Council attained some of its most significant victories and greatest growth, becoming the largest and eventually the most important public union in the city. Throughout the following year, thousands of additional public workers came under the DC 37 banner and those of its affiliated locals, including hospital aides, school aides and clericals, cleaners, chemists, librarians, actuaries, institutional barbers, exterminators, lifeguards, court reporters, area service coordinators, block workers, and mortuary caretakers.

During the first ten months of 1966, the Council added 6,000 new members to its roster, enabling it to speak for a total of 82,000 city employees. DC 37 was also in the midst of other important organizing drives that were bringing in hundreds of members weekly in such areas as the public library systems and quasi-public institutions like museums. Brooklyn Library employees showed the way to colleagues in other boroughs when they voted to have AFSCME represent them. This decisive victory served as a strong catalyst for similar action among employees of the other systems, requiring the creation of new library locals.

Fiscal Difficulties

In the spring of 1966, however, Gotbaum expressed serious concern over the large deficit that drained Council resources, resulting from the tremendous expenses entailed in the welfare strike, the hospital elections, the clerical organizing drives, and the ongoing campaigns to displace the Teamsters. To ease this fiscal crisis the executive director fired eight employees, in addition to cutting down expenditures for grievance representatives. He secured approval for a constitutional amendment increasing per capita dues from $2.10 to $2.50 monthly, but only when a local's membership received an increase in wages at the collective bargaining table. The Council was also forced to borrow $300,000. The Council requested help from the International president and solicited short-term loans from more affluent Locals.[1]

In contrast to Wurf's frequent hostility to staff organizations in earlier years, this strained financial situation did not deter Gotbaum from negotiating a new, amicable contract with the staff's union, the Federation of Field Representatives, providing for a general increase in wages. Salary increases were also awarded those top administrators not included in the staff Union.By the end of 1966, the Council was operating on a reduced deficit with the expectation that the budget would be balanced the following year. The high costs of earlier organizing drives and strike activities, and the low per capita financing was gradually being remedied by increases in membership and dues. The upward curve of membership continued throughout 1967 with dues checkoff helping to regularize the Union's income. When Beverly Dabney, a children's librarian in Brooklyn, signed a green checkoff card she became the 50,000th member. In 1967, income finally exceeded expenses, enabling the Council to begin paying off its huge debts. It also afforded Gotbaum an opportunity to move the Union into new activities, such as community organization and political action, essential to preserving any long-range gains made at the bargaining table.[2]

The Cleaners Organize

Somewhat representative of the dramatic growth of Council membership were developments involving Custodial Employees Local 1597. When it first entered the city picture in 1965, no union was certified to speak for building cleaners on a citywide basis. The organizing task of its rank-and-file leaders was not easy, for they had to convince disheartened and demeaned cleaners, who worked on day and night shifts in buildings dispersed throughout the city's sprawling counties, that DC 37 would fight for a more decent way of life. When they weren't ignored, they were mistreated. City bureaucrats did not take kindly to having their authority over unskilled, primarily black laborers diminished by an intervening union. One of the primary explanations for the success of any local was personal commitment and undeviating support by rank-and-file activists, and this small local had them.

After two years of organizing, they were able to call for and win representation elections against Local 237. Negotiations resulted in an impressive contract: a good annual salary, cash raises, the establishment of a welfare fund, and a more dignified title. Changes in the attitude and behavior of the predominantly white administratorship showed greater sensitivity and better treatment of workers. A shop steward and union representative were at their side at grievance hearings, and they were given a chance to move up the job ladder through training programs planned by the union in cooperation with the city. All this added up to heightened personal dignity, increased financial well-being, and a deepening sense of security.[3]

Servicing the growing membership proved to be an unrelenting and demanding task, requiring imagination and perseverance to fulfill the needs and increasing aspirations and expectations of recruits. As new locals were formed and old ones expanded, staff helped draw them steadily into the Council's framework, offering services to their membership and expertise for organizational development. DC 37 facilities continued to grow as communication networks were fashioned to tighten relationships between locals and the Council. In the meantime, Gotbaum was increasingly successful in keeping Wurf away from New York. Not until the late 1970s, when relations between the two became strained to the breaking point, did the International president resort to destructive interventions. By that time, however, the Council's executive director had secured an impregnable base through an expanding membership, increased Council loyalty among rank-and-file members and most local leaders, and his leadership of public employee unions during the city's fiscal crisis.

THE SECOND CONFRONTATION: TEAMSTERS LOCAL 237

In early 1966, the Council initiated a citywide campaign to challenge the Teamsters for exclusive bargaining representation for some 3,500 Housing Authority caretakers, maintenance men, exterminators, storemen, and other blue-collar titles. As part of the drive, Council leaflets and PEP portrayed Teamster head Bill Lewis and Vice-President Barry Feinstein as insensitive, business-type unionists who acted as "flunkies for the bosses" and resorted to "back door deals" with management.

Housing boiler room firemen were promised their own local with control over their own affairs, election of their own officials, and the power to decide policies, set their own bargaining agenda, and participate in the Council's decision-making apparatus. The firemen were also offered the clout of DC 37 as the largest trade union of public employees in the country—they were given professional help with grievances and support in lobbying efforts for legislation. Organizers, who spread out among the housing projects, pledged discount buying, summer camps for children, pension counseling, and vacation tours. After years of representation by the Teamsters, firemen in the Housing Authority continued to receive one of the lowest salaries of private or municipal workers in the boiler room. And caretakers, doing work similar to that of laborers in the parks, received far less.

In contrast to their previous overconfidence and slipshod campaign during the hospital elections, Teamster leaders Bill Lewis and Barry Feinstein poured tens of thousands of dollars and every available resource and experienced staffer into the fray, including traditional Teamster tactics. This time, Feinstein was as active and as committed as the AFSCME staff, for he raced from one housing project to another, pushing his members and stewards. He utilized longstanding contacts with management to make things difficult for DC 37 organizers. Organizing leader Bert Rose and his colleagues were often evicted bodily by Teamster goons from housing projects. Feinstein was determined to win this election, for his union's survival was at stake.[4]

A representation election was scheduled, but the Teamsters at first threatened a job action. Feinstein and Lewis made clear that their local was prepared to "hit the bricks" against any "phony deal." The "deal" to which they alluded was the decision of the Labor Department to hold elections among blue-collar titles, which the Teamsters could ill afford to lose. Feinstein then charged that DC 37 green cards were "forgeries" and, therefore, elections were unnecessary. Somehow he had managed to secure lists of those who had signed the AFSCME cards requesting an election, whereupon his field staff immediately set to work pressuring them in traditional Teamster fashion. Increasing numbers of these petitioners indicated to management that they had not really meant to ask for new elections and requested revocation of their green card applications. Eventually the Council was able to validate more than the minimum number of cards required, which was 30 percent of the total work force. The outcome of the election clearly indicated that Feinstein had done his work well, for the majority decided to remain with the Teamsters. The AFSCME drive to destroy Local 237 came to a grinding halt. This defeat, however, was somewhat compensated by Council victories among clerical workers and other units in the Teamsters' bailiwick.[5]

As a result of a historic union contract with the city in December 1966, 17,500 employees of the nonsupervisory clerical force received salary increases. Most important was that this agreement withdrew 20,000 employees from the restrictive wage regulations of the Career and Salary Plan, which had become so inequitable that raises of $50 or less on promotion had become common. This new contract played a vital role in insuring two significant victories for DC 37 over the Teamsters, and helped swell the ranks of clerical employees who won exclusive bargaining rights under the Council banner. As a result of a lengthy campaign, the nonsupervisory clerical workers in the Housing Authority cast a decisive vote for DC 37. The following month, in an election of Department of Health clericals, the vote was even more overwhelming. In 1967 Hospital Local 420 defeated the Teamsters for bargaining rights for elevator operators and laundry workers. With these setbacks Bill Lewis could no longer hope to acquire significant numbers of public workers, and it was clear that the future role of the Teamsters among city employees would be severely limited. Shortly thereafter, a disheartened Lewis died and was succeeded as president by Barry Feinstein.

An unexpected outcome of these developments was the initiatives by Gotbaum and Feinstein to bring a halt to their civil war. A number of factors led to the truce. These jurisdictional struggles had all but bankrupted their respective treasuries and exhausted their staffs. In light of the latest election results, it made little sense to continue the conflict. Furthermore, the new Teamster head discovered that Victor Gotbaum was different from Jerry Wurf, whom he disliked with a deep passion. Feinstein viewed the latter as "wild, irascible, and volatile," who would stop at nothing to destroy an opponent. The Teamster leader was particularly angered by Wurf's "red-baiting campaign" against his father. He found Gotbaum a "reasonable, normal, logical guy that he could talk to and...deal with." Besides, Feinstein was not encumbered with Bill Lewis's traumatic defeat in the hospitals election, or with an unyielding drive for revenge and exoneration.[6]

Shortly after the OCB opened its doors for business, Chairperson Gotbaum of the MLC offered the first olive branch to Feinstein by facilitating his election as a member and officer. In January 1968 they signed a treaty of peace prepared by Teamster counsel Louis Yavner. Both agreed to respect the collective bargaining relationships each had with the city; to consult and amicably resolve disputes; to conduct organizing campaigns only in unorganized areas; to work together to gain recognition of the agency shop, exclusive recognition, and exclusive checkoff; and to jointly seek legislative action. In essence, the agreement apportioned the bulk of the municipality's nonuniformed employees, excluding the teachers, to DC 37, with little more than 10,000 public workers remaining with Teamsters 237. During the years that followed, the two drew ever closer, even cooperating in strike decisions.[7] With the exception of some subsequent raiding by Al Shanker and his United Federation of Teachers, there was no longer any viable opposition to AFSCME in New York.

THE THIRD CONFRONTATION: BUILDING COHESION

The key to mobilizing the diverse membership and locals into a cohesive force was to deliver on bread-and-butter issues and to improve conditions at the workplace. During these early years, Gotbaum and chief negotiator Dan Nelson displayed their skills at collective bargaining sessions with the city, and in facilitating representation elections. Their goal was to enable the Council to speak on behalf of the overwhelming number of city workers not organized by the teacher and uniformed groups. In addition, the Council's leadership was committed to revising significantly the Career and Salary Plan in order to free those public employees trapped in civil service regulations that severely restricted wage and pension gains.

History was made among white-collar workers in December 1966, when the first union contract to cover some 17,500 employees of the city's nonsupervisory clerical force provided for significant salary increases. In addition, some 20,000 employees were withdrawn from the wage regulations of the Career and Salary Plan, enabling clerical workers with extensive service to begin receiving more deserving compensation. A major precedent resulting from this contract was a guarantee of a decent raise upon promotion.[8]

With these contractual developments behind it, a strong movement evolved within the Council for the creation of a citywide local for all employees in clerical occupations. Dolores Berg, president of Local 1784 (Hospital Clerical Workers) contended that locals based on craft would prove more effective, and urged development of a citywide unit. Tom Hagan, venerable activist and president of Clerical–Administrative Local 1549, supported her by pointing out that in the Parks Department there had been more unity around occupation than there would have been with an industrial format. Pat Caldwell, vice-president of Local 371 (Social Welfare) explained that welfare clericals also favored a citywide unit, convinced that their interests had been neglected because of the industrial structure.

Viewing this development as a positive strategy for enhancing the power base of the Council, the leadership pushed members to authorize creation of one, all-encompassing local for Clerical–Administrative and related titles. With this reorganization and voluntary mergers, Local 1549 became the largest single unit of government clericals in the nation. Its potential of over 20,000 members was reached by the early 1970s, and with unified interests gave immense strength to Council negotiators during the years that followed. This local, first under Tom Hagan and then Al Diop, also played a vital role in Gotbaum's conflicts with the International president.[9]

1967–68: MORE VICTORIES!

There had been a time when civil servants were willing to exchange higher salaries for job security and pensions. By 1967, however, with wages and retirement income still not abreast of those in the private sector, and the bulk of public employees organized by unions that had helped raise their expectations and aspirations, changes in strategy were necessary. For the first time unified negotiations were commencing on a new contract on behalf of some 120,000 city employees by one public worker union. Having attained the magic figure of majority representation of virtually all civil servants covered by the Career and Salary Plan, excluding the uniformed forces, DC 37 was alone at the collective bargaining table, opposite City Hall's representative. Gotbaum was determined to push for wage scales and improvements in pensions and work conditions commensurate with those in private industry.

Heading a 40-member negotiating committee from the Council, Gotbaum was well briefed by Dan Nelson, head of negotiations, whose extensive knowledge proved invaluable. As a result of long, arduous meetings with local presidents and their negotiating committees, some 65 fringe benefits were selected for bargaining that related to the workweek, shift differentials, hazard pay, time and leave, health insurance, pay practices, retraining and reassignment, personnel practices, career development, and transfers, among others. Herbert Haber, representing management, responded that the list was far too long. Without experience in collective bargaining, workers wanted to correct everything at once. He insisted that problems of some 20 years' standing could not be resolved in a single contract.

Obviously, the two sides in this highly adversarial bargaining process had started from opposite points of view and expected to gradually find their way to a compromise. Negotiations proceeded slowly and arduously through the hot summer months and on into the fall, with steady progress being made in a number of areas. In the meantime, other units outside the citywide process continued to act on their own set of negotiations. Toward the end of summer, for example, the first citywide bargaining certificate for prevailing-rate workers was awarded to Locals 924 and 376, which gave the Council exclusive representation rights for 6,000 laborers in all city agencies.[10] By the end of 1967, after half the items were resolved, DC 37 called upon the OCB to designate a third-party mediator to assist in breaking an impasse. Involved were issues which, over the years, the city had refused to discuss on grounds that no union represented a majority of workers. Dan Nelson insisted that the time had come to agree upon major improvements in seniority, promotions, pensions, overtime, and summer work hours.

Council negotiators benefited from two external events—the transit negotiations and the sanitation strike. In a cliff-hanger settlement in early January 1968, the transit workers secured a contract with a tremendous breakthrough in pensions. This immediately became a model for other public unions, including DC 37. It provided for vested pension rights after 20 years of service, and pension payments for workers at least 50 years old. Gotbaum's reaction provided newspaper headlines when he commented, "We're licking our chops." Within days, he stalked out of a mediation session threatening to strike "selective departments," unless they were awarded the same gains as Transit. About the time mediations resumed, the sanitation workers resorted to a wildcat strike for some nine days. Not covered by the OCB process, and in defiance of the Taylor Law, John DeLury's powerful Uniformed Sanitationmen's Association (USA) broke off negotiations with Lindsay's representatives over demands for substantial wage increases and assumption by the city of additional contributions to the pension system. Undaunted by the mayor's request for the National Guard, the striking union facilitated existing tensions between Lindsay and Governor Rockefeller. Finally, the negotiators agreed to a confusing face-saving formula proposed by the governor. It provided for binding arbitration and a pay raise higher than the citywide pattern.[11]

As the final mediating sessions began in the sanitation dispute, City Hall announced a general settlement with DC 37 negotiators. The single most important accomplishment was a major overhaul of the pension coverage for city employees, with changes of such magnitude that retirement income was increased approximately 40 percent over existing plans. This new program provided a minimum annual pension of 55 percent of the final year's pay (or average of the best three years, whichever was higher), after 25 years of service, at a minimum age of 55. "Heavy duty" outdoor employees were afforded the opportunity to retire at age 50, after 25 years of employment. Whereas under the old system employees and the government each paid 50 percent into the pension fund, under the new formula the city assumed two-thirds of the contributions. These new pension plans required subsequent affirmation by the state legislature, which would be a mere formality.

In addition to the new pensions, the agreement made reduced summer work hours a contractual right, guaranteed 11 paid holidays, and provided for shift differentials, cash pay for overtime, and improvements in virtually every phase of the city's rules and regulations governing employment, except wages, which were to be negotiated at a later date on an individual title basis. This settlement was to run for three years, through June 1970. In the meantime, Gotbaum and Nelson accomplished two breakthroughs that would have major impact for municipal unions in the future: one extended the scope of collective bargaining to include virtually all issues affecting city workers, and the other established an impartial grievance procedure that provided greater access and equity. Both objectives were integrated into the operations of the newly established OCB.[12] Soon after, the state's Court of Appeals handed the Council another victory when it rejected a suit by the Teamsters Local 237, which had challenged Lindsay's grant of exclusive checkoff privileges to unions formally chosen as collective bargaining agents. The financial worries of the Council were now at an end.

Within little more than two years after assuming office, John Lindsay's labor negotiators had concluded settlements with DC 37 that began to overtake those won by unions in private industry. This did not mean, however, that AFSCME members were suddenly thrust to the top of the scale of salaried workers. Prior to their association with unions in 1966, many municipal workers' wages had fallen far behind private industry levels. In a number of instances, municipal employees were being paid poverty-level wages, and had far to go before they could attain a decent standard of living. In other areas, such as fringe benefits, overtime, and pensions, Dan Nelson insisted that Council unionists still lagged behind their counterparts in the private sector. Generally, the public was unaware of the need for City employees to catch up with private industry colleagues and only heard the media underscore "big" wage settlements, giving the impression of overpaid public workers. Recalling that the average hospital worker's wage was $4,400 before the most recent negotiations, Gotbaum insisted that while the latest increase of $1,000 was sizable, it was not unreasonable in light of the fact that the United States Bureau of Labor Statistics set a moderate living standard in New York at $10,195 for a family of four.[13]

Membership in the Council continued to spiral with the greatest increases in the Schools, Professional and Cultural, and Hospitals Divisions. DC 37 claimed a membership of over 65,000 by the end of 1968, a marked rise from the year previous when the 50,000th member had been honored.

Subsequent to citywide collective bargaining talks in 1967–68, individual unit contracts had to be negotiated. The basic structure of the bargaining process in New York City was on three levels. The first was the citywide contract, which covered areas uniform for all employees, with DC 37 the bargaining agent for most nonuniformed city employees. The second level was the individual unit contracts, or title bargaining. These covered wages, expanded grievance procedures, contributions to the DC 37 education fund, aspects of training programs, and special working conditions for some departments. A third level was the departmental or supplemental contract. This encompassed working conditions that had to be uniform within an agency and were negotiated for all Council employees within a department (e.g., defining safe working conditions and rights of transfer).[14]

Early in 1969, unit contracts provided 28,000 clericals and 19,000 hospital aides and technicians with salary increases of $1,100 to $1,500 over a 30-month period, averaging 8 percent annually. They were guaranteed a minimum salary of $6,000 by the end of the contract, raising thousands of workers above the poverty level for the first time. This was a stunning landmark for public workers at the bottom of the ladder, and Mayor Lindsay welcomed them as "firm taxpayers." Welfare fund contributions by the city increased to $125 per employee by 1970, which enabled the Council to bolster benefits endangered by rising inflation, and to provide those services increasingly neglected by the nation's welfare state. The education fund was finally extended to hospital and clerical groups.[15] It was part of union strategy that a breakthrough in gains for one unit could become a trend setter for others. However, it took strenuous efforts by the leadership to educate members to be patient and wait their turn.

BARGAINING PROCESS: INSIDE THE UNION

In many ways, DC 37 fulfilled Big Bill Haywood's dream of "One Big Union." But at the same time, the many titles, the wide divergences in salary, status, and background, and the extremes in working conditions, constituted a constant challenge to negotiators. Jealousy and tensions arose among members over increases in salary and fringe benefits. And the victories of other municipal unions inevitably sparked demands for at least the same from Council members. By fostering a comparatively broad participation of members and local officers, the top leadership was made aware of the demands and concerns of unionists. In turn, the latter were compelled to hear the many requests of co-workers in other titles and the problems confronting them in other agencies, inducing a good deal of give-and-take in developing a final agenda for collective bargaining. A brief review of prebargaining illustrates the complex, educational process.

The bargaining process is where local and chapter heads assume major roles, for they generally select committees for unit or title bargaining. For the citywide contract, the divisions were represented by their locals. Through issues of PEP, newsletters, and fliers, bargaining goals were solicited from the membership rather than left solely to these committees. Prior to each set of negotiations, these representative committees met with a staff member of the Research and Negotiations Department to help clarify and specify their objectives. Generally, these committees were willing to follow the pattern set by the larger locals, although there have been times when a committee's demands were unrealistic. On the other hand, these groups do make important contributions and adjustments to the traditional economic pattern. After a committee develops a set of proposed demands, they are generally ratified by the membership.

The bargaining process between Council staff and a local's negotiating committee continues after negotiations have begun with the city. During this stage, Council negotiators continue to play the role of mediator, helping local committee members to determine what they really want and what they are willing to surrender as trade-offs. Local presidents are almost always present at citywide negotiations, for they serve as conduits of information to their members. In this manner, Dan Nelson's staff sought to make members of local negotiating committees feel they were active participants. Collective bargaining negotiations within the union, therefore, serves as an educational experience for local leaders and as a means of exchanging information for top Council negotiators.

Union leadership, meanwhile, underscored the need for locals to cooperate in fashioning a realistic bargaining agenda so that a unified force could confront city negotiators. Although this extensive preliminary bargaining system was in place, it did not automatically guarantee compromise and flexibility. Much time, patience, and intramural pulling and hauling were required before the union's demands were ready. Somewhat typical were the difficulties that arose preparatory to negotiations for the second citywide contract, scheduled to commence in April 1970.

Negotiating chief Nelson was troubled by the accumulating demands of locals, a sum which was far too costly for the city. The head of the Council's welfare fund felt that the city should double its aid and there was strong pressure for the city to make a larger contribution to pensions, to pay premium wages to all those who worked on Saturdays and Sundays, and to provide cash payments for involuntary overtime. Nelson urged local leaders "to start shaping our promises to something that more closely resembles a realistic package." After five months of internal wrangling, they reached agreement on a more responsible agenda.[16]

Not only did the AFSCME leadership respond to the pressures of the membership, but it also indicated new directions. The membership had to be educated, for example, as to the importance of more long-range goals such as education, training, health, and security programs, which provided the union with resources that helped develop its creative career and college programs. Not all of the memberhsip sought to take advantage of these broader offerings, especially in the early phases of union building, when they were attracted to such immediate issues as increased wages. Over the years, it was the union's leadership that brought these items to the bargaining table. As an astute participant put it, these achievements were due primarily to "innovative leadership—not so much because of membership pressures, organizational process or environmental factors."[17]

THE BARGAINING PROCESS: CONFRONTING CITY OFFICIALS

As the bargaining process was under way for DC 37, the TWU negotiated a settlement with the city during the first days of 1970, which included a major breakthrough in the form of a fully paid, noncontributory pension plan. Gotbaum sought the same provisions for his members since, as he put it, "This is the name of the game in labor relations." The *Daily News* attacked the "king-size" settlement, underscoring the city's fiscal difficulties in confronting a projected $1 billion deficit in its 1970–71 budget. It feared that "tough-talking Gotbaum" would demand the same. Between April and June, Nelson, Gotbaum, and Council representatives made considerable progress in negotiations with Herbert Haber and other city representatives. One of the most promising aspects of these talks was that, in contrast with other labor negotiations, they were carried on in an atmosphere of quiet discussion, without resort to recurrent strike threats.

Dan Nelson viewed the final agreement as including a good deal that was new and unexpected—improvements on benefits and consolidation of earlier gains. Shift differentials were awarded to practically all, and those who put in authorized involuntary overtime would get straight-time cash instead of time off. Everyone required to work on a holiday was awarded a cash premium, and extended sick leave was provided for all job-connected injuries.[18]

The new pension plan was hailed by union negotiators as "the impossible dream come true." It provided for 50 percent of an employee's pay, after 20 years of service, at age 55. The Council attained, for the first time, a guarantee of 100 percent pension after

40 years of service. The terms of the "New Career Pension Plan" had, by and large, jumped DC 37 members ahead of the pension plans of other city employees, including uniformed services. Herein lay the danger to the new pension agreement. Traditionally, police and firefighters had been the pace-setters in pension benefits since their funds were first established.

This second citywide agreement was eventually signed and ratified unanimously. The pension arrangement had to await action by the legislature in Albany. Under state law, New York City could not make substantive changes in its retirement systems without approval of the legislature and the governor. Traditionally there had been no difficulty in securing legislative approval. But times were changing.[19]

The *Daily News* immediately launched a vigorous attack, and was joined by a chorus of much of the city's press, radio, and television, denouncing the whole pension business as "getting out of hand." The *News* insisted that private industry and business could not arrange retirement at full pay for their people, but civil servant unions, like DC 37, could "put the bite on the taxpayers for such pensions." The public seemed unable to find governmental officials "brave enough to resist such robbery."

Gotbaum was elated, in winning the "highest" pension benefits for public employees in the nation. To blunt the rising chorus of protests from the media, civic groups, and other union critics, he sought to remind the public that the great numbers of Council members were on the lower rungs of the pay ladder and that their newly revised pensions, when approved by the state legislature, would merely bring them close to, not above, a humane level of retirement income. With reference to the more highly paid professionals and skilled workers, he emphasized that these pensions were a way of encouraging them to remain at their city jobs longer, rather than retire at a relatively young age to take another job. The police and firefighters were jealous of the DC 37 leap forward since they felt that in comparison to the average public servant, their work involved far greater risk.[20]

THE PENSION FIGHT:
"THE FATTEST, SLOPPIEST STRIKE"

Having long resented Gotbaum's tirades against his Taylor Law and the DC 37 leading opposition to his candidacy, Governor Rockefeller was adamant in his hostility toward this new pension plan. Generally suspicious of the big city and its big unions, upstate Republican lawmakers came out strongly against the new "giveaway." Despite traditional endorsement of local pension initiatives, the governor and Republican legislative leaders refused to permit the 1971 state legislature to vote on these new pensions. The patience of the rank and file was running out, for they were terribly upset by the steady media blitz and public attacks on them. One of their supporters at this time, Congressman Edward Koch, fired off a telegram to the Republican leaders, insisting that "collective bargaining agreements already made in good faith must be honored and unions' bargaining rights in future contracts must not be restricted." As far as newspapers were concerned, only the *Amsterdam News* and the civil service weekly, *The Chief*, condemned the role of the Republicans.

Exacerbating the situation and adding fury to the frustrations of labor leaders, was Rockefeller's bill establishing a commission to oversee all pension proposals, factoring their costs and evaluating their impact. Angered by the intransigence of Rockefeller and the Republican lawmakers, Gotbaum warned that "they leave me no recourse but to visit upon this city the biggest, fattest, sloppiest strike we have ever seen."[21]

In a final attempt to force state consideration of the pension agreements, Feinstein and Gotbaum resorted to a strike which, in the end, proved costly and self-defeating. DC 37 pursued a selective strike strategy, limiting the number of involved locals. Some 8,000 workers, largely from the blue-collar work force in sewers, parks, and incinerators, were involved. Parks and beaches were closed, and raw sewage was permitted to flow into the waterways of the city and suburban areas. The Teamsters gave special drama to the first day of the strike when its bridge tenders "opened" 27 drawbridges, bringing much of the city's traffic to a standstill on one of the hottest days in June. Thousands of fuming suburbanites and city residents were trapped in their cars, unable to move.

The strike boomeranged, for the union's actions did not impact upon state lawmakers but embittered great numbers of city and suburban dwellers. In two days it was all over. OCB officials worked doggedly for an agreement, which labor quickly accepted; the pension bill would be presented again at the next legislative session, and if it did not receive proper consideration and enact-

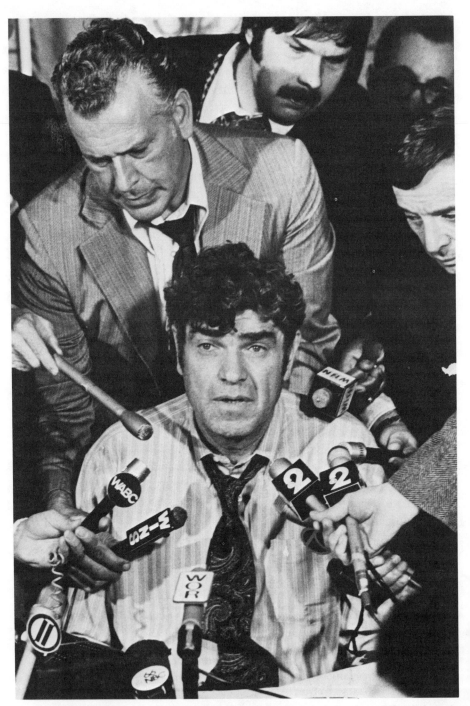

Embattled Gotbaum and Teamster leader Barry Feinstein seek to defend their decision to halt traffic as a protest against the refusal of Governor Rockefeller and Republican legislative leaders to permit a vote on pension agreements reached with the Lindsay administration in 1971.

ment, the city would offer an alternative plan to circumvent state involvement.

For weeks, the barrage of media attacks against public unions continued unabated. Public resentment welled up against DC 37 and its director, ignoring completely the provocative role played by Rockefeller and Republican lawmakers. While the *Daily News* denounced the strike as a "dastardly crime," the *New York Times* attacked it as "illegal and irresponsible." Tom Wicker, usually considered a friend of labor, stormed that these public workers sought private gain at the expense of the citizenry. In more biting language, James Reston warned that while labor had organized in order to fight the arbitrary powers of employers, ". . .it is now using the power of violence to achieve its own ends."

The DC 37 leadership and its members were obliged to assume the responsibility for pay lost for one or two days on strike, and a Taylor Act penalty of one day's pay for each day out. The contributions from locals amounted to $600,000, and from that of the Council and International some $150,000. The monumental task of paying thousands of union members who had struck took months of staff time. Eventually, the union also had to pay Nassau County $13,000 to defray its legal expenses incurred in a $1 million lawsuit filed against the union for permitting raw sewage to pollute its beaches.[22]

Feinstein admitted, years later, that he had misjudged the consequences of his action, and viewed the strike as a failure. He explained, "It was a last-ditch effort at a moment in time when we felt that there was still a glimmer of hope of bringing the bill to a vote. . . . It didn't work but it seemed the right thing to do at the time." Sensitive to the stinging criticsm hurled at him from all sides, Gotbaum sought the assistance of a public relations firm in presenting the union's views. Selected notables and friends of DC 37 signed newspaper advertisements. The union bought commercial time for its own TV program, and Gotbaum appeared in a never-ending round of interviews. The membership had to be reassured by individual mailings that the strike was justified.

Suddenly, prior to new wage negotiations for nonuniformed public employees, the city claimed it was unable to give more than cost-of-living increases and the usual fringe benefits. Since 1966 the Lindsay strategy had focused on raising wages and improving pensions, for most contracts had provided for raises of 8–10 percent annually. Thousands of hospital workers at the bottom of the lad-

Copyright © 1971 New York News Inc. Reprinted by permission.

der had received higher percentage increases so as to lift them from a status "no better than that of a welfare recipient." To attract qualified professionals, and in attempts to forestall raids by private industry, the wage increases for nurses, lawyers, accountants, and other professionals had been about 10 percent. But with an economic crisis now afflicting the nation and the city, Lindsay asked DC 37 to temper its demands for further gains.[23]

THE WORKPLACE: IMPROVING CONDITIONS

Besides the delivery of excellent contracts between 1966 and 1970, the Union was concerned with conditions in the workplace.

Speaking of Biggest, Sloppiest, Nastiest ...

Copyright © 1971 New York News Inc. Reprinted by permission.

Perhaps the most dramatic and frustrating example of the Council's involvement in such situations was with the public hospitals. After Local 420 members complained bitterly of distressing work conditions, a number of studies and governmental investigations described the inhumane treatment of hospital workers, poor and inadequate equipment, dangerous physical conditions for patients, and a chronic shortage of trained personnel at some hospitals. Over $100,000 of new equipment was said to be unnecessary and unusable at Fordham and had been turned over to its voluntary affiliate.

Major deficiencies in all 21 municipal hospitals were uncovered by a study of the United Hospital Fund, such as lack of professional and supporting personnel, mainly nurses, serious deficiencies in plant maintenance, and shortages of essential supplies. A five-month audit by the comptroller disclosed that a "morass of mismanagement" had shortchanged patients and taxpayers. "Through ignorance or abdication of responsibility, the Hospital Department," he concluded, "just doesn't know what is going on." He found misplacement, misuses, loss of equipment, waste and larceny, inadequate patient care, supplementation of doctors' payrolls by voluntary hospitals in violation of affiliation arrangements, conflicts of interest from persons being on two payrolls, and diversion of funds to items not properly expendable under the affiliation program.

At Lincoln Hospital in the Bronx, where city doctors complained bitterly about shortages of equipment, State Senator Seymour Thaler found two unused, fully equipped endocrinology laboratories. He charged the city with losing over $100 million the previous four years due to payroll padding and other abuses by voluntary hospital doctors and administrators. He blamed the affiliation program for most ills, adding that this experiment had not raised the quality of service within the municipal hospital system.[24]

In response, top hospital administrators and city officials characterized Thaler's charges as "irresponsible," a "gross exaggeration," and "heartless and reckless." A New York Times editorial called the senator's charges "lurid," "sweeping," and "unsupported." And yet, before the end of 1966, Mayor Lindsay conceded "neglect and decline" in the city hospitals and recognized that many of Thaler's charges were valid. But, he maintained, the previous administrations were at fault.[25]

Within a few months after assuming the editorship of the union newspaper, Bernard Stephens realized that the hospitals provided PEP with its first opportunity to pursue a new, investigatory role. As a result of extensive research and photography by reporter Steve Lichtenstein, more details of debilitating conditions in municipal hospitals were uncovered. He found roaches and rodents at many hospitals, while tuberculosis patients at Kings County had no sheets or pillowcases, lying on pillows used by other patients. The rate of this disease afflicting workers at the hospital was enormously high when compared with other units of the system.

Despite a "crash program" of repair and renovation begun under a "state of emergency" decreed by Commissioner Joseph V. Terenzio, Stephens and Lichtenstein collated extensive damning material, including dramatic photographs of a deteriorating hospital system. In one PEP issue, in late 1967, Stephens set aside half of its 20 pages for the first of a series of indictments of hospital administrators, charging waste, corruption, and negligence. Shortly before the series began, the findings were incorporated in a lengthy letter to the mayor in which the union's leadership charged the hospitals with widespread waste and inefficiency along with a conspiracy to downgrade and destroy the entire city system, "so that it can be turned over piecemeal and at bargain basement prices to the voluntary hospitals." Tens of millions of dollars were reported to have been handed over to the voluntaries through the affiliation program, "much of it proven to have found its way into the pockets of doctors and administrators, while the city hospitals are starved of funds to the point where lives of patients and employees are actually endangered." The city had made available large sums of money to the voluntary affiliation hospitals without red tape and without detailed explanations, while its own hospitals were strapped by lack of funds to repair deteriorating facilities and to fill openings where personnel was desperately needed. The letter ended with a request that the mayor condemn these conditions and reaffirm that "the city believes in and will reconstruct a municipal hospital system second to none."[26]

On the day that Stephens and his staff were busily preparing the final copy of the hospital exposé, the editor was suddenly called to Gotbaum's office. There he found Terenzio and two assistant commissioners. The union head asked his wary editor to listen to the commissioner, who had read the union's letter to the mayor detailing the deplorable hospital situation. Terenzio was also aware that he was about to be blasted in the Council's newspaper. The commissioner displayed deep concern about the deplorable conditions, contending that the unsatisfactory state of affairs was the accumulation of years of underfinancing, inadequate maintenance, insufficient replacement of equipment, and marginal inventories of supplies. In his defense he insisted that he was correcting these deficiencies as expeditiously as possible. The commissioner then requested that he be permitted to have inserted, alongside the exposé, his own explanation. While Gotbaum seemed receptive to the request, Lillian Roberts exploded, "I'm tired of winning victories in the dark." Because of her daily, intimate contact with hospital workers depressed by enervating working conditions, she insisted that Stephens go to press immediately. Despite his rationale for momentary postponement, and under pressure to make a plane, Gotbaum turned to Stephens as he left and commented, "I'm leaving the decision up to you."[27]

Within hours, the printing presses began to roll, and the brightly colored PEP front page read in bold black headlines: "Exposed! The Plot to Destroy the City Hospitals." The lower part displayed a picture of an overcrowded ward in a city hospital. Inside was a series of stark color pictures showing broken windows in Bellevue's employees' lounge, collapsing walls at Lincoln, the bedpan sterilizer at Kings County taped shut, ceilings collapsing at Cumberland, decrepit beds with torn mattresses at Greenpoint, a pool of stagnant water on a broken floor in a kitchen at Kings County, and a tub full of soapy water with a pair of hands replacing a broken dishwasher at Seaview.

In a slashing attack against Terenzio, Roberts denounced his failure to provide decent conditions, charging him with attempting to unload the municipal system instead of preserving it. Public hospitals, she insisted, had to be preserved because in many parts of the city there were no other facilities for the needy, disadvantaged minorities who often found admittance to voluntaries difficult, if not impossible.[28]

Learning that City Hall was discussing the lease of Bellevue to New York University, and of other municipal hospitals to voluntary institutions, the DC 37 leadership quickly threatened to close down the entire hospital system. The mayor and his top health aides responded, initially, by denying that there was any plan to lease or sell city hospitals other than James Ewing to Memorial Cancer. But the city comptroller, Procaccino, immediately labeled the mayor's denials false, insisting that his office had information on discussions already held with voluntary hospitals concerning the "leasing or turning over" of Coney Island, Greenpoint, Seaview, Delafield, Bellevue, and Ewing. He warned the Lindsay administration that he would not permit this giveaway, especially in light of new state and Federal resources to help subsidize the city system.

After first denying the union's list of charges, City Hall began a quiet, steady retreat. The union's exposé and the spotlight from Senator Thaler and other investigative bodies insured changes in strategy. Lindsay suddenly requested additional funds for emergency renovations and for rebuilding several municipal hospitals. Assistant Commissioner Howard Brown admitted what PEP had alleged all along, that Medicaid and Medicare could pay for most of it.[29]

Confronted with the threat of DC 37 to resort to the courts for speedier action, and alerted to the forthcoming report of his own special committee, which would reveal "deplorable conditions" in the hospitals, Lindsay invited Gotbaum and Roberts to City Hall. The mayor promised that the city would not go out of the hospital business. Conceding that he had been unaware of the seriousness of conditions, he expressed his willingness to upgrade the hospitals. Before the DC 37 leaders he directed Commissioner Terenzio to immediately prepare a timetable for correcting the situation. Implementation of the general hospital cleanup was soon evident in the individual institutions.[30]

These were momentary successes, however, in a never-ending battle with hospital administrators. During the months that followed, the municipal hospitals seemed to remain in a state of perpetual crisis.

SUMMARY

In the context of taking command of this growing union, Gotbaum and his colleagues confronted a work force that required constant attention. Improving conditions in the workplace was of major significance, but was only one of many challenges to which the leaders and staff had to respond.

The first phase of Gotbaum's leadership was characterized by tremendous growth in Council membership. In the process, he successfully prevented his predecessor from interfering with his leadership and control of the Council, made peace with Feinstein of the Teamsters, and delivered to the members a series of contracts which dramatically improved their economic status, heightened their dignity, and expanded their expectations and aspirations. The union's growing cohesion and influence made it far more effective at the bargaining table and when pressuring for humane working conditions. During a period when organized labor was generally on the defensive, if not declining, DC 37 displayed its increasing strength and effectiveness. Within a few short years, the union was able to raise the basic minimum wage of exploited hospital unionists from $3,500 to $7,000, and deliver to them and their families extensive medical and educational services. Although serious problems remained in the public hospitals and elsewhere, and the base pay provided only the barest subsistence, the rising spirit and loyalty of union members was increasingly apparent, particularly in Hospital Local 420.

In the next chapter, we turn to institution building as the Council and its leadership develop the organization and recruit a talented staff to serve members in what was to become a pioneering effort in the union movement.

NOTES

1. Finance committee minutes, April 14, 1965; April 14, May 3, and July 13, 1966.

2. Finance committee minutes, July 13 and September 27, 1966; DC 37 executive board minutes, January 11, February 23, 1967. The executive director's salary was increased from just over $15,000 to $18,000 on October 1, 1966 and to $21,000 on July 1, 1967, along with an expense account. Associate directors were increased from $12,000 to $15,000; negotiations director from $10,400 to $12,500; special representatives from $9,620 to $11,800.

3. PEP, April 19, 1967, p. 2; August 23, 1967, p. 5. Among the early activists and voluntary organizers were John Crumedy, Dorothy Brown, Dorothy McLean, Herbert Hynes, Foster Burton and Joe Jacone.

4. Public Employee Press, April 29, 1966, p. 8. Also, leaflets issued by "Housing Authority Division of DC 37," April 15, 20, 22, June 8, 9, 20, 1966; Al Santiago to Bert Rose, May 5, 1966.

5. The Chief, October 21, 1966, p. 1; District Council meeting minutes, November 22, 1966; interview with Barry Feinstein, April 22, 1981.

6. Interview with Barry Feinstein, April 22, 1981.

7. Executive board minutes, December 13, 1967 and January 10, 1968. Also, interviews with Barry Feinstein, April 22, 1981; Bert Rose, September 16, 1981; Louis Yavner, April 18, 1982.

8. New York Times, December 10, 1966, p. 34; December 11, 1966, p. 36. Public Employee Press, December 14, 1966, p. 3. When the Career and Salary Plan was adopted in 1954, public employee unionism was in its formative stages and could not challenge the contention that it exemplified the most advanced thinking in the field of personnel management. Twelve years later, a vast majority of city employees belonged to unions. Lindsay accepted the advice of the Budget and Personnel directors, and of organized labor that the pay plan regulations and salary grade structure, accompanying the Career and Salary Plan, constituted a hindrance rather than a help in collective bargaining and in the recruitment and retention of qualified personnel. The mayor then proposed to exempt from the general pay plan regulations those civil service titles for which unions held valid

collective bargaining certificates. Thus, the Career and Salary Plan would no longer be used as a basis for wage negotiations for most of DC 37 members.

9. *Public Employee Press*, January 25, 1967, p. 3; December 27, 1967, p. 4. Evelyn Seinfeld, "Total Population of Divisions and Certain Locals—Historical Trends," July 21, 1982, DC 37 library files. Interview with Al Diop, March 2, 1984.

10.Under Section 220 of the Labor Law, wage rates of laborers were negotiated with the city comptroller. For purposes of collective bargaining on other labor relations matters, including grievances, however, all agencies were directed to deal with DC 37 and Locals 376 and 924.

11. *New York Times*, January 2, 1968, p. 36; January 3, 1968, p. 38; January 16, 1968, p. 30. Charles Morris, *The Cost of Good Intentions*, New York: W.W. Norton, 1980, pp. 103–106; Raymond Horton, *Municipal Labor Relations in New York City*, New York: Praeger Publishers, 1973, pp. 82–83; James Underwood and William Daniels, *Governor Rockefeller in New York*, Westport, CT: Greenwood Press, 1982, see especially pp. 230 and 311, note 84.

12. *New York Times*, January 28, 1968, p. 1; February 27, 1968, p. 1. *Daily News*, February 27, 1968, p. 3. For the full contract, see *Public Employee Press*, February 28, 1968, pp. 3–9.

13. *Public Employee Press*, March 29, 1967, p. 2; *New York Times*, October 25, 1967; April 12, 1968, p. 51.

14. Seymour Mann and Sheldon Mann, "Decision Dynamics and Organizational Characteristics: The AFSCME and NYC District Council 37." Paper delivered at American Political Science Association, San Francisco, California, September 2–5, 1975, pp. 25–26. Contracts that were to be effective on January 1, 1974, involved 17 units and 25,000 workers; those to be effective on July 1, 1974, embraced 28 units and 80,000 employees. By January 1, 1975, contracts for 12 units had to be negotiated for over 3,000 employees, and by July 1, 1975, contracts for 18 units involving more than 8,000 public sector workers had to be concluded. At any one moment, there were some 50 to 100 sets of negotiations under way. To their utter confusion and frustration, Nelson and his negotiating staff soon learned that what was legally or practically citywide had to be separated out from title issues at virtually each round of negotiations, and that what was purportedly bargainable under the New York City Collective Bargaining Law and Civil Service procedures was not always clear.

15. *Public Employee Press*, February 7, 1969, p. 3. *New York Times*, February 7, 1969, p. 1.

16. Dan Nelson memoranda to Gotbaum, November 12 and 13, 1969; interview with Alan Viani, February 26, 1982. The full citywide bargaining committee reached its conclusions at a weekend retreat after hearing reports from John Boer on civil service and career development; Lou Aliperta on the workweek, overtime and shift differentials; David Jacobson on pensions; Gerald Brooks on time and leave; Fannie Fine on personnel and pay practices; and Irving Baldinger on health and security.

17. Mann and Mann, "Decision Dynamics;" p. 40.

18. *Daily News*, January 5, 1970; p. 4. The gains in pension and health fund benefits were clear in money terms alone. It was expected that Council members would soon be receiving more money through higher retirement allowances, in-

creased take-home pay because of lower pension contributions, and better reimbursement for dental and medical bills. The city's per capita contributions to the health and security funds were increased substantially to $175 in January 1972, and to $250 a year later.

19. *Public Employee Press,* August 28, 1970, pp. 4–5; November 20, 1970, p. 3. Other civil service groups in the city had the 50 percent concept, but none of them was guaranteed a rate of 2.5 percent for each year up to 40 years of service.

20. *New York Times,* July 8, 1970, p. 39. *Daily News,* July 9, 1970, p. 53.

21. *New York Times,* May 4, 1971, p. 51. Edward I. Koch to Earl W. Bridges and Perry Duryea, May 6, 1971; *The Chief,* June 16, 1971.

22. *Daily News,* June 8, 1971, p. 39; *New York Times,* June 9, 1971, p. 43; *Public Employee Press,* April 22, 1972, p. 2. interview with Julius Topol, March 17, 1981.

23. *New York Times,* October 14, 1970, p. 1; November 18, 1970, p. 1; December 13, 1970, p. 85. Since 1966, Haber's Labor Relations Office had negotiated 438 settlements, of which only 43 went to fact-finding because of a temporary impasse.

24. *New York Times,* October 6, 1966, p. 1; October 12, 1966; p. 1, October 15, 1966, p. 1; November 2, 1966, p. 1; November 13, 1966, p. 70; November 15, 1966, p. 49; November 30, 1966, p. 51; December 8, 1966, p. 1. Under the affiliation program, public hospitals were supervised by a sister institution in the voluntary system, allegedly to improve personnel training and update treatment and facilities.

25. *New York Times,* December 10, 1966, p. 50; December 13, 1966, p. 46; December 19, 1966, p. 1.

26. *New York Times,* October 24, 1967, p. 1; *Public Employee Press,* October 25, 1967, p. 3.

27. *Public Employee Press,* December 27, 1967, p. 6. Also, interviews with Bernard Stephens, February 2, 1981; and Lillian Roberts, September 28, 1982.

28. *Public Employee Press,* October 25, 1967, p. 9.

29. *New York Times,* October 26, 1967, p. 63; November 14, 1967, p. 37. *Public Employee Press,* November 15, 1967, p. 3; December 6, 1967, p. 4.

30. Gotbaum and Roberts to John V. Lindsay, November 20, 1967; *New York Times,* December 16, 1967, p. 1.; December 24, 1967, p. 22; *Public Employee Press,* December 27, 1967, p. 6. At Bellevue, six new bedpan flushers were ordered; bedpan flushers were repaired in three wards; the amount of linen allocated was increased; several hundred new mattresses were contracted for delivery, along with new beds and other patient furnishings; the flooding in the clothes house, due to clogged pipes, was being remedied; and garbage in the elevator shaft was removed. At Greenpoint Hospital, the major locker areas were painted; two new respirators were ordered for immediate delivery; the defective bedpan flusher on Ward 3-A was made operational; broken wheelchairs were replaced; new equipment was distributed promptly to the in-patient service on high priority; and a major repair of the boiler was in progress. And on and on it went for emergency repairs at Lincoln, Queens General, Sea View, Coney Island, Kings County, and other city hospitals.

11
Inside Union Bureaucracy

Bureaucracy is an unavoidable consequence of modern society. The things the union movement does cannot be accomplished unless an organized group of men and women are employed to put its policies into effect. Once Gotbaum secured his position, he turned his energies to building the internal structure of the union. The major focus of activity under Wurf's direction had been organizing the unorganized. Thus, field activities were the primary concern of his staff. Charismatic and messianic in his zeal, Wurf concentrated on external affairs, neglecting internal management. Further, he demonstrated that he could not readily share power, refusing to delegate authority to subordinates; those who worked closely with him as organizers frequently found him interfering in their work. And when he became involved in the campaign for the presidency of the International, his attention to internal administration suffered even more. In taking command, Gotbaum found the administrative affairs of the Council in disarray and the allocation of responsibilities unclear.

In the following pages we examine the emergence and maturation of the DC 37 administrative organization and the key figures selected to help manage it. As outlined in Figure 11.1, four major components of the union's organization are examined: the executive director, top management, the departments, and the divisions.

The basis of the DC 37 structure is the local, for the size of its membership determines the number of representatives it elects to the delegates council, the highest policy-making body of the union. In turn, every two years the delegates council elects an executive

Successful collective bargaining negotiations involve careful planning, research and team effort by the union's bureaucracy. Director of Research and Negotiations since 1973, Al Viani (right) is joined by Al Diop (left), longtime president of Clerical Administrative Local 1549 and Stanley Hill (center), then staff director of the Clerical Administrative Division. Hill succeeded Lillian Roberts as Associate Director in 1981.

board, whose principal officers include the president, secretary, treasurer, 15 vice-presidents, and the executive director. In addition, the "five percent locals," those whose memberships constitute at least five percent of the Council's total, each elect a vice-president. It is the executive board, chaired by the president although influenced primarily by the executive director, that is key to the union's power structure, for it determines policy positions which are reviewed but rarely overturned by the delegates council.[1] It is the executive board that serves as the coordinating and centralizing mechanism of the union. Despite the Council's growth and influence, however, the large locals retain considerable autonomy, and the presence of their respective leaders as vice-presidents on the executive board serves as another mechanism for local input. As with any federated system, the ongoing relationships between locals and the executive board is a dynamic one, and, on occasion, a point of tension in the union's internal politics. Nevertheless, over the years the District Council has become the predominant element, the unquestioned advocate in the negotiations process and the prime agency for delivering services to members directly.

The leadership of the Council is vested in the office of the executive director. The constitution affords him substantial power to develop and supervise the organization, interpret board policies, determine the strategies of collective bargaining legislative affairs, control the internal communications system, and make important appointments. Thomas Cronin, political scientist and student of the U.S. presidency, has suggested that leadership and management are not the same. Although an effective manager may often be a successful leader, and leadership requires a number of the skills of the manager, there are basic differences between the two. "Leaders," he writes, "are the people who infuse vision into an organization or society. At their best, they are preoccupied with values and the long-range needs and aspirations of their followers. Managers are concerned with doing things *the right way.*"[2]

GOTBAUM AS MANAGER

Recognizing the need for tighter structure, Gotbaum began to shape the Council organization and establish specific procedures. Since the policies, personnel, and tone of the organization were essentially fashioned by the executive director, it is important that we review some of the major influences affecting his behavior.

Professor Eric Polisar of Cornell's School for Industrial and Labor Relations had been an adviser to Wurf and continued in that capacity under the new Council leadership. Youthful, bright, and totally dedicated, he shared Gotbaum's enthusiasm as well as his values and orientation. They enjoyed each other's intellectual exchanges, spending endless hours discussing, and often heatedly debating, union policies and contemporary politics. As an invaluable adviser and boundless source of vital information, Polisar guided

FIGURE 11.1: Organization of DC 37

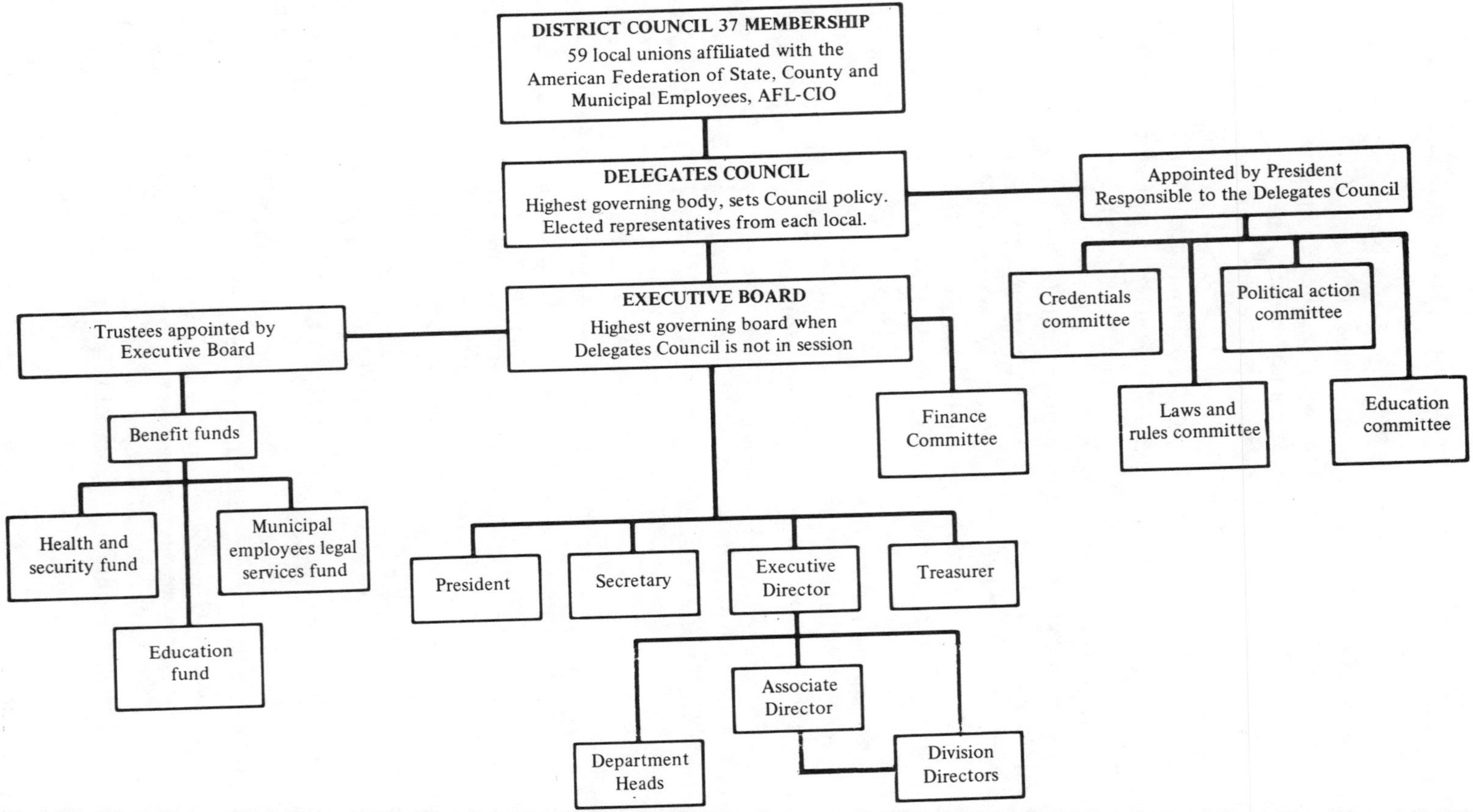

the new director in building the internal structure of the union. He counseled executive board members, local officials, and those revising the Council's constitution. Polisar also sought to serve as a mediator between Gotbaum and Wurf, easing developing tensions caused by the efforts of the new International president to retain the reins of power in New York City. Polisar's untimely death in July 1968 was a serious blow to Gotbaum, for it meant the loss of his closest and most helpful adviser in the early development of the Council's bureaucracy. For a time, it left him disheartened and depressed.

Another key figure was Sakiko Miyashiro, known to all since Chicago days as Saki. In 1966, she was brought to New York as executive secretary to Gotbaum. A mild-mannered, unassuming, and deceptively quiet Hawaiian, Saki gave herself to the cause of unionism. Sensitive to the director's needs and aspirations, and quickly mastering communications with the influential in government, business and politics, she has calmly juggled incessant telephone calls and appointments with a judicious temperament, comparative ease, and the utmost of quiet efficiency. With a strong commitment to organized labor and to the rank and file, she senses what should be brought to Gotbaum's attention and acts accordingly. When she deems it necessary, she makes her position clear on vital issues and sensitive personnel matters. By resorting, occasionally, to her form of "silent treatment" of the executive director, she has been able to convey a questioning attitude and ensure reappraisal of a decision.[3]

ORGANIZATIONAL IMPERATIVES

A major challenge to the new leadership was the need to integrate the disparate character of the union, the independent traditions among large locals and the differences of status, income, race, and education among members. Gotbaum realized that internal cohesion and unity were essential to effective collective bargaining and influencing public policies. To further these goals, a departmental organization, headed by his own appointees, was put in place by the director. In addition, a team of three administrators was selected as part of his top management. While building the centralizing mechanisms, however, he recognized the need for vitalizing and encouraging the local as a basic element in the growth of the Council. To ensure and enhance the input of locals, a divisional structure was established.

Gotbaum's recruitment policies reflected the dual federated structure: professionally trained outsiders for the departments and rank-and-file leaders for the divisions. While recognizing the importance of "business unionism" set down by Samuel Gompers, he sought staff who shared his broader societal concerns. Another important aspect of his personnel policies was to identify individuals who were experienced self-starters, who could assume and retain major responsibilities on their own initiative. The executive director's style was to delegate substantial authority and encourage development of new ideas and simply "not cluck over them." He reportedly insisted, "I'm not a grad of Harvard Business School nor an expert in public administration. I only know my own needs as an administrator. Basically, I try to select competent staff and then let them run the show. It's hands off."

Gotbaum found it difficult to discharge incompetent staff members. Generally, he hesitated to act, hoping that somehow these individuals would leave of their own accord or simply fade away. Only when he suspected that they were disloyal to the Council or to Lillian Roberts would he act decisively. Consequently, there were some staff members who were retained long beyond their period of effectiveness, who created, as a result, internal dissension, interpersonal tension, and occasionally a critical emergency. It was labor consultant Lois Gray who, when reviewing the Council's training needs, noted that, "The size and complexity of organizational structure and the lack of free-flowing networks of communications have, from time to time, resulted in unanticipated crises."[4]

TOP MANAGEMENT

When Gotbaum took over DC 37 there were two hold-over associate directors; one soon resigned and the other retired in a few years. Under the constitution, associate directors are designated as the director's assistants, but are required to have executive board approval. Their assignments are ambiguous, left to the director to determine. Lillian Roberts advanced from special representative to division director of hospitals, and finally, to the second most important post in the Council, associate director in charge of organization. Responsible for overseeing field operations managed by the divisions, her work included supervision of grievances, monitoring field staff activities, and handling external agency relationships. Division directors reported directly to her. Not only was she responsible for directing important staff operations but, because of her close personal association with Gotbaum going back to Chicago days, she came closest to playing the role of a confidant to the executive director. Having developed a deep loyalty to the labor movement, she was one of a small number of black leaders who saw unions as an agency for greater equity and social justice for minorities. Along with her commitment and idealism, she had the strength to stand up to, argue with, and even challenge, Gotbaum. The latter held her in high esteem, respecting her limitless devotion to the rank and file, her understanding of minority thinking and problems, her judgment in and insight into union problems, and her gentle but determined handling of city officials.

A second associate director, Edward Maher, was charged with administrative in-house matters involving staff, housekeeping relating to the physical quality of headquarters, and logistics with regard to conferences, transportation, and demonstrations. Having come up through the ranks from special representative to assistant to Jerry Wurf, his appointment was an attempt to transfer the loyalty of the old-timers to the new leadership. While formally part of top management, Maher did not play as intimate a role in the decision making of the executive director as did Roberts. But his administrative activities freed Gotbaum of details that he disliked. In later years, interpersonal difficulties between some staff members and Maher evoked tensions, eventually leading to his retirement.

The Council treasurer, Arthur Tibaldi, has played an increasingly important role at the top level of leadership. In effect, he can be viewed as another associate director. Tibaldi began his civil service career as an accountant and volunteer organizer for DC 37. He soon became president of his local, a position he still retains. After reviewing the accounting practices of the Council and finding them in serious disarray, he accepted the invitation of the executive director to take a leave of absence from his city post and create the union's Finance Department. Elected treasurer of the Council, his part-time assignment soon became full time. Mild-mannered and unobtrusive in style, he emerged as the principal fiscal adviser to the director, the Council's business manager, its chief property officer and the major link between the executive director's office and the quasi-independent boards of trustees that govern the union's special funds—Health and Security, Education, and MELS.

Tibaldi brought onto his staff Shaurain Farber, and together they built the financial system and established procedures for the organization, reducing the steep fees formerly paid to outside firms. As his importance rose within Council circles, Tibaldi displayed a rigorous conservatism in the disposition of union funds. Yet his sensitivity and positive response to the Council's innovative spirit won him increasing respect and admiration from imaginative staff members. Known for his honesty and integrity, proponents of new proposals often solicited in advance his advice and guidance as to their financial feasibility. If there is a legitimate and responsible way, Tibaldi will find it. Personnel matters are also under his direction, and he now negotiates new contracts with the internal staff unions.[5] This top management of the Council clearly reflected the executive director's personnel policies: two came from outside the New York union and two from the rank and file. They shared his progressive advocacy, and they represented the typical balanced ticket sought by the best of politicians—women and men of a variety of ethnic and religious backgrounds reflecting the union's membership.

THE FIRST TEAM: DEPARTMENTS

Within a year after taking command, Gotbaum put into operation an expanded departmental structure, the specialized professional arm of the Council. He created his own in-house legal staff, expanded the collective bargaining services into the Department of Research and Negotiations, vitalized the union newspaper, and established the Departments of Education as well as Political Action and Legislation. Shortly, thereafter, he created Health and Security.[6]

Research and Negotiations: Daniel Nelson

Daniel Nelson served for 15 years as an economist and research specialist at the ILGWU. When Gotbaum sought professional experienced assistance for collective bargaining, he was frequently referred to Nelson. Impressed with his commitment and independence of mind, Gotbaum convinced him to head the Council's Department of Research. In the intervening years, until his unexpected death in August 1973, Nelson became a source of strength in the negotiations process. With only three aides he conducted the entire operation for the tens of thousands of union members. On short notice he also wrote briefs, researched issues, and served as adviser to Gotbaum on a wide range of complex economic matters. The negotiations director had phenomenal command of statistics and could quickly grasp the import of discussions, making him a respected figure among city representatives. His sharp mind and speedy decision making endeared him to Gotbaum, staff members, and local officers, and he soon became an institution at DC 37. During the most difficult of negotiating sessions, when both sides were tensely locked in battle, he could generally be relied on to come up with a compromise to lower tensions.

Legal Department: Julius Topol

Gotbaum was soon convinced that with the expense of outside legal consultants mounting steadily, and his need for constant legal advice and guidance, he could use an in-house legal staff. In 1966, shortly after the executive board approved the idea, he selected Julius Topol, associate general counsel of the ILGWU.

For 20 years, Topol, a soft-spoken intellectual, had been in private and labor practice, becoming an expert in utilizing the Taft–Hartley Act to protect union organizing drives in the South. His imaginative approach and progressive advocacy attracted Gotbaum's attention. Although anxious to leave the ILGWU, Topol made the move with some misgivings, for he knew little about the public sector. Immediately, however, he was thrust into the legislative phase of the new collective bargaining law evolving under Mayor Lindsay's administration. From that moment he was actively involved in the public work scene in New York. He hoped that by replacing mayoral domination (typified by Robert Wagner's role playing) with an impartially designed procedure under the OCB, it would help avert the need for public worker strikes.

Topol developed a close working relationship with Gotbaum on the legal aspects of union work. He observed that Gotbaum did not share the broader aspects of his thinking with others, except possibly with Lillian Roberts. Instead of a cabinet style of consultation, Gotbaum tended to work individually with each department head. During the long period of the fiscal crisis, he depended increasingly on Jack Bigel for financial guidance in complex, drawnout negotiations. It was then that Topol saw an opportunity for more imaginative involvement in developing a prepaid legal service for Council members and thereupon asked to be relieved as general counsel and assigned new responsibilities.[7]

Public Employee Press: Bernard Stephens

Since 1967 the International Labor Press Association has given PEP more commendations than any other union newspaper. Within a 14-year period, it won 66 major awards. The judges' commentary on one of these occasions seems to capture the essence of the newspaper's quality:

> Issue after issue, this hard-charging publication pounds away at local, national and international problems, always concentrating on what it all means to the individual workers. Profiles, human interest features, job and community interests, classified ads and strong graphics combine with a hard news punch to produce a first-class union newspaper. This journal will have no trouble competing with the commercial press in the homes of its members.[8]

The newspaper provides a key communication network for members, particularly local officers, staff and activists. In a 1973 survey of Council members, the report disclosed an unusually high readership for a union newspaper: 64 percent of overall membership responded that two newspapers they read frequently were PEP and the *Daily News*. Among union activists, however, some 78 percent were frequent readers of PEP.

Tall, warm-hearted, and soft-spoken, Bernard Stephens had been part of the radical student movement at New York's City College in the 1930s. He followed a progressive political path throughout his adult years, and during the 1960s was an outspoken opponent of the war in Vietnam. For 12 years he had been managing editor and then acting editor of the newspaper for the Retail, Wholesale and Department Store Workers. When his union president succumbed to pressure from the AFL–CIO to suppress antiwar sentiments in the organization's paper, Stephens decided it was time to leave. Disenchanted with the sterility of the extreme Old Left and repelled by the increasing conservatism of most unions, Stephens made himself available when he learned that DC 37 was in search of a newspaper editor.

Stephens was immediately impressed with Gotbaum's "freshness, vibrance and imaginative quality," which he found sadly lacking among other union leaders. Recalling him as "less doctrinaire or rigid than most," he felt that the Council leader exhibited a youthful enthusiasm and optimism that infected those about him. Advised that he would be given a free hand in running the paper, Stephens accepted the job, even though it meant a reduction in salary.[9]

During the next 15 years, the new editor developed the biweekly *Public Employee Press* (PEP) into one of the crucial communication mechanisms of the Council and a star among union newspapers. When he took over in 1966 he found a patchwork publication produced by two dedicated, hard-working individuals, June Ringel and Steve Lichtenstein. The new editor brought to his assignment a well-planned concept of what he wanted PEP to become, modeling it on the United Auto Workers' publication, *Solidarity*. The newspaper was to be an educational tool and stimulate increased participation of members in union activities. In addition, it would expose wrongdoing among public and private institutions and crusade for social justice and human concerns. While quiet in personal demeanor, Stephens' journalistic style was hard-hitting and formidable. In the muckraking tradition of Lincoln Steffens, the investigatory reporting of PEP made it a fighting partisan paper for municipal employees. Gotbaum responded warmly and gave Stephens freedom and financial support.

The media have often criticized the city's civil servants for laziness and neglect in attending to their responsibilities. In one of its biting editorials, the *New York Times* on June 29, 1971, p. 36 suggested that

> The prevailing attitude among public employees here seems to be one of how little work they can do for how much more pay. One can see the clerks at work; chatting with each other, settling personal financial accounts, catching up with their newspaper reading, or just daydreaming.

Shortly thereafter, PEP reporter William Schleicher paid a surprise visit to the offices of the *Times* and snapped a number of revealing photographs. When cornered by security guards, he held on to his camera tightly, claiming his rights under freedom of the press. Eventually, one of the editors recommended that he be released, possibly appreciative of the fact that arresting Schleicher might prove damaging to the public image of the *Times*. In the following issue PEP ran a dramatic spread of pictures, showing *Times* employees chatting, relaxing, and seemingly "daydreaming." Under the photos, the reporter wrote that "Many *Times* staffers were hard at work. We simply pointed our camera at those who were not working. That's selective reporting, à la the *Times* editorial."[10]

Walter Balcerak, a gifted writer guided by a concern for the membership, won an award for an article showing how an average worker confronted spiraling inflation. Its "humanistic spirit" attracted the judges. Richard Niles's art has for years added an exceptionally attractive graphic quality to the paper's design. A union member who eventually formed his own company, artist Stan Glaubach gave his time to the paper with little remuneration because of his dedication to the labor movement and DC 37. The staff reporters—Geri Ruth, Bill Schleicher, Alan Howard, Michael Rosenbaum, and others—up from the ranks, have been skilled at giving stories a strong human quality. They artfully weave stories with cogent, readable prose for a readership with varied educational backgrounds.

Other key figures on the first team included Sumner Rosen at Education (the first to leave, in a little over two years, and who was replaced by Bernard Rifkind) and John Corcoran for Political Action and Legislation. This first group included highly specialized experts with an extensive labor background. They appreciated the bread-and-butter concerns of workers as well as the broader viewpoint of the executive director. In addition, they were attracted to DC 37 for the wide scope it afforded them and the opportunity for innovation.

AN EMERGING SECOND TEAM

Al Viani, who replaced Daniel Nelson in Research and Negotiations in 1973, was a young social worker. He emerged as an active rank-and-filer at a critical moment in the history of Local 371, becoming its president, and then was selected by Nelson as his assistant. Mastering the skills of the negotiating process, and with a keen ear for the feelings of members, Viani expanded the department to assist in the growing complex of activities required of the burgeoning union. With the help of Bart Cohen and Marcia Lamel, rank-and-file recruits, and Reuben Rosenberg, the department staff became increasingly proficient in the bargaining game. In the process, Viani developed a practical, much utilized library to assist locals and Council staff in their daily search for information on contracts, salaries, titles, and statistical data. Even city officials find it useful, often calling for a varied assortment of information. Operating in an incredibly crowded space, with shelves of reports and documents overflowing onto tables, chairs, and the floor, librarian Evelyn Seinfeld knows exactly where to find almost any information requested.

Research and Negotiations recruited an academically trained economist, Dr. Carol O'Cleireacain, who was assigned responsibility for analyzing data on wages, pensions, and benefits, and for preparing pertinent background material for Council bargaining strategy. She also reviews and collates pertinent information relating to other public unions and cities across the nation, and prepares special position papers on the cost of living, the impact of inflation on workers, and economic trends.

The growing outreach of the union was a response to increasing attacks on public workers and requests for information, policy positions, as well as interviews with Gotbaum. In 1974 Edward Handman, who had served previously as consultant, was appointed to head Public Relations. A few years later all publications, including PEP, were placed under his responsibility as head of the department. But the newspaper continues to operate on its own, edited by Walter Balcerak, since Bernard Stephens's retirement.

After a long search Beverly Gross was appointed to replace Julius Topol as general counsel in 1977. It was with some reservations that top management accepted its first woman as a department head, particularly for the Legal Department. This may have been due to personal prejudice, their own anxieties or an uneasiness as to how this appointment would be received by other staff members and among the locals. With time and tireless devotion to the needs of the membership, she won acceptance for her professionalism, directness and mastery of work responsibilities. Like many of her colleagues in other departments, Beverly came from a strong union background. And her legal experiences with city and state governments, particularly in the field of human rights, strengthened her knowledge of, and sensitivity toward, discrimination against minorities and women, insuring a successful affirmative action program within her department.

In taking command, she systematized the department, allocating to all the lawyers an equitable share of the grievance cases that reached arbitration. Her own responsibilities include litigation, larger policy questions, and legal assistance to the Council, the locals, and staff. Through persistent attendance at meetings of locals and Council bodies, and by having Legal staff steadily available, she helped overcome the feelings of distance between lawyers and union members.[11]

Nat Lindenthal's replacement at Health and Security was Roslyn Yasser, who served for some time as acting administrator. Again, the uneasiness and hesitancy in selecting a woman to head a department was clearly evident. But during the months that followed, her warm interpersonal relationships, respect for department employees, and her ability to master the intricacies of vast programs won her universal acceptance and respect. The "acting" was soon dropped before administrator, and in a period of rising consciousness the union took increasing pride in having women head two important departments.

THE INEVITABILITY OF OLIGARCHY?

Robert Michels, Will Herberg, and Clark Kerr have concluded that in organizations, including unions, there is a tendency for power to concentrate at the top. As functions multiply and responsibilities increase, the very nature of the organization facilitates an oligarchical structure. The trend is toward complete bureaucratic administration—that is, a group of professional functionaries, especially selected and trained, comes to control organizational life by replacing the more primitive self-administration of the rank and file of earlier days. Thus, as unions become functioning, sophisticated structures, there is less and less need for members to be active, except on those rare occasions of direct conflict with management. Although not necessarily the fault of leadership, so the argument goes, it is the normal run of things. Members accept this state of affairs because they don't want self-government, but prefer, instead, protection and service, their "money's worth" for their dues.[12]

This view holds that members are traditionally apathetic, that soon the old "fire" is gone and the early organizing militancy is dormant. With membership interest waning, leadership assumes greater discretion, facilitating increased organizational conservatism. Upon examining the multifaceted programs and services offered by DC 37, in this and subsequent chapters, it is clear that bureaucratization enabled union officials to assume and exercise increased powers. But this did not necessarily determine the way in which they were to be exercised. Staff authority and discretion did not automatically follow a conservative path in DC 37, but continued to produce reformist goals, impulses, and achievements. Michael Hayes offers an explanation that poignantly applies to the departmental staff and their programs. In paraphrasing the work of James Wilson and others, Hayes suggests that

> Only in organizations, where maintenance problems are largely solved will slack resources or surplus profits exist sufficient to permit the discretion necessary to attract and hold professionalized staff members interested in purposive rewards. Moreover, only such groups will possess the combination of resources, prestige, and professional reputation necessary for effective influence on behalf of reformist objectives.[13]

In DC 37, staff members were given broad scope in their respective tasks and exceptional opportunities for their "reformist" impulses. While many were attracted by decent union salaries, key members knew they could enhance their professional standing with the support of the Council's expanding resources. Sharing Gotbaum's vision bolstered their enthusiasm for innovation and commitment to change.

DIVISIONS

The divisions constitute the union's field operation, for they are the direct link to the locals and the membership. The divisional structure serves to accommodate two equally important pressures that sometimes pull the Council and its leadership in different directions. The centripetal force represents the need for cohesion at the Council level, facilitating effective bargaining, efficient protection for processing grievances and extending benefits. The centrifugal tug is from the grass roots, expressing the needs and concerns of the membership, largely through the locals and their leadership. Local pressures have the potential for divisiveness and fragmentation, requiring, as a result, that Council leadership and staff be alert to the needs and sensitivities of these units and work closely with them.

Each division is headed by a director and assistant director, appointed initially by the executive director, and supervised by the associate director for organization. Other staff includes Council representatives, paid by the union, and full-and part-time grievance representatives who are on released time from their municipal jobs. Whereas in other unions local presidents usually perform organizational grass-roots work, DC 37 Council and grievance representatives (often called reps) carry on many of these responsibilities. However, a number of local presidents and officers are also on released time and perform similar tasks. Indeed, it is often difficult to distinguish between them. Almost all reps are drawn from the rank and file, many having served previously as shop stewards.

Council reps play a key role in servicing locals, for they assist with organizational problems and the planning of meetings. They are expected to maintain close, ongoing contact with locals and their membership, insuring a continual flow of communication between the grass roots and the Council leadership. They are also the link between locals and department staff, insuring that services reach members efficiently and effectively. They are expected to encourage greater utilization of the extensive services and benefits provided by the Council.

The Council comprises 59 locals, the largest of them having substantial treasuries which help augment their independent tendencies. Several of them have a continuing tradition of suspicion of Council leadership. John Boer, one of the Council's early presidents, described Gotbaum's "inheritance" of certain locals, in 1965, as a bunch of "petty baronies." As recently as 1980, labor editor Michael Oreskes of the Daily News wrote that "The district council he heads is not a kingdom, and Gotbaum is not a king. It is, in fact, a loose amalgam of independent locals, some of which have become increasingly activist over the last two years. . . ."[14]

The wide social and economic disparities among the membership have the potential for fragmenting Council unity. In 1973 some 70 percent of those in high-status, best-paid positions were concentrated in the predominantly white Professional/Cultural Division. Lower-income members were mainly in the Hospitals Division, where some 77 percent were black. The educational spread follows similar patterns—the Professionals have the highest level of education, with 83 percent holding college degrees or having had some college-level work. At the other end of the scale, some 58 percent of the hospital workers did not have a high school diploma. Differences in income also indicate the substantial distance between members at the lowest end of the scale, including those hovering near poverty, and those at the highest. Again, the lowest paid were among the hospital workers and the highest, the professional groups (Table 11.1). The blue-collar workers, with far less formal education than the professional/technical employees enjoy, nevertheless, a relatively good income, having benefited from early participation in the union's development and a series of helpful wage agreements.

In 1973, more than half the membership was male, but within five years women comprised some 60 percent of the union. Among the divisions, Blue-Collar was mostly male, the Professionals 70 percent male, while Clerical–Administrative and White-Collar were overwhelmingly women, 80 and 70 percent, respectively. Only in the Hospitals Division was the ratio more equitable.[15]

Blue-Collar

In the Blue-Collar Division of over 12,000 members, laborers constitute the largest segment among motor vehicle operators, custodial assistants, climbers and pruners, gardeners, and stationary firemen. Skilled, semiskilled, and specialized workers are found among technicians in sewage disposal plants as well as among animal keepers. The blue-collar membership is organized into 22 locals, their sizes varying considerably. Some 16 grievance representatives, a majority of whom are also elected officials of their locals, service the membership. Since creation of the Comprehensive Employment and Training Act (CETA) program (discontinued under

TABLE 11.1: Total family income by division, 1973

Income (in dollars)	Total sample	Blue-Collar	Hospitals	Administrative/ Clerical	White-Collar	Professional/ Technical
Under 18,000	19.6	3.4	51.0	26.0	20.3	6.5
8,000–12,000	21.1	24.5	28.4	23.5	14.19	16.5
12,000–16,000	24.5	46.8	10.2	21.5	23.7	23.3
16,000–20,000	17.0	16.8	5.4	16.5	14.9	24.2
Over 20,000	17.7	8.6	4.9	12.6	26.2	29.6

The School Division was not included in this survey since it was conducted during the summer months. Figures are percentages of each class.

the Reagan administration), the largely male, Italian-American makeup of the division has been altered considerably as a result of increased membership by blacks, Hispanics, and women.[16]

Hospitals

More than 12,000 members are organized into Local 420, with chapters in a large number of municipal hospitals. Workers are employed by the Health and Hospitals Corporation, with some of the titles serviced by other divisions. Included in Local 420 are hospital aides, nurse practitioners, household and institutional aides, security guards, and an assortment of medical assistants and technicians. More grievances are handled by the Hospitals Division than any other, due primarily to poor working conditions in the city's hospitals. With workers dispersed among units in various parts of the city, and with a three-shift round-the-clock operation, it has taken considerable effort for this division to become a well-organized and cohesive unit. This has come about largely through an active staff, face-to-face relationships among workers who share common backgrounds, and the heavy utilization of Council services.

Over the years, hospital workers have become some of the most loyal and dedicated supporters of the Council and its political and economic activities. Compared with other divisions, its members gave the union the most positive rating for wages won, solving grievances, and improving working conditions. Recently, however, the president of Local 420 and the Council leadership have been engaged in a bitter, internecine conflict that has shattered a previously warm relationship.[17]

Clerical–Administrative

With over 27,000 members in one local (1549), the Administrative/Clerical Division is the largest in the Council. Its workers are found throughout city departments under the mayor's jurisdiction, involving some 30 managements, and include stenographers, typists, messengers, telephone operators, and various levels of clerks. The local is subdivided into 40 chapters and their officers, along with over 20 staff members, play an important role in servicing the membership. Well over 80 percent of the division are women, and its members are the major users of the education fund, particularly the high school equivalency and college programs.

One of the largest delegations of the Council's active political cadre has come from this division. Although well financed, and with all the potential for independent tendencies, this local has maintained close and harmonious relations with the Council and its top management. Local president Al Diop sits with Gotbaum on the AFSCME International Executive Board (IEB) and, over the years, has consistently sided with him, alone, against Jerry Wurf and the rest of the IEB. Diop was primarily responsible for the local's cooperative spirit, encouraging extensive participation of members in all Council programs and events. At the Solidarity Day march on Washington, in September 1981, well over a third of the estimated 20,000 delegation from DC 37 came from Local 1549. At least 1,000 of its members can be called on for participation in any major political action or public demonstration. Mostly black and women, many of them experienced harsh discrimination in the private sector before entering public service. As a result, they understand the connection between what they do politically and the union's power to deliver good contracts and to insure increased dignity at the workplace.[18]

White-Collar

Formerly part of the Clerical/Administrative Division, the White-Collar Division came into existence in 1973. It includes over 12,000 employees and services seven locals. While it covers many of the same titles as clericals, these college assistants, cashiers, court reporters, interpreters, and others are in the nonmayoral agencies such as the Board of Education, Board of Higher Education, Off-Track Betting Corporation, Judicial Conference, the Metropolitan Transit Authority, and the Triborough Bridge and Tunnel Authority. Because of the great number of locations and varied managements, it is difficult for the division staff to make frequent visits to worksites and service members. Off-Track Betting, for example, has some 150 branches open six or seven days a week, making it difficult to schedule meetings and broadcast important information. When comparing this with other divisions, there is apparent need for intimate and direct involvement of its director in collective bargaining negotiations because many of the

FIGURE 11.2: Percentage of DC 37
membership by division (1981)

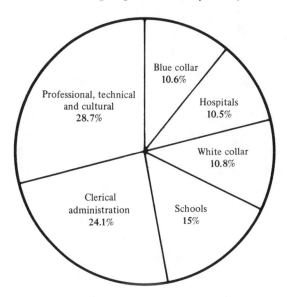

Blue collar
10.6%

Professional, technical
and cultural
28.7%

Hospitals
10.5%

White collar
10.8%

Clerical
administration
24.1%

Schools
15%

locals do not fall within the Council's citywide contract. The division director also represents newer locals which lack the experience and traditions associated with the negotiation process.[19]

Schools

Some 17,000 members work for the Board of Education and constitute one large local (372) in the Schools Division. Most are part-time workers, including school lunch orderlies, family paraprofessionals, loaders and handlers, school neighborhood workers, and school crossing guards. Local president Charles Hughes has been a decisive factor in galvanizing these workers into a cohesive force. Through his unyielding efforts and charismatic appeals to members to take pride in their work and the union, he has been able to elevate the role and importance of support services in New York's public schools. As with the Clerical/Administrative Division, stewards have been recruited for a decentralized training program in the field which was developed by Beryl Major in the Council's Education Department. These trained stewards are an important supplement to division staff in servicing the membership at the individual schools.

Appreciating the needs of his part-time, mostly black female membership, Hughes has utilized local funds and the Council's many services to enlist their support and active participation through prizes, jobs, social events, and other attractions. The servicing of members in some 900 schools and 32 community school districts is a tremendously complicated task. Not only must staff attend local and chapter meetings but must also observe school board sessions, where budgetary and personnel decisions affect Local 372 members. The local also has its own lobbyist in Albany, supplementing the work of Norman Adler by concentrating on school legislative proposals.

Professional, Technical and Cultural

Twenty-six locals in the Professional, Technical and Cultural Division add up to more than 32,000 members in some 300 titles. Comprising one-third of the division are the city's cultural institutions, which include professionals, blue-collar, clerical, and technical workers. They are deemed "quasi-public" employees, since they are not part of city government. The remainder of its membership are the professionals who work primarily for mayoral agencies such as engineers, architects, technicians, public health nurses, physical therapists, librarians, accountants, social workers, and assessors, among others.

It is within this division that Locals 371 and 375 have, until recently, sought to maintain a distant relationship with the Council, tending to keep administrative contact to a minimum and managing a number of their own services. Among the Professionals, morale had been reported to be low during the 1970s, due in part to the feeling that salaries had not been kept commensurate with their skills and educational backgrounds. The division was likewise upset by internal personality differences among staff which was eased with the appointment of Guido Menta as director in 1979. Since most members in this unit are professionals, quite often with college and university backgrounds, they see little need to use the Council's educational services, except to claim tuition reimbursement for graduate or professionally designed programs for certification or improvement of job performance. But they do utilize health and security benefits, visiting dentists and receiving medical attention regularly.[20]

MEMBERSHIP PROFILE

By 1969 the power base within DC 37 shifted dramatically. In the early years of its development, the laborers and motor vehicle operators, overwhelmingly white, male, and of Italian descent, had been the pillars on which Wurf built the Council. They provided the dedication and the zeal necessary for the initial organizing campaign.

With the passing of the years, however, they were outnumbered by new recruits from Hospitals, Schools, and Clerical workers, as noted in Table 11.2. Large blocs of black workers and a sizable proportion of women began to enter public service during the 1960s, which altered the complexion of the membership as well as its base of power and influence (Fig. 11.2).

GRIEVANCE PROCESS

It is generally unknown to the public that once the terms of a collective bargaining agreement are accepted, the union and its managers must devote themselves to continuous implementation

TABLE 11.2: Population of divisions, 1968–1981

Division	1968	1970	1975	1981
White-Collar*	5,342	6,577	11,034	12,403
Blue-Collar	9,958	11,296	12,695	12,180
Professional/Cultural	13,721	22,809	27,339	32,750
Schools	9,572	12,936	16,525	17,124
Hospitals	11,179	12,982	14,444	12,085
Clerical/Administrative	7,404	12,457	24,746	27,543
Total	57,176	79,057	106,783	114,085

*White-Collar came into existence as a distinct division in 1973. Until then, it was a section within the Clerical/Administrative Division. Therefore, the White-Collar numbers for 1968 and 1970 can be added to the latter division.

Source: DC 37 Library, Research and Negotiations Files.

and enforcement of the contract. "Though neither an obvious nor an especially glamorous activity," writes Neil Chamberlain and his co-authors, "policing of the labor agreement helps set the tone of, and give definition to, a labor–management relationship." Indeed, the grievance procedure, an integral aspect of this activity, is "the heart of collective bargaining."

It is in this phase that individual and collective grievances, disputes, and problems are handled as an inevitable aspect of daily life at the workplace. At the same time, experience with grievances affords staff an insight into possible issues for the next round of bargaining. Except for the Board of Education, divisional grievances are processed along similar lines: a four-step procedure defined in the citywide agreement and further detailed in unit contracts. Shop stewards usually file the initial grievance and are often the first to confront management with a complaint. The grievance rep may be involved in this initial phase, but plays an integral part in succeeding steps.

The division director usually discusses with the staff member responsible whether to appeal to the third step, but will definitely be consulted on proceeding to the fourth, which is arbitration. This final step is a financial responsibility of the local and involves the Legal Department. At any given time the Council's arbitration docket averages well over 1,000 cases, with 400 new ones added every quarter. Since assuming her post as general counsel, Beverly Gross convinced union leaders and staff to permit her office to train grievance reps to handle the less complex arbitration cases, freeing her department to cope more readily with its heavy case load.[21]

SHOP STEWARDS

The steward has always been the central figure in monitoring members' problems and advocating their interests. "We simply could not do without them," explained Al Diop, for he sees them as a crucial extension to the overtaxed divisional staff. With increasing use of paid personnel, the role of the steward has shown signs of decline. However, renewed interest in the mid-1970s, inspired by Lillian Roberts, encouraged recruitment for and improvements in their training. Besides assisting in the grievance process, they constitute an important core of union activists who also help identify potential leaders. With one recent exception, division leaders and staff have been drawn from the rank and file, most of them participating initially as shop stewards.[22]

DIVISION RECRUITMENT

Since the union does not maintain a leadership training program, except for shop stewards, it is left to individual members to take advantage of available opportunities. By the union paying tuition fees, encouragement is given those who attend Cornell University's programs in leadership training, and those at the union's campus college. Those who make the jump from lower-level Council assignments to staff and management positions serve, according to Gotbaum, as models for others to follow and so he sees no need for a formal leadership training program. "In a short time," he contends, "members knew that careers in the union were possible. We created it, they saw it and made use of it."[23]

BUREAUCRATIC DIFFICULTIES

With maturation came indications of the organizational growing pains that are typical of the endless efforts to build the union's service structure. By 1973 the membership had reached over 100,000 organized into almost 60 locals. Council staff, meanwhile, grew from 120 in 1967 to 635 in 1981 (Table 11.3). The divisions have become sizable bureaucracies, increasing two and one-half times in eight years. The payroll of the Council rose from $1.3 million in 1970 to $6.1 million by 1980, excluding the expenses for Health and Security, Education, and MELS.[24]

The union's bureaucracy operated under constant pressure to expand benefits, create new programs, extend the organization's political influence, improve the grievance process, and of course, negotiate improved contracts. During its maturation throughout the stressful decade of the 1970s, the union also had to confront the city's fiscal crisis. Although discontent developed among the city's work force, and a number of other municipal unions experienced leadership turnover, wildcat strikes, and internal turmoil and factionalism, the Council's response to the crisis showed comparative unity and stability.

TABLE 11.3: Growth of District Council 37 Bureaucracy

Technical and Support Personnel	1967	1970	1975	1981
Professional Staff in Departments				
Accounting	2	2	4	5
Executive Office	5	7	8	11
Legal	3	4	7	9
OSHA	—	—	—	7
Political and Legislative Action	3	3	4	5
Publications and Public Relations	4	5	8	8
Research and Negotiations	4	3	7	9
Subtotal	21	24	38	54
Clerical and Other Support Personnel in Departments	19	30	51	66
Department Subtotal	40	54	89	120
Field Staff				
Division Directors	4	5	6	6
Assistant Division Directors	5	5	6	6
Representatives	22	29	40	34
Released Time Representatives[a]	16	50	61	57
Secretaries-Typists	4	8	13	13
Field Staff Subtotal	51	97	126	116
Health and Security Plan				
Professional Staff	5	10	66	83
Clerical and Other Support Personnel	24	71	113[c]	147
Health and Security Subtotal	29	81	179	230
Education Fund[a]				
Professional Staff		5[b]	9	20
Clerical and Other Support Personnel		3	7	13
Education Subtotal		8	16	33
Municipal Employees Legal Service[a] (Mels)				

Technical and Support Personnel	1967	1970	1975	1981
Professional Staff			6[d]	74
Clerical and Other Support Personnel			8	62[e]
Mels Subtotal			14	136
Total	120	240	424	635

[a]Includes Benefits Fund and those paid mostly by City government.
[b]For 1971, when Education Fund began.
[c]The large increase in personnel was due to expansion of the data processing system.
[d]In 1975 Mels was begun as a pilot project.
[e]Included as support personnel are the legal assistants or paraprofessionals.
Note: This table was compiled with the assistance of Evelyn Seinfeld, Librarian, Research, and Negotiations.

GOTBAUM'S MANAGEMENT

DC 37 had its share of difficulties which contributed to tension and personnel changes among a number of staff members. As has often been noted, an institution is often the lengthened shadow of its leadership. In the Council, Gotbaum's direction gave the organization its form and basic character. His style was informal, and he dealt most comfortably with staff on an individual basis in his office rather than in the more formal setting of group leaders' meetings.[25] This informality was frequently interpreted by some staff as an open invitation to his office, bypassing the chain of command through Lillian Roberts, chief of field operations. She felt increasingly that these end-runs undermined her position.

Gotbaum also preferred to deal with staff as need demanded. While responsive to their problems and issues concerning department or division matters, he tended not to share decision making in evolving high-level policies, or seek staff counsel in making a number of strategic decisions affecting the bureaucracy. While group leaders' meetings were held monthly, little of fundamental importance occurred, except for Gotbaum's communications, which set a certain tone and updated recent political, economic, and union developments. The more important decisions were reached in less formal settings.

The PEP editor visited regularly to discuss Gotbaum's editorial page, and informed him of the themes and major stories of forthcoming issues. It was not his style to interfere with the PEP operation or with that of any unit of the bureaucracy, instead allowing very wide scope for staff discretion. Preparation for contract negotiations involved working closely with Nelson and then Viani, of Research and Negotiations, when he would also be briefed on pertinent economic information and general trends. When it came to testifying before legislative committees, Gotbaum turned to John Corcoran and later Norman Adler for advice, and to Ed Handman for a helpful draft; but in the political arena he often went his own way. Not until Adler had been on the scene for several years and gained his confidence did the executive director share his thinking with and solicit the reactions of his political lobbyist. With the possible exception of Lillian Roberts, there were few whom the DC 37 director consulted intimately on a regular basis. While Gotbaum was in touch with staff directors in affairs affecting their respective departmental operations, a number of them felt that with the passing years he shared fewer and fewer key questions with them. Had he retained the openness of earlier years they felt that he could have avoided certain costly mistakes.

The union's power grew and with it Gotbaum's influence, a general source of pride to Council staff and members. This development, however, meant increasing demands for his involvement in external affairs, affording him less and less time for internal matters. A number of staff began to complain of inadequate communication between themselves and the director, leading, at times, to feelings of estrangement and isolation from important events and decisions. They also sensed an impatience on his part, as he hurried from one meeting to another. As his stature grew in the world outside, staff members began to treat him with increasing reverence. Some interpreted Gotbaum's power in a manner that made it difficult for them to consult him with what they now perceived as petty matters. Even those at the highest levels of union management reached the stage where they avoided engaging him in forceful argument, even when they thought him wrong or not in full command of the facts. When some individual did confront him head-on, a momentary angry reaction or outburst insured further withdrawal from public questioning or challenging.

At first a number of these exchanges took place in the more

open arena of group leaders' meetings, but soon they took on the appearance of monologues. Dan Nelson, Lillian Roberts, and on occasion, Viani and Adler, would argue with the executive director in the confines of his office. Many of these were heated debates with Roberts. It is far more understandable that staff members on the lower levels should feel insecure and thus not speak up—it is less so with top echelon. From Gotbaum's perspective, direct questions or challenges were not acts of disrespect or disloyalty. He understood these exchanges as the normal results of organizational growth and personal differences. It is illustrative that relatively few staff members have left DC 37 over the years, which was in sharp contrast to the "revolving door" at the AFSCME headquarters in Washington.[26]

ROBERTS AS FIELD DIRECTOR

The close relationship with Gotbaum, built on long, bitter union battles, gave Lillian Roberts an increasing sense of security, helping her emerge as an outstanding black labor leader. The increasing numbers of black women streaming into Council ranks turned to her as a model and source of tremendous pride. Working in tandem with the executive director, she relieved him of organizational details he disliked intensely. She in turn enjoyed close personal relationships with the membership, keeping her office door open to members troubled with personal concerns.

With time, however, signs of strain developed between Roberts and some of the division chiefs, and eventually with the president of Local 420. Taking orders from a black woman was not easy for a number of staff leaders. Several felt she lacked the administrative talent to direct the overall operation, while others questioned her choice of certain personnel, alleging they were based more on friendship rather than competence or skill. Insecure in dealing with intellectuals friendly to Gotbaum, she tended to surround herself with those she knew best from union ranks. It was during the fiscal crisis that she began to feel left out of Gotbaum's decision making, as he came to depend increasingly for guidance on Jack Bigel, Felix Rohatyn, and others outside the Council. Staff members who differed with and remained cool toward Roberts sometimes took their problems directly to Gotbaum. Viewing these acts as disrespectful, Roberts brought them to the attention of her director. He, in turn, sought to rectify the situation by issuing a special memorandum reminding the staff to follow the hierarchical lines set down by the union's table of organization.[27]

SIZE CREATES STRAIN

As the divisions evolved into their own sizable bureaucracies, while each of the departments expanded into new areas and services, it was inevitable that increased size would strain the union's cohesiveness and close personal relationships of staff members. Gotbaum was aware of these developments and their impact on his own leadership, for he was soon defending his inability to visit and meet regularly with expanding locals, membership, and staff. "If I go to too many local meetings," he explained, "then I have to forego continuous involvement with the political and economic leaders of the city. This type of union leadership and responsibility has not characterized trade union officers in the past."

Although the top leadership and staff could readily walk about headquarters in the initial phase of the union's development, that became increasingly difficult by the 1970s, when an exploding Council bureaucracy found itself spread among different floors and, at times, in separate buildings. Personal and informal contact with top leaders became less and less frequent. By the time headquarters was moved to a permanent site at 140 Park Place/125 Barclay Street, one heard talk about "the fifth versus the fourth," denoting the separation in attitude between top management and departments on the fifth floor and the divisions, locals and grass-roots operations on the fourth floor. In one of his reports to group leaders, Gotbaum lamented the fact that division directors, department heads, and the top management "do not talk to each other. Even at the group meetings we seem to hold back."[28]

Supervising the large number of Council and grievance reps operating in dispersed parts of the city also created difficulties. Monitoring where reps are and constantly checking up on them is an unpleasant task for directors. Among some reps, a routine approach to work took hold. While many performed well, loafers and incompetents tended to demoralize responsible staffers. Those who did not perform were reminded by Gotbaum that they had to behave as vigorous advocates of their members and confront management more aggressively:

> Too many of you have treated the administration as though they are political friends. You can be polite and friendly. You do not need to be vulgar—but they represent a different interest than you do. The members suspect that when you are too nice, you are selling them down the river.

> In grievances, stop seeing management's side of it. It's the members' interests we must pursue. That's why we are in service.[29]

A major attempt was made by Gotbaum to resolve a number of these bureaucratic problems. He outlined to division and department heads and their staffs a series of organizational changes that amounted to a basic tightening of the structure and a modification of their daily work patterns. He urged the staff to conduct business in a more orderly fashion, following the formal line of command through their department and division directors, and then to the associate director for organization, Lillian Roberts, before coming to him. To improve communications, directors were told to hold monthly staff meetings. To promote greater accountability, he asked that evaluation reports on all personnel be prepared twice annually by supervisors, and that they identify individuals who showed potential for promotion. Continuous, on-the-job training was to be instituted immediately by the Education Department to insure that division staffs were informed about contracts, knew the grievance process, and learned skills useful for improving the organization of locals. In divisions, greater priority was to be accorded to improving the operation of locals, their organization, the quality of meetings, and the recruitment and training of stewards.[30]

This was a challenging agenda, necessitating a determined change of attitude by staff. Some of the suggestions were implemented, but other changes had to await gradual replacement of certain personnel. However, many of the bureaucratic problems experienced by the union were inevitable signs of growth and development and must be evaluated in terms of the overall effectiveness of the organization in achieving its major goals. This will be dealt with in the following chapters.

SUMMARY

In taking command, Gotbaum completed his initial goals: securing his own base, eliminating jurisdictional disputes with the Teamsters, winning the support of his growing membership with good contracts, improving grievance machinery, and creating a responsive bureaucratic organization. In establishing the DC 37 organizational structure, his strategies included developing a strong, centralized Council while accommodating legitimate demands for local autonomy, expanding the service arm of the Council, recruiting outside professionals and experts to manage the departments who shared his progressive ideas, and selecting field personnel from within who represented the polyglot makeup of the membership.

The chapters that follow will detail the staff's role in shaping the political arm of the union and its extensive educational, health, and legal services. Only after this review of the DC 37 bureaucracy can its role in meeting the needs and aspirations of union members be judged fairly.

NOTES

1. Locals within the jurisdictional area are required to affiliate with the Council, but may appeal to the International to remain outside of it. The major standing committees of the executive board include Finance, Political Action, and Education.

2. Thomas Cronin, "Thinking About Leadership," *Presidential Studies Quarterly,* 14 (Winter 1984):25.

3. Interviews with Sarah Gotbaum, October 2, 1981; Bertram Perkel, December 27, 1982; and authors' observations.

4. Interview with Victor Gotbaum, March 6, 1984; Lois Gray and Sandy Lenz, New York State Industrial and Labor Relations, Cornell University, "Preliminary Analysis of Staff Training Needs and Possibilities," undated, although approximately 1974 or 1975, p. 1. Every department head required the freedom to operate without interference of the executive director.

5. Seymour Mann and Sheldon Mann, "Decision Dynamics and Organizational Characteristics: the AFSCME and NYC District Council 37," paper presented at the American Political Science Association, San Francisco, California, September 2–5, 1975, pp. 6–7. Interviews with Arthur Tibaldi, December 6, 1982; Roslyn Yasser, November 16, 1982. Also, authors' observations of executive board meetings, 1978–81.

6. Technically, Education, Health and Security were agencies paid for by

special funds provided by the city, won by the union in negotiations. The heads of these agencies are called administrators. However, in the daily operations of the union and in the formulation of major policy, they play a role difficult to distinguish from that of departments. Those departments that service the union but are not included in this study are Mailing and Printing and Accounting. In the mid-seventies, the Municipal Employees Legal Service was established.

7. Finance committee, executive board, October 10, 1966. Interviews with Julius Topol, March 17, 1981; Bertram Perkel December 27, 1982. See Chapter 15, section on MELS, "Legal Care With a Union Label."

8. Wayne Parsons, Charles Kadushin and Bogdan Denitch, "Preliminary Report: Study of Members of DC 37," AFSCME Bureau of Applied Social Research, Columbia University, February 1974, pp. 7–8, 32–33, hereafter cited as BASR. Also, *Public Employee Press*, December 23, 1977, p. 6; November 26, 1982.

9. Interview with Bernard Stephens, February 2, 1981.

10. *New York Times*, June 29, 1971, p. 36; *Public Employee Press*, July 16, 1971, p. 3; interview with William Schleicher, February 10, 1984.

11. Interview with Beverly Gross, November 11, 1982, and authors' observations.

12. Will Herberg, "Bureaucracy and Democracy in Labor Unions," in Richard Rowan and Herbert Northrup, eds., *Readings in Labor Economics and Labor Relations*, Homewood, IL: Richard Irwin, 1968, p. 342; and Clark Kerr, "Unions and Union Leaders of Their Own Choosing," *Ibid.*, pp. 248–249.

13. Michael Hayes, *Lobbyists and Legislators, a Theory of Political Markets*, New Brunswick, NJ: Rutgers University Press, 1981, p. 85.

14. *Daily News*, June 22, 1980, p. 5. Parsons, Kadushin and Denitch, "Preliminary Report: Study of Members," p. 6.

15. Memorandum from Evelyn Seinfeld to Alan Viani, "Demographic Breakdown of DC 37," March 16, 1978, research and negotiations file.

16. Interview with Andy Lettieri, director, Blue-Collar Division, May 19, 1982. As will be noted below, grievance representatives are considered staff members of the Council's divisions, yet those who also hold elective office in their locals can obviously carry on independently of headquarters if they wish.

17. Parsons, Kadushin and Denich, "Preliminary Report: Study of Members," pp. 11–12. This dispute will be discussed in the final chapter.

18. Interview with Al Diop, March 3, 1984.

19. Interview with Marty Lubin, White-Collar Division director, May 10, 1982.

20. Authors' observations, Professional Division Conference, Friar Tuck Hotel, Saugerties, N.Y., Spring 1980; Interviews with Guido Menta, October 20, 1981 and March 18, 1982; and Louis Albano, president of Local 375, April 4, 1984.

21. Neil Chamberlain, Donald Cullen and David Lewin, *The Labor Sector*, 3d ed., New York: McGraw-Hill, 1980, pp. 235, 239; interview with Beverly Gross, November 1982. In the Blue-Collar Division, a grievance rep may help the steward and processes the second step; a council rep would also be involved from the third step on.

22. Interviews with Lillian Roberts, September 28, 1982 and Beryl Major, head of steward training, April 15, 1982. Tom Jennings, director of the Schools

Division, did not come from the DC 37 ranks, but did have prior experience as a shop steward. He was originally recruited to assist Gotbaum in his campaign for the International presidency. Interview with Tom Jennings, April 15, 1982.

23. Interviews with Bernard Stephens, February 2, 1981; Alan Viani, March 10, 1981; Victor Gotbaum, October 13, 1981; Brenda White, October 13, 1981; As the union has matured, a number of rank-and-file members have come up through their local and divisional responsibilities and moved into departmental staff positions, generally considered the province of outsiders who have been professionally trained. Among those who have made this transition include: Guido Menta, Brenda White, Bill Schleicher, Geri Ruth, Beryl Major, Marcia Lamel, Nat Lindenthal, Alan Viani and Bart Cohen.

24. Edward Handman to Victor Gotbaum, "Some thoughts for your thoughts on organization," undated, probably 1973 or 1974; Lois Gray and Sandy Lenz, New York State Industrial Labor Relations, Cornell University, "Preliminary Analysis of Staff Training Needs and Possibilities," undated, probably 1974 or 1975; Gotbaum to department heads et al., "New DC 37 Procedures and Guidelines," March 7, 1974; interviews with many division directors, department heads, Council staff, and local officers.

25. Group leaders' meetings included the executive and associate directors, division and department directors, assistant directors, and key staff.

26. Interviews with Murray Gordon, April 28, 1980; Bernard Stephens, February 2, 1981; Julius Topol, March 17, 1981; Al Bilik, October 21, 1981; and Bertram Perkel, December 27, 1982; Joseph Goulden, *Jerry Wurf, Labor's Last Angry Man,* New York: Atheneum, 1982, pp. 227–230. Another close consultant entered the scene when Betsy Flower Hogen became Victor Gotbaum's second wife. This bright young woman, who loved many of the same things that he did—politics, tennis, and a younger circle of friends—had worked on Mayor Lindsay's staff and developed a large network of contacts in government and politics. A skilled and friendly administrator, this new relationship quickly developed into one in which Gotbaum respected and sought her views on various union and political matters.

27. Victor Gotbaum to division and department directors and staff, March 7, 1974.

28. *Ibid.*; interview with Gotbaum, May 11, 1981.

29. Victor Gotbaum to department heads, associate directors, division directors, assistant division directors, "New DC 37 Procedures and Guidelines," March 7, 1974, Gotbaum files.

30. *Ibid.*

12
Political Machine, Union Made

"Politics," suggested Max Weber, "means striving to share power or striving to influence the distribution of power." Unlike the private sector, unions in the public service operate totally within the political system. Although collective bargaining processes matured in New York City, and organized labor brought its demands to the negotiating table, this in no way diminished the importance of political action. Indeed, politics affected intimately the negotiation process itself. Spero and Capozzola put it succinctly when they wrote:

> The more recent upsurge in direct bargaining, however, has in no way diminished organizational interest in the use of political tactics. An abundance of political weapons are available that may be distinguished from collective bargaining but have an impact on the form and scope of the bargaining that takes place.[1]

The framework for collective bargaining is shaped by political actors, which include the governor, the mayor, the state legislature, the city council, as well as the judiciary. Many issues that come before these decision makers closely affect public workers: the size and allocation of budgets, the provisions of civil service laws, and policies concerned with health, education, welfare, libraries, and cultural institutions. Furthermore, collective bargaining and legislative policy making often intermesh. What cannot be won at the bargaining table is often placed on the union's legisla-

239

Political Action director Norman Adler speaking to Assemblyman Denis Butler at the Council's annual legislative breakfast to discuss the union's legislative goals for 1980. This was but one of many lobbying techniques developed for each legislative session in Albany.

tive agenda. And lobbying often serves to protect the gains won in collective bargaining.

In this chapter, we review the Wurf legacy in political action and detail the major developments under Gotbaum's directorship. Of particular importance is the conversion of the growing DC 37 membership and other union resources into an operation reminiscent of the old political machine. During the 1970s, the union emerged as one of the key political forces in the city and state. Its influence varied, depending on a number of factors: the contemporary political scene, party control of legislative bodies and the governor's office, Democratic party factionalism, the influence of other unions, the role of pressure groups, and public opinion.[2]

THE WURF LEGACY: POLITICS IS OUR BREAD AND BUTTER

The Wurf legacy included a deep appreciation of political action and the importance of the union's involvement in the political life of the city and state. During the decade of 1955–65, the union's political thrust was constrained by a variety of factors. The first priority was to organize public workers and to build the locals. Second, because the union's resources were limited a relatively small staff was busily engaged in signing up workers and collecting dues. While appreciating the need for political action, Wurf found it difficult to delegate responsibility and, particularly in the political arena, tended to maintain personal command of developing policy, strategy, and tactics.

Wurf did permit creation of a legislative committee, which carried on the detailed lobbying activities at the state capitol. A small core of union activists—volunteers devoted to the cause—gave their time and energies, and carried an incredible burden during the regular sessions of the legislature. Attendance at legislative committee meetings was uneven; not all the locals participated, and of those that did, few were on a regular basis. This left the bulk of responsibility on the shoulders of a handful of members. The committee met more regularly during the course of a legislative session, which, at that time ran for only three months. It had no support from a permanent staff, having to operate largely on its own. It was essentially through "on-the-job" training that they learned the intricacies of the legislative process, helped prepare and prefile bills, sought out sponsors for union proposals, monitored the calendar for bills to be endorsed or opposed, testified before appropriate committees, and guided their bills through each of the chambers. A glance at the chart below indicates the breadth and detailed character of select items on the legislative agenda during two typical sessions, 1957 and 1962.[3]

DC 37 legislative program: Select items

1957

Social security to supplement existing pension plans;

Premium pay for overtime work, including time and one-half for overtime, double time for work on Sunday or legal holidays, and a 10 percent differential for night work;

Increase the city's share of pension contributions to three-quarters of the total from its present half share, with a corresponding reduction in employees' contribution;

Retirement at best single year's salary, rather than the present method of taking the best five years' pay to determine the amount of the pension;

Optional retirement at half pay after 20 years of service.

1962

Allowing unemployment insurance items to be negotiated at collective bargaining process;

Amount of insurance coverage on loans for retirement system to increase from $2,000 to $3,000;

Beneficiary of retired employee choice for an annuity in place of lump sum payment;

Reclassify administrative and clerical employees of NYC Community College of Arts and Sciences and community colleges under Board of Higher Education to Gittleson administrative titles so that their work will be equated with those at four year colleges.

Unlike the congressional committee system in Washington, where members stayed on for many years to establish seniority, state lawmakers often remained in Albany for comparatively short periods, insuring steady changes in personnel. This frequent turnover impelled the Council's legislative committee to be constantly alert and make new contacts to maintain communication and to enlist dependable allies. The group also determined when to mobilize rank-and-file members in Albany or in a legislator's home district, and when to launch a letter-writing campaign. Unable to cope with the wide range of legislation, the committee was often obliged to call on individual locals to assist in lobbying.

The committee also published, on an ad hoc basis, a special

legislative bulletin sent to lawmakers urging support of union proposals. Political columns were prepared for issues of the union newspaper, describing current bills, indicating its location in the legislative process, and directing readers in the practical "how to's" of letter writing and lobbying. The committee held meetings during summer months, preparing the groundwork for the forthcoming legislative program and session, and served as the coordinator of political action groups among the larger locals. In addition, it lobbied the city council for home rule messages required under state law for Albany lawmakers before they could consider certain local issues. The latter included such important items as workers' rights, grievance procedures, and a host of civil service regulations.

Every fall, a well-publicized legislative conference brought together hundreds of key activists from the many locals to hear from and exchange views with noted labor leaders, influential party officials from Democratic and Republican ranks, and key lawmakers. Legislators were alerted to the union's agenda for the upcoming session. To instill pride and confidence in their own members, and to impress the invited notables, these meetings were held at prestigious hotels. Lobbying became more onerous as the legislative work grew in complexity. Greater expertise was necessary than volunteers could provide and lawyers were increasingly involved in bill drafting. For the 1960 legislative session the Council hired a lobbyist to assist with its work in Albany. With Wurf's attention drawn, at first to organizing in the early years, and then to challenging Zander for the presidency, a more effective lobbying effort appeared essential. No matter how dedicated and skilled, volunteers were no match for a full-time staff.

A small group of volunteers participated in the Political Action Committee (PAC), which was closely controlled by the executive director. Wurf understood and appreciated the linkage between the union's lobbying efforts and the electoral base to which lawmakers had to come for support every two years. Attention was thus given to endorsing candidates and allocating the Council's limited resources among them. His strategy focused on targeting a number of races, preferably at the earliest stage (the primaries) when the union's input might make a significant difference and be more visible. The union's efforts included letters to members in districts of endorsed candidates, urging them to register and vote. Volunteers sent into a district to ring doorbells, to distribute leaflets at busy shopping corners, and to assist at a candidate's headquarters included shop stewards and small cadres of activists from key locals. Union members were also canvassed at home or telephoned and, on election day, a final concerted drive was organized to get out the vote.[4]

With its own printing press the union produced an extraordinary number of hard-hitting leaflets for endorsed candidates. Despite the advent of the television era, these activists and the limited resources of the union were important factors in determining the eventual outcome of close legislative races . Only in statewide and national contests did the new medium play a major role.

Wurf was a skilled strategist and sought constantly to maximize the limited DC 37 resources. Candidates who proved supportive of the members' interests—Democrats and some Republicans, liberals and conservatives, reformers and regulars—received some union assistance. On most occasions, Wurf took up the cudgels to oppose boss-dominated candidates, especially those who had refused to support union proposals. While he generally sought alliances with Democrats, because he tended to find them more liberal and pro-union, on occasion he opened lines of communication to Republicans. Since at least one chamber of New York state legislature often came under the influence of the GOP, he understood the value of having some friends among Republicans. Typically, at the union's legislative conferences, he saw to it that leaders of both major parties were seated on the dais to address his members.

Despite an overall conservative voting record, William Conklin of Brooklyn won DC 37 backing because of his sympathetic treatment of public service workers. Between 1956 and 1962, he supported some 90 bills dealing with social benefits for, and specific concerns of, Council members. John Marchi, Staten Island Republican, won Council support because he had been a loyal friend to public employees and supported many proposals of major assistance to New York City. Others included Assemblyman Lucio Russo, Republican–Conservative (58 A.D., Staten Island) and Edward Amann, Jr., Republican–Conservative (59 A.D., Staten Island). In his run for a U.S. Senate seat, conservative Brooklyn Democrat John Cashmore won the union's backing because of work favorable to public employees and his opposition to the Condon–Wadlin law.

Throughout this period, endorsements of political candidates were made largely at the behest of Wurf. "It was all in his head," recalled an involved rank-and-file leader, although "formally the selections went to the Council." Through the union's newspaper, and at local meetings, members were reminded to vote for Council-backed nominees. Political action included registration drives among unionists. Eventually, each member was put into the union's computer system, identifying party affiliation and district—an easy way to target members during campaigns.[5]

Throughout the 1950s and on into the early 1960s the political impact of DC 37 was not major, but it could help make a difference when part of a wider coalition. The time had not yet come when the Council could flex its political muscles and make lawmakers sit up and listen carefully. Only with the advent of a new administration, a greatly enlarged membership, and the appointment of full-time personnel would DC 37 be singled out as an increasingly potent and independent element on the political scene.

GOTBAUM'S POLITICAL SCENE

Upon assuming the directorship of the Council in 1965, Gotbaum soon realized that certain political developments were intimately affecting the role and potential influence of the union, and that he would have to respond to them individually and quickly: the union's state legislative agenda was increasing in size and scope; the overwhelming dominance of Republican Governor Nelson Rockefeller in legislative decision making severely circumscribed the Council's ability to get its proposed policies acted on in Albany; and the statewide Democratic party organization was seriously fragmented and ineffectual.

The Legislative Condition

The Council's state agenda had grown steadily and substantially and there were no signs of abating. At the beginning of each succeeding session, a longer, more complex set of proposed bills was placed in the legislative hopper on behalf of DC 37. Even though the collective bargaining process was strengthened during the 1960s, and victories were won increasingly at the negotiating table, the union's goals in Albany continued to expand. Part of this growth was the result of the Council adding new groups of workers and titles to its ranks who required, under state law, specific action by the legislature, e.g., workmen's compensation, improvements in pension systems, certification, a host of work rules and civil service regulations, as well as policies affecting workers' health and safety. In addition, the Council was concerned with the state budget, for many provisions affected the wages and working conditions of city workers. With the increased size of the municipal deficit, the city turned annually to the state for assistance. By 1962 a little over one-fourth of the city's expense budget was dependent on state and federal aid. Ten years later, that figure jumped to just under one-half. In this decade, state aid to the city rose from one-half billion dollars to more than two and one-half billion—a fivefold increase.[6]

In addition to the growing Council agenda, the legislature was a source of bills that had to be monitored constantly by the union for possible negative impact. City managers sought legislation to improve, from their perspective, the administrative process by modifying state rules or regulations, which the union might view as harmful to its members. With the enlarged scope of policies came changes in the legislative structure and process of decision making. Sessions grew longer each year, extending into the summer. The complex and detailed character of bills became overly burdensome for the union's small volunteer core charged with lobbying in Albany. More knowledgeable and professionally skilled personnel were needed on a full-time basis. Building networks and learning the points of access necessitated closer relations with decision makers, especially the speaker in the assembly and the majority leader in the state senate. These key actors provided the leadership in each chamber, and were authorized to appoint and remove members of legislative committees and shape the legislative agenda.

There was also a marked increase of staff assigned to the legislative leadership and to committee chairpersons. A host of aides, administrative assistants, counsel, and researchers with specialized knowledge had become a key element in the work of the legislature. Lawmakers, in turn, became increasingly dependent on their staffs for information and guidance. Volunteer activists of the Wurf days were no match for this growing cadre of influential professionals. And Gotbaum was fully aware of these political facts of life.

Governor Rockefeller

In addition to the Council's sizable legislative agenda during the 1960s and the early 1970s, the union confronted a Republican governor of unusual strength and influence in the legislative process, and with whom they had unfriendly relations. First under Wurf and then Gotbaum, these tensions turned to outright bitterness. Rockefeller did not take kindly to militant public service unions, especially those that persisted in defending the right to strike.

In his earlier years as governor, Rockefeller worked skillfully in building his reputation as a liberal Republican. He reached out to the more traditional, conservative arm of the private sector, craft-controlled unions, through Peter Brennan, chairman, and Raymond Corbett, executive director of the state AFL–CIO, and Harry Van Arsdale, president of the Electrical Workers and head of the Central Labor Council in New York City. He cemented warm, ongoing friendships with them and a strong base of support. The governor's myriad public works in Albany and throughout the state served as important sources of employment for craft workers, particularly in the construction and electrical fields.

For years, increasing hostility marked public relationships between socially conscious DC 37 and other public workers on the one hand, and the conservative craft-oriented unions on the other. The latter found the aggressiveness and militancy of these burgeoning public service workers discomfiting, as well as a direct challenge to their jurisdictional claims and political and legislative influence. Brennan and Corbett fought the right of public service unions, for example, to organize engineers and other craft workers on the city payroll. They actively opposed bills introduced by DC 37 that called for exclusive representation of many titles among city workers.

Finally, the craft unions and DC 37 differed markedly in their political orientations, the former being among the most conservative in the nation, focusing narrowly on trade union issues. Once having endeared themselves to the governor, they became his loyal and devoted followers. He appreciated these differences and played them to his distinct advantage, consciously reaching out to the craft segment of the labor movement with honorific appointments and new construction projects. In these ways he was able to strengthen his liberal image and at the same time challenge the newly emerging public union.

Contributing to the hostility between the governor and DC 37 was the passage, in 1967, of the Public Employees Fair Employment law, more popularly known as the Taylor law. Formulated by a committee appointed by the governor, it replaced the much hated and much abused Condon–Wadlin law. While providing a basis for organizing and bargaining with public workers, AFSCME and other public service unions vigorously attacked the provisions forbidding strikes and its judicially imposed penalties for violations.

Democratic Machine, New York Style

By the 1960s, the urban political machine had changed markedly. Except for Daley's hold on Chicago, most cities had evolved smaller, more decentralized organizations which controlled distinct districts or wards. Ted Lowi noted that "New York became a loose, multi-party system with wide-open processes of nomination, election, and participation: Chicago became a tight one-party system."[7] In New York, highly fragmented political enclaves were now scattered throughout the city and state, and within five counties, citywide negotiations proved increasingly difficult. The erosion of a strong centralized party system left leaders of the separate county organizations and small local fiefdoms in control in the Bronx, Brooklyn, and Queens.

In Manhattan antagonism between old-style regulars and the younger, postwar generation of reformers within the Democratic party also contributed to the city's contentious politics. Although Meade Esposito ran a countywide operation in Brooklyn, a number of small organizations controlled specific local areas, insuring frequent factional struggles around elected officials, e.g., Assembly Speaker Stanley Steingut and groups of black leaders competing for control in Bedford-Stuyvesant. In the Bronx, reformers tried, in vain, to challenge the regular organization, enabling the latter to continue its effective hold on the county through individual "arrangements" with a variety of local neighborhood groups. Queens was less centralized but dominated by several key figures, including its borough president and Councilman Matthew Troy.

In Robert Wagner's last campaign for mayor in 1961, when most of the city's remaining political "bosses" refused to support him, he was able to put together a winning coalition of his own, with the assistance of private sector (primarily craft) unions. It was evident then that the old citywide party organization was gone from New York. But many of the functions it formerly performed still had to be carried on. What were those functions? And who would fill the vacuum left by the old pros?

GOTBAUM'S RESPONSE

Having secured his base through the hospital elections, Gotbaum could now devote more attention to organizing the union's political activities. He recognized the need for a permanent lobbying operation in Albany and a coherent, stable electoral presence in the city. With an increasing membership dispersed throughout the five counties, he sought to integrate them into a potent, year-round, grass-roots operation for lobbying, registration drives, election campaigns, and other political activities. He was anxious to build a constructive image in the community through closer ties with neighborhood groups.

Early in 1967 John Corcoran was appointed the first director of political action and legislation and served for the next nine years. Recommended by Murray Gordon, a mutual friend and prominent labor lawyer, Corcoran brought to the union extensive experience and an affable and endearing personality. He shared the liberal-social orientation of the executive director and promised he would monitor "the entire range of legislation proposed in the assembly and senate—social, educational, economic, poverty and welfare, not just labor laws."

Corcoran was familiar with the labor movement, having helped organize the workers at Consolidated Edison. He understood the unique concerns of public employees as a result of his work as a fireman and as president of the Uniformed Fire Officers Association of New York, Local 854. In this capacity, his key activity was to lobby Albany lawmakers, which brought him into close contact and working relationships with important legislators and politicians around the state. Corcoran had been admitted to the bar after attending law shcool at night. This added to his skill in overseeing bill drafting and the legislative work of the union, and an easygoing personality and his Irish-Catholic heritage facilitated contacts with many of the state's lawmakers and politicians. Socially sensitive and caring, he sympathized strongly with the need to improve the economic and social well-being of blacks and other minorities, and was dedicated to the concept that they be effectively integrated into the labor movement. For two years he had served in Nigeria, assisting black workers and their fledgling labor movement, underscoring his determination that unions enroll minorities into their rank and file and leadership ranks far more vigorously.[8]

A PROFESSIONAL LOBBYIST

In Albany Corcoran labored strenuously to build the union's presence, networking and contacting lawmakers and their staff, as he laid the groundwork for more effective input. Full-time representation in Albany afforded the Council a closer involvement with the details of legislative decision making—pre-filing of bills, the daily activities of committees, sudden changes of the calendar, monitoring floor debates, and recording the votes of legislators.

By keeping on top of legislative developments, Corcoran improved the union's timing for mobilizing its forces, when needed, pinpointing each strategy to mesh closely and more effectively with the legislature (e.g., when to call for a letter-writing campaign and to whom it should be targeted; at what point it would be useful to bring a delegation to Albany, or whether it should be sent to the home constituency office; and when to mobilize the union's top leadership). Letter writing was encouraged for those members who were directly affected by the content of specific bills.[9] As the resources of the union grew, Corcoran filled busloads of members for special lobbying efforts at the state capitol.

Although Corcoran focused largely on Democratic lawmakers and their staffs, he felt increasingly that the union had to reach out to Republican lawmakers as well. This conclusion grew out of two important realities of the political scene: Governor Rockefeller dominated legislative matters, and at least one chamber, sometimes both, were controlled by the Republican party. New York governors inherit a constitutional framework that provides for strong leadership in both legislative and administrative arenas. Bolstered by executive budget making, item veto of budgets, and extensive appointment authority, the governor is invested with significant powers and an unbroken tradition of energetic leadership. The political party mechanism strengthens this influence, if patronage and executive resources are used skillfully. Direction of the legislature, especially when controlled by the governor's party, can often be another source of strength.[10]

Rockefeller's effusive personality, as well as his skill and personal resources enhanced his authority and outreach to lawmakers. Assisted by his wealth and extensive network of friends, he attracted staff skilled in policy making, financial matters, and public relations. His long tenure as governor, from 1959 to 1973, gave him mastery over the details of the legislative process and positioned him as a key figure in providing certain incentives sought by lawmakers. To the leaders of DC 37, however, he was considered an anathema, an opponent of their overall interests.

Time and again Corcoran found himself frustrated by the influential role of the governor and general intransigence of Republican lawmakers on issues of direct concern to DC 37. Each year his attempts to soften the Taylor law failed, as did the union's bill for an agency shop.* Nevertheless he felt that some Republicans could be wooed from the governor's camp, if only the union would extend its growing electoral resources to them. But Gotbaum was not receptive to his suggestions, maintaining his commitment to the Democratic party and its New Deal image. Gotbaum had developed an intense personal dislike for Rockefeller and could not bring himself to cooperate with his political organization. Deferential to the will of his executive director, Corcoran did not press his case intensively. As a result he often found himself fighting rearguard actions in the legislature, particularly during budget periods. For DC 37 the legislative record was less an indication of Corcoran's skill than the overwhelming influence of Rockefeller.

Guido Menta, assistant director of political action, helped link DC 37 to a Republican leader and facilitate a new union strategy.

---

*An agency shop requires all employees covered by a union contract to pay dues to the union, in return for expenses involved in collective bargaining negotiations and other services rendered, although they are not required to join the union.

Through Guy Vellela, Republican assemblyman from his district, Menta arranged for Gotbaum to meet State Senator John Calandra, a powerful GOP figure, to discuss the agency shop. Calandra had resisted at first, complaining that the union had never shown any interest in Republican lawmakers. But once the union leader and the lawmaker met, they developed a better understanding that has continued to this day. This initial opening proved immensely useful in the years ahead.[11]

ELECTORAL POLITICS: A MACHINE IN THE MAKING

Alongside his lobbying operation in Albany, Corcoran launched the union's electoral activities. Required, however, to spend an inordinate amount of time upstate, he delegated major responsibility for this grass-roots operation to his department colleagues: Guido Menta was assigned political action and Elizabeth Feinstein community relations. Menta was young, energetic, and articulate. He came up through the ranks of the blue-collar, heavily Italian contingent within the Council. As with other staff appointments, Menta's assignment indicated Gotbaum's preference for recruiting rank-and-file members for Council posts, encouraging them to seek careers within the union through active volunteer participation.

Menta's responsibilities included enlargement of the volunteer efforts of the PAC.* At first, the extended outreach to the members was a difficult objective. "Participation," explained Menta, "did not evolve easily or automatically but had to be cultivated, requiring persistent and patient staff effort." Menta and Feinstein appeared before meetings of locals, always trying to make the connection between wages, pensions, and working conditions, on the one hand, and political action on the other. Eventually Menta succeeded in establishing a political action contact in each of the locals to facilitate a steady flow of communication between the Council's PAC and the local's membership. The larger locals, like 1549, 371, 372, and 420 were able to establish their own political action committees to augment electoral work and to strengthen the union's lobbying efforts. This was particularly evident when the needs of the local's membership coincided with a DC 37 bill introduced into the legislature.

---

*PAC hereafter refers to the Political Action Committee appointed by and responsible to the Executive Board. It is not an independently funded committee.

Sharing the political work with Menta at headquarters was Elizabeth Feinstein, a young activist whose assignments included training some 250 members annually for lobbying and electoral campaigns. As Gotbaum's reputation as a political activist and involved liberal reformer spread to an increasing number of groups and causes, Feinstein frequently received messages from the executive director informing her that he had just met with a union or civic coalition or attended some community meeting. Once the executive director had committed the support of the Council, it was up to her to follow through on the union's promises. Before very long Feinstein found herself very much involved with other unions and with ethnic, political, women's, and consumer organizations.[12]

At the same time a consistent collaboration evolved between three labor leaders—Jan Pierce of the Communications Workers of America, Ed Gray from the UAW, and Victor Gotbaum. These three worked together in the political arena, and shared a profound dedication to educating the members of their respective unions on broad social and economic issues beyond their traditional bread-and-butter concerns.

Political participation among DC 37 members grew steadily, reaching its height during the 1970s when monthly PAC meetings filled two rooms with close to 300 in attendance. PAC work became the pride of the Council; it was a watchdog group ready to be mobilized for electoral campaigns and legislative lobbying. With the union's political action commitment growing in size and scope, the endorsement of candidates was formalized through a screening committee, selected by the PAC, although they required ultimate approval by the delegates council. According to Corcoran and Menta, only on rare occasions did Gotbaum intervene in the selection process for local candidates. The executive director was more actively involved in determining strategy and tactics for statewide and national candidacies.

To prepare volunteers drawn to political action, the department organized classes on an ad hoc basis in the techniques of organizing registration drives and for developing skills in other electoral work. Occasionally the AFSCME International office sent professional staff to assist, but its general orientation did not focus adequately on the unique conditions found in the city. Persistent efforts were made to politicize members, to get them registered and enrolled in a party, preferably Democratic. In a sample of union members taken in 1973, some 85 percent of respondents reported that they were registered, a substantial number when compared to the city's average of 68 percent. Included in this high turnout were hospital workers—primarily black women, low in status and income—with an 80 percent registration figure. Most political analysts had tended to characterize them as nonpolitical types.

Although the union included a conservative-oriented tendency in its ranks, particularly among blue-collar Italian-American workers, Council members expressed an overwhelming Democratic preference. Some 60 percent of the former group reported having voted for Richard Nixon in 1972, while the majority of DC 37 members had cast their ballots for George McGovern. This survey indicates that the union's Democratic followers were traditional New Dealers concerned mainly with socioeconomic issues. But even the conservative element was supportive of the union's positions on some economic questions.[13]

Corcoran shared Gotbaum's concern that larger segments of the membership be drawn into the union's political activities and that special efforts be made to involve the growing numbers of blacks and women joining the union. Recalling his days as a civil rights activist and his Nigerian experience with black workers, the political director actively sought minority participation. Registration drives were targeted to increase minority voting strength, while special efforts were made to recruit blacks for volunteer work with the PAC. Identification of promising talent often resulted in encouragement that they run for local office and an eventual appointment to Council staff.

One of many individuals who blossomed under the guidance of DC 37 was Charles Hughes. As a young school lunch aide and a member of Local 372, he was an inexperienced, insecure unionist who at first declined the nomination to the Council's executive board in 1965. However, as a committed activist, he attended the union's political action classes and workshops, learned how to write leaflets, make speeches, canvass voters, and manage campaign headquarters. With the encouragement of Gotbaum, who urged him to become involved in Council affairs, and with the aid of the union's training classes, he developed and sharpened his political and managerial skills to such a degree that he moved steadily up the ladder. By 1968 he not only became president of his local but soon headed the Council's increasingly important PAC. Today,

Hughes is a fervent orator in the tradition of Martin Luther King, a sophisticated and imaginative leader of some 18,000 unionists in Local 372, a longtime member of the Council's executive board, and the continuing head of its influential PAC. He has been sought after by mayors and even by a President of the United States.[14]

FUNCTIONS OF THE POLITICAL MACHINE

Sociologist Robert Merton articulated the essence of the role of the political machine when he insisted that it performs certain latent functions that are necessary to a working polity that is, not being carried on by other institutions. He wrote:

> Proceeding from the functional view, therefore, that we should *ordinarily* (not invariably) expect persistent social patterns and social structures to perform positive functions *which are at the time not adequately fulfilled by other existing patterns and structures*, the thought occurs that perhaps this publicly maligned organization is, *under present conditions*, satisfying basic latent functions.[15]

One important function of the old machine was to link voters to the political system, servicing their individual needs, making the complexities of the political world understandable, and prodding them to cast their ballots. The machine had been instrumental in helping newcomers, largely European immigrants, to adjust to their new political environments through ethnic representation and by providing a variety of assistance in an unfamiliar setting. DC 37 was well on its way to performing this function, for its registration and get-out-the-vote drives brought significant numbers of citizens into the political arena. Whenever possible, the union's staff helped newcomers to the city, as well as its own members, providing access to public officials and guiding them through a bewildering bureaucratic maze to a benefit to which they were entitled but which they might not otherwise secure.

Another vital function performed by the political machine was the selection of candidates for public office. In former years political aspirants usually had the support of a party organization as the base for election campaigns. It was the machine which provided financial help and a core of seasoned volunteers who carried around nominating petitions and rang doorbells. By the 1970s, however, the typical political machine was far weaker, its resources meagre, its patronage hardly lucrative, and the volunteer contingent disappearing. The expanding DC 37 resources included fiscal assistance as well as an increasing core of activists experienced in organizing many of the city's neighborhoods. The heightened professionalization of politics—the use of experts in polling, public relations, and fund raising—further displaced the old-style political operation. Here too, the Council, with its sophisticated staff and trained experts in the new-style politics offers candidates vital support services: professional advice, legal assistance, media expertise, and attractive printing and graphics. DC 37 staff learned to package candidates for local appeal, equal to those in the employ of private firms. The large, well-trained core of phone bank volunteers provides another important source of aid to candidates in districts where canvassing is no longer appealing.

A third function of the old machine was to provide services to members and neighborhood residents that no other institution performed—inspectors for election day, jobs for new arrivals and those thrown out of work, and cutting down red tape. While civil service rules expanded, and examinations became the entrance to city employment, residents still needed to gain access to a variety of governmental agencies. Patronage remains a concern of the city's population, for young lawyers and insurance brokers seek clients, older attorneys want judgeships, professionals need business contacts, and the average citizen still requires an assortment of help. Favors in cutting through the mammoth bureaucracy continue to be a pressing concern (e.g., help in receiving unemployment and social security benefits, legal advice, and filing complex applications with various city agencies). Tenant–landlord disputes continue to require mediation. Citizens complain of inadequate public services, deteriorating housing, unpaved streets, embattled schools, crowded health facilities, and insufficient police protection.

The panoply of services and assistance must be performed by some institution, and if the local political club is no longer in a position to be helpful, then others have to do the job. Among those who stepped into the vacuum was DC 37, for its staff knew the access points for immediate telephoning, or could offer the legal or professional support requested. However, a word of caution is in order. The Council could, through its political arm, help members and citizens. But its outreach remained limited by the restricted resources available to it under the Corcoran regime, as compared with later years when the Council's political work matured still further in scope and variety, made possible by enlarged fiscal resources.

A fourth latent function performed by the machine was its ability to mobilize diverse interests and forces into a coalition for election day—the aggregation of interests. The process of bargaining and compromising involved a delicate web of relationships and trade-offs among differing factions, and careful balancing of diverse ethnic, religious, and nationality groups. Most scholars characterize pressure groups as being single-minded, narrow in interest, unable to coalesce with others into an electoral coalition, and leaving in their wake a highly pulverized politics. However, aggregations of voters remain a necessary function of politics, and while the party has weakened in respect to this task, we have found that under the Council banner, its leadership has put together a number of winning coalitions by performing the machine's function of negotiation and compromise. While not always capable of cementing the highly fragmented political factions in the city, the Council was generally able to aggregate a left-oriented coalition of other unions, minorities, blacks, women, Jews, reformers, independent Democrats, and many community groups. The conventional wisdom that interest groups focus on interest articulation does not apply here. Indeed, because of the interpenetration of the union and the party, at times they found themselves in a reversal of roles.[16]

THE CLUBHOUSE REPLACED

Many of the old machine organizations were weakened or simply disappeared, although cliques of politicians continued to operate in select parts of the city. Among unions and other pressure groups, the DC 37 political arm constituted one of the more stable and sophisticated operations. While not controlling the political scene, it nurtured its resources carefully, allocating them to the more promising candidates. Table 12.1 contrasts the resources provided by the old, typical clubhouse and those of New York's

TABLE 12.1: Resources provided in election campaigns: DC 37 and old clubhouse compared

Resources provided by old clubhouse	Resources provided by DC 37
Volunteer-activists	Volunteer-activists
Canvassing	Canvassing
Management of candidates' headquarters	Management of candidates' headquarters
Distribution of leaflets	Distribution of leaflets
Registration drives	Registration drives
Carry petitions	Carry petitions
Election-day pull	Election-day pull
Ethnic endorsements	Ethnic endorsements
	Telephone bank
Access of political club	Political action department
Professional advice	Professional advice
Legal assistance	Legal assistance
Financial Aid	Financial Aid
Contacts and coalitions with other unions and groups	Contacts and coalitions with other unions and groups
Access to city agencies	Access to city agencies
	Public relations*
	(leaflet writing, graphics and design, printing press, outreach to media)

*The growing importance of public relations is a more recent phenomenon. Candidates are more dependent on images created by a host of professional people; surveys and polls are new, more expensive tools for sensing voter views; fund raising has also become a fine art.

AFSCME. Union resources are organized in a way to distinguish the volunteer-activists from the paid staff of the political and other departments of the Council's bureaucracy.

These substantial resources emerged as a result of the continuing growth of the Council which reached over 100,000 by the early 1970s, and meant a steady, substantial income. During electoral campaigns the large battery of telephones, unused after regular work hours, was converted to political canvassing, creating an "evening clubhouse" atmosphere. And the skill with which these resources were utilized became an important aspect of the political action staff. To replace Corcoran, who retired in 1976, Gotbaum chose Dr. Norman Adler, a young, confident political science instructor from Hunter College. Attracted to Gotbaum's progressive orientation and frank style, Adler also appreciated the resources and the vast potential of DC 37 as a political setting for implementing his own political activism.

POLITICAL ENTREPRENEUR

Adler was a rare combination of theorist and pragmatist, bringing to the Council energy, enthusiasm, and skill. Building on Corcoran's legacy, he created an updated union-made version of the political machine. It soon won the respect and admiration of public officials and other unions throughout the city and state. Self-assured and impatient with what he viewed as incompetence and sluggishness, he set high standards for those who worked alongside him. His total commitment, sometimes bordering on brashness, soon converted most of those who worked with him into ardent admirers. His previous experience had been outside the labor movement, primarily as a college instructor and community activist. He enjoyed the Byzantine world of politics and quickly mastered the techniques of electoral campaign work.While teaching he continued his political activity, serving as a paid consultant in a variety of campaigns. With an extraordinary opportunity to use his academic training and field expertise, he eagerly assumed the challenge offered him by DC 37, moving the department into new directions and extending its reach still further. Helping him achieve these goals were the invaluable resources of the Council, its large and varied membership, the professional expertise of other staff members, and ready access to funds and a printing press. Most important of all, he had won the support and confidence of the executive director. The latter's growing reputation as a dynamic union leader with a progressive social outlook afforded Adler a setting in which he could thrive.

The new political director quickly immersed himself in union affairs, mastering Council issues and identifying the personnel he could tap to help fashion his department's programs. Dynamic in style, he expected staff members to perform at their peak of energy and concern. He soon developed a network in the Council, identifying those who could be helpful with legal advice and information on health, education, and publicity. The availability of the union's own printing press was a resource of immense importance, making it easy for him to offer free or at-cost leaflets and brochures to candidates, pressure groups, and community organizations. After observing operations at the education department, he was able to package a unit for the Council's stewardship training programs containing basic facts about political action and the importance of registration and voting. At local and division weekend retreats organized by the Education staff, Adler made certain that his department had a major input, offering workshops in targeting and getting out the vote, preparing campaign literature, and showing films on political campaigning, lobbying, and techniques for the recruitment of volunteers.[17]

Attentive to the specific needs of locals, Adler keeps close contact with them, sharing information on lobbying efforts on behalf of bills having immediate concern to them. Since local officers are always anxious for favorable publicity, Adler insures that a PEP photographer is present at a meeting between local presidents and some notable, such as a legislator or key public official. Photographs and an accompanying news article are then published in PEP, a local's newsletter, or a publication of the Political Action Department. Always out on the hustings, no matter where he is, the political director constantly seeks to make friends, build support, and encourage membership involvement.

Soon after assuming office, Adler centralized the various programs of his department, linking his own lobbying activities in Albany closely to general electoral work. Although staff assisted in both areas, he retained exclusive control over the design and execution of policies and strategies. Explaining this decision, he contended that "there was an important inter-relationship between lobbying and elections. I want Albany legislators to know that behind my lobbying efforts are the electoral resources of DC 37 and its political clout which I personally dispense." Thus, in delegating authority to his staff, he nevertheless continues to supervise them at most every step of the way.

At Albany he is alert to ways of extending the union's influence. He built the upstate office into a year-round operation, expanding the clerical staff and bringing in more professional assistance. Adler hired an attorney, formerly a student intern, to help draft and review legislation on the spot, instead of waiting for the response of busy legal staff based at New York headquarters. With legislative demands growing in complexity, and sessions running into summer months, the Albany office was able to monitor a larger range of issues for the union. It became a permanent listening post even when the political director was not present, enabling the union to identify immediately any alteration in points of access, such as changes in rules and procedures, new appointments to committees, and modification of strategies by legislative leadership.[18]

Adler rented an apartment close by his Albany office, enabling him to utilize his social hours more effectively by inviting lawmakers, legislative staff, and politicians who might be helpful in his lobbying enterprise. Known for his culinary skills, visitors enjoy Adler's delicacies within the informal setting of a home atmosphere. The attraction of such an opportunity becomes understandable when one realizes that Albany, like many state capitols, has a limited social and cultural life and hotel accommodations that are not unusually appealing. Adler remains attentive to such minute important details.

The Council lobbyist brings special skills to the union's endeavors. They include his ability to translate complex research and technical data into pragmatic, useful material for policy making, and to argue cogently and forcefully with busy lawmakers and their staffs. At times direct conversations with committee members can keep an unfriendly bill from getting onto the floor. Sensitive to the pressures and demands on legislators, Adler makes his argument in a clear, crisp fashion. Confident of his own growing effectiveness, but helped by general recognition of the union's powerful political muscle, the political director extended his network of Albany contacts, the key to successful lobbying. Illustrative of his expanding friendships was the informal gatherings in his Albany office of lawmakers or labor lobbyists around bagels and coffee or giant hero sandwiches.[19]

Drawing on his experience with internship programs at Hunter College, the political director annually selected several exceptional undergraduates students to work with him in Albany. Through contacts with former colleagues, he pressed them to send the best they could find. In short order his young cadre of amateurs was converted into a sophisticated group of involved and dedicated assistants. He taught them the intricacies of the legislative process by lecturing to them and rushing them into committee meetings, hearings, and discussions in which they could observe the "system." They learned to monitor legislative calendars, keep concise notes on bills, research issues, and prepare testimony for committee hearings.

The demanding schedule Adler set for himself and his associates created a spiral of ongoing activities. Typically during a legislative session the marching orders for the week were given each Monday morning, directing staff to the key points of lobbying work. Leaving little to chance, he sought to keep abreast of relevant goings-on at Albany. Away from the office, he would often be seen outside a committee meeting ready to buttonhole lawmakers, exchange information, press for votes, or urge some strategic by-play inside or outside the legislative chamber. He expected the same intensity from his staff, including the young interns, who anxiously and amazedly watched him operate around the clock.

The Council's Annual Legislative Conference, initiated by Wurf and carried forward by Corcoran, was continued under Adler, but with a tightened agenda and increased membership participation. Preliminary to the conference, he organized an all-day meeting of representatives from the locals to identify and prioritize a number of preferred legislative items. While this proposed legislative program had eventually to be approved by the executive board and the delegates council, rarely, if ever, was the agenda modified. In the process of this preparation, Adler sought to educate these key activists on the issues involved. Kits with background material were distributed beforehand to stimulate wide-ranging debate and discussion. At the same time these debates served as a preliminary testing ground for subsequent presentations to lawmakers. In the process, the political director and his staff became increasingly familiar with local leadership and their primary legislative concerns. Appraising his reputation within the union, Adler realistically underscored the importance of being a successful lobbyist in Albany. The locals, he felt, "really care little about my political work, campaign course stuff—the meat for them is the legislation—the bread-and-butter items."[20]

The legislative conference also served as an opportunity to reach lawmakers and their staffs before the new session got under way in Albany, so as to familiarize them with the DC 37 agenda and to show off the union's extensive resources and increasing strength. The morale and pride of Council members mounted when they observed, or read in PEP, that noted political leaders were coming to their union headquarters or to attend the legislative conferences. These meetings also served to enhance the Council's reputation as a growing political force, for lawmakers noted the presence of a large number of their colleagues. In turn, the conference gave these legislators an opportunity to be seen by the core of key union activists and their top leadership. These elected officials enjoyed the publicity, especially their pictures on programs and the news stories in PEP, which reaches some 100,000 families throughout the city.

OUTREACH TO THE REPUBLICANS

Adler quickly recognized, as had Corcoran, that the union's role in Albany was severely handicapped by its continued close association with the Democratic Party and Gotbaum's coolness to Republicans. Since the senate and at times the assembly were controlled by the Republicans, this simply did not make sense to the new department head. And on those occasions when Democrats won a majority in the assembly it was often by a narrow margin. Under the state's constitution, two-thirds majorities of both chambers were required for a number of important legislative matters, further enhancing the role of Republicans. In addition, Republican lawmakers, especially from upstate areas, did not suffer the high rate of turnover of city Democrats, who often sought judgeships. Thus, the former accumulated maturing experience and seniority in the legislative process. Adler felt that by friendly overtures to select Republicans, the Council could enhance its effectiveness in Albany. This seemed especially true in light of the negative consequences of the influence of Raymond Corbett, head of the State Federation of Labor, upon Republican governors and lawmakers, because of his unsympathetic attitude toward public service unions.

After Adler's increasing insistence, Gotbaum finally agreed to alter union strategy. It was then that tactful overtures were made to certain legislators from the dominant party, assuring them that their cooperation in Albany would be remembered at election time. Explaining this new approach to DC 37 members in 1976, the political director insisted that

We have realized that we must be blind to party affiliation when it comes to deciding who our friends are. The three Republican candidates endorsed have taken our positions, often in the face of heavy pressure from their own party, on matters vital to the union: pensions, aid to the city, prevailing rate bargaining, and funds for libraries and school.[21]

One of the most valuable rewards of this new outreach to the Republicans was the link forged with Senate Majority Leader Warren Anderson. In Binghamton, the upstate heartland of Republican strength, Anderson was associated with an influential law firm, one of whose partners served as the Rockefeller's family attorney and as a prominent fund-raiser for the national Republican party organization. As Rockefeller began to pay attention to his future on the national scene, leaving state politics to others, Warren Anderson became interested in his own possibilities for the governorship. Obviously an association with an important liberal labor constituency downstate, such as DC 37, could be useful. The Republican legislative leader proved receptive to a number of items on the agenda of public service workers, ingratiating himself to Gotbaum by endorsing the agency shop, one of the most controversial bills introduced annually by the Council. This proposal would make payment of union dues obligatory, insuring that "freeloaders," as Gotbaum called nonmembers, would contribute their share of the expenses for the union's collective bargaining staff, grievance processors, and for increased benefits and services provided all public employees covered by negotiated contracts.

Gotbaum and Adler vigorously pursued the legislature on behalf of the agency shop. If enacted, they knew it would provide the union with a dependable source of income. As senate majority leader, Anderson played a critical role in facilitating enactment of the agency shop in 1977. Deeply appreciative, the DC 37 executive director responded with a "Salute to Anderson" reception at Council headquarters, in cooperation with some 400 friends from other public service unions. Not long afterwards, "Andy" Anderson graciously acknowledged the "generous contribution" made by DC 37 to the New York State Republican Campaign Committee Funds, as well as the Council's endorsement of 13 Republican legislative candidates for the 1978 elections. Satisfied with the outcome, the senate majority leader sent Gotbaum a proposed list of legislative committee appointments, anticipating that the labor leader would be pleased with his assignments.[22]

During this same period, the Council's director became increasingly disenchanted with the conservative behavior of a number of Democratic leaders. In his columns in the union newspaper, he complained bitterly about state Democrats coming to look more and more like the typical Republican. In caustic tones, he lashed out at Democratic governor Hugh Carey, who won election in 1974 on campaign promises to insure a tight budget with cuts in education, welfare, and revenue sharing with cities. Carey's critique of "too much government" as the source of the state's fiscal difficulties caused Gotbaum to compare it with traditional, short-sighted Republican rhetoric. To his union supporters, Gotbaum warned that he was not yet ready to join a Republican fellowship: "While I am just about ready to give up on Democrats in this state, you will have to forgive my hesitancy in embracing the Republicans." Although leading Democratic lawmakers were unhappy with the new DC 37 Republican strategy, particularly Senate Minority Leader Manfred Ohrenstein, Gotbaum was delighted with some of the legislative payoffs.[23]

Republicans supported by DC 37
in 1978 elections to state legislature

Candidate	District	County
Guy Velella	80 Assembly	Bronx
John LoPresto	35 Assembly	Queens
John Calandra	34 Senate	Bronx
John Flynn	35 Senate	Bronx/Westchester
Martin Knorr	15 Senate	Queens/Kings
Christopher Mega	21 Senate	Kings
John Marchi	24 Senate	Staten Island
Roy Goodman	26 Senate	Manhattan
Joseph Reilly	14 Assembly	Nassau
John Flanagan	7 Assembly	Suffolk
Joseph Bruno	41 Senate	Parts of Columbia–Saratoga
Hugh Farley	44 Senate	Parts of Montgomery–Fulton–Hamilton, Schenectady–Saratoga
Anthony Gazzara	14 Senate	Rockland

LABOR COALITION:
PUBLIC EMPLOYEES CONFERENCE

Confronted with traditional conservatism and legislative obstructionism by Raymond Corbett and the State Federation of Labor, Adler sought friends among other public service unions. In 1977 he felt the time was ripe to draw together a coalition that included participants in the city's Municipal Labor Committee and key upstate organizations such as the Civil Service Employees Association (CSEA), police, firefighters, teachers, transit workers, nurses, and others. In all, 22 organizations representing over 750,000 public workers were brought together in the Public Employees Conference (PEC), which was chaired by Barry Feinstein of the Teamsters. By then the Teamster head had drawn close to Gotbaum on an organizational as well as a personal basis. Despite personality clashes and strong ideological differences, teacher leader Albert Shanker accepted Gotbaum's invitation to join the new alliance and serve as one of its vice-presidents. (See Table 12.2)[24]

PEC members agreed quickly on a common legislative agenda, focusing on such key concerns as the agency shop, pension buyback for veterans, passage of OSHA, improvement of retirement benefits for lower paid workers, and modification of the Taylor Law. Many PEC affiliates had their own representatives in Albany who could be mobilized quickly to assist in more unified lobbying endeavors on behalf of their common objectives. In essence it was the DC 37 political director who kept in close command of PEC activities in Albany and successfully pressed the groups to contribute funds, campaign literature, telephone banks, and doorbell ringers during election campaigns of lawmakers who had proven themselves supportive of the overall goals of public workers. In this fashion the Council's political clout was extended, through the unions allied with PEC. Adler threw these organizational resources into election campaigns as early as possible, preferably before the primaries. Somewhat typical of this long-range planning was his success, during the spring 1979 legislative session, in winning PEC commitment to actively support Democratic lawmaker Anthony Semminario. The latter had barely squeezed through in the last legislative elections in a traditionally conservative, often Republican, 31st Assembly District in Queens. At a strategy meeting in his

Albany office, Adler secured specific commitments of money and in-kind services long before the 1980 elections. This early support not only helped insure Semminario's reelection but enhanced the roles of DC 37 and PEC, both in the city and upstate. And this selective strategy helped secure new important points of access for DC 37.

In 1979 an additional staff member was appointed to direct lobbying at City Hall. For the next few years affable, knowledgeable Vincent Montalbano monitored the daily work of the city coun-

TABLE 12.2: Public Employees Conference Officers

CHAIRMAN
Barry Feinstein
Local 237, IBT

CO-CHAIRMEN

Victor Gotbaum	William McGowan	Albert Shanker
DC 37, AFSCME	*CSEA*	*United Federation of Teachers*

OFFICERS

John Lawe	Al Sgaglione	Robert Gollnick
Treasurer	Corresponding Secretary	Recording Secretary
Local 100, TWU	*NYS Police Conference*	*NYS Professional Firefighters*

BOARD OF DIRECTORS

Anthony Abbate	*Subway–Surface Supervisors Association*
Richard Basoa	*Correction Officers Benevolent Association*
Sam DeMilia	*NYC–PBA*
Joseph Dominelli	*NYS Chiefs of Police*
Ed Jennings	*Uniformed Fire Officers Association*
Jim Jennings	*AFSCME*
Jack Jordan	*NYCHA–PBA*
Al Mandanici	*Correction Captains Association*
John Maye	*NYCTA–PBA*
Harold Melnick	*Sergeants Benevolent Association*
Ed Ostrowski	*Uniformed Sanitationmen's Association*
Dr. Murray Schneider	*NYSC of AFSA Locals*
Frank Sisto	*Sanitation Officers Association*
Richard Vizzini	*NYC Firefighters Association*
Jack Zuckerman	*Council of Supervisors and Administrators*

cil, Board of Estimate, the mayor's office, and administrative agencies. By devoting full-time staffers to city relations, the union was able to improve its access to legislators and their staffs, facilitate last-minute changes in budget items, as well as call up of members for special lobbying endeavors on short notice. For example, when funds were cut in the city's budget for school crossing guards, libraries, and several cultural institutions, Montalbano put into gear the full panoply of lobbying and human resources available at the union, only a "stone's throw from City Hall itself." He also directed an aggressive campaign for voluntary payroll checkoff for political activities. In 1980 he finally secured city council endorsement of the political checkoff only to have a hostile Mayor Edward Koch dub it a union "slush fund" and veto it. Koch's general popularity and strong influence over city council members kept his veto from being overridden.[25]

Montalbano's work was similar to the lobbying strategies employed at the state level—memos to city council members explaining the DC 37 position on specific bills, preparation of testimony for hearings, legislative luncheons, timely visits with lawmakers and staffs, developing contacts with local party organizations and community groups, mobilizing letter-writing campaigns and telephone brigades, and organizing delegations to visit with legislators. He also helped deliver extensive electoral support to legislators and new candidates friendly to DC 37.

ELECTORAL STRATEGIES:
THE DC 37 MACHINE MATURES

Under Adler's leadership electoral activities were linked integrally to his lobbying operations. While expanding the union's grassroots thrust and electoral involvement in the city, he also became involved in select legislative races upstate, seeking to increase the number of AFSCME friends at the state capitol. When not in Albany or at his New York desk, he was often found at the local clubhouse in Brooklyn, extending his network of politician–friends influential on the Albany scene, including Stanley Steingut, speaker of the assembly (1974–78), Stanley Fink, majority leader and successor to Steingut as speaker, Melvin Miller, and others. Alongside these local Democratic party strongholds scattered throughout the city and other groups organized for elections, the DC 37 political operation was often more than their equal. Adler's skill and driving energy quickly won the confidence and admiration of Gotbaum, assuring the former wide latitude in dispensing the union's resources. With vigor and care, he nurtured friends and tightened commitments. As Gotbaum's interest turned to the larger scene, and Lillian Roberts became increasingly occupied with the Health and Hospitals Corporation and internal union matters, many political decisions were left to the political director. Adler was sensitive to Gotbaum's authority however, and always sought his advice on strategic decisions. Within the parameters of the potential influence of DC 37, the political director adhered to several carefully designed strategies to target its valuable resources. The Council fulfilled its promise to assist friendly lawmakers running for reelection, but especially those holding key leadership positions in the assembly and senate. Secondly, candidates in marginal districts were also aided when it appeared that DC 37 resources might make a difference. While this strategy was first pursued under Corcoran, the expansion of union resources and the more selective targeting under Adler increased the number and impact of these decisions.

Examples of this marginal strategy occurred as early as 1974, when seven of eleven tough races were pinpointed for special attention and investment of resources by DC 37. In upstate Ulster County, a conservative, unfriendly Republican assembly floor manager was targeted by DC 37 and defeated in the elections, as was Vito Battista, another hostile lawmaker from a Brooklyn–Queens district. Assembly Speaker Steingut, close friend of the Council and a powerful political figure, was allocated $25,000 and an equal amount in services in a bitter primary battle. The union also paid close attention to special elections. Since these usually involved the smallest of electoral turnouts, Adler felt that union involvement in these instances could make a major difference. Typical of this strategy was the assistance offered Eliot Engel in his tough bid for an assembly seat in 1977 from the Co-op City district in the northeast Bronx. Despite the fact that the regular Democratic candidate also had Republican endorsement, Engel managed, with aggressive support from PAC members who flocked into the area, to squeeze through by a razor-edge 99 vote margin out of 14,000 cast. Another example of critical union help in a special election involved Democrat Louis Freda who, in 1979, won in a Republican stronghold in Brooklyn's Bay Ridge section.

Another predictable strategy was to give encouragement to those with a progressive orientation. With the increasing strength of conservative forces in the state, and the appearance of extreme right-wing pressure groups during the 1970s, DC 37 assured those who shared its general outlook that they could count on the union. A bitter and crucial battle in Staten Island between moderate liberal and extreme conservative views centered on John Marchi's 1978 race for reelection to the state senate. The widespread conservative forces in the county drew together behind an opposition candidate in the Republican primary, which was particularly threatening to Marchi. The Council mobilized its full resources on Marchi's behalf as it allocated over $4,000, utilized its telephone bank, printed leaflets, and sent a battery of volunteers to help run his campaign headquarters. Selected from among those who lived on Staten Island, they were representative of Marchi's blue-collar and white ethnic constituents. In addition, Adler conscripted vital support services from six other unions associated with the Municipal Labor Committee.

In the face of the national Republican sweep behind Reagan in 1980, New York voters managed, on the whole, to retain their liberal state and local officials. This was due in part to the work of progressive organized strength as represented by DC 37 membership and its political arm. In its year-end report, the Political Department assumed credit for vital assistance given in the primary victories of 40 of 45 liberal candidates, and in 43 of 48 election-day races.[26]

AFSCME endorsements in New York continued to reflect, as well, the ethnic and racial composition of its membership, for Adler warmly supported the union's outreach to minority communities. In turn, representatives from these groups were well aware of the union's social advocacy. Active minority voices strengthened by the Council included Tom Fortune, Angelo Del Toro, Herman Farrell, Jr., Al Vann, Major Owens, Carl McCall, Joseph Galiber, Olga Mendez, Robert Garcia, David Dinkens, and Basil Paterson. Involved civil rights, ethnic, and community groups could generally rely on a contribution from the Council or one of its locals in the form of dinners, seats at theatre benefits, and journal advertisements. As a result of its grass-roots activities among the city's minorities, the union extended its political presence throughout the five counties and beyond. When Stanley Steingut, speaker of the assembly, was defeated in a bruising Democratic primary, the minority constituency in his district voted for him, primarily because of the special outreach and active support of his candidacy by DC 37.

A final strategy which enhanced the Council's political clout was its assistance to select suburban and upstate candidates. While support of Democrats was generally easy to pursue, its Republican strategy sometimes made Gotbaum restless and uncomfortable. On occasion it required endorsing a candidate who, while supportive of many of the union's legislative proposals, was nevertheless distinctly conservative in his approach to most other issues. One such race involved the candidacy of Republican Fred Warder in the Poughkeepsie area for the state senate in 1978. Although Warder ran with Conservative party endorsement, the union nevertheless afforded him considerable assistance, including the assignment of a political staff member to coordinate his campaign. The Council input was recognized by Warder as playing a significant role in his reelection. The race firmly cemented the relationship between Warren Anderson and the union, giving him the edge necessary to continue his party's control of the senate chamber.[27]

FIGURE 12.1: Adler's political operation

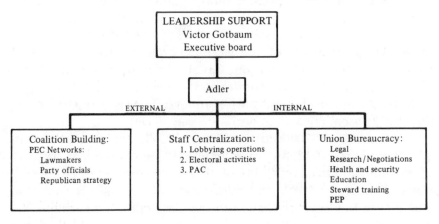

SUMMARY

By 1981 DC 37 had one of the most effective and sophisticated political operations in the city, if not the state. Its lobbying operations were skillful and influential at many levels of government. Constrained during the Rockefeller years, it blossomed once he left the state scene, making significant strides with the aid of key Republican lawmakers, but particularly Warren Anderson, the senate majority leader. Council lobbyists won the agency shop, OSHA, the career pension opener, and select items in the state's budget. Additionally, they were effective in preventing harmful legislation from passing, such as revision of the insurance laws which would eliminate abortion coverage, Mayor Koch's civil service "reforms," and elimination of drug addiction instructors from the budget. The staff also took credit for its energetic work protecting the budget of the City University of New York and keeping Metropolitan Hospital open.

At the same time, the outer limits of DC 37 influence were clearly evident: the agency shop legislation required periodic renewal and intense lobbying endeavors, the Taylor Law remained on the statute books, pensions negotiated with the city were no longer ratified automatically by the state legislature, and public service unions suffered another serious setback when the legislature enacted a pension law reducing benefits to new public workers. In these and other instances, the forceful rhetoric of Gotbaum and the intensive lobbying by Adler were of little avail.

Electoral activities became more professionalized and increasingly effective under Adler's leadership. By targeting marginal districts and by allocating resources judiciously and effectively, he enhanced the influence of the Council dramatically. Figure 12.1 summarizes Adler's operation. On the broader electoral front—citywide, statewide and national political contests—DC 37 was, of course, a smaller element among diverse factors influencing the eventual outcome of elections.

During the 1970s and the 1980s, DC 37 was generally consulted by local, state, and even national Democratic leaders as to its position and the availability of its resources in key electoral contests. As early as 1969 the Council served successfully as a vital element in Lindsay's reelection to the mayoralty. Increasingly, the Council's executive director and political arm assumed leadership roles in the formation of liberal–progressive coalitions for major electoral contests. In partial recognition of the union's political clout, Gotbaum was soon involved on the national arena within the Democratic Party, playing an important role in altering its rules for national conventions and primaries, opening them to women and minorities. He had become an important broker, aided by his own union's effective political machine.

Finally, the union's reputation as social advocate for a wide range of issues and causes—fair justice, economic equity, ecological protection, anti-nuclear and disarmament goals, abortion prerogatives, and women's rights—was widely heralded by progressive groups. An endless line of individuals and organizations sought to associate themselves with the Council and to tap its resources.

NOTES

1. Sterling Spero and John Capozzola, *The Urban Community and Its Unionized Bureaucracies*, New York: Dunellen, 1973, p. 82.

2. A substantial source of information for this chapter has been personal observation by the authors and involvement with the leadership of DC 37 for more than a decade. Jewel Bellush, a political scientist, was a former colleague of Norman Adler at Hunter College and, over the years, provided student interns for the union's Political Action Department.

3. Legislative committee minutes, 1969; Wurf files, DC 37. In 1959, for example, Committee attendance ranged from 7 to 22. Included among the most active cadre were John Boer, Victor Thompson, Harry Levine and Nathan Simon. The following list of expenses for 1958 indicates the limited funds available for the committee's lobbying work: telephone, $150; typist, $75; postage, $300; legislative news, $500; bill drafting, $250; Nathan Simon, drafting, $231; legislative index, $225; telegrams, $800; personal services, $2^{1}/_{2}$ men for a maximum of 2 days per week, $2,250. The total expenses came to $4,781. DC 37 legislative committee minutes, December 18, 1958.

4. Jerry Wurf and Harry Levine to DC 37 members in the Bertram Podell district, August 24, 1962; Jacob Gilbert Campaign, 1962; Wurf files.

5. *Public Employee Press*, October 26, 1962, p. 4; taped interview, John Boer, August 15, 1983.

6. Frank J. Macchiarola, "The State and the City," in Robert H. Connery and Gerald Benjamin, eds., *Governing New York State, The Rockefeller Years*, Montpelier, VT: Academy of Political Science, 1974, p. 114.

7. Alexander B. Callow, Jr., ed., *The City Boss in America*, New York: Oxford University Press, 1976, p. 311.

8. Victor Gotbaum to John Corcoran, December 5, 1967; *Public Employee Press*, December 27, 1967; p. 4; interview with John Corcoran, November 4, 1981.

9. *Public Employee Press,* January 17, 1969, p. 10. In a survey undertaken in 1973, 9 percent of Council respondents reported that they had sent at least one letter to a state official that year. In actual numbers this amounted to approximately 10,000 letters. Wayne Parsons, Charles Kadushin and Bogdan Denitch, "Preliminary Report: Study of Members of District Council 37, AFSCME," Bureau of Applied Social Research, Columbia University, February 1974, p. 32.

10. See Bernard Bellush, *Franklin D. Roosevelt as Governor of New York,* New York: Columbia University, 1955; Jewel Bellush, "Herbert Lehman as Governor of New York," Ph.D. dissertation, Columbia University, 1959.

11. Interviews with Guido Menta, November 22, 1978, and October 20, 1981.

12. *Ibid.,* and interview with Elizabeth Feinstein-Cook, November 10, 1983.

13. Wayne Parsons, Kadushin, and Bogdan Denitch, "Preliminary Report: Study of Members, DC 37," Bureau of Applied Survey Research, Columbia University, February 1974, p. 16.

14. Charles Hughes to DC 37 executive board, December 17, 1965; interview with Charles Hughes, October 30, 1981.

15. Robert Merton, "The Latent Functions of the Machine," in Edward Banfield, ed., *Urban Government,* New York: The Free Press of Glencoe, 1961, p. 181.

16. In 1976, for example, DC 37 led coalition building in each of the congressional districts, putting together tickets for delegates to the national convention. In Chicago, under Daley, the machine organization under his control forced interest groups, including labor unions, to be aggregated by the Democratic party.

17. Department of Political Action and Legislation, Annual Report, 1976, section on division and local conferences, unpaged, union files.

18. Alan G. Hevesi, *Legislative Politics in New York State,* New York: Praeger, 1975; Interview with Norman Adler, May 12, 1980. Adler's lobbying activities were observed by one of the authors on May 13 and 14, 1980.

19. Author's observations of Adler, May 13, 1980. Adler spoke to 9 of 13 committee members as they left the room on a bill concerned with initiative and referendum reform, explaining the weakness in the proposed legislation.

20. Interview with Adler, February 4, 1982.

21. Minutes, PAC meeting, October 22, 1976, Department of Political Action files.

22. Warren Anderson to Victor Gotbaum, January 18 and December 26, 1978; Edward Maher memo to Norman Adler, September 19, 1978.

23. *Public Employee Press,* February 11, 1977, p. 2; interview with Elizabeth Clark, December 7, 1981. Ms. Clark was a staff member of a Democratic state senator.

24. Author's observation of PEC meeting, May 13, 1980. PEC organizations included: Teamsters Local 237, DC 37, CSEA, the United Federation of Teachers, Transport Workers Union Local 100, New York State Police Conference, New York State Firefighters, Subway–Surface Supervisors Association, Correction Officers Benevolent Association, New York City Police Benevolent Association, New York State Chiefs of Police, Uniformed Fire Officers Association, State AFSCME, New York City Housing Authority Police Benevolent Association, Correction Captains Association, New York City Police Benevolent Association, Sergeants Benevolent Association, Uniformed Sanitationmen's Association, Sanita-

tion Officers Association, New York City Firefighters Association, Council of Supervisors and Administrators, and Nassau-Suffolk Council of School Administrators and Supervisors, Local 12.

25. During the 1980 session of the city council, five DC 37 priority items were adopted, three as home rule messages. They included political contributions by voluntary checkoff, supplemental pension benefits (COLA), increase of city contributions to Medicare premium, creation of medical review board for disability retirement disputes, pension buy-back for employees in the Rent Control Agency. Under the New York state constitution, certain legislative matters require a home rule message, i.e., approval of the local governmental body. In this instance, it meant the New York city council.

26. Political Action Department, Annual Report, 1980, department files.

27. Interview with Adler, November 16, 1983.

13
Political Participation

Men and women are not, by nature, political animals, for many do not see the connections between politics and their personal lives. There are more immediately important, or more interesting, things to do than participate in the civic arena—earning a living, raising families, and enjoying what limited leisure there is. Ambitious union members may prefer to pursue careers that also impinge on time for relaxation. Distances between work and home are often considerable, particularly in New York City. And for most women, some 60 percent of the Council, their double lives have meant caring for families while earning a living. Researchers often claim that low-income and minority populations are not drawn to active politics. However, the rather intensive membership involvement in the DC 37 political action program indicates that these obstacles do not necessarily discourage participation. In this chapter, we examine the strategies of the leadership and staff, the inducements offered, and the variety of programs that are purposefully developed to encourage healthy, vigorous, participatory politics.

LEADERSHIP

Gotbaum and Roberts have always been strong advocates of the broadest possible participation of members in union affairs and political action. In the first place, they believed that active involvement was an essential ingredient of democracy. Second, through their cooperation members provided an additional vital resource

Typical of DC 37's political efforts on behalf of causes beyond its own bread and butter concerns is support of Cesar Chavez and the farm workers' organizing drives. Charles Hughes (second from right) PAC Chair and president of Schools Local 372, along with other Council members, join Chavez in New York to pressure the Defense Department.

for the union by extending its political influence with governmental officials, by expanding the horizons of negotiators in evolving policy for collective bargaining sessions, and in enhancing the union presence in broader community and national issues. Finally, they supported the linkage of politics and education vigorously, believing that members had to be persistently reminded of the close ties of politics to their lives in concrete and specific ways.

In his study of AFSCME workers, political scientist Julian Baim concluded that "The ability of DC 37's leadership tó mobilize its workers should not...be underestimated. DC 37 is considered a potent force in New York City and state politics precisely because it can generate enthusiasm for union-supported candidates and issues among its members." Along similar lines, a Columbia University study found that the union successfully mobilized large numbers of people on various political issues. Staff were recruited who shared a commitment to extend membership participation. Political Action Directors John Corcoran and Norman Adler warmly embraced the philosophical outlook of the top leadership and labored diligently to broaden involvement.[1] This was no easy task for staff. As Corcoran noted in a memorandum to Gotbaum, "I detect a general feeling of pessimism when the recruitment of volunteers is mentioned. I have no reason to subscribe to such feelings and will not until we have made some real effort to recruit volunteers." He believed that the program would succeed when sufficient individuals were convinced of the need for political action and were given a useful role to play.[2]

INCENTIVES TO PARTICIPATION

According to Mancur Olson, a *latent group* is a large organization in which a single individual does not make a noticeable difference in its workings. Since such people do not feel they are making a contribution, Olson concludes, there is no incentive for them to participate. He contends that "...an individual in a 'latent' group, by definition, cannot make a noticeable contribution to any group effort and since no one in the group will react if he [sic] makes no contribution, he has no incentive to contribute."[3]

DC 37 can be viewed as a latent organization. Because of its success in attaining the agency shop and dues checkoff, large numbers of workers automatically become members. Thus, the union acquired a stable membership and a secure source of financial support. Participation, as a result, appeared less urgent. Improvements in wages and working conditions subsequently won at the bargaining table seemed to evolve automatically, offering little inducement for involvement in union affairs. Therefore, suggests Olson, separate and selective incentives are necessary to stimulate a rational individual in a latent group to act in a group-oriented way. Since most members were unwilling, of their own accord, to volunteer the time and energy necessary for constructive participation in political activities, then attractive incentives were necessary to stimulate involvement. As an old Manhattan political sage, District Leader George Washington Plunkitt, remarked, "When a man [sic] works in politics, he should get something out of it."

Another way of expressing this has been suggested by Robert Salisbury and James Wilson as the "exchange theory." This views the leader–follower relationship as similar to that of a businessman and customer. The leader is conceived as the entrepreneur of the enterprise, who provides the initiative for organization and the "capital," with the "products" to be sold to the general public. Thus, in a voluntary organization the products are the various incentives that attract and retain followers. The incentives or benefits can be classified as of three general types: material, solidarity, and purposive.

Material incentives include immediate payoffs (usually monetary) and, in the instance of a union, improved wages, hours, and working conditions. Also part of the reward system are the individual favors a union can bestow, similar to the help extended by the old-style political clubhouse, such as helping members get children into college or finding a summer job, cutting red tape in a city agency, or assisting a worker in getting priority treatment for housing.

Solidarity incentives have social roots and include the enjoyment and pleasure one receives from socializing with others, deriving a sense of friendship and comraderie. This also involves honors and awards that win respect and admiration from one's peers. As one study concluded, "Collective solidary [sic] incentives are derived from the congeniality and the social attractiveness of the group." As has often been the case in DC 37, one's picture prominently displayed in a newsletter or one's name in the union paper, gives an individual inestimable pride.

Purposive incentives are cause-related and are more ideological in character, such as working for world peace, social justice, women's rights, and environmental protection. These benefits, however, are generally of a collective genre, not immediately rewarding to the individual who participates in such activities. "If the environment is cleaned up," suggest Ruth Scott and Ronald Hrebenar, "all inhabitants of a geographical area benefit, not just the group membership."

These three categories of incentives, however, cannot always be clearly delineated. At times a combination of incentives are at work on an involved individual. Along these lines, Hrebenar and Scott have suggested that, "Solidary [sic] benefits are usually combined with purposive and material benefits to make political organizations more attractive to a wider range of potential members who may not be highly motivated by these latter benefits." On occasion, they maintain, politically oriented organizations retain a percentage of their membership primarily on social incentives.[4]

The DC 37 political action staff, in cooperation with a number of leaders from the various locals, showed an understanding of the members' attraction to select incentives as a motivation for participation in political projects. Table 13.1 summarizes the variety of inducements offered the DC 37 membership. It should be noted that specific activities often provided members with different combinations of incentives. For example, lobbying generally achieved concrete results, such as winning major benefits through legislative enactment. At the same time, the lobbying effort offered members a social activity, an opportunity for group solidarity, and friendship. Politics has its enjoyable aspects, such as the socializing during a day's outing to Albany or Washington with other workers. In both the Parsons, Kadushin and Denitch and Baim surveys, as many as half the respondents reported that they "enjoyed participation" in union activities, and many described it as "fun."[5]

In addition, different inducements tended to attract different members of the Council. While demonstrations for civil rights inevitably drew a significant representation of white members, even larger delegations of the union's black constituency were always evident. Social workers and librarians have tended to be more supportive of ideological issues, those concerns that go beyond immediate bread-and-butter matters, such as arms control, the nuclear freeze, Central America, and the environment. The delegation, for example, that journeyed to Pennsylvania to participate in the Three-Mile Island demonstration against reopening a flawed nuclear energy plant included a large representation of members attracted to its purposive character. Overall, AFSCME people have been motivated by material appeals. However, while material considerations constitute a strong incentive, top leadership and staff have, through a variety of incentives, newspaper articles, and educational offerings encouraged participation in more purposive programs.

TABLE 13.1: DC 37 incentives for political action

Material	Solidarity	Purposive
Raffles, door prizes	Attending PAC meetings	Women's conference
Good food	Demonstrations, marches	Three-Mile Island demonstration
Discounts at stores	Conferences	Earth Day
Weekend at vacation resort	Lobbying	Coalition on El Salvador
Lobbying* Campaigning*	Campaigning	Martin L. King Day
Gifts (carry bags, leather cases, ties, home appliances)		Lobbying
Favors		

*Lobbying for material inducements would include legislative proposals that members from a particular local are pursuing.

MILBRATH'S HIERARCHY OF POLITICAL INVOLVEMENT

In his study of participation, Lester Milbrath suggests that activist citizens cluster around three types along an active–inactive continuum, as noted in Table 13.2. The levels of participation constitute a hierarchy of costs in time, energy, and skills. The Level of involvement and knowledge required for the tasks performed vary considerably.[6]

At the top of Milbrath's diagram are placed "gladiatorial activities," those that require the greatest expenditure of energy, personal commitment, and skill, as when holding public and party office, running as a candidate, soliciting funds, or attending a caucus or strategy meeting. A second rung of participants are in "transitional activities," which include attending a political meeting or rally or making a financial contribution to a party of a candidate. They are labeled transitional because these participants may move from time to time from one category to another or simply become

TABLE 13.2: Hierarchy of Political Involvement

GLADIATORIAL ACTIVITIES Holding public and party office Being a candidate for office Soliciting political funds Attending a caucus or a strategy meeting Becoming an active member in a political party Contributing time in a political campaign
TRANSITIONAL ACTIVITIES Attending a political meeting or rally Making a monetary contribution to a party or candidate Contacting a public official or a political leader
SPECTATOR ACTIVITIES Wearing a button or putting a sticker on the car Attempting to talk another into voting a certain way Initiating a political discussion Voting Exposing oneself to political stimuli
APATHETICS

Source: Lester W. Milbrath: *Political Participation,* Copyright 1965 Houghton Mifflin Company. Used with permission.

political dropouts and join the apathetics. As will be noted below, the exhortations from the union's leadership, staff, and articles PEP persistently urge political involvement; the incentives described above constitute an integral part of this encouragement. An invitation to a free weekend conference at an attractive resort hotel is but one of many "come-ons," as was a week-long cruise in the Caribbean.

At the next and lowest level, one finds "spectator activities" which involve voting, wearing a button, putting a sticker on the car, or initiating a political discussion. Outside this hierarchy of the politically involved are the "apathetics" or nonparticipants. Milbrath suggests that ranking of items in the hierarchy may vary from election to election and from time to time. The rankings shown in the diagram are based on percentages of Americans who engage in that particular behavior. It is generally estimated, for example, that less than one percent engage in the top two or three activities, while about 4 or 5 percent join a party, work in a campaign, and attend meetings. About 10 percent make monetary contributions and 13 percent contact public officials. As one descends to the bottom of the diagram, 40 to 70 percent of the citizenry are exposed to political messages and vote in any given election.

As a hierarchy of costs and skills, Milbrath's analysis is a useful

The widely acclaimed telephone bank of DC 37 in action at Council headquarters.

tool, when modified and adapted, for understanding the scope of
political activities in DC 37 and the level of participation of its
members (Table 13.3). Where possible we will indicate the size of
the activist core and identify the participants.[7] Gladiatorial activities in the union include four major channels for member participation: the volunteer–active core, the PAC, the course offerings in
political action, and the legislative conference.

TABLE 13.3: Hierarchy of Political Involvement in DC 37*

> **GLADIATORIAL ACTIVITIES**
> Being hard-core activists
> Participating in political action committee
> Attending courses in campaign/lobbying
> Becoming a member/active of a political party
> Contributing a time to campaign**
> Attending Legislative Conference

> **TRANSITIONAL ACTIVITIES**
> Participating in community associations
> Making a people contribution
> Lobbying
> Ad Hoc actions

> **SPECTATOR ACTIVITIES**
> Reading PEP regularly
> Attending education, women's and other conferences
> Voting
> Youth programs

> **APATHETICS**

* Adapted from Milbrath's Figure 1, "Hierarchy of Political Involvement"
** Campaign activities include phone banks, staffing candidate headquarters, election day operations, canvassing voters, petitioning, literature distribution and technical assistance.

Source: Lester W. Milbrath: *Political Participation,* Copyright 1965 Houghton Mifflin Company. Used with permission.

VOLUNTEER–ACTIVIST CORE

The Political Action staff concedes that there are difficulties in attracting the Council's constituency to politics. "There is no doubt about it," underscored Associate Director Vincent Montalbano, "we have to work at it all the time." The staff estimated that in recent years, 150–200 members have constituted a hard core of dedicated, dependable, and skilled activist–volunteers, available at a moment's notice for campaigns, lobbying, legislative hearings, public demonstrations, and other forms of involvement (Table 13.4). In the course of a typical campaign, other activists from the PACs of large locals add substantially to the initial core.

In a 12-month period, the Political Department was able to channel the energies of some 600 volunteers in 45 primaries and 50 general election contests. In 1978, when John Marchi, a Republican state senator, faced his serious primary fight he survived largely through the dedicated assistance of scores of volunteers

TABLE 13.4: DC 37 political activity, 1980

Activity	Number of participants
Albany lobby for agency shop	300
City Hall lobby for passage of pension COLA	250
Three-Mile Island protest demonstration, Harrisburg, Pennsylvania	100
Washington, D.C. demonstration in protest against U.S. involvement in El Salvador	200
Election Day canvassing for President Carter	1,000

Source: Political Action Department, annual report, 1980.

from an assortment of locals. On primary day alone over 100 members spread out in his community to ring doorbells. At the same time, DC 37 stimulated the cooperation of the Uniformed Firemen, the Teamsters, and the Police Benevolent Association, among others.[8]

The telephone bank has evolved as a vital element in the political operation of the union, especially in New York City, where increasing numbers of apartment dwellers refuse to open their doors to bell ringers. In the course of a normal political campaign, half a dozen or more telephones are operated constantly by retirees during daylight hours. Many of these retirees, who are uneasy about traveling to and from union headquarters at night, are veteran local and Council officeholders who have already made significant contributions to the union during the last decades. They know how to canvass and organize, and are therefore most effective. After regular work hours much of the union headquarters is transformed into a telephone operation. It is then that a substantial number of gladiator volunteer–activists, a majority of them from the Clerical–Administrative Local 1549 and the School Support Services Local 372, stream into the building from all parts of the city. Every night during a political campaign, at least 80 of them telephone registered voters in designated districts, including most of the 100,000 AFSCME members. Free sandwiches, cake, and coffee are provided each night during the campaign. Those who volunteer at least six evenings are invited after elections to a night of socializing, cocktails, and an overflowing buffet of food.

Certain issues stimulate greater response by specific groupings within the union. The Retirees Association, for example, which has become an increasingly important resource under the leadership of President Eliot Reif and Staff Coordinator Eleanor Litwak, can produce a dependable core of experienced and committed activists for issues of special concern, such as social security, pensions, health insurance, and subway and bus tolls for senior citizens. A smaller but influential number of these retirees can be relied on to journey to City Hall, Albany and Washington in support of general political activities of the Council. On the other hand, blue-collar and professional locals have been far less involved in the entire panoply of political programs, although individuals from these locals are attracted and represented in the activist core.

Milbrath indicates that contributing time in a political campaign is a gladiatorial activity. However, the DC 37 members who fit this category are generally of far greater experience, better trained, and more deeply committed than the typical campaign volunteer. Milbrath also found that as an individual became more involved in politics the engagement was "in a wider repertoire of political acts and moves upward in the hierarchy from the less frequent to the more frequent behaviors." This applied to Council participants as well.[9]

POLITICAL ACTION AND
LEGISLATIVE COMMITTEE

A second group of gladiators are members of the PAC. Under Wurf the committee was essentially an informal, ad hoc operation of a limited number of people. Meetings were infrequent and involvement was sporadic. John Boer, long-time activist, former Council president, and now a much-involved member of the Retirees Association, recalled that "Wurf carried political action around in his head." Gotbaum called for a more organized and expanded committee, involving monthly meetings at headquarters. During Corcoran's leadership of the department, between 80 and 90 local representatives attended PAC meetings regularly. This number was expanded by Norman Adler to between 150 and 200, with increases occurring during important election campaigns or when a controversial issue or popular guest speaker stimulates member interest.

Since PAC is, technically, a creature of the Council, its membership is not set by any constitutional provisions or bylaws. The committee chair is, however, designated by the Council, on the initiative of the executive director, and is authorized to select the other officers and designate members for various subcommittees. Adler noted that rarely are formal votes taken on candidate endorsements or issues. Most matters, he insisted, were worked out through consensus, and subcommittee recommendations on candidate screening and policy recommendations were usually endorsed.[10]

The department persistently stimulates membership involvement. Adler moved his office to the fourth floor, where division and local offices are located, enabling him and his aides to maintain closer communication with every level of the organization. A monthly newsletter reaches some 5,000 of the Council constituency, informing those who have participated in political activity of new or ongoing programs, highlighting the work of individual members by name, and spotlighting their pictures, all in an endeavor to encourage involvement.

Meetings of PAC convey the atmosphere of a big, old-fashioned clubhouse "pow-wow," as people pour into the bright meeting room, cluster in talkative groups as friends find each other, save chairs so that they can sit together, and line up for sandwiches, dessert, and drinks. Since members come directly from work, the opportunity for some good food and socializing helps give the gathering a festive and social quality. It is at these meetings that individuals are stimulated to participate and to recruit colleagues from their locals. PAC also serves as a vital intervening link between the formal political party and the volunteer workers who do the district or precinct work. The spirit of the evening usually engenders the feeling among members that by associating together they can be politically effective. In his description of political clubs, James Wilson captures some of the same qualities evident at a PAC meeting:

> ...The club creates a set of proximate inducements to supplement and reinforce the ultimate ones. Both are essential; neither will suffice alone. These proximate rewards derive from the act of associating together, and include opportunities for office, power, and prestige in the clubs; the sense of approval from one's fellow members, and the opportunities for sociability which are in part dependent on club work and contribution of money or effort.[11]

At these meetings, members hear current news of the political situation affecting the union, reports from Albany and Washington, and review the work of the screening subcommittee, which recommends candidates for endorsement. PAC recommendations on candidates and policies are then sent on to the Council's executive board and delegates council for final approval.

Chairing the PAC is Charles Hughes, who has served in this capacity almost continuously since 1968. He brings the strength of one of the largest delegations to PAC and understands the necessity of incentives to attract participants and increase PAC vitality. Hughes is a charismatic leader who is popular with union audiences, which have responded well to his flamboyant style of oratory. He senses the mood of his audience, and responds accordingly. Raffles and door prizes have also helped to insure a consistently large turnout.

UNION PRECINCT WORKERS

Campaign and lobbying courses constitute a third gladiatorial activity. To increase participation and improve the skills of volunteers, Adler organized campaign training as a professorial program directed specifically to the needs of the Council. As a college teacher he taught campaign strategy, and as a paid consultant he served in a number of campaigns. Utilizing his academic background and practical experiences, he evolved a program that proved to be particularly suited to the electoral objectives of DC 37.

At least once a year, twice when there were important elections, between 100 and 125 Council unionists attended his campaign courses, in addition to one designed especially for school board elections. Sessions were held on four consecutive Saturdays at union headquarters, where kits were distributed containing the latest election laws and regulations and detailed techniques of leaflet writing, canvassing, and managing a campaign headquarters. Adler directs the course, lectures on various aspects of campaigning, and selects guest speakers skilled in fund-raising techniques, targeting voters, budgeting, and organizing registration drives.

The response to the course has been enthusiastic. Its reputation for presenting the nuts and bolts of campaigning has spread among politicians and candidates, motivating many to send staff and volunteers. Adler encourages this outreach as another service extended to DC friends and as a way of enhancing the union's reputation. Because of such educational programs, the union is able to offer candidates endorsed by the Council a well-trained group of workers who are easily mobilized and generally more reliable than the average campaign volunteer. Some members who take the union's courses have become more active in neighborhood organizations while others join the PAC of the Council or their local.

In cooperation with the Retirees Association, one-day workshops have been offered for newly involved participants, focusing on techniques for telephone bank volunteers. Few are former activists; most are late bloomers who desire to remain active and who are eager to contribute their time and talents.

It is not unusual for graduates of the campaign course to utilize the knowledge gained to challenge the established leadership of their local, or simply to enhance their skills in political work. At one refresher meeting, a young black woman recounted her experiences in running for the board of trustees of her local. "Because of the course," she explained, "my confidence was raised, enabling me to have the guts to run for office." Based on what she had learned, she prepared her own campaign leaflets and recalled the suggestion that candidates could help themselves by "projecting" their own image through some visible technique. Her response was to wear a bright red jacket as she campaigned among her fellow workers. She believes that the resultant recognition helped improve her outreach and facilitated her success at the election polls.[12]

Always the teacher, Adler applied his classroom talents to the creation of a lobbying course. Given twice each year, it is devoted to the strategies and techniques for effective lobbying. Content is related to the level of government and the issues confronting individual locals and the Council. The program includes the organization of the legislative system, the process of decision making, the importance of the legislative staff, the presentation of testimony, and the perceptions of lawmakers concerning lobbying. This one-day course is packed with invaluable information. Vital data are prepared and packaged beforehand for the students. To encourage participation, unionists who take the course are selected for special lobbying days in Albany. This means a break in their usual regimen, a day of socializing, and meeting important political personages. When proposed legislation requires a special lobbying endeavor, Adler knows those course graduates who can converse readily and effectively with legislators. Attendance varies from 80 to 125, with the largest representation coming from Locals 371, 372, and 1549.

In addition to regular course offerings, the staff organizes special workshops and seminars at weekend conferences or monthly meetings of locals. Petitioning and organizing registration drives are discussion topics often used to stimulate increased involvement. Political skills have also been introduced as part of the shop stewards' training programs.

Political Action instituted the legislative conference in 1976, a one-day meeting to draft a program for the Council in preparation for the forthcoming session in Albany. This constitutes the fourth gladiatorial activity. Topics cover a wide range of issues— improvement of working conditions, resolution of on-the-job problems, the Taylor law, pensions, civil service, occupational health and safety, and the agency shop, among others. Based on the remarks of a number of guest experts, discussions in workshops, and the needs of locals, members and staff put together a series of proposals that are recommended as the Albany legislative package for the following year. Rarely does the Council's executive board alter these suggestions.

TRANSITIONAL ACTIVITIES: COMMUNITY ASSOCIATIONS

Transitional activities include attendance at community association meetings, lobbying, a monetary contribution to the PEOPLE (Public Employees Organized to Promote Legislative Equality) fund, and participation in some special ad hoc activity. When Gotbaum first suggested creation of a department for politics, he envisioned the union building a relationship with communities where its members live. His hope was that more AFSCME unionists would be drawn by effective strategies. Fully aware that political work in an electoral campaign was extremely important, although performed within a relatively short time frame, Gotbaum was determined that members should be involved between election campaigns as well. Attempts to formalize a neighborhood presence over the years proved difficult and generally produced less than the desired attendance. Staff targeted the heaviest concentrations of membership in the city, and at the head of each of these developing community associations appointed a coordinator. At first the goal was to recruit new participants from the locals, but in actuality it was the staff that had to be assigned this responsibility.

Preparations and follow-through require considerable attention and commitment for community organizing. The first association was established in 1972 in Staten island and served the entire county. Meetings were held sporadically over the years. With a potential of some 1,200 out of a population of close to 60,000 residents in Co-op City in the Bronx, the Council's community association reported an average attendance of 50 at meetings. By 1981 the number of associations had reached eight, representing all five boroughs.

Meetings focused largely on two areas of interest: publicizing benefits available to union members in education, health, legal and personal services, and resolution of community problems. Except for the Harlem group, most of these associations did not become ongoing community organizations. Meetings are held three to five times a year, and while the attendance hovers around 30, the associations serve as a potential core for more heightened political activity.

Staff member Gloria Smith, the coordinator of the Harlem group, explained that when she took over the association there was little interest and poor attendance. Gradually, through persistent telephoning and a very personal outreach, she was able to improve participation markedly; for a given election she can draw as many as 150 committed volunteers.

Smith's success with the Harlem community association has not been repeated elsewhere. Building a community presence on an ongoing basis proved far more difficult than anticipated. Evening meetings are no longer attractive to people who travel long distances to their jobs, put in a full day, and fear going out after dark. In addition, once the rush hour ends, there are long intervals between trains on deserted platforms. Those who constitute the activist core tend to perform their political activity within their locals, at the Council's headquarters, or during a campaign at a site where there is movement and people. Many are also drawn to the union building, near City Hall, where volunteers feel closer to the hub of activity.

Community issues are not necessarily the same as union issues.

For example, "solving" the housing problems of members is far more difficult, certainly much more complex, than the request for an increase in wages brought to the bargaining table. The same applies to neighborhood safety, cleanliness, transportation, and schools. Finally, mobilizing individuals for participation is one of the most difficult, time-consuming activities. Rarely do they respond spontaneously. Such cultivation requires, at the very least, paid expert staff with the time, resources, and patience to build a lasting field operation. Vincent Montalbano, who was responsible for the local political arena, acknowledged that dedicated leadership was an essential element for successful political mobilization of the city's communities. The catalyst had to exude enthusiasm and the spark for activating others, for developing an organizational infrastructure, and for maintaining the programs and interest of participants. In summation, the community association serves as a potential source for recruiting individuals, largely on an ad hoc basis, for brief, specific periods, and for such immediate goals as a voter registration drive, election day canvassing, or neighborhood clean-up day.[13]

PEOPLE FUND

After a bitter, acrimonious campaign, the Council won the right of its members, in 1980, to join PEOPLE, a special checkoff from wages which permits regular contributions to a political fund. This payroll deduction can only be used for candidates and lobbying activities on the federal level. Initially, Mayor Koch vehemently opposed it as a "slush fund," vetoing a City Council bill but later allowing it to be brought to the collective bargaining table. The union pays a per capita fee toward the city's expenses for administering the checkoff. To enlist members the union has organized a special outreach under Brenda White, former associate director in Political Action.

Volunteers assist White in bringing the message to DC 37 unionists, pressing them to sign up at local meetings, conferences, or at work. Inducements to participate include gifts to those who sign up members, such as a trip for two to Hawaii or a freezer full of meat. Based on her experience, White feels that the gifts are attractive and influence participation. It is still too early to know the full potential of this new income, but it is already evident that it provides a larger and more stable source of money than the union's usual political fund-raising activities.

As with many other activities, among the first to join PEOPLE, and the largest contributors have been members of Schools Local 372 and Clerical-Administrative Local 1549, workers with incomes at the lowest level among unionists. Equally significant is the fact that this fund was introduced at a time when union dues were increased and the erosion of income by inflation remained a serious problem, particularly for those at the lower ends of the salary scale. Furthermore, school aides are mostly part-time workers! It is evident to those involved that a key element in enrolling large numbers remains the leadership of individual locals. Despite personal appeals by White and other staff, the key has been the committed and consistent support of presidents in encouraging their members to join.

According to Milbrath, making a donation may be a first act in becoming a gladiator or simply part of remaining a spectator. Busy and wealthy individuals often look on a monetary contribution to politics as a substitute for personal participation. But Milbrath and others have found that most contributions come from the activists. This applies to DC 37 as well, but what is particularly significant is that many of those who do give to the PEOPLE Fund have little "extra" in their paychecks. It is they who are making a larger personal sacrifice, certainly more than the well-to-do contributor known to fund raisers.[14]

AD HOC ACTIVITIES

A lobby day is held at least once each session in Albany, that focuses on the key issues of concern to the Council and individual locals. Delegations vary between 80 and 100 well versed individuals. With the legislative sessions running longer, the Political Action Department has been relying increasingly on organized letter-writing campaigns and group visits with individual lawmakers in their home districts.

A relatively high number of participants comes from the hospital workers, who are considered by most scholars of political behavior as having the least political efficacy because of their low income, limited educational background, and experiences with discrimination. Mostly black, and some Hispanic, they turn out one of the highest numbers for lobbying activity. Of those surveyed in Local 420, 25 percent said they wrote or personally lobbied legislators. On those occasions when a particularly important issue affected workers directly, and this linkage was clearly communicated to the membership, substantial numbers would join lobbying actions. For example, when an unemployment insurance proposal excluded part-time workers, impacting directly on the school aides, Local 372 and President Charles Hughes sent four bus loads of angry members to Albany.[15]

Included in the transitional category are the union's ad hoc activities, which occasionally involve new people who may become more active in other areas of politics. Examples include mobilizations and demonstrations, usually one-day affairs. The march on Washington in 1975 was organized to support New York's last-ditch efforts to avoid bankruptcy by urging federal financial aid. In cooperation with other unions, the Council directed the mass effort and organized some 600 buses, with over 25,000 from the Council, alone. Other activities have included Labor Day parades, civil rights mobilizations, and protests against military terror in El Salvador. While some of these activities have been classified as gladiatorial they are considered transitional as well, because participants may only join in a one-day event or become more permanently involved in other activities. The hard-core activists are usually found among those participating in these ad hoc programs.

SPECTATOR ACTIVITIES

Reading PEP regularly, registering, voting, and attending one of its conferences constitute the major spectator activities in DC 37. The Council is proud of its prize-winning union newspaper which, according to Parsons, Kadushin and Denitch (Columbia University) and Baim studies, is read often by as many as two-thirds of the membership, and fairly often by another 23 percent. The highest percentage of readership is found among the clericals and blue-collar workers, while the professional–technicals are among the lowest.

The union produces a higher turnout for registration than that found in the general electorate. Eighty-five percent of those surveyed for the BASR sample registered, as compared to the general population's 68 percent. Among the union's registered voters are a large number of low income and minority citizens and a high percentage of women. The Columbia University sample found eighty percent of the hospital workers, 93 percent of respondents in the clerical division, and 95 percent in the white-collar division were registered, which were incredible figures. Since the findings of scholars generally show low turnout for these populations, in all likelihood the day-to-day activities of the union, and its special registration campaigns have had a marked impact. Over the years, PEP and the Political Action staff have devoted great efforts to increase registration and election turnouts. During the campaign of 1972, when George McGovern headed the Democratic ticket and many members expressed little enthusiasm for his candidacy, almost 70 percent of those unionists said they voted for him. Only among the more conservative blue-collar workers did a majority support Richard Nixon.

Not only are overwhelming numbers of Council members registered, but they also tend to vote regularly. Despite low turnouts by the general public in primary elections, almost half of the union's respondents vote in them often, and another 22 percent fairly often. These are very substantial figures. Despite this large voter turnout, however, Parsons, et al. and Baim surveys found that a relatively large number of union members expressed feelings of alienation from the political process. About half of those surveyed felt that they didn't really have any say in government, and as many as two-thirds concluded that those in power cared little about them.[16]

This apparent dichotomy between attitude and behavior may be accounted for in the union's role as an involved and caring intermediary between its constituency and the body politic. The widespread malaise toward politics, which began to engulf the nation in the late 1970s and resulted in a precipitous decline in voting, inevitably affected union members. However, the DC 37 newspaper, staff, and top leadership served persistently as more positive, intervening elements, reaching large numbers of members with their appeals to perform one of the simpler acts of politics, that of voting. In other words, while Council unionists share some of the general public's feelings of alienation, the active-volunteer cohort does not.

There is, in addition, a strong congruity between the opinions of union leaders and their followers on such political issues as support of welfare state programs, a pervading New Deal liberalism, and voting for national Democratic candidates. The exception to sharing this common political outlook is found primarily among blue-collar laborers who tend to be more conservative and supportive of Republican candidates. Nevertheless, this latter group has adhered traditionally to a strong union consciousness, from the founding days of the Council. Overall, Denitch concludes that "there seems to be a reasonable fit between the attitudes of the leadership of District 37 and its press, and the attitudes of the members on economic issues."[17]

WOMEN AND POLITICS

Women's conferences, which began in 1978 as annual, day-long affairs, are a third spectator activity. The 150 women, and a scattering of men, who attended the first meeting, grew to some 500 within three years. Participants represented the various categories of union membership, the largest delegations coming from Locals 372 (Schools) and 1549 (Clerical-Administrative). What made these conferences unique, even for the women's movement, was the large numbers of blacks and Hispanics. The issues highlighted included wage equity, comparable worth, the role of the media, spouse and child abuse, alcoholism, reproductive rights, and women in government and union politics. In contrast to the first conference, where the main bulk of participants constituted the traditional activists and local officers, by 1981 the tremendous outpouring included many who had never attended a Council-sponsored event before.

Close observers note the distinctive role of women in political action. In a recent study analyzing the participation of women in seven unions in New York City, including DC 37 Custodial Employees (Local 1597), it was disclosed that women did not hold as many elective or appointive positions as men, although they were found to be the union's backbone in daily affairs. Women attended more meetings, went to more social and educational events, and filed more grievances than men. However, the higher the union post, the fewer women in leadership, despite the fact that the most active women were shop stewards and committee members. Although more women than men ran for office in the Custodial Local, as compared to other unions, more men tended to be elected.[18]

The explanation of why more women did not seek higher office was that most of them felt that they needed greater preparation for leadership, particularly education and information on what the union had accomplished, and what it takes to be a leader. Men, however, did not use this rationale for not running for office. Women tended to be less confident than men in pursuing leadership responsibilities offering home responsibilities as their reason for not seeking office. When compared with other unions in the study, DC 37 illustrates greater opportunity for expanding its leadership potential among women. The authors found women custodials far more education-conscious than their counterparts in other unions, and that they took more courses than their male colleagues. With this evident interest in education among female members, the Council may well have a significant core of women ready for leadership who need greater acceptance from the male members.

YOUTH AUXILIARY

Attentive to the need for encouraging participation in union activities, Adler has worked to attract members to union headquarters through a varied assortment of programs, not all political in character. In cooperation with the Education Department, Youth Day was created for high school students and their union parents to introduce them to the variety of careers available, and to prepare those interested in going on to college by offering SAT courses. In 1979 some 600, many from minorities, attended the Council's career planning conference to assist them in selecting colleges and applying for financial aid, and introduce them to careers. Other activities, more social in character, included tours of museums, picnics, and sports festivals.

According to Milbrath, a person needs a strong push from the immediate environment to move from spectator to a more active type of participation. Perhaps these youth programs and other Council services will provide some much-needed stimulation for the children of unionists, and help many of them break out of the traditional patterns of discrimination that weigh heavily on those who grow up in isolated ghetto environments.

SUMMARY

Political participation is an important goal at DC 37, for it is viewed as enhancing the interest of public employees in their union and extending the Council's influence. A panoply of political activities and material inducements are offered to attract unionists to the political arena, ranging from educational programs and workshops to door prizes and free weekends at vacation resorts. The number of Council unionists involved over a typical year, in at least one of the broad range of activities described in this chapter, approximates what Lester Milbrath has described as the active citizenry in society. This suggests that about 10 percent of the membership performs some political act. It's cadre of volunteer–activists is comparatively well trained and constitutes an invaluable resource for public candidates who no longer have available to them the traditional party machinery.

Large numbers of women unionists participate in gladiatorial activities. They run the telephone bank, crowd PAC meetings, register for political action courses, and usually predominate in lobbying delegations and at public demonstrations. Among them are dedicated groups of black women, drawn largely from Locals 372 and 1549, as well as from Hospitals Local 420 in more peaceful times. In the process, a number of competent leaders have emerged from among these activists. Sparked by the Political Action Department and encouraged by the union's leadership, black women, in particular, have become increasingly involved in political action on every level.

NOTES

1. Julian Baim, ''Work Alienation and Its Impact on Political Life: Case Study of District Council 37 Workers;'' Ph.D. dissertation, political science depart-

ment, City University of New York, 1981, p. 286; Wayne Parsons, Charles Kadushin, and Bogdan Denitch, "Preliminary Report: Study of Members of District Council 37, AFSCME," Bureau of Applied Social Research, Columbia University; February 1974, p. 16.

2. Memo, Corcoran to Gotbaum, August 8, 1968 and June 20, 1969, Gotbaum files.

3. Mancur Olson, *The Logic of Collective Action*, New York: Schocken Books, 1968, p. 50.

4. Ronald Hrebenar and Ruth Scott, *Interest Group Politics in America*, Englewood Cliffs, NJ: Prentice-Hall, 1982, p. 19; James Wilson, *Political Organizations*, New York: Basic Books, 1973, Chapter 3; Robert Salisbury, "An Exchange Theory of Interest Groups," *Midwest Journal of Political Science*, 13 (February 1969):1–32.

5. Parsons, Kadushin, and Denitch, "Preliminary Report: Study of Members," p. 9; Baim, "Work Alienation," p. 274. Also, interviews with many rank-and-file participants at a variety of Council conferences.

6. Adapting the roles played at Roman gladiatorial contests, in ancient times, Milbrath has labeled each category accordingly. Lester W. Milbrath, *Political Participation*, Chicago: Rand McNally, 1965, Chapter 1. See Joel Seidman et al., *The Worker Views His Union*, Chicago: University of Chicago Press, 1968; Arnold Tannenbaum and Robert Kahn, *Participation in Union Locals*, Evanston, Il: Row, Peterson, and Co., 1958.

7. Milbrath,*Political Participation*, p. 19. We do not have exact figures for each of the categories, but we do have data for specific activities, and some general impressions based on observations for more than a decade. Our main purpose in utilizing Milbrath's diagram is to show the character of the activities and intensity of involvement. It is important, for our purposes, to identify the dependable, solid group of some 150–200 activist-volunteers who can be recruited quickly for a wide range of sophisticated political work.

8. Attendance sheets, October 16, 1978, Department of Political Action files. Interviews with Vincent Montalbano, March 3, 1981; and Norman Adler, October 26, 1983.

9. Milbrath, *Political Participation*, p. 20; Interview with Vincent Montalbano, March 3, 1981. See Parsons, Kadushin, and Denitch, "Preliminary Report: Study of Members"; and Baim, "Work Alienation."

10. John Boer tape recording, August 15, 1983. The largest locals, those with 5 percent or more of the membership, send five or six delegates to the PAC; the middle-sized, three or four; and the smallest, one or two. In addition, Council members may, on their own initiative, participate in PAC meetings and programs.

11. James Wilson, *The Amateur Democrat*, Chicago: University of Chicago Press, 1962, pp. 170–171.

12. Interview with Chris Willis, October 17, 1981. Attendance at this particular refresher course included 25 participants, of whom 11 were black, several Hispanic, and 14 were women.

13. Political Action, annual report, 1977; interview with Gloria Smith, December 30, 1981.

14. Milbrath, *Political Participation*, p. 24; Alexander Heard, *The Costs of*

Democracy, Chapel Hill: University of North Carolina Press, 1960; DC 37, "A DC 37 Delegates and Shop Stewards Guide to PEOPLE Check-Off," brochure, files. Interview with Brenda White, October 26, 1983. By January 1983, 3,545 members had enlisted with PEOPLE, contributing $90,000 annually. By September, some 6,500 had joined, raising the fund to approximately $150,000. At that time, the average contribution ranged from $13 to $39 each year.

15. Bogdan Denitch, "Summary Report on the Study of Members of District Council 37 AFSCME, and Evaluation," Bureau of Applied Social Research, Columbia University, undated, p. 9. PAC minutes, May 19, 1977, including a summary of the "Albany Report" by Guido Menta.

16. Parsons, Kadushin and Denitch "Preliminary Report: Study of Members," pp. 1, 7-8, 16-19, 26. Baim, "Work Alienation"; see especially Chapter 4.

17. Parsons, et al. "Preliminary Report," and Denitch, "Summary Report," p. 8; see especially p. 9.

18. Barbara Wertheimer and Anne Nelson, *Trade Union Women: A Study of Their Participation in New York City Locals*, New York: Praeger, 1975, pp. 85-87, 89. Also, authors' observations.

14
Learn, Baby, Learn...
While You Earn, Baby, Earn

Adult education has had a long and noble history in the United States, but it has invariably been denied to one of the largest audiences and potential constituencies, the working class. DC 37 provides a model for creative programming that reaches workers at all levels and provides channels for sharpening skills and advancing into professional or para-professional careers. Education has always held a high priority within the Council's development, and the scope of the program and the varied opportunities it provides have won nationwide attention and praise.[1] In this chapter we examine the factors that helped to spark the union's programs and their utilization by the membership. They include four major components: general education and training, labor education, the DC 37 college, and the retirees program.

EDUCATION AND TRAINING

The union's drive for expanding educational opportunities has been a product of at least five factors: union leadership, skilled staff, the needs of members, inadequate programs by city agencies and the climate of the 1960s.

Leadership and Staff

Perhaps the single most important explanation for the union's educational thrust was the commitment of its top leadership, be-

The pride of union members who took advantage of the Council's career ladder training program is evident in this class of nurses aides who have just graduated to become licensed practical nurses.

ginning with Jerry Wurf and followed by Lillian Roberts, Victor Gotbaum, and Education Directors Sumner Rosen (1965–68) and Bernard Rifkin (1968–76). Roberts was a driving force behind the major push for education, focusing particularly on those workers trapped at the bottom, in dead-end jobs. Through on-the-job training as a hospital aide in Chicago, she assumed the responsibilities of a nurse. She understood the pressures, anxieties and frustrated aspirations of Council members, and was convinced that a hands on program, appropriate counseling, and targeted tutoring could provide the stimulation and guidance necessary to help workers advance to higher posts. Having experienced the sense of entrapment by inadequate education and limited background, Roberts conveyed a zealous, almost missionary, dedication to upgrading workers through education and job training.

Gotbaum shared her commitment, recognizing the relationship of education and training to enhancing one's opportunities for economic and social mobility and a sense of individual worth. "The one natural resource of our nation that remains most neglected, most wastefully ignored," he stated, "is the natural overwhelming desire of humans to learn, to develop their capacities, to expand their abilities and to enjoy greater personal and material rewards from the work they do."[2] Another aspect of Gotbaum's interest in education and training was his determination to build the Council into a cohesive and effective force. As the major organizational phase approached completion, he sought to draw independent-minded locals and the disparate membership into the orbit of a centralizing Council. Through extensive services to unionists and their families, he hoped to win their allegiance. Education proved to be one of the key service arms of the union and played a major role in galvanizing support and unity. Not long after taking over as executive director, Gotbaum brought Roberts's ideas to the bargaining table and eventually won creation of a special fund for education and training.

Members' Needs

Influencing the design of the Council's educational goals was the makeup of its membership. Organizing success during the 1960s had been most impressive among hospital and clerical workers, including substantial numbers of women from minority populations who held the city's most menial jobs. The Kerner Commission, in its study of the nation's urban riots, concluded in 1968 that "the single most important cause of poverty among Negroes was the heavy concentration of workers in the lowest end of the occupational scale." Thousands of new AFSCME members had little or no high school education, were unable to read or write, or lacked the skills required for a rapidly changing city. As late as 1975, 58 percent of the hospital workers and 31 percent of the blue-collar laborers had not completed or ever attended high school. Limited by inadequate backgrounds and having to support families, few could afford the time or expense to continue their education. In the early 1970s the total family income of well over half the hospital workers and as many as one-fourth of the clericals was under $8,000. While many workers did not return to school for fear of failing, large numbers were still unaware of the possibilities for advancement.[3]

Thousands of civil servants were aware that no matter how hard they worked, or how promising their potential, there appeared to be no bright future for them. Opportunities were usually limited to two or three advances. Restricted promotional lines were evident for clerical employees, who could not qualify for administrative positions or certain technical and professional career lines. Substantial numbers of public workers served as assistants to higher-level public employees and possessed the skills necessary for these advanced jobs, some even performing them, but they could not be appointed because of a missing credential. In the blue-collar area, attendants wanted to move ahead in the Parks Department but had no program for achieving this goal. Laborers would have welcomed the opportunity to become automotive mechanics, or to learn how to operate various kinds of equipment used in city construction and repair work.

Response of City Officials

In the initial phase, the interest of the Council's staff was not matched by most city officials. The focus of attention for the latter was on other more pressing matters. Influenced by a civil service orientation, they believed that the way to advancement was through individual effort, by utilizing the traditional educational institutions. Most officials did not see their responsibility as preparing workers for promotion or for upgrading their skills. When a city task force investigating personnel problems for Mayor Lindsay neglected to explore the needs for education and training among low-income workers, Gotbaum complained to the mayor that "Nowhere, as far as we can discover, does the report address itself to the fact many city jobs are dead-end in nature, thus contradicting the very notion of career development as a meaningful one for those who hold or will hold these jobs."

In a report on the city's training programs, personnel expert David Stanley of the Brookings Institution concluded that:

> Despite the obvious importance of well-trained local government
> employees, the study's findings on the subject of employee train-

ing and education indicate little interest on the part of unions and considerable inactivity on the part of management. Training is a low-priority union objective, *except where a few aggressive unions have tied it to promotions.* (authors' emphasis)[4]

High-level administrators and academicians generally looked critically at the idea of government assuming responsibility for upgrading employed civil servants, for they feared that fresh, new ideas would be cut off without outsiders replenishing city agencies. Consequently, many departments and agencies were without training or upgrading programs. And among those giving some attention to training, such as hospitals, the focus was limited to higher-level professionals. Programs that were instituted came as a result of specific requests by unions; budgets for these purposes were small, and the trainers themselves usually inadequately prepared. Finally, a number of professionals in public employment did not take kindly to the idea of training on the job as an alternative to their own preparation through years of formal schooling, based on what they believed were higher standards for certification. As one city official conceded, "The city government did not see training as a long-term investment." A study undertaken for the Lindsay administration in 1966 did recommend that every city agency commit itself to the concept of career development, insisting that management had the responsibility to relate dead-end jobs to career lines. Unfortunately, these suggestions were not generally implemented.[5]

Climate for Change

The timeliness of the union's proposals proved to be an important asset in its drive for educational opportunities. Sparked by the civil rights movement and the war on poverty, the 1960s ushered in a series of new national programs. President Lyndon B. Johnson's "Great Society" included expanding educational and manpower training programs for the low-income and unskilled class, particularly for minority populations in urban centers. New resources were made available for these purposes, primarily through federal grants.

In the course of the DC 37 hospital organizing campaign, Sumner Rosen met with representatives of the U.S. Department of Labor and secured a commitment to cooperate with a project for training, promoting, and licensing low-level hospital workers. This included preparing nurse's aides to become licensed practical nurses (LPNs). Eventually, a $2.4 million grant was made. Armed with this Federal help, the union pressured officials and hospital administrators to respond positively and quickly. While Mayor Lindsay was supportive, nurse supervisors and middle management in hospitals generally did not like the idea. Their attitude toward the large numbers of black and Hispanic hospital aides often revealed cynicism concerning the possibility of converting this work force into professionals. When the federal program was first proposed, a number of officials dared the union to produce as many as 100 aides who could qualify for such a program. Eventually, some 3,000 applied on the first offer of such a program.[6]

Rosen's Initiatives

In 1965 Gotbaum created the Education Department and recruited Dr. Sumner Rosen as its first director. An economist and college instructor, he had first met Gotbaum in Turkey, where both helped train the leadership of a newly emerging trade union movement. After his appointment to DC 37, Rosen consulted with many labor educators in search of models on which he could build the Council's programs. But he quickly learned that public service unionism was vastly different, and that he would have to develop new programs and approaches. Rosen continued the promotional test preparation programs initiated by Mildred Kiefer under Jerry Wurf, which helped prepare mostly clerical workers for promotional examinations, the traditional civil service route to advancement. The program was expanded under Rosen to cover examinations in accounting, business administration, and a variety of technical and professional subjects. Before long, the Education Department became an in-house civil service training school, competing effectively with older private institutions. As their members' intermediary, the union criticized unfair questions and worked closely with city examiners to insure that preparation courses dovetailed as closely as possible with test expectations.

A second area on which the education director focused was the shop steward training program. In addition to calling on Al Nash of Cornell University to serve as an adviser in developing the curriculum, Rosen sought to build into the training program a strong sense of trade union and worker consciousness. Perhaps the most notable contribution Rosen made to the Council was his innovative efforts in creating a career ladder program. Sensitive to the concerns of the impoverished, he recognized that one of the characteristics of poverty was the low level of skill of poor workers and the general lack of opportunities for advancement. It was inevitable, therefore, that he should be attracted to Lillian Roberts's interest in improving workers' skills. During his first six months at DC 37 he helped Roberts organize hospital workers, prior to the critical elections in December 1965, and gradually won her respect and trust. Generally suspicious of intellectuals with academic credentials, and questioning their overall commitment to the labor movement, Roberts accepted his advice, for both shared a deep belief that the union should provide its low-paid workers with a way out of their menial assignments and opportunities to enhance their sense of dignity.

Careers, Union-Made

In a letter to all nurse's aides, DC 37 detailed a new training program to prepare them for the position of LPN. They were warned that they would be confronted with a tough series of courses and long hours of class work, in addition to their regular weekly 20-hour hospital assignments. Careful screening by the union reduced the 3,000 applicants to three groups of approximately 150 each. The program turned out to be a source of pride for the Federal government as well as the Council, for it proved to be one of the most successful sponsored by a trade union. DC 37 tutors worked closely with participants for at least six weeks prior to the start of training and continued throughout the program. The built-in tutorials and personal consultation with Education Department staff played a significant role in reducing the projected dropout rate. After 14 trying months, 422 graduated from an original class of 462, and 96 percent received state licenses.[7]

Nurses's aides who advanced to oxygen technicians were also accorded an opportunity to attend a community college program to become inhalation therapists. This was not only a more highly skilled and well-paid professional position, but such individuals were in scarce supply in 1971. The educational program was further expanded when several community colleges of the City

University made available courses leading to the Associate in Applied Sciences degree, which enabled DC 37 hospital workers to become experts in the use of complex and dangerous life-saving equipment such as iron lungs, oxygen tents, resuscitators, and respirators. Following the initial success of these upgrading projects, the Council finally secured the cooperation of the hospital system in developing a training program to enable nurse's aides to become registered nurses through a combination of classroom work and clinical experience.

Nurse's aides were also offered a technology program which enabled them to become inhalation, ambulance, oxygen, and obstetrical–gynecological technicians. Training was done on released time from hospital assignments with assurances of promotion and salary increases on successful completion of course requirements. Beyond the numbers of members affected by these programs by 1968 (700 students), was the pride and dignity afforded the workers—a change in uniform symbolized advancement and improved status. The success of these programs became the model for other careers: for dietary aides to rise to supervisory positions; housekeeping aides to senior assignments; motor vehicle operators to dispatchers and garage directors. By the end of 1968 the career ladder concept was well under way, and city officials joined in planning or approving new directions.[8]

Changing Command

Upon leaving the Council, after two and a half years, Sumner Rosen could look back with a feeling of accomplishment on one of the more highly regarded career programs in the city. In the process, he demonstrated that they were not only cost-effective but had raised the morale of workers tremendously. This, in turn, strengthened Gotbaum at the bargaining table for, as a result of negotiations, he was able to win city support for expansion of career ladder projects. A successor to Rosen was found in Bernard (Bernie) Rifkin, a long-time trade unionist with extensive educational and administrative experience. Rifkin was an imaginative, practical, down-to-earth educator, who was not overly impressed with the goals, training, and measuring rods of professional educators. At times, a latent hostility surfaced toward university-trained academics, for he was moved by a deep and abiding commitment to the practical aspects of trade unionism. As a socialist organizer for Norman Thomas's presidential campaign in 1936, he allied himself with the progressive wing of labor. Subsequently, he worked as a labor relations specialist with the American Agency for Development in Japan, Iran, and Bolivia, as well as in labor education with the UAW.

Rifkin headed the Council's Education Department for almost a decade, expanding into new, creative areas, including the DC 37 college. He believed that the traditional, formal approaches to education, with a heavy focus on credentialism, were unwarranted, if not discriminatory, and that if afforded appropriate opportunities and preparation, most workers could achieve a level of intellectual development equal to that of the average college graduate. Thus, he turned his creative mind and nervous energy to opening college doors, and further stimulated expansion of the allied health career programs. He pressed for increased financial support from the city for the high school equivalency (HSE) program, for example, which flourished under his direction. Supported by a heavy input of remedial and tutorial help, school aides, custodial workers, and others caught in the lowest level of employment, and who had not attended or completed high school, were able to climb out of dead-end work. While the Council originally allocated the $10,000 Rifkin requested for the program, by the end of its first year the cost had spiraled tenfold due to its unexpected popularity. Since these students were residents of the city, Rifkin urged that the costs be defrayed by City Hall.[9]

Education Fund

A major breakthrough for the Council's educational activities occurred during the 1969 round of collective bargaining. At that time, the city agreed to Gotbaum's request that it assume the financial responsibilities for the union's training and career program for almost a third of the Council's members. The result was an education fund to which the city agreed to pay $25 for each member in the Clerical–Administrative and Hospital bargaining units. Besides covering the costs of the program, the fund paid for administrative expenses and the salaries of most members of the union's Education staff, including the top administrator and associate and assistant administrators. In later years, the fund was extended to other bargaining units in the Council until virtually all were covered. While city officials must approve projects, DC 37 controls the character and direction of career training and education of its members.

From the union's perspective, its involvement in educational programs enabled it to build a substantial and popular record of achievement. Servicing individuals in this fashion enhanced the leadership's position and contributed to the Council's growth and influence among the locals. Through such wide-ranging services the Council helped pull its fragmented parts together behind common goals. The hands-on approach of the Education staff also proved invaluable in linking training to real jobs and opening new opportunities for workers. Furthermore, those who sat in classes with other adults who confronted similar problems found themselves in more comfortable settings. The great diversity of unionists attending classes and special programs and their association with most of the Council's locals helped fashion greater cohesion, loyalty, and respect for DC 37 and its growing staff.[10]

From the city's vantage point, reaction to union-directed education programs was mixed. Officials were divided and uncertain as to their role and responsibility for training and educating the civil service work force. Lindsay and his staff believed that friendly and cooperative bargaining with a powerful DC 37 could ultimately be of inestimable help in his aspirations for higher office, and so they endorsed the Council's programs. Most permanent career professionals did not view training and education for those at the bottom as part of their responsibility. They felt that individuals could, and should, take advantage of traditional forms of education to get ahead. At the same time, the city's small staff of trainers differed with this view and wanted to participate more actively in planning the training of public employees. But their minuscule budgets constrained their ambitions.

To stimulate use of its expanding educational activities, the department campaigned constantly through the union's newspaper, pep talks at local meetings and conferences, and widespread distribution of career pamphlets and brochures. Strategies were explored for encouraging members to raise their expectations and aspirations and to seek new careers through greater utilization of union-provided opportunities.

Staff sought to create new careers by working closely with individual locals. But it took a special type of expertise to bridge the gap between the traditional academic approach to credentialism and the practical needs and capacities of individuals to develop appropriate skills for new responsibilities. Identification of an appropriate training curriculum required ongoing collaborative efforts with city officials, who often had the necessary knowledge for creating effective programs. Eager to insure success, union staff urged small classes and extensive remedial and tutorial assistance. They also assured participants that upon completion of career development courses they would be rewarded with salary adjustments and/or promotion. When the nurse's aide technician program did not, at first, receive the necessary authorization for automatic salary increments from the Department of Hospitals or the Civil Service Commission, the union interceded successfully. And when an allied health career program was threatened with bureaucratic snares and delays, Council staff cut through to a positive conclusion. If a promotions test was promised by the city, the union saw to it that it was given.[11]

In the process, many obstacles had to be overcome by these aspiring public workers: family obligations, anxiety about returning to a school situation, fear of failure, and the considerable distances between work, school, and home. Counseling and extensive tutoring were offered to help mitigate these problems. Care was taken to meet the special needs of groups, such as organizing separate classes for custodial and clerical workers, to make them less apprehensive and uneasy. In these small groups, they were encouraged to move into the HSE course or take a civil service test.

DC 37 Operates a Workers' School

By 1972 over half a million dollars was being expended annually for a wide variety of educational programs, equal in size to an average city high school. For the first time in their lives, thousands of city workers who were severely handicapped by limited education and isolation from the mainstream of economic opportunity found doors being opened to them for career, salary, and status improvements. Others were attracted by the opportunity to master English and attain a high school diploma or college degree. Contrasting the program of New York AFSCME with those of other unions in the nation, Brendan Sexton, former head of education

Many of the union's educational courses offered before and after work hours include basic skills, preparation for high school equivalency tests, and technical training of the greatest variety.

at the UAW, noted that "The educational offerings planned and administered under the auspices of the fund are more varied and far-reaching than any similar programs organized by any other union in the United States."[12]

Test Preparation

Review and brush-up courses, which help prepare members for promotional examinations, are among the most popular because of their close linkage to salary and job advancement. In one 12 month period, over 1,500 members attended eight weeks of classes for senior clerk, junior building custodian, rent examiner, assistant assessor, senior investigator, recreation director, and building custodian for libraries, among others. Whether test preparations insured better grades is difficult to prove, but at the very least they helped workers ease anxieties prior to test-taking. In addition, the Education staff carefully prepared a curriculum around the demands of a particular test.

As the union's membership expanded, the staff sought new channels for encouraging upgrading. For example, the city's custodial employees Local (1597), which grew from 200 to 2,500 members over a three-year period, required a special course, designed in conjunction with the Board of Education, to equip custodial assistants with the skills necessary to prepare for a promotion examination to junior building custodian. The course not only opened career ladder doors for hundreds of low-level workers, but marked a milestone for the Council in its relations with a city agency. For the first time, a department agreed that if custodial assistants completed the course successfully and then passed the examination, thus making the eligible list, the city would not hold an open competitive examination for the title. Previously, supervisors of custodial workers were secured from private industry.

Overwhelmed by the requests of 10,000 members to register for a promotional examination course in 1971, the staff experimented with an eight-week presentation over local television. Booklets and test materials were also carefully designed for easy comprehension. In addition, periodic general test preparation courses cover reading, mathematics, vocabulary, and test-taking techniques.

Basic Skills Development

Designed to improve reading and mathematical skills, and to prepare participants for the HSE examination, courses were first introduced in 1967. What began as a small experimental program for school aides and custodials became, within months, a venture with a long waiting list. A majority of students entering the program during its first year had a reading ability between the sixth and ninth grades of elementary school.[13] Once having completed the equivalency examination program, participants were in a better position to enter a career program or move into more difficult test preparation courses.

After the city assumed the costs of the equivalency program, the union expanded it at headquarters and moved out onto sites at or near the workplace. By January 1970, over 650 hospital employees were in the HSE program out in the field. The issue of expansion through decentralizing the program to the outer boroughs evoked considerable staff conflict. Not until months after Sean Gibney took over as administrator in 1978 was the debate finally resolved. The nub of opposition to decentralization was the fear of losing clients, particularly the large numbers in the program who would not otherwise visit headquarters where other activities might attract them. In the fall of 1981, the decentralized program grew as fast as space could be found, doubling in size and yet not affecting the numbers participating at headquarters. Members never reached before by union programs were now participants with good attendance records. As Gibney enthusiastically reported, "We have simply created a new market." Decentralization of HSE required moving tutorial and counseling services to field locations as well. HSE became a primary focus of staff commitment under Gibney. This changed the department's thrust from one of college preparation, under previous directors, to more basic education.[14]

Classes were organized at three levels, according to student performance. To handle those at the lowest state of preparation, education counselors sought, through individual interviews, to determine the type of support services each one required, such as individual tutorials, special reading clinics, or psychological assistance. By 1980, according to staff analysis, three of four union students passed the HSE courses, while two of every four passed the state examination. These are deemed "extraordinary" figures, in light of the fact that the union accepts everyone who registers, in contrast to the public school system, where a prescribed level of knowledge is required for admission. Even those who do not ultimately pass the state test have been afforded an education experience in which they inevitably improve some of their basic learning skills. As Kathy Schreier emphasized, "We use HSE more than just for the diploma. It helps us reach substantial numbers of members below the acknowledged secondary level. It's basic education as well."[15]

The director of the basic skills program underscored the fact that many of those who come to these courses are often illiterate or have little command of English. Although a considerable number are unable to pass the HSE examination, they have learned enough, in the process, to be able to fill out forms and write a memo. The mere recognition that they have developed some reading and writing skills often fosters a sense of confidence and strengthens their resolve to move ahead. Included in basic skills is English as a second language, an important project for the increasing numbers of the work force from Hispanic countries. Placement tests assign students to one of three levels. Unfortunately, the dropout rate for this particular program turned out to be high, but the retention rate seems to have improved in recent years because of an increase in services by education counselors. The reading improvement program was designed for workers who could not read or had less than a fourth grade level of comprehension. Run on an individual basis, tutors drawn from the union's Retirees Association are given special training and a modest remuneration. Wandering through union headquarters, one often finds in empty nooks and crannies two people huddled over a book, one usually youthful, the other a greying, elderly retiree. This one-on-one relationship is usually a productive one for both individuals.[16]

The spirit behind DC 37 education programs is best captured by the title of one of its pamphlets, "Learn Baby, Learn...While You Earn, Baby, Earn." Education was literally sold to Council unionists to protect jobs and insure security and advancement. Repeatedly pursued as an entitlement at each round of contract negotiations, demands were made increasingly for extending educational benefits. Articles in PEP, talks at local meetings, and special workshops at conferences publicized and demonstrated the value of the education fund. A constant flow of publicity was evident in the stream of Council brochures, leaflets, and posters listing courses and workshops, in addition to a hotline telephone service which still provides information on class schedules and newly developing activities.

Safety Education

The health and safety of workers on their jobs has become another concern of the DC 37 leadership and staff. It has been largely the work of staff professionals who educate and sensitize workers to its importance. After several years of legislative battles, the political arm of the union pushed through one of the most advanced state Occupational Safety and Health Acts (OSHA). While enforcement in the public service depended on governmental agencies, it was largely left to the unions to initiate application of the act to work situations. Consequently, Gotbaum appointed additional staff to focus on job conditions. In competition with groups throughout the country, DC 37 won a federal grant for developing an educational and training program for workers. As a result, additional staff was recruited, giving the Council one of the largest health and safety units for a union of its kind in the nation. Special workshops and classes are conducted regularly for stewards, members, and health and safety committees in various locals. These committees are urged to work closely with management in resolving job-site problems and monitoring work situations for violations of OSHA or of some city code or the union's contract, which entitles workers to "adequate, clean, structurally safe, and sanitary work facilities." Because of ambiguity in the law and the union contract, it is the responsibility of committee members to interpret their meaning as applied to the workplace. When the committees confront an intransigent management, they often seek the help of PEP staff to dramatize a particular situation with photographs and statistics. According to Marcia Lamel, Health and Safety coordinator, and Kathy Schreier in Education, the most meaningful and useful aspect of the program is the education and training of workers. Increasing awareness and sensitivity to their work conditions helps flag those problems requiring professional assistance from staff.[17]

College Programs

College programs include tuition reimbursement for courses taken at approved institutions, DC 37 contracts with individual schools for special programs, and the union's own college at Council headquarters administered by the College of New Rochelle. Tuition refunds have been provided by the city for over a decade, enabling public employees to enroll at any of numerous institutions. Over the years, education fund reimbursement for tuition costs has increased from $50 to $450 per semester. This arrangement enables members to pursue undergraduate or graduate work, which does not have to be job related.

The union has also contracted with a number of schools for special programs which often serve participants as a test for performing at college level. At the New York City campus of Cornell

University's School of Industrial and Labor Relations, for example, a special credit program was developed in labor studies, women's issues, and communication skills. Designed to develop an understanding of the labor movement, it offered a more advanced intellectual challenge to registered students.

A group of courses, focusing on business administration, human services, urban studies and public administration, was offered in cooperation with LaGuardia, Hunter, Baruch and York Colleges of the City University as a transitional or preparatory phase for those interested in pursuing college work. On the initiative of Hofstra University, a program was instituted with a focus on labor and human services aimed at preparing a select group of city workers for leadership roles in confronting urban social problems.[18]

For members with a high school level education, a developmental skills program (formerly called the College Preparation Program) was established by Rifkin. It was designed to meet the needs of students who required additional reading, writing, and mathematical skills for college performance. Study techniques, refresher courses, workshops in management of time, and setting realistic goals were among the offerings. Group and individual remedial help were included with support from an educational counseling unit.

Education Counseling

In 1976 an education counseling service was organized with one full-time and five part-time professionals. Between 1977 and 1978 some 800 unionists were seen individually by counselors and 735 others participated in group counseling, which has been particularly useful since it brings together workers with common education backgrounds who share similar anxieties about returning to a school situation. While individual counseling is available, heavy demands on this relatively small staff requires group strategies. Workshops are offered in study skills, curriculum planning, and setting achievable goals.

Given the diverse educational offerings of the union, counseling has become increasingly important in helping workers to select the appropriate sequence of courses. Particular attention is accorded to those at the lower levels of public service who, according to counseling director Joyce Dudley, "need a good deal of help in setting, or indeed, wanting to have goals...and then to guide them to select reachable goals." Dudley claims that counseling services have contributed to high retention rates in the various courses. Utilization of the counseling service has been greatest among younger workers, retirees, and those in the process of career changes. Since the fiscal crisis there has been an increase in worker anxiety concerning job security, facilitating a greater sense of urgency for additional education and training. Recently alerted to employee concerns about the possible impact of the new word processor machines being installed in city offices, the Education staff has developed a training program to assist thousands of affected public workers. A learning laboratory was developed to give individualized instruction in basic skills, particularly to those who need help in test preparation and in training programs. Almost half of the students using the lab are participants in the HSE.[19]

Growth Pains: Administrative Problems

Given the haste in exploring, initiating, and implementing programs, and confronted with the difficulties involved in identifying experienced personnel who could meet the needs of the DC 37 membership, it was inevitable that the Education Department would experience organizational problems. There was over-extension in some areas and a lack of clarity in others, with too little attention to determining priorities. Assignments were often ambiguous, goals remained unclear, and jurisdictional squabbles and personal conflict were evident. The style and interests of Rosen and Rifkin, though different, focused on exploring new areas for workers' development—the former on careers, the latter on opening the doors for continuing education.

After Rifkin's departure, it was difficult to find a suitable replacement, due largely to the fact that recruitment for union education draws on a relatively small number of individuals with the necessary background. The turnover of administrators between 1976 and 1978 due to incompatibility and personality clashes exacerbated the department's difficulties.[20] Some changes were made, eventually, in the organization and assignment of responsibilities. High school equivalency and skills development were consolidated and all the career development activities were brought together. Although a uniform set of personnel procedures and other management controls were established, the department continued to lack a standardized registration and record-keeping system for its wide variety of programs. As a result, vital information was not collected for registered students.

After a number of personnel changes, Sean Gibney was appointed administrator in 1978. Sparked by the protest movements of the 1960s and by progressive developments within the Catholic church, Gibney worked with the poor and then entered the field of adult education. Bringing to DC 37 a well-formulated administrative approach, he restructured the department, clarifying staff responsibilities and establishing a new focus for the Council's education activities. While cutting back on the time and energies committed to the college-oriented programs, he expanded the decentralization of high school equivalency offerings. His overall goal for the next few years was to concentrate the vast education activities of the organization on meeting the primary needs of low-income, poorly educated public workers. The education fund doubled between 1974 and 1978, reaching over $2 million annually.[21]

Participation in Education

The popularity of these various programs has been underscored by DC 37 leaders, the staff, and a number of outside consultants. According to Gregory Smith, director of Worker Education and the Training Policies Project of the National Manpower Institute, the outreach of adult education programs to working-class populations has been quite limited. He underscored the fact ''...that one of the single largest audiences and potential constituencies for continuing education and training programs is currently not taking advantage of existing opportunities presents a significant public policy challenge.'' According to Smith, even when such courses were offered without cost to union members, generally only four to five percent took advantage of them. However, he found that the DC 37 utilization rate was double that of most other unions. Of some 80,000 Council members, approximately 8,000 enrolled annually between 1974 and 1978.

The most extensive study of the Council's program concluded, ''The fund has attracted thousands of workers to its wide variety of educational programs and services.... Many workers who had been out of school for years have been motivated.'' Dean Lois Gray of Cornell's School of Industrial and Labor Relations found the popularity of its educational services to be relatively extensive, considering that "These people work, have families and confront problems of many urbanites these days, the fear of going out evenings." The union's staff underscored the point that the Council is viewed as a pacesetter in education, for other unions throughout the nation make persistent requests for information and descriptive materials, as well as for suggestions to fill job vacancies.[22]

The largest constituency eligible for education programs is women, many of them heading households. And yet they manage to overcome obstacles and the city's geographical spread, and take the bus and subway to jobs, homes, and union headquarters in downtown Manhattan, where most programs are offered. Despite these difficulties, membership utilization is substantial. When the licensed practical nurse training program was first announced, 37 percent of all nurse's aides applied, obliging the union to choose applicants by lottery. Retention rates were considered high, with some 90 percent reportedly graduating. Over the years, the heaviest enrollment has been in the HSE, college tuition refunds, and test preparation programs. When some courses were given on television, the staff estimated that close to 3,700 participated in the administrative assistant career program and at least 5,000 in the supervisory clerk position in income maintenance. In a typical year, about 8,000 register for courses, with selections made from an extensive variety of offerings (Table 14.1).[23]

Participation has been strongest among those in the Clerical–Administrative Division, with 44.6 percent of all registered students, followed by White-Collar unionists with 18.3 percent. The Blue-Collar and Professional Division members make least use of the union's education programs. These contrasting numbers are partly understandable since Clericals make up one of the two largest constituencies in the fund, with 22.9 percent of the Council's membership in 1974. Although professionals constituted 26.4 percent of DC 37 unionists, many of them already hold college degrees, so that the need for additional education has not been as pressing. Nevertheless, 296 professionals took courses at metropolitan colleges or with the College of New Rochelle at union headquarters in 1974. A number also pursue masters-level work or utilize programs to enhance their professional backgrounds. Accountants and real estate assessors, in particular, are attracted to the Council's certificate programs.

TABLE 14.1: Student enrollment in education programs, DC 37, for September 1977–August 1978

Special college programs	1,271
High school equivalency	744
Clerical skills	761
Career advancement	1,215
Channel 13/WNET	91
Income maintenance	60
1407 accounting	133
Cornell Labor Women	96
Hofstra/Release Time	70
Developmental skills	615
English as a second language	120
College of New Rochelle	1,759*
Brooklyn decentralization—HSE	100
Tuition refund students—fall and winter 1977–78	944
(Refund dollars fall/winter—$117,529.54)	
Municipal personnel program	149
Annual Total Students Serviced	8,128

*Enrollment in all courses. This figure is not a count of students in the college. The total does not include all students tested for possible program entry.

Source: Trudy Anschuetz, "DC 37 Education Fund/Department Annual Report Highlights," June 9, 1978.

COLLEGE WITH A UNION LABEL

In 1972, the vision and imagination of two men helped bring to fruition establishment of a four-year, accredited college at DC 37 headquarters, a first in labor education. With an unbounded creative energy, Bernard Rifkin viewed continuing education for workers as an integral part of opening opportunities for new careers and broadening individual capacity. At the College of New Rochelle in Westchester County, a young assistant professor, Thomas Taaffe, had been evolving a new outlook on educating older students. Adults, he concluded, learned best in an environment that related their daily lives and work to education. The traditional college of youngsters, direct from high school, did not provide an appropriate setting for mature, adult populations.

Rifkin was attracted to Taaffe and his ideas, for both agreed that there were too many rigidities in traditional school systems, that curriculums were artificially segmented into distinct disciplines, that programs were unrelated to life experiences, and that most college offerings discouraged workers from pursuing further study. Both viewed formal education as too narrowly oriented to an elite type of student, from middle class cultures, therefore neglecting workers and lower-class populations. A more open, flexible, and experimental approach would better serve the working adult student. Taaffe explained, "We wanted to redefine the B.A. in terms that would make sense to working adults, and to broaden the areas of knowledge around interdisciplinary course offerings." By the early 1970s, the small, Catholic College of New Rochelle launched a novel program called the School of New Resources. In search of a new clientele to replace its declining enrollment, the school's leadership opened its doors to a more flexible, nontraditional program aimed at older adults. Open to innovation, the college's president, Sister Dorothy Ann Kelly, was attracted to the idea of serving a working-class constituency. With Taaffe's proposal in hand, Rifkin went directly to Gotbaum and Roberts, who quickly gave the idea their blessing, excited that the membership would have their own college. Thomas Taaffe became its first director.

The DC 37 campus was established by a simple contract between the College of New Rochelle and the union. Students eligible for education fund benefits were to receive tuition refunds, and others could apply for financial assistance from a variety of federal and state sources. Given a free hand, and with a minimum of bureaucracy, Taaffe immediately set to work evolving a process for admission, selecting temporary faculty and organizing the curriculum. A notice in the union's newspaper announcing the college's opening stimulated 457 applicants, whereupon Taaffe resorted to a lottery for selection of the first class of 130. They were attracted by the idea of their own school, and by the knowledge that the students would be of similar background and would share many of the same anxieties about returning to the classroom. It appeared far less threatening than the traditional college. As one student subsequently remarked, "It's different here. I find I have a lot to contribute, the teachers respect what we've learned the hard way, and we all learn by a give-and-take process."[24]

Keeping admission requirements to a minimum, the focus was on exit rather than entrance. When applying, the student had only to show proof of completion of high school and pass a short five-part test to determine skills in reading and writing. Based on the test results, certain courses were suggested. Initially, however, there were no requirements, for the school's founders were insistent that adults could decide for themselves how best to pursue their educational program. Their life and work experiences had enriched their backgrounds and provided a more sophisticated attitude than that of younger students. The basic task of the college was to provide an academic setting in which students could evaluate these experiences and link them realistically and constructively to the academic subjects they studied.

Program: Flexibility and Change

The framework of the program originally comprised three basic elements: credit equally apportioned among life experience, a set of interdisciplinary core courses, and an individual project, developed with a faculty adviser, related to the student's job or personal interest. Eager to encourage the innovative program, the founders did not believe in requirements, nor were they enthusiastic about the need or value of remedial work. On the other hand, while excited and supportive of the college, some members of the Council's Education Department felt that the students needed requirements, specific direction, and more remedial assistance than was planned or available. These differences began to surface in 1973. At a meeting of the top Council officers and those administering the new venture, Gotbaum cautioned that college was not necessarily for everyone, and that a program in which students were destined for failure, because they lacked basic skills for college-level work, might only prove counterproductive. He urged that remedial work be given more serious attention.[25]

After several years, the college began building more structure into its program and provided greater remedial facilities. Among the new requirements were language arts, a quantitative skills course, and core seminars. For elective work, the program provided for a concentration from among five areas: communications, foreign languages, letters, psychology, and social sciences. The labor studies concentration offered at Cornell's School of Industrial and Labor Relations was more traditional in scope and organization. This program could serve as a major concentration toward the degree, which included courses in labor history, labor economics, labor law, arbitration, manpower planning, economics of poverty, and public administration. Courses were also assigned levels of difficulty, and students had to select a distribution among them toward graduation.

The six-credit core seminars were designed to familiarize students with the various disciplines offered at a traditional college, "develop skills of historical perspective, increase their resources for life-learning," and integrate their experiences with subject matter. Each student is required to prepare a special project, providing an opportunity for independent study, and for integrating experience and background with newly acquired knowledge. An integral part of the program includes student participation in planning their own curriculum, suggesting new courses, and involvement in independent study.

Financial support for the college has always been constrained, insuring a limited and overworked administrative personnel and an inadequately paid instructional staff. Faculty was originally recruited on an ad hoc, part-time basis, including a number of renowned individuals who held other full-time posts, but who were excited by the idea of a workers' college. Few instructors had the time to attend faculty meetings or schedule student conferences. In recent years, however, greater stability has been sought through creation of a more permanent faculty for the School of New Resources, centered in New Rochelle, and by making a number of part-time adjuncts regular appointees with additional assignments to advise and evaluate student projects on the union's campus.

Over the years, 60 percent of the students have been women, 30 percent were black, and their ages ranged from 30 to 60, with half of them earning less than $8,000 in 1974. After 1975, when a new city contract enabled retirees to attend a special morning program, the age level increased significantly. The largest group of students, however, some 70 percent, have been from the Clerical–Administrative Division (Local 1549).[26]

LABOR EDUCATION

Labor education, in an enlightened, forward-looking union like DC 37, prepares individuals for participation and leadership, and

reaches into the broader concerns of unionism as a reform movement and as a force for social justice. It encompasses at least two
broad goals: to energize the internal organization of the union, and
to broaden the understanding of workers about the historic and
contemporary roles of the labor movement. These include steward training, leadership identification and development, and cultural and recreational activities to improve the lives of workers.

Perhaps no progam is so basic to internal union organization,
its democratic development, and achievement of its ultimate goals
than training shop stewards. Its program directors, drawn ultimately from the union's membership, have shown competence, enthusiasm, and sensitivity to the changing needs of the Council.
Heading the program since 1979, Beryl Major is an articulate, dedicated, and masterful teacher who has come up from the ranks. In
her capacity as a union leader she serves as a model to other young
black women. She targets her training program to the particular
constituency with which she works, tailoring it to their needs. Included in the basic steward course are union organization, advocacy of workers rights, grievance procedures, and analysis of
contracts. With the passing years, new material was added and the
increasing variety and scope of benefits available to members and
their families made explicit. Stewards are now alerted to personal
and psychological problems that may afflict fellow workers and the
need for referral to the union's Personal Services Unit. Other components include encouraging participation in the union's education
offerings and its varied political action programs. Beryl Major
has underscored steward training as the Council's primary grass-
roots effort to insure its own vitality, maturation, and membership involvement.

Course materials are oriented to the practical, daily, on-the-job
problems in clear language and with graphics prepared by the
union's in-house technicians. Slides and film present real-life situations to facilitate role playing, class discussion, and improved
communication skills through observation, debate, and analysis.
Since participants include those who have not completed high
school, this basic course serves to broaden knowledge and encourage critical thinking. At the conclusion of one series, a participant suddenly blurted out, "This course has blown my mind.
I never realized that I could even give all those different arguments
to management." Another student was moved to comment, "Learn-

ing the grievance procedures has helped build my self-confidence. I really never thought I could do it—take on management."[27]

Stewards reflect the wide diversity and character of the union, for a large number of women and minority groups are well represented, as are workers in hospitals, schools, and elsewhere. Successful steward experiences often provide the spark for members to continue their education and seek advancement through new careers. Trainers in steward courses help identify students who demonstrate potential for leadership, for they themselves were spotted in similar training programs or while serving locals as shop stewards.

Identification and development of leadership has been essentially an informal, ad hoc venture, for there is no organized leadership training program. As far as Gotbaum is concerned, "People just know that by seeing who goes where in this union and the opportunity patterns that it provides, members just know how it works." A former staff employee and close associate of the executive director explained that it was known policy to bring competent rank-and-filers into administrative positions. Through an extended network of interpersonal contact and friendship among local leaders and Council staff, individuals are regularly identified as having potential for leadership. They are expected, however, to grow into their responsibilities through on-the-job-training, and any further education or professional skills are to be sought by members on their own initiative.

Gotbaum and the Council support several programs designed for leadership development by Cornell University's School of Labor and Industrial Relations. The Labor Studies Program in Liberal Arts has sought since 1969 to improve the formal education of Council leaders and to keep them abreast of the latest trade union developments. Courses in economics, history, labor law, and legislation are offered, with a focus on labor. These course offerings can be applied toward a labor concentration at the union's college or at some other institutions of higher education. Both Rifkin and Gotbaum were successful in urging local officers like Charles Hughes of Local 372, staff members like division director Guido Menta and assistant director Patricia Caldwell, and shop stewards like Ina Tranberg to attend to gain an understanding of the U.S. labor movement.

RETIREES: TOO OLD TO WORK, TOO YOUNG TO DIE

U.S. society has been enormously successful in prolonging life, allocating substantial medical resources and talent toward this end. Too little attention, however, has been given to exploring meaningful social roles for older adults. Formed in 1968, the Retirees Association of DC 37 initially focused on recreation and education. Its long-time secretary, John Boer, viewed its early purpose as "an alumni society," with little influence or significant membership involvement. But as inflation eroded their fixed pensions, and they were faced with threats of medicare cutbacks in an increasingly conservative national climate, the organization began to expand its activities. With the appointment in 1976 of Eleanor Litwak as full-time staff coordinator, the association blossomed. Her imaginative skills and sparkling energy offered retirees new channels for participation in the union's educational, recreational, and cultural activities, and involvement in its political work. By 1981 the association had grown to 20,000 and was increasing rapidly, with a functioning chapter in Florida. Although a large group of retirees come to union headquarters, where most programs are offered, attempts were made to reach those living in distant areas of the city who face an assortment of difficulties in getting to downtown Manhattan. Litwak has sought to decentralize some activities, an effort strengthened by a monthly newsletter edited by Elie Barr.

The association membership reflects the longer life expectancy of women while the heaviest enrollees are of Jewish origin, illustrative of the large numbers who sought city employment during the Great Depression. Sensitive to the multicultural and ethnic composition of the Council, Litwak has, with the cooperation of Local 372 president Charles Hughes, reached out to recent retirees among minority groups. Programs for retirees run the gamut of members' interests, especially since the union successfully bargained with the city to bring them within the education fund. They participate in the High School Equivalency program, receive college reimbursements, and attend the campus college. Among the most motivated and dedicated of students, 35 of them graduated in 1981 from the DC 37 College of New Rochelle. Over 1,500 are attracted each week to the association's rich array of cultural, craft, recreational, and health activities, where top experts are recruited to conduct classes of particular relevance to senior members. Formerly a college history instructor, Litwak has developed one of the nation's outstanding continuing educational programs for senior citizens. A self-help program called "Not to be Alone," gives increasing support to those who recently experienced death of a spouse or other trauma. The resulting close friendships have even facilitated a marriage! During daylight hours at Council headquarters, retirees are seen busily rushing from one classroom to another, and then meeting for lengthy luncheon discussions in the basement cafeteria. Others are in various cubbyholes and corners assisting young Council members with basic reading and math skills, as part of the tutorial program.

Sensitive to the dynamic potential of senior citizens in U.S. life, Litwak has sought to energize them as a political constituency for the union as it seeks to give progressive leadership and direction to elder colleagues. Members are urged to volunteer for the telephone bank, campaign headquarters of candidates, letter writing, and lobbying legislators in Albany and at City Hall. In 1976, 10,000 retirees were telephoned by association members urging them to vote for Jimmy Carter. Armed with pertinent data, and articulating the needs of the elderly, Litwak and other retirees often testify before governmental committees on social security, health, and welfare. When the Reagan administration threatened severe cutbacks in a wide range of services to senior citizens, she was instrumental in helping organize "Save-Our-Social Security" (SOS), as well as all-day conferences on medicare and health legislation which identified strategies for effective lobbying efforts in Washington. Litwak and the union leadership know, however, that the full potential of retirees in the life and politics of the nation is a distant goal, but they are heading in that direction.

SUMMARY

The wide variety of programs offered to DC 37 members serves as a model for other unions as well as adult education institutions across the country. Among important elements in its success, at least three stand out. First, staff skill has linked workers' training and education needs to relevant and well-planned curriculums for test preparation, basic skills, the career ladder programs, counseling

services, and activities for retirees. Second, since the union has assumed the responsibility for delivering these services, it has heightened the confidence and trust of its own members. Finally, the
deep commitment of the union's leadership is evident in the high
priority accorded education and in the expansive range of programs, from the three Rs to a college degree.

NOTES

1. Gregory Smith, preface to Jane Shore, *The Education Fund of District Council 37: A Case Study*, Worker Education and Training Project, Washington, D.C.:
National Manpower Institute, 1979, pp. v–vii.
2. Draft for pamphlet on education and upgrading, February 4, 1971.
3. *National Advisory Commission on Civil Disorders Report*, New York: Ban-
tam Books, 1968, p. 254; Shore, *The Education Fund*, p. 9; Seymour Mann and
Sheldon Mann, "Decision Dynamics and Organizational Characteristics: The
AFSCME and NYC District Council 37," paper delivered at the American Political Science Association, San Francisco, September 2–5, 1975, pp. 12–13. Also interviews with Bernard Rifkin, September 15, 1982; Sumner Rosen, September 22,
1982; Lillian Roberts, September 28, 1982.
4. Victor Gotbaum to John Lindsay, July 14, 1966; David T. Stanley, *Managing Local Government Under Union Pressure*, Washington, D.C.: The Brookings Institution, 1972, p. 46.
5. *New York Times*, June 27, 1966, p. 1; *Public Employee Press*, July 1, 1966,
p. 8; Sumner Rosen, "Not Jobs Alone...Careers," *Public Employee Press*, March
29, 1967, p. 5.
6. *Public Employee Press*, December 24, 1965, p. 8; *New York Times*, November 15, 1966; p. 61; interview with Sumner Rosen, September 22, 1982.
7. *Public Employee Press*, April 1, 1966, pp. 1, 8; August 23, 1967, p. 17; January 17, 1969, pp. 18–19. Helen Gaillard, a 61-year-old grandmother, recalled this
lengthy, time-consuming training period as one in which her apartment constantly
looked like a "cyclone." But she maintained, "It's been worth it."
8. *Public Employee Press*, May 8, 1968, p. 10. Bertram Bolt, a 50-year-old
nurse's aide who had labored with challenging courses, advanced to the post of
oxygen technician and moved among his patients with new-found pride as he
wore his white clinical jacket, white shirt, and necktie. It was among these thousands of hospital workers that the Council won profound gratitude and a deep
commitment of support for its many activities, including political action.
9. Harold G. Pollard, director of career development, DC 37, testimony
presented to the New York State Senate Standing Committee on Labor and Industry, August 27, 1968. Shortly thereafter, the city did agree to assume the costs
of the high school equivalency program, although direction and management remained within the union.
10. Hereafter, the education fund will be referred to as the fund or ed fund.
While the heads of departments in the union are called directors, in Education

the title is administrator because of the language in the contract. For purposes of this study, these terms will be used interchangeably.

11. Memorandum from Victor Gotbaum to presidents of all locals, January 5, 1968; memorandum, Harry Pollard to Rifkin, April 4, 1968.

12. Brendan Sexton, principal investigator, "An Evaluation of the Education Fund of DC 37," New York State School of Industrial and Labor Relations, Division of Extension and Public Service, Cornell University, July 1982.

13. The test involved 8 hours of reading comprehension and 2 hours for mathematics, including some algebra and geometry. Classes were offered every work day for 2 hours, mornings and evenings, to accommodate all work schedules. A small sampling of the first group in the program disclosed that almost 70 percent passed the equivalency examination on their first try. In 1969 this figure reached 80 percent. Of those who failed, a majority came within five percentage points of passing.

14. Education Department activities report, January 15, 1970; High School Equivalency end term report, 1980. Also, interviews with Sean Gibney, March 18, 1982; Kathy Schreier, March 18, 1982; Michael Brailove, April 23, 1982; Ronald Fordham, April 29, 1982; Rose Pizonnia, April 29, 1982. In recent years, an average of some 500 students enroll annually at headquarters, and over 1,200 attend the decentralized program.

15. Interviews with Sean Gibney, March 18, 1982; Kathy Schreier, March 18, 1982, and January 24, 1984. In late 1983, Ms. Schreier succeeded Mr. Gibney to the post of administrator.

16. English as a second language, end term progress report, September 10–December 17, 1981.

17. "1983 Survey of Fourteen Union Occupational Safety and Health Programs," Washington, D.C.: Public Citizen Health Research Group, January 1984, pp. 7, 8, 11, 14. Also, interviews with Richard Winsten, assistant director of Political Action, March 18, 1982; Kathy Schreier, January 25, 1984; and Marcia Lamel, February 10, 1984.

18. Workers receiving reimbursement for college courses totaled, in 1971–72, 1,178, and in 1976–77, 2,586. Contracted programs are distinguished from other college programs mainly because of funding arrangements. The education fund usually pays tuition directly to the serving institution while, under a contract, the student pays the fee and then may be reimbursed through the ed fund tuition refund program and/or other financial assistance programs. Shore, *The Education Fund*, p. 26; interview with Kathy Schreier, March 18, 1982.

19. Joyce Dudley to Trudy Anschuetz, July 13, 1978; interview with Joyce Dudley, April 29, 1982. Three of the early counselors were former members of DC 37, products of the union's workers education programs who had returned to school in their later years and became role models for their clients.

20. Memorandum, Seymour Mann to Gotbaum, Roberts, Tibaldi, Maher, re: Some Follow-up Comments and Observations on Sean Gibney's Preliminary Report on the Education Fund, November 30, 1978, p. 2. Among the administrators who served for relatively short terms included Ernie Weiss, Irving Rosenstein, and acting administrator Seymour Mann, who was also an assistant to Gotbaum and Roberts.

21. Seymour Mann, "Review of Selected DC 37 Education Programs and Activities," July 25, 1974. Also, interviews with Kathy Schreier, April 15, 1982; Sean Gibney, April 23, 1982; Ronald Fordham, April 29, 1982.

22. Data on the exact numbers of students and utilization of various programs are not available. Records are inadequate because, according to the staff, time for gathering such information has been limited. Other reasons offered are inadequate funds and the need for a costly, computerized system. See Shore, *The Education Fund*, p. 93, and Mann, "Review." Also, interviews with Michael Brailove, April 23, 1982; Lois Gray, May 12, 1982.

23. Draft report, "Education and Career Upgrading," corrected by Lillian Roberts, February 4, 1971, attached to memo from Roberts to Rifkin. See also "Educational Fund Programs In Operation, December, 1974, and their Utilization." With annual utilization of courses averaging around 8,000, Table 14.1 indicates the breakdown in student registration.

24. *Public Employee Press*, September 29, 1972; *Sunday News*, July 15, 1973; Seymour Mann, "Review of Selected DC 37 Education Programs and Activities," July 25, 1974, pp. 21, 28–32, Education Files. Also interviews with Bernard Rifkin, September 15, 1982; Tom Taaffe, November 3, 1983.

25. *Public Employee Press*, March 31, 1972; Seymour Mann, "Education Report," 1974 Gotbaum files; DC College, New Resources, program curriculum, fall semester, 1972; memo from Bernard Bellush to Gotbaum, Rifkin and Taaffe, "Summary of Meeting," May 7, 1974.

26. Memo from Tom Taaffe, director, DC 37 campus, to authors, "Graduates of DC 37 Campus," Feburary 1984. Interview with Taaffe, November 3, 1983. Among those awarded degrees by 1977, over 100 had been accepted by graduate schools. Some 30 percent who graduated felt that they had earned increases in salary or won promotions because of their college work. Although a substantial number did not report any subsequent advances, they did express feelings of pride and self-worth in having achieved a college degree. By 1984, 1,000 graduates will have received a B.A. degree from the DC 37 college.

27. Interview with Beryl Major, April 15, 1982; Jewel Bellush, "Observation Report of Shop Steward Class," May 6, 1982.

15
Expanding Union Services: The Lifeblood of DC 37

As a mediating structure in the delivery of human services, DC 37 is a trailblazer in exploring strategies and in extending benefits. Throughout its history, the Council has been attentive to the health and educational needs of its members, at first negotiating for reimbursement of medical costs and then, by the 1970s, exploring the feasibility of its own delivery system. At least three major goals were the targets of the union's program to broaden the services to members: the desire to make available specialized, technical developments in the health and legal fields; to offer these services free of bureaucratic red tape and impersonal care; and to be within the limited parameters of financial feasibility. By 1981, its health programs reached over a quarter of a million people, including the families of Council members and retirees. Over its 40-year history, the DC 37 service arm matured under the impact of a number of factors: organizational needs, leadership commitment, skilled staff and consultants, the inadequacies of the private sector, and gaps in public policies. In this chapter we describe two encompassing programs, the Health and Security Plan (H/S) and the Municipal Employees Legal Services (MELS).

ORGANIZATIONAL NEEDS AND LEADERSHIP

Benefits have long been offered as incentives for joining a union. As far back as the mid–nineteenth century, the Amalgamated Society of Engineers in England provided a wide range of

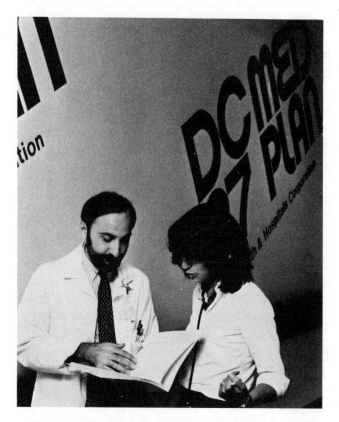

The union has assumed direct responsibility for the delivery of an expanding variety of health services to its members through Med-Plan and other pioneering endeavors.

services to its members. Labor historian G.D.H. Cole explained, "The essential basis for the 'New Model' [in trade union organization] was a close combination of trade and friendly activities. . . . [the Engineers] provided for all its members a wide range of benefits, ranging from dispute and unemployment benefit to sickness and superannuation benefit. . . . In short, it was a Trade Union and a Friendly Society almost in equal measure."[1]

In major DC 37 organizing drives, a key appeal to public workers was that the Council would serve them better than would competing unions. Services also remained important for maintaining support and enthusiasm among union members. The primacy of loyalty in trade unions, and the vital role that servicing played, should not be discounted nor derided. A recent AFL–CIO publication underscored these factors when it maintained, "There is a race to assist members in solving 'off the job' problems and the prize is loyalty. Organized labor cannot afford to lose this one."[2] Along similar lines, specialists in social welfare policy highlighted the importance of servicing members, for they recalled, "A labor union is a membership organization. Some segments of public opinion notwithstanding, union leaders remain in power only so long as they tend to their store—i.e., provide service to the membership."[3]

Another organizational imperative was the need for cohesion. At the start of Gotbaum's tenure, the Council was characterized by dozens of independent locals, each representing different occupations and titles, with a membership drawn from a wide range of educational backgrounds, income, and status. Service provided a crucial strategy for galvanizing and integrating these diverse elements within the Council and in support of the leadership. Many functions normally performed by locals in other unions were assumed and managed by the Council as the parent body. With 85 percent of the membership served by H/S, administrator Roslyn Yasser pointedly noted, "This frequency of contact creates a significant bond between the plan, its members, and the union." The larger membership and expanded treasury enabled the Council to develop one of the more extensive service programs in the nation. The days of the small organization had passed, and as Mancur Olson noted, "It appears that in many unions. . .in the present day, not much strength can be gained from constituent small groups, . . .and with the growth of the average local, a union may also not be able to support itself any longer by providing social benefits."

Throughout their careers in New York, the leadership teams of Wurf, and then Gotbaum–Roberts, were firmly committed to bringing the broadest range of human services to Council members. New ideas were encouraged, challenging ventures explored, and even in the face of severe constraints evoked by the fiscal crisis, Gotbaum agreed to Julius Topol's concept of developing legal services for members. Roslyn Yasser noted that "Vic was ahead of the field itself."[4] Gotbaum was particularly sensitive about the inadequacy of the private health and legal sectors in meeting the minimum needs of workers. Roberts, who identified closely with minority workers, knew from personal experience that basic health needs of many were sadly neglected. Her determined battle to prevent the closing of city hospitals under the Lindsay and Koch administrations was one of many struggles in response to their desperate plight. She knew from first-hand observation that hospital emergency rooms were often utilized as a substitute for a doctor's office. As they worked side by side, Roberts and Gotbaum shared a dream that their union would service members better than any other, and that DC 37 would be a role model. The legislative struggle for the agency shop was but one of many indications that the Council's leadership sought resources primarily to improve the union's service arm. And when that goal was finally achieved, DC 37 had a stable and dependable source of funds to enable it to pursue a better life for its members.

THE UNION AS MAGNET TO EXPERTS

In its recruitment of human service staff, the Council attracted many individuals with unusual expertise and commitments who also knew that the union's setting provided expansive scope for innovation. The DC 37 reputation as a pacesetter in servicing workers drew a number of professional consultants who shared the union's idealism and devotion to its members. In one grant application to test a new service proposal, consultants insisted, "This service-oriented psychology of DC 37 was necessary to conduct this study." Heading the list of consultants who played a major role in encouraging new servicing directions was William "Bill" Michaelson, president of the United Store Workers (affiliated with the Retail, Wholesale, Department Store Union), and a close friend of Gotbaum. It was largely through his efforts that the Council achieved its greatest advances in providing health care services in a number of areas. A key source of constant advice and guidance, and "a wiz in financial arrangements," it was Michaelson who helped organize the hypertension program, the second surgical consultation, and who suggested that the union deliver its own health services. It was also Michaelson who convinced H/S staff that "it could be done. He was a tower of strength and stimulation."[5]

A colleague of Gotbaum from college days, Hyman Weiner had remained in contact with the union leader since both shared a strong commitment to workers. His associates at the Industrial Social Welfare Center of Columbia University's School of Social Work, who worked closely with DC 37 on a number of projects, included John Sommer and Sheila Akabas, and a graduate student, Roslyn Yasser. Weiner was one of the guiding figures who pioneered strategies for bringing preventive medical and mental health care to working-class populations. Not only did he believe that the world of work should constitute an important concern for social workers, but he concluded, as a result of combining practical field experiences with theoretical analysis, that the workplace and the unions provided an important network for communication and support, as well as a means for locating and helping workers. In its early years, direction of H/S staff was drawn largely from outside professionals, who did not understand the Council's structure, and who contributed to tensions evoked by personality differences. The resultant turnover in leadership finally led Gotbaum to turn inward and select Nat Lindenthal as administrator. Lindenthal had come up from the union ranks, rising from shop steward among caseworkers to division director. With strong administrative skill he was able to systematize the benefits program into a well-organized and efficient service arm. However, while effective at his work, he demanded undeviating loyalty from his subordinates, to the extent of terrifying some of them, while, at the same time, requesting complete independence from his superiors in decision making. Soon, he, too, was forced to leave the union.

In 1978 Roslyn Yasser was appointed to replace Lindenthal as administrator of H/S. Her initial experience at DC 37 had been as a graduate student of social work assisting in the establishment of the Personal Services Unit (PSU). Creative, bright, and sensitive to human foibles, her warm personality and enthusiasm as administrator engendered stability and calmness. Handling millions of fund dollars annually, members of the board of trustees, union treasurer Arthur Tibaldi, council auditor Harvey Nuland, and lawyer Bertram Perkel, helped keep the complex systems financially viable and the administration honest and responsible.[6]

HOLES IN THE PROFESSIONAL NETS

Despite the nation's postwar advances in health technology, the growing numbers of trained doctors, dentists, and lawyers, and the expansion of other human resource professions, working-class populations generally remained underserved or often simply neglected. Oriented to middle-class clients, and more comfortable in tending to their needs, the health and legal professions were generally not as responsive to the average worker.

Even in its expansionary period, the U.S. welfare state did not always reach working-class populations fairly or equitably. Many programs designed to provide public care neglected workers or reached them inadequately, although Medicare was a substantive improvement for the elderly. Researchers found that workers tended to dislike most anything that smacked of charity or free clinical care. But benefits provided by the union had the distinct advantage of avoiding any stigma, for they were sold by the leadership and staff as a worker's right, for which they paid dues, and were not a handout. In addition, in various ghetto communities throughout the city, where many DC 37 members lived, professionals were leaving in droves for more stable, upper-class clientele. Quality care of many Council members was poor, and a substantial number of them were without family doctors or had never gone to a dentist. "We were shocked," admitted Yasser, "by what we found among working people in the level of the health needs they required when we started to serve them ourselves."[7]

The Council's Health and Security Plan began in 1963 when the Motor Vehicle Operators (Local 983) successfully negotiated with the city to contribute $50 per capita annually toward a welfare fund. The money was used initially for life insurance, disability, and hospital care. From these modest beginnings, the plan expanded to include a wide array of benefits for employees and dependents, although some services were offered only to workers. By 1981 the benefits available to employees and their dependents included: catastrophic medical, second surgical consultation, dental, prescription drug, optical, health and pension counseling, and social service crisis intervention (Personal Service Unit). Those benefits available only to employees included: death, accidental death and dismemberment, and weekly disability income.

Members were eventually permitted to select from among several health programs offered by the city—the Health Insurance Plan (HIP) or Group Health Insurance (GHI) were most popular. A prepaid, all-inclusive service with centers throughout the city and in Nassau County, HIP provides a comprehensive set of health care facilities, including a family doctor, specialists, and laboratory services. GHI is essentially a reimbursement arrangement, dependent on a fixed scale that proved increasingly inadequate as the fees of private physicians, particularly specialists, skyrocketed.

PERSONAL SERVICES UNIT

In 1971, John Sommer and Sheila Akabas helped the union establish the PSU. This social service crisis intervention program made professional help available to members with problems relating to family, finances, health, accident, and death. The Council's executive director urged members to utilize this service explaining, "We live in a hectic, anxious world, with pressures and tensions exerted on individuals and families from all sides.... it's no reflection on you or your family if you turn to your union for experienced, professional help." Although PSU utilizes both individual and collective counseling, group strategies are pursued more extensively, since the union seeks to reach as many members as possible. This approach encompasses a wide range of subjects which, for retirees, include: finances, health, leisure, work opportunities, insurance, and availability of benefits. For widows and widowers, help is provided to enable them to cope with their traumatic distress. PSU also offers advice to those with long, debilitating illnesses, identifying sources for special help and treatment and arranging placement in rehabilitation facilities. In situations of mental disability, it offers short-term therapeutic counseling.

The unit's hands-on approach helps link members, in a personal way, to other services. Not unlike the old political machine, with its roots in the local community, the union offers direct assistance to members and their families. As Robert Merton put it, "Public issues are abstract and remote; private problems are extremely concrete and immediate." The PSU offers advice on how to find housing and identifies individuals and appropriate agencies. Replacing the politician, the professionals at PSU help cut red tape in the bureaucratic agencies of the city, which have grown bulkier and more distant from clients. The city's complex forms and impersonal treatment tend to frustrate members and leave them demoralized. PSU staff, bolstered by the expansive influence of the union, can frequently make a simple phone call which produces the right contact and sets the wheels rolling for a speedy and constructive solution. As part of this developing process at PSU, the city agreed to underwrite the cost of two counselors to help develop strategies for the handling of alcoholic workers in an endeavor to help them on their jobs. PSU's heavy case load involving garnished wages influenced development of a consumer education and advocacy program, in which city officials cooperate in training unionists as advocates for fellow members who have been treated unfairly. In addition, consumer education programs are offered regularly at local meetings, conferences, and workshops, and through articles in PEP.[8]

DIRECT CARE, UNION-DELIVERED

The staff at H/S found increasing numbers of workers having difficulty finding good dentists and adequate medical care in their deteriorating communities. Observing these developments, Bill Michaelson urged DC 37 to assume the direct delivery of health services. Most unions, he found, had taken the safe road of simply providing the members with health benefits, leaving the character and quality of the services rendered to independent professionals. Unafraid to take on the medical and dental establishments, Michaelson had experimented with the direct delivery of services in his own, small union. Gotbaum was immediately receptive and according to Michaelson, "showed great courage to assume such a responsibility." By taking over the direction and delivery of services, the union would not only become the focus for complaints from dissatisfied members, but would encounter considerable opposition from those closely associated with other health programs. As a result, three programs were organized, providing for dental, medical, and vision care centers. In January 1971, the first union dental plan was established, providing low-cost care for the entire membership. Over 2,000 dentists in the metropolitan area agreed to adhere to the H/S schedule of fixed charges for a variety of dental treatments. In turn, DC 37 agreed to reimburse 75 percent of the client's bill.

Shortly thereafter, however, major professional dental associations openly criticized this arrangement of fee fixing, including the Dental Society of the State of New York, the 11th District Dental Society in Queens, and the 2nd District Dental Society in Brooklyn and Staten Island. After a steady flow of resignations from dentists, DC 37 felt compelled to complain bitterly that these professional groups were consciously seeking to undermine and destroy the union's plan by "persuading, threatening, or coercing any licensed dentist" to discourage their participation. Gotbaum let loose with a blast against the "upper-middle-class bias" and insensitivity of these dental associations to minorities and to lower-income workers, for they were "putting money over the needs of society." In response, the Secretary of the State Dental Society claimed that fixing fees insured substandard work. Another dental spokesman argued that the plan "harms the patient–dentist relationship by encouraging the establishment of clinics which become impersonal because their success depends on turnover."[9]

By 1979 as much as half the membership utilized the union's panel of dentists, while others selected their own and were reim-

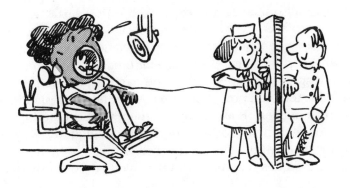

bursed according to the fee schedule. However, in the process of monitoring the services, H/S staff became concerned with rising costs and the poor quality of care offered many of their members. In reviewing the dental claims for that year, they found that preventive services, the most utilized yet the least costly, were overtaken by reconstructive work, which absorbed 40 percent of all dental expenditures. The staff concluded, "This and other evidence indicates that many of our members get more treatment than they need for dentures and bridgework because there's more money in it for the dentist. . . . We would like to encourage treatment based on the patient's need instead of the dentist's 'greed,' and more focused attention on preventive work." Yasser, meanwhile, complained that members were getting work "below acceptable standards of quality."

The union then experimented with a large dental center, which was owned and operated by a private dentist. When set up in lower Brooklyn, the borough containing the Council's largest concentration of members, it serviced the members of families under the plan, including children up to the age of 19, or 23 if full-time students. Each individual was assigned a regular dentist, and major attention was focused on preventive care, fillings, and periodontal work. Not long afterwards, in order to improve monitoring and control costs, this experimental arrangement was replaced by the union's self-operated center.[10]

A Council-operated center was opened in Brooklyn in 1980, to be directed by dentists with long experience, with an emphasis on preventive care. A group of young recruits, hired after completing dental school and a year's residency, was attracted to group practice, because it afforded them a rich experience under caring supervision, which enhanced their future career. In order to contain the costs of high salaries and expensive benefits, these young dentists were replaced every three years. Yasser contends "Members love the young dentists because they care and show concern." With treatment monitored carefully, the care has been of marked quality. When specialists are needed, they are hired on a per diem basis. In 1981, the plan processed 100,000 dental visits, including over 21,000 for children. Because of the success of the first center and by the long waiting list of members, a second center was planned for lower Manhattan. The plan is self-insured, which means that the union assumes responsibility for covering costs. By displacing the insurance company, which formerly protected the union against cost overruns, the staff has been able to cut expenses for processing and administering claims. Educational campaigns at local meetings, conferences, and through PEP urge early use of dental services before conditions require more expensive care. Dental claims absorb 45 percent of the total health expenditures, the largest benefit provided, costing approximately $23 million a year. It is the largest such dental service in the country.[11]

Med-Plan

As part of contractual negotiations, municipal unions in New York won health insurance coverage for doctor services and hospital care, with HIP offering the most comprehensive arrangement. Except for well-run centers, however, DC members reported growing dissatisfaction with its care and treatment. In response to these complaints, and after four years of skilled and imaginative input by Michaelson, DC 37 staff designed its own delivery system of comprehensive health care for the entire family. In 1979, Med-Plan was opened to the first 6,000 subscribers of a prepaid group practice. Run by the city's Health and Hospitals Corporation (HHC), the arrangement is a complex of contracts among HHC, New York University Medical School, and the union. Physicians are employed on a full-time, salaried basis, within the Bellevue Hospital complex, where Med-Plan members are serviced by the hospital and by staff of the medical school. It was largely due to this experience that the union's staff discovered the generally poor level of care their workers were receiving in many ghetto areas of the city. According to Lawrence Morgan, the Council's health planner, those who subscribed to Med-Plan were generally an "adverse selection," an older, more sickly, and expensive population than usual, with increasing health problems. To this group were soon added the retirees. In its relatively few years of operation, the carefully monitored and supervised care demonstrated heightened utilization of preventive medical services, which cut costs tremendously.[12]

Because of the constant pressure of rising medical costs, and the fact that Med-Plan was not located at a central, convenient point of access, the number of subscribers in the program has had to be expanded considerably to help cover costs. Membership, as a result, was opened to other unions in the MLC.

Vision Center

Over the years, members and their families have received reimbursement for eye examinations and glasses, with a panel of doctors agreeing to service city workers at a fixed fee. However, with these services tending to range from inadequate to poor, the H/S staff set to work in search of another arrangement. With the help and encouragement of consultant Dr. Jessie Rosenthal, DC 37 organized its own vision care service, which turned out to be a unique, high-quality facility. Open to all members and their families, it is conveniently located in downtown Manhattan, with optometrists drawn from the clinical staff of the state university's college of optometry. These doctors quickly learned, for example, that many of the previous prescriptions of private opticians had been written poorly or incorrectly assigned. It was expected that some 10,000 members would avail themselves annually of a free eye examination, comforted by the knowledge that included in the service, at no cost, were lenses and frames every two years, and more often if required.

In addition to these three major health delivery systems, a se-

ries of important new services were offered DC 37 members. Since 1972 the union has provided second surgical consultations, a program which has become popular throughout the country. Another innovative service has been the hypertension screening and treatment program offered at various sites throughout the city, some of which are run at the workplace as well. Workers suffering from high blood pressure have been identified early, avoiding subsequent complications and burdensome expenses. With many workers on their feet for long periods, the union responded to their pleas to provide podiatry as a service, and which is now offered free to everyone at the Med-Plan center. In the first three months of operation, between September and December 1981, over 3,600 patient visits were made. Likewise, with an increasing number of retirees on the list of subscribers, audiology has been added. This involves lengthy procedures and several examinations before hearing aids are prescribed. In the instances of podiatry and audiology, the H/S staff pursued the task of offering these services without advance guarantee by the city that they would subsequently become part of a negotiated benefits package.[13]

The drug benefit covers the cost of prescription drugs, including insulin and allergens. The medication, however, must be purchased from participating pharmacies, which have agreed to the H/S fee schedule. Except for retirees, members pay a small 75-cent fee for each prescription. Expenditures for drugs have mounted considerably, reaching 6.5 million dollars by 1979. The annual cost per employed member that year was about $66 while for retirees it was more than double that. By 1981 drugs absorbed 30 percent of all medical benefits, the second largest expediture. Finally, the staff of H/S and Med-Plan scheduled special group discussions and a variety of education programs in an endeavor to meet the overall health needs of members, covering such topics as smoking, diet, problems of adolescence, and concerns of retirees. Benefits and their utilization have grown steadily as the Council successfully negotiated steady increases in the city's contribution.[14]

With the nation's changing mood, and a political leadership in Washington which has been moving the country in the direction of drastic budgetary cutbacks and severe shrinkage of welfare and human services, the Council's expanding health care programs have become increasingly important. As a provider of sophisticated health services, DC 37 stands as a beacon of hope and care to unionists everywhere.

LEGAL CARE WITH A UNION LABEL

Using the principles of prepaid medical care, another innovative Council venture was creation of the Municipal Employees Legal Service (MELS) plan. Two events provided the impetus for the new program—the fiscal crisis and the civil rights movement. Clearly evident by the early 1970s, the city's financial difficulties placed severe constraints on the budget, made contract negotiations increasingly arduous, and severely limited union demands. As a result, the Council's leadership sought to expand services as a strategy for improving the quality of life of workers and their families. Secondly, the civil rights struggle helped sensitize many professionals to the unmet health and legal needs of the country's poor, minority, and working-class populations. Legal services, for example, were increasingly recognized as fundamental to helping individuals achieve fair and equitable treatment. Without the aid of a lawyer, individuals frequently could not assert their legitimate rights as tenants, consumers, or potential clients of a government service. Legal difficulties could be as burdensome as medical problems. The DC 37 counsel, Julius Topol, was well aware that the legal profession served workers, the poor, and minority groups inadequately, especially after he began to receive a stream of requests for legal assistance from the union's PSU. PSU staff estimated that as many as one in four of their clients needed some form of legal aid, but such costs were generally prohibitive.

Typical of a working-class clientele, many union members were often uncomfortable, if not fearful, of approaching lawyers. Others simply did not know how to select an attorney. Topol was at a loss as to how his staff of lawyers, experienced in labor–management relations, could become involved in the personal problems of public workers. At this time, Topol read about a prepaid legal program under way in Shreveport, Louisiana, sponsored by the Ford Foundation. The possibilities of such service for Council members attracted him and he discussed the matter with Gotbaum. Although under intense stress due to the developing fiscal crisis, the executive director approved Topol's request for released time and funds with which to pursue the idea. Topol recalled, "Most any other labor leader would have said it was a nice idea, but now is not the time for such a venture. Vic had the imagination and courage."

It was then that Topol approached Sheila Akabas, who had assisted in the establishment of PSU. Challenged by the idea, she organized a team to study the general proposal, drawing on both the social work and law school faculties at Columbia University. Aided by Akabas's skill and access to the foundation world, this talented group set to work drawing on the model of prepaid medical programs. To identify the primary legal needs of members, the clerical workers were selected for an initial survey. One in six reported that they had confronted situations that they felt required legal assistance, but they had never consulted a lawyer. Over 60 percent of respondents attributed this decision to prohibitive costs. As many as one-third did not know how to select an attorney, nor how to evaluate legal competency. Most members expressed the need for legal assistance on such matters as credit, fraudulent merchandise, garnishment of wages, tenant–landlord relations, non–work-related accidents, estate planning, and a host of family problems, including divorce, separation, child custody, and support. Based on these findings, the team designed a pilot project to explore the services the union could offer, how they could be most effectively organized, the strategy for linking legal and personal problems, and the question of financial feasibility. A proposal was submitted to the Ford Foundation, underscoring the need to bring professional services to low-income populations, the union's reputation as a socially concerned organization, and its responsiveness to the needs of poorly paid minority populations.

The team emphasized the fact that many professionals had resisted efforts to find ways for delivering legal services to working-class populations. Another attractive element of the proposal was the possibility of creating a system that was cost-effective and which put into place such arrangements as a closed panel of salaried lawyers. Finally, the application encompassed new directions and actors, involving social workers early in the process. "In real life," they explained, "there is often no easy line between law problems and social problems. We assumed that early preventive counseling may eliminate later dispute." Since the idea proved so challenging and the proposal was so well presented by a group of acknowledged experts, the Ford Foundation suggested that the pilot project be converted into a permanent program, for which they would increase the initial modest request of $35,000 to a grant of $250,000![15]

In October 1974, as the initial phase of the experiment, Topol opened an office that was restricted, by lottery, to a limited number of members. Two programs were established—one offered free comprehensive coverage in almost all civil matters to 1,500 workers and their families; the other provided assistance with consumer affairs for 25,000. The project provided opportunities for experimenting with different modes of handling cases, including identifying areas for utilization of paralegals. Techniques were also developed for collaborative efforts between lawyer and social worker and maximum utilization of their respective expertise. Standardized handling of routine tasks was identified, and methods were devised for monitoring case progress from initial interview to closing.

Considerations, Constraints, and Challenges

Development of a permanent package of legal benefits proved no easy task, for a number of issues had to be resolved and tradeoffs made. One critical matter, for example, involved the varying needs of different constituents within DC 37. Due to extremes in income and education levels, the consultants recognized the necessity for offering an all-encompassing program that would service the union's heterogeneous population. If the permanent program were to gain and retain broadly based membership approval, the union leaders had to spread the program benefits as widely as possible. A mixture of social idealism and pragmatic considerations eventually shaped the cost-benefit decisions.

In addition to cost considerations, intensity of need was another determining factor. Food stamps and debt management, for example, were chief concerns among low-income hospital workers, while estate planning and will preparation attracted middle-class members. Since food stamps were survival matters for members with incomes just above the poverty line, MELS included assistance in this area. Another difficult decision involved handling complaints of housing code violations, primarily from lower-income tenants. While those were pressing, the MELS staff excluded them as a practical matter because they required more time, energy, and personnel than was available, and because uncertain outcomes often left clients disgruntled.

Matrimonial matters, however, cut across the membership and were quickly recognized as an area for inclusion. But even this service evoked cost issues, since a contested separation often involved extensive personnel time. Given the fund's limitations in the original program, the staff decided to charge $300 for more complex marital difficulties. Consumer problems were also selected because they affected members of all social and economic backgrounds. While bankruptcy difficulties were costly, often complex, and on many occasions involved social work staff, MELS did not hesitate to include them in the permanent package, for it viewed the service as a "social imperative to relieve distress of the individual whose debts were out of control." Although debt and bankruptcy initially tended to involve families with household incomes of less than $12,000, a number of families in the higher income brackets also utilized the service. Problems with administrative agencies tended to attract those in middle- and lower-income brackets.[16]

Union-Made Legal Care

After one year in operation, sufficient information had been gathered to enable Topol and Gotbaum to plan for the extension of the legal package to the entire membership. With the city in the midst of the most critical phase of its fiscal difficulties, expenditures for new or expanded benefits were not negotiable. With little to show members of any positive gains in 1976, Gotbaum pressured City Hall to at least commit itself to the new legal service. However, to underwrite the expenses involved, Gotbaum appealed, in turn, to the membership to allow part of their COLA to be set aside for the city to utilize as payment for the program. Under this arrangement, one dollar would be taken out of each member's

COLA every two weeks, or $26 per year. Although members were asked to sustain the initial cost, Gotbaum was convinced that once the city committed itself to the MELS program the union could secure direct municipal contributions in the next contract.

In the process of securing general Council approval, Gotbaum appeared before each bargaining unit to explain the importance of the new service and the rationale for his strategy. Faced with a no-gain contract, the MELS plan offered workers some hope for better days, enabling DC 37 to create a new service that was concrete, visible, and extremely useful. Twelve of the larger locals, encompassing some 80,000 members and their families, agreed to participate.

In the initial phase of the plan, major attention was given to family problems related to divorce, separation and annulment, child support, alimony, and custody. Since these cases were heard in the city's family court, workers were encouraged to represent themselves, and MELS prepared self-help material to guide them. MELS did assume responsibility for divorces that went to trial, but this was not burdensome, since 90 percent were not contested. MELS covered problems that arose in the purchase of goods and services, and where the amounts were $100 or less, advised members how to represent themselves in a small claims court. Also included were debt-related problems, such as preparation of wills, and difficulties with government agencies involving social security, Medicaid, Medicare, special income-raising subsidies, and food stamps.

MELS was officially launched in 1977 as a permanent program, enabling Topol to move out of the Legal Department to direct this unique, challenging idea, and one of the biggest prepaid legal ventures in the country. This innovative program came at a propitious moment in his career, since he had begun to feel less useful to, and more distant from, Gotbaum during the fiscal crisis. The executive director was turning increasingly to Jack Bigel and others for advice and guidance at a crucial stage in the history of the union and the city.[17]

Humanizing Legal Care

Basic to the MELS program was a different relationship between lawyer and client. "MELS viewed its clients as 'legally competent' persons who would accept casehandling responsibilities, who had every right to understand the legal issues and to participate actively in selecting options, and who were capable of evaluating whether the office had served them well." Behind this view was a more humanistic and concerned philosophy, oriented toward helping clients solve their personal legal problems. The office staff was trained for a hands-on approach, to help in filling out "threatening" forms, and to treat individuals cordially and respectfully. In the selection of the MELS legal and administrative staff, warmth, patience and understanding were among the qualities sought. "No one sits and waits," explained Topol. An intake process was carefully designed with legal assistants screening phone calls to determine the appropriate lawyer and to schedule interviews.

The pilot program produced important information to insure improved utilization of legal assistants, often called paralegal aides. For example, using them as generalists with wide discretionary power proved costly and inefficient. No matter how intelligent, devoted, and closely supervised, legal assistants fared much better as specialized experts than as generalized sub-lawyers. They helped prepare the uncontested matrimonial calendar, bankruptcy, and other routinized documents, and negotiated settlements in select consumer disputes not involving opposing attorneys. Perhaps their most innovative use was as lay advocates. Since administrative agencies permit nonlawyers to appear before them as client representatives, their presence proved invaluable. As a result, MELS created an Administrative Agencies Unit, run by the legal assistants, under an attorney's supervision, which handled public assistance, food stamps, Medicaid, disability and retirement benefits, SSI, Medicare, and veterans' benefits. Also assigned to them were disputes with public utility companies, credit rating charges, school suspension, and eligibility for rent subsidies (Table 15.1).[18]

Another important aspect of the program was to identify clients with personal problems and link them with social workers on the staff. It was not long before social workers were viewed as "invaluable" to both lawyers and clients. The social workers quickly educated and sensitized the legal staff as to their skills and usefulness in identifying personal and family problems. Training sessions were held to assist lawyers in introducing the social service component to clients. Social workers also offered direct assistance to

TABLE 15.1: Social work utilization by legal case category

Legal case Category	Legal cases	Social work cases	Social work cases as percentage of legal cases
Divorce, complex	52	18	34.6
Debt and bankruptcy	322	78	24.2
Housing eviction matters	170	33	19.4
Administrative agencies	118	16	13.6
Divorce, simple	455	42	9.2
Purchase of goods and services, public utilities, and credit rating	263	16	6.1
Separation agreement	36	2	5.6

Source: "Final Report for Ford Foundation," p. 61.

clients in dealing with emotionally distressing aspects of their case. When lawyers recommended bankruptcy in severe financial situations, for example, the social service staff usually intervened to assist the client in preparing a family budget. They also facilitated a better understanding of the legal aspects involved, and thus improved the client's participation in decision making and in the possibilities of avoiding a recurrence of the problem. Social service usually improves the quality of legal benefits, as in divorce actions, where the amount of alimony or child support is at issue, and can help prepare a more realistic budget reflecting the client's income, resources, and expenses. Innovative uses of social work approaches have been utilized at MELS, as with the application of advocacy strategy before government administrative agencies, and in contacting clients who had not kept appointments, which is usually an indication of some social problem. Six months into the permanent program, the social service referral rate was about 10 percent of the clients, a figure that has remained constant.[19]

Funding, Coverage, New Benefits

At the 1979 bargaining sessions, a new arrangement was formalized for providing benefits to Council members. The three funds—education, health and security, and legal—were consolidated into a single "benefits fund" toward which the city agreed to contribute $400 per capita (raised to $450 in 1980). MELS coverage now reaches all members and their families, as well as retirees. Within five years, MELS coverage grew over 50 percent, and its trustees voted to expand services to transactions involving the purchase and sale of a home; representation in family matters involving disputes over support, custody and visitation; arrangements to serve as guardian of a child; adoption of a child; and the changing of one's name.

Between 1977 and 1981, approximately 40,000 cases were handled by MELS. The largest number involved wills, a little over 30 percent, with matrimonial and debt cases adding up to about the same figure. Eviction cases doubled in four years, indicative of difficult economic situations confronting workers in this period, while consumer matters averaged ten percent.

To accommodate the doubling of locals in MELS in three years (1978–1981), the staff grew as well. In 1981 there were 61 lawyers, 22 legal assistants, and 56 administrative support staff. The program's consultants believed from the start that the plan would attract a number of lawyers because of its innovativeness, the job security it offered, and the interest and social concerns of those who preferred to represent workers. Its director of systems and planning, Helen Johnson, found this to be true, since a large pool of attorneys continue to be attracted to MELS. Another factor that made MELS attractive was the "softness of the job market for younger lawyers," for over 1,500 filed applications in the initial recruitment drive. Retention has been remarkably stable, since few left during the first five years of operation. Johnson suggests that a key element in the low turnover rate is that "they are all committed people; there is no question that 95 percent come because they are interested in servicing workers. These are idealistic young people similar to those found in legal services for the poor."

MELS adheres to an active and aggressive affirmative action program, "seeking women and minorities for staff positions from top to bottom and across the board." While successful in attracting minority social workers, legal assistants, and clericals, the plan has not been able to recruit as many minority lawyers as it would like. Due largely to its modest salary scale, as compared to the private sector, black lawyers can do better elsewhere. With a 50 percent black clientele, the directors of the plan are not content with a 15 to 20 percent minority representation in its legal staff, which includes blacks, several Hispanics, and Asian-Americans. While there were no "senior" minority lawyers as of 1981, this will probably change in the near future, for a number of the staff will soon attain the required five years' experience. Women have been attracted to the plan because of liberal maternity policies, which permit three-year leaves and opportunities for work sharing.[20]

As with other DC 37 services, MELS organized a variety of programs to educate members on legal affairs. Materials prepared in lay language explaining legal programs clearly were distributed at local meetings, workshop sessions, and union conferences. Relevant articles in PEP periodically highlight an activity with graphic illustrations. Special well-attended conferences have been designed on consumer credit, marriage and divorce, and family violence. A conference on credit, borrowing, and family budgeting, held on a beautiful Saturday, attracted some 100 members. At a crowded marriage and divorce conference, topics included preparation for marriage, the emotional, sexual, and legal aspects of separation, violence in families, financial difficulties, child custody, and single parenting.

Accountability

The growth of MELS has been monitored attentively by the union, the Ford Foundation, and Columbia University's Law and Social Work staff. The plan has also built accountability systems into its operations, with time sheets, case-closing review, and a "tickler" system. The last was developed to bring open cases to the attention of staff lawyers at regular intervals. Assisted by the computer, time-sheet data are aggregated, showing the amount of time staff spend on each case and the days a case has been open. Similar cases could easily be scrutinized and compared for guidance, enabling staff to identify unusual delays or utilization of colleagues. This became the precursor of the monthly Team Case Activity Report, an important mechanism for reviewing cases in the permanent program.

Evaluation at MELS takes various forms. Supervisors are in daily contact with individual attorneys, reviewing open cases, convening staff meetings, and examining cases with the help of the computerized system. Written evaluations are submitted periodically to the administrator, after consultation with the attorney and supervisor. In addition, clients are given an opportunity to evaluate the service through a questionnaire. In 1981, based on a 40-percent return, clients indicated a very high level of satisfaction with the accomplishments of and treatment by lawyers and other personnel.

Another attribute of MELS was the opportunity it afforded for experimentation, particularly in the use of legal assistants and social workers. During the pilot period there was evident duplication of work by attorneys and paralegals. Shifting gears and moving into new directions, MELS officials allocated increased responsibilities and independence for the legal assistants in handling cases involving administrative agencies. With lawyers available for supervision, better planning and more targeted training helped prepare them for more extensive involvement. Experimentation also led to increased specialization among lawyers, which improved efficiency in the delivery of services. Assisted by manuals and standardized will forms, the legal staff was able to sharpen its skills in select areas. Thus, the original emphasis on a team approach was modified, shifting staff to specialize in distinct areas.

These developments at MELS have also been used for teaching purposes at Columbia University. The collaborative efforts of law and social work faculty continued at the university, where an interdisciplinary course was instituted. Many students were stimulated to apply their professional skills to a working-class population, as DC 37 became their laboratory. Finally, and perhaps most exciting, it was MELS which served as the model for the legal program adopted by the UAW. Until recently, it was the UAW which had been the pacesetter for unions and unionists throughout the nation. That role was being assumed increasingly by District Council 37 in New York.[21]

SUMMARY

The unique aspect of DC 37 benefits has been the willingness of Council leadership to assume responsibility for the direct delivery of services in health, dentistry, optical care, and legal assistance. While unions have fought for health and security benefits over the years, DC 37 has been a trailblazer in finding innovative ways to insure that members receive quality care and dignified treatment. The union is willing to answer to its members in an area that involves complex administrative and fiscal arrangements. With a highly motivated and skilled staff, and a leadership willing to assume responsibility for the overall outcome, the Council has made a seminal contribution to the servicing of union workers. At a time when these services are escalating in cost, and when the Federal government is actively reducing its support of such programs, public service workers at DC 37 can be comforted by the care and concern their union has shown in organizing and delivering human services as part of its determination to improve their quality of life.

NOTES

1. As quoted in Mancur Olson, Jr., *The Logic of Collective Action*, New York: Schocken Books, 1968, p. 72.

2. AFL–CIO Department of Community Services, *Community*, September–November, 1978, p. 16.

3. Hyman Weiner, Sheila Akabas, and John Sommer, *Mental Health Care in the World of Work*, New York: Association Press, 1973, p. 44.

4. Mancur Olson, Jr., *The Logic of Collective Action*, p. 74; The DC 37 Health and Security Plan, December 1-3, 1980. Also, interviews with Julius Topol, March 17, 1981; and Roslyn Yasser, January 11, 1984.

5. Sheila Akabas et al., "Putting Secondary Prevention to the Test: A Study of an Early Intervention Strategy with Disabled Workers," *Journal of Primary Prevention*, 2 (Spring 1982):186. Also, interviews with Yasser, January 11, 1984; Lawrence Morgan, February 10, 1984; and Bill Michaelson, March 27, 1984. An important figure who was also helpful in advising on financial considerations, and actively sought constructive ways to insure fiscal reliability, was Council treasurer Arthur Tibaldi.

6. They were aided in this venture by staff members Hyacinth Lloyd, Hermina Gonzalez, Jeanette Alkoff, Lawrence Morgan, and James Smith.

7. Herbert Gans, *The Urban Villagers*, New York: The Free Press of Glencoe, 1962, pp. 136-141, chapters 11 and 12; Jewel Bellush and Murray Hausknecht, eds., *Urban Renewal. People, Politics and Planning*, Garden City: Doubleday, 1967; Jewel Bellush and Stephen David, eds., *Race and Politics in New York City*, New York: Praeger, 1971; Bertram Brown, director, National Institute of Mental Health, "Foreword," in Weiner, Akabas, and Sommer, *Mental Health Care*, pp. 11–12; Jewel Bellush, "Indispensable Facilities: In Defense of Municipal Hospitals," *New York Affairs* 5, no. 4 (1979); Paul Kurzman and Sheila Akabas, "Industrial Social Worker as an Arena for Practice," *Social Work*, January, 1981, p. 53. Also, interview with Yasser, January 11, 1984.

8. Robert Merton, "The Latent Functions of the Machine," in Edward Ban-

field, ed., *Urban Government,* Glencoe, IL: The Free Press, 1961, p. 183; Roslyn Yasser and John Sommer, "One Union's Social Service Program," *The Social Welfare Forum,* 1974, pp. 112–120; DC 37, *Personal Services Unit,* May 1978.

9. *Wall Street Journal,* July 15, 1971, p. 23; interview with Bill Michaelson, March 27, 1984.

10. The DC 37 Health and Security Plan, Background: Leadership Conference on Benenfits Fund, December 1–3, 1980; Roslyn Yasser, speech at Public Employee Conference, Williamsburg, VA, November 11–14, 1981, H/S plan files.

11. *DC 37 Health Benenfits for You and Your Family,* pamphlet, January 1, 1979. The dental plan allows for an expenditure of $1,000 for each individual annually. For a detailed fee schedule, see pp. 6–19. Interview with William Michaelson, March 27, 1984. Data from Ernie Walker, H/S plan staff, March 3, 1984.

12. Interview with Lawrence Morgan, February 10, 1984. He claims that because of Med-Plan, hospital utilization has been cut by three times.

13. Interviews with Ernie Walker, January 24, 1984; and Dr. Jessie Rosenthal, February 10, 1984. By 1984, some 25 percent of DC 37 members used the Vision Center.

14. The DC 37 Health and Security Plan, Leadership Conference on Benefits Fund, December 1–3, 1980, Table 1. Pamphlet.

15. Sheila Akabas, "Initial Findings: Study of Need for Legal Services Among Clerical Worker Members of District Council 37," Industrial Social Welfare Center, Columbia University School of Social Work, no date, MELS files; proposal to the Ford Foundation on Municipal Legal Services Plan, A Study of Legal Services Program for a Working Class Population," submitted by District Council 37, AFSCME, Columbia University School of Law and Columbia University School of Social Work, 1974, p. 1. Also, interviews with Julius Topol, March 17, 1981; and Gerald Mann, administrator of MELS, January 11, 1984.

16. MELS Fund, Inc., "Projections for Pilot Period," January 7, 1976; "Final Report to the Ford Foundation on Municipal Employees Legal Services Plan," submitted by DC 37, Columbia University School of Law and Columbia University School of Social Work, September 1978, pp. 26–28. Hereafter cited as MELS "Final Report." Also, Helen Johnson, "Mels After Ten Months," *New Directions,* 3, nos. 5 and 6, September–October and November–December 1978, not paged.

17. MELS, "Final Report," p. iii; interviews with Julius Topol, March 17, 1981; and Helen Johnson, October 15, 1982. The city agreed to contribute to MELS in 1978.

18. MELS, "Final Report," pp. 47, 74. For case histories, see pp. 49ff.

19. MELS Fund, Inc., "Interim Report to the Ford Foundation," December 19, 1975, pp. 13–14; "Final Report," p. 61. The "Final Report" includes the specific breakdown of cases, as shown in Table 15.1.

20. MELS, Department Files, "Trends in Kinds of Legal Matters Brought to MELS, 1977–1981," February 23, 1982; MELS staff roster, March 2, 1982; interviews with Helen Johnson, October 15, 1982; and Gerald Mann, January 11, 1984.

21. "Final Report," p. 72; summary of questionnaire, January 29, 1981, pp. 3, 9, 34; After a client is served by MELS, a questionnaire is sent to elicit client's evaluation of the staff's assistance. "Course Outline and Reading List for 'Delivery of Legal Care to a Trade Union Population'," Appendix H, "Final Report to Ford Foundation," pp. 136ff.

16
In the Shadow of Crisis

The burden of blame for the city's financial collapse during the 1960s and 1970s depends on one's politics and orientation. One school of thought identifies individuals or groups perpetrating giveaways, fiscal gimmickry, irresponsible financial "leadership," and gouging the public trough. Among the accused are Mayors Wagner and Lindsay, Comptroller Beame, black welfare "chiselers," overpaid and overpensioned city workers, greedy bankers, and real estate barons. Even the "invisible" hand of the free market is singled out as a cause for the problems, spun off by suburbanization, deterioration in the cores of the city, and a general regional slowdown. Another interpretation points to the process of capitalist accumulation, a system of economic development and growth shaped by capital's desire to accumulate greater and greater profits rather than providing for social needs.

What follows is a short review of what went wrong, in order to set the stage for some of the more dramatic events that unfolded between 1974 and 1976, and which are dealt with in the following chapter. It is not a full-scale analysis, for that constitutes another book in itself. Overall, the various causes of the fiscal crisis can be grouped into two categories, long-range and more immediate factors.

THE LONG-RANGE FACTORS LEADING TO THE CRISIS

A City in Change

With the perspective of the 1980s, the steady downturn of the previous decade becomes more apparent. It was no temporary,

Felix Rohatyn, investment consultant and a key figure during the fiscal crisis of New York City in the mid-1970s comments on the responsibilities of public worker unions and the banking community while addressing a biennial educational conference of DC 37.

short-lived decline or slowdown in the economy. The continual loss of jobs in New York over a 30-year period, experienced in other older industrial cities of the northeastern, mid-Atlantic and mid-western states, was particularly evident in manufacturing enter-prises. At the opening of the 1960s, New York was still a manufac-turing center with more industrial employers than any other city in the world. Almost a million of its 8 million population, or one-fourth of the work force, was employed in producing goods like food and baked goods, beer, apparel, and printing. Industry, how-ever, was hardly visible, and as Jason Epstein observed, was "tucked away in old lofts in odd corners" of the city.

> There were no great steel mills or automobile factories to dom-
> inate the city's economy or its landscape. More than a third of
> the city's factories employed fewer than twenty people each,
> New York's industry was nondescript and, like much else that
> supplied the city's vitality, largely invisible.[1]

With the passing years, dramatic changes occurred, many of them profound in their long-range effects. Manufacturing was declining rapidly. Between 1958 and the mid-seventies, the city lost over 400,000 jobs, a decline of 40 percent representing over $3.5 billion in wages. In one year alone, some 115,000 positions disappeared in all categories. An increase of some 47,700 jobs in the five-year period between 1964 and 1969 was more than offset by a decline of 68,000 in the next five years. The city's printing industry, which produced 18 percent of the nation's output, dropped to 12 percent within a five-year period. Between 1960 and 1975, one-third of the printing jobs disappeared.

Like other aging industrial centers in the Northeast and Midwest, New York steadily lost jobs in the industrial sector. At the same time, however, expanding employment opportunities were provided by the steady growth of commercial and administrative functions. The managerial and technical changes that ushered in the service society were characterized by a major shift in the private sector from production to administration and servicing activities associated with finance, information, communication, entertainment, and education. For New York and other central cities it meant a transition from the factory to the office building as the central element of social organization.

Approximately one of every five jobs in the central administrative offices and auxilaries of U.S. firms were soon housed in New York. The larger the business, the more likely are its headquarters to be located there. Among the top 100 corporations, for example, some 40 percent were in New York City, and in many instances these firms were the leaders of their respective industries. The headquarters of manufacturers are heavily represented in the city.

A major activity that attracts corporate headquarters has been the city's financial community. New York has led in employment among financial centers in the total number of jobs in finance, insurance, and real estate. In fact, this total is larger than that of the next five largest municipalities combined. Expansion in employment alone was significantly larger than the next three centers taken together; the largest numbers of workers have been employed in finance, brokerage institutions, and banking. Nine of the fifty largest life insurance firms were in the city. As one urban specialist observed, the factors facilitating these enterprises locating in New York include "the need for knowledge in a hurry, the need to perform functions in close proximity to one another, and the possibilities for external economies."[2]

The city also served as a corporate headquarters with a tremendous concentration of specialized enterprises and services such as advertising agencies, management and consulting services, computer installations, and statistical services. New York's cultural and entertainment activities and expanding hotel and restaurant facilities have made the city attractive for the headquarters for many enterprises. Other attractions include a sophisticated communications network, mass transportation facilities, expansive public utilities, publishing, and design and sales in apparel. Another aspect of significant technical change was the suburbanization of the New York area, along with the rest of the country. This was accompanied by a precipitous decline in the middle-class population, creating a substantial loss of the city's tax base, paralleled by the retention and increase of dependent populations. Households followed employment opportunities to the suburbs and, with the jobs and people, so did the service industries catering to both the needs of manufacturing and residential projects.

The levels of per capita local costs were higher, and growing faster, than those of surrounding suburbs. Because of demographic, economic, and social developments beyond its control, the city's budget gaps increased steadily as its revenue base contracted. Retail sales, personal incomes, and property values—the bases for taxation—were growing more slowly in the central city than in its environs. In the 1973 edition of *Setting of National Priorities,* Schultz et al. spotlighted a key problem when they concluded, "The resulting change in the city's economic and demographic structure increases its need for public expenditures—for welfare, crime control, and social programs—while reducing its ability to pay for them."[1]

Substantial increases in public sector activities constituted a third aspect of change affecting the city. Housing and urban redevelopment subsidies, new services in welfare, the anti-poverty programs, and manpower training were among the expanding activities of the welfare state in the 1960s. In turn, New York increasingly became the home of people in need of these programs and benefits. It had a greater concentration of individuals in need of public help, especially the aged and the poor, compared to the suburbs. Crime rates were higher, streets and air dirtier, while density and congestion required expensive services to control traffic and maintain lighting and street repair. Between 1950 and 1970, the aging population, those 65 and over, increased from 8 to 12.1 percent. Families below the nation's median income level rose from 36 to 49 percent. Likewise, the welfare case load, which mounted steadily for some two decades, quickened its rate of growth between 1965 and 1969. While a quarter of a million people received welfare grants in 1948, by 1965 the figure reached half a million, and then doubled within four years.

Spurred by the plight of blacks and Hispanics, the nation and city responded to desperate conditions in health and education by launching a commendable but restricted war on poverty, which included model cities, aid to education, Medicare, Medicaid, and improved social security benefits. This expanded into financial support for attacking the problems of pollution, transportation, and sewage treatment. As one of Mayor Lindsay's top aides put it, "The country's underlying prosperity made it all possible." Through a series of categorical grant-in-aid programs, local affairs were literally revolutionized as new programs and activities were stimulated and funded. But federal support was not limitless, and once Washington's share was phased out, the local government was left with "an expensive program, a high standard of service, and an organized set of supporters." In addition, the state sector under Governor Rockefeller also expanded its activities. While a number of programs had been around for decades, what was new in this liberal expansion of government was, according to a Lindsay staff member, "its grandiose expectations. The conquest of disease, the conquest of ignorance, the technocratic hegemony that New Dealers dared only dream about seemed finally within reach."[3]

Demographic Changes

While the total city population remained stable during the period 1960 to 1970, its demography revealed dramatic changes: the number of nonwhites jumped from 1.1 to 1.8 million, most of them blacks. Puerto Ricans, meanwhile, increased from 600,000 to 800,000, and at least 400,000 more came from other Spanish-speaking countries. Paralleling these shifts was a precipitous decline in the white population from 6.1 million to 4.8 million, accompanied by an increase in aging whites and a large number of young people in minority populations. Blacks and Hispanics were disproportionately represented among laborers, operatives, and service workers. And where they made gains in the crafts, clerical, professional, and technical occupations, their wages did not reflect parity with those of whites. Additionally, minority populations were showing increased numbers of unemployed, exceeding whites by a large margin.

Despite prosperous incomes, generally, for whites and for a growing minority middle class, the city's welfare rolls mounted rapidly between 1960 and 1970. While this growth was rooted in demographic and economic transformations under way in the city, it was also stimulated "by the more liberal income criteria, changed attitudes, and new political organizations which characterized the latter part of the 1960s." Consequently, large numbers on welfare were receiving allowances not much less than wage rates paid substantial numbers of low-income workers in apparel, hotel, restaurant, and clerical jobs. By April 1972, nearly half of the city's Hispanics were on relief, and almost a third of the blacks, as compared with less than 4 percent of the white population. The poor lived for the most part in slums, further exacerbating their situation and limiting their upward mobility. The growing poverty was reflected by the rate of unemployment—some 240,000 people were registered, but certainly not all were accounted for, among the beneficiaries of unemployment insurance. The rates for black youth unemployment reached 34.9 percent and would worsen with the passing years.

The increase in public employment constituted the fastest-growing sector in the 1960s, for all levels of nonagricultural government employment combined increased from 11.2 to 14 percent. In New York alone, the figures rose from 8.2 to 11 percent. While the number of federal workers in the city remained stable at about 100,000, state and city employment showed the largest increases, especially in education. Before the end of the decade, the numbers of local government workers, excluding those in education, rose from 188,700 to 253,900. It was this increase in city jobs that absorbed some of the slack in the private sector. By 1972 there were over 400,000 city workers, including those in education, or one for each 20 city residents. Accompanying this wave of public worker growth was the tremendous expansion of unionization among new city employees. New York was known widely as being a "union city," its teachers, transit workers, police, firefighters, and sanitation workers having flexed their muscles and demonstrated their strength and influence at various periods of the twentieth century. By 1972 Raymond Horton found six unions participating in the collective bargaining process encompassing 70 percent of all city workers. By that time, interjurisdictional conflicts had all but come to an end, assuring each group unchallenged control of its respective membership.[4]

Eroding Tax Base and High Labor Costs

The city's tax base was seriously constrained and unable to respond to the burgeoning needs of its dependent populations. Revenues were lost, along with jobs and the top tax base, as a result of the exodus of business and of the middle- and upper-middle-income groups. Professor Dick Netzer noted that almost every budget message presented by the city's mayors during the 1960s included references to "various pressures increasing city government spending." All of them complained that the rate of increase in expenditure far exceeded "the rates of increase in the revenue provided by the city's own revenue sources or from state and Federal aid under provisions existing at any given moment." All this pointed to an almost fivefold rise in external assistance, which "came to a screeching halt" in 1969.

High labor costs accounted for part of the rise in city expenditures, but controversy continues to rage as to the extent of its impact on the expense budget. A team of Syracuse University researchers found city expenditures for common municipal functions relatively "normal" during the period 1965 to 1972, as measured by both per capita level and growth rate, as well as labor costs, as compared with other cities. "Both the rates of city government employees per city resident and the average level of wages appear well within the range experienced by most large cities."

Along similar lines, Professor Charles Brecher of Columbia University discovered that once allowance was made for the variations in functions, the city's rate of increase in its expenditure proved typical of large municipalities. He contended that among the ten largest cities, New York ranked seventh in rate of increase per capita in expenditures for functions common to all municipalities, and for cities with responsibilities similar to New York's, there was little variation in the rate of expenditure growth.[5]

Urban economist William Tabb concluded that between 1965 and 1972, 31 percent of the city's increased labor cost was due to an enlarged work force, 46 percent to inflated prices, and 23 percent reflected higher real wages for public workers. Additionally, he believed that expenditures for retirement had to be examined more carefully, contending that about a third was caused by more workers covered, a half to price increases, 4 percent to enlarged contribution rates, and only 12 percent to improvements in real wages. With respect to the salaries paid public employees, a Congressional Budget Office (CBO) study concluded, "New York is generous but not the most generous of large cities." Reflecting that New York's cost of living, as measured by the Bureau of Labor Statistics intermediate family budget, "is higher than all but that of Boston; its wages are not particularly out of line." Admittedly, city employees were provided more fringe benefits than elsewhere, including pensions and health insurance.

As for city and state welfare expenditures, William Tabb found that two-thirds of the costs were Medicaid payments to doctors, pharmacists, hospitals, and nursing homes, "not cash payments to the poor. A proper investigation of where the welfare dollar goes, of who benefits from 'welfare abuse,' of who the 'chiselers' are, would not focus on the poor."[6]

Social Welfare Burdens

The city had very little control over public assistance expenditures. New York state determined need standards, eligibility criteria, grant levels, and other conditions of public aid. As a result, New York carried greater responsibilities than most other cities, for many of them could share growing costs with counties, state governments, or special districts, particularly for welfare and health care services. New York was one of 21 states that required its local governments (counties) to contribute support in the form of cash assistance for aid to families with dependent children (AFDC) and toward Medicaid payments. The local responsibility was highest in New York, ranging from one-fourth to one-half of the non-Federal share. The state required that the city pay 25 percent of the AFDC cost and 50 percent of the cost of the Supplemental Security Income and general assistance programs. Only six other states required any local sharing of the cost of these three programs, and their formulas for sharing the cost were less severe for local governments.

Although in 1961 the welfare expenditure share of the city's expense budget was about 15 percent, by 1975 this had catapulted to approximately 29 percent. For fiscal 1976 the total amount for social assistance was $3.69 billion out of a total expense budget of $12.55 billion. In addition, the Federal reimbursement formula at the time for AFDC programs provided that New York (and 12 other states) received a 50 percent reimbursement while other states received a higher Federal contribution. Furthermore, the Federal formula did not take into account geographic variations in living costs, public aid receipts and payment levels, and economic conditions, nor the special ethnic composition of New York City's population. In comparing the city's standard functions with those of older cities on a per capita basis, the CBO found that the former were not out of line. In fact, they were lower than San Francisco, Baltimore, and Boston.

Adding to pressures on the city to do more were the "punches" it was forced to sustain from Washington. The overall tax structure had not been known for its equitable or fair treatment of lower-class populations, nor were its policies responsive or hospitable to the needs of the burgeoning population of newcomers. The Democratic administrations, according to Patrick Moynihan, had formulated programs that were "underfinanced and oversold." Academics like Seymour Melman decried the inequities in Federal aid when it was based on the contributions of city taxpayers to the nation's coffers. New York was singled out as one of the dramatic examples of a governmental unit giving far more than it received in return, being seriously shortchanged by the Federal government's extensive aid to the Southwest. With the Republican sweep in 1968, Federal aid to cities was cut back. By the end of the decade, Medicaid costs skyrocketed in hospitals and nursing homes, while the city's share of welfare costs went up by more than 20 percent.[7]

New York responded to progressive movements in the past, encouraging the municipality to assume increasing responsibility for consequences of industrialization and urbanism. It created a city university, an extensive municipal hospital system, a transportation network, and was among the first to build low- and middle-income housing. As Douglas Yates put it, the city "has been asked, and has taken it upon itself, to behave as if it is a national welfare state." Further, he explained, "You cannot have Britain-on-the Hudson River and have the combination of aspirations and capacities work. . . . If you get a hundred new Federal programs to be administered in the city, you are going to break an already loosely managed system, and that's what began to happen in the sixties."

The city's tax share for welfare and Medicaid in 1970–71 was $696 million, more than all the revenue gains combined since 1966 from improvements in unrestricted state aid programs and from all the new and increased city taxes. President Nixon, meanwhile, was in the process of dismantling the Federal programs that had produced so much new help since 1964. This was particularly painful for the city in light of its increasing dependence on outside assistance since the Great Society programs. Cutbacks in formula programs shifted the unpleasant impact of service reduction to the city. Retrenchment and cost-conscious Federal agencies pressed New York officials to make the painful decisions. Unrest associated with the cuts often forced the city to take the brunt of the growing discontent. Further restrictions resulted when, in August 1971, President Nixon imposed a version of wage and price controls that lasted for two years.

In addition to the austerity in Washington, the situation was equally depressing at the state capitol, where Governor Rockefeller found his own house under increasing pressure to contain expenses. He had spent extraordinary sums, particularly through the escape hatch of special authorities that allowed heavy borrowing outside the state's budget. Furthermore, various programs had been poorly managed at the state level, one of the most dramatic being the spiral of Medicaid costs. State construction authorities built scores of new nursing homes, providing the most "lavish standards of care" at tremendous costs. State officials neglected to oversee the rates and service of what Charles Morris called "a vulturish private nursing home industry. Medical institutions and medical providers of all kinds distinguished themselves by a degree of rapacity simply not found in other places." In response, the governor made across-the-board cuts in aid to localities, including New York City. Wherever one assigns responsibility, the impact of all this was a burden for the city taxpayer and the budget "balancers" at City Hall. According to Dick Netzer, the city's traditional functions such as firefighting, police, environmental protection, and parks received little support from external sources and, in combination, constituted two-fifths of the city's financial problem.[8]

Gimmickry and Mismanagement

A final factor contributing to the city's fiscal difficulties was its generally poor accounting procedures and loose financial management. Juggling figures had long been "an open secret," as administrations postponed the day of reckoning while amassing an imposing debt. As mayor, Abraham Beame was forced to confront a fiscal crisis that he helped create as comptroller through his roll-over strategy. Ken Auletta suggested, "Everyone has his favorite villains, but the chief culprit of New York's fiscal crisis is mismanagement." And once the city's access to the financial markets was cut off, according to Charles Morris, "The result of the accumulated gimmicks was exposed in a way that anyone could understand: the city's commitments were massively greater than its income; unless the city could keep on borrowing, there was no way it could pay its bills."

The city was not alone in its questionable fiscal practices. Under Governor Rockefeller the state had utilized "moral obligation bonds" which allowed it to borrow beyond the limits of its constitutional restrictions. The total cost for the Albany Mall project, which was well over 1 billion dollars, never appeared in a state budget. Indeed, the state and city were often partners in the borrowing game, since many of the latter's ventures necessitated state approval and inevitably invited the governor's involvement as legislative leader. The state's fiscal condition also affected the "health" of city bonds.

By 1970 all of the major elements of the final breakdown were in place: a national economic decline reducing tax revenues while at the same time compelling larger public expenditures, a growing budget gap, a credit market unable to absorb the increased borrowing demands placed on it, and high interest rates demanded of a municipality already in serious economic straits. The city's eroding fiscal condition was unraveling at the seams, at the same time as the larger budget scene—regionally and nationally—also revealed challenging economic difficulties as planners scrambled for help. A new era was being ushered in—"the new politics of less."[9]

THE IMMEDIATE FACTORS
CONTRIBUTING TO THE CRISIS

Other factors, more short-range in character, gave the fiscal crisis a dramatic appearance that was almost a distraction from the long-range changes under way. A national recession, inflation, and loss of investor confidence in the city's "credit health" constituted some of the immediate elements of the crisis. The CBO identified investors' attitudes as essentially "psychological," in light of the fact that the city's long-run economic outlook, which determined its ability to pay off debts, was not much different from the situation one or two years previous. While noting that this was highly "speculative," the CBO pointed to several recent events as probably contributing to investor anxiety, including the temporary default of the New York State Urban Development Corporation (UDC) and the collapse of Penn Central Railroad, Lockheed Corporation, and the Franklin National Bank. As the CBO study put it:

> Any hint of financial instability may send them scampering away. Investor uncertainty becomes a self-feeding process, for the fewer the number of persons willing to lend the city money, the greater the probability of default and the greater therefore the uncertainty, and indeed, the risk.

Not only did fiscal conditions in the city create investor nervousness, but various activities of Governor Rockefeller, and his sudden departure from the state scene to become vice president, contributed to their uneasiness. Rockefeller had increased the state's debt from $1.97 billion in 1961 to $13.37 billion at the end of his 15-year administration, a sevenfold rise. The invention of "moral obligation" debt had dramatically changed the nation's credit markets and provided handsome profits and tax-exempt income for banks and individuals. And even when warned that the financial condition of UDC was seriously endangered, the banks appeared satisfied and protected, as long as Rockefeller held the reins of power. It was a state investigating commission which reported that "because they (managers) were assured that UDC had an excellent relationship with the governor," they did not feel the moral obligation bonds were in danger. "Given Mr. Rockefeller's preeminent position in the political power structure of the state," the report continued, "this was no small assurance."

A number of market conditions also fed into general uneasiness. Both long-term and short-term borrowing by the municipality rose steadily, from almost $36 million in 1970 to a new high of some $64 million in five years. Mayor Lindsay and his top aides, as well as many other close observers of the city scene, failed to recognize that the economic recession of 1969 was turning out to be exceedingly long. Charles Morris noted that the vigor and optimism of the 1960s continued to express the spirit of the administration, long after the decade was over. The city's prestige as a world capitol and its booming downtown and financial districts gave it a false sense of healthy growth and relatively low unemployment. But Morris was aware that the 1970s were a new era and called for wholly new financial policies. "In previous years, when the city had been overextended, business and watchdog groups had wrung their hands and raised alarms but economic growth and mild retrenchment were always enough to restore the city to basic health." But this was no longer the case.[10]

Erosion of Fiscal Base

The continuing recession contributed to investors' insecurities and augmented the city's difficulties. Illustrative of the recession's impact, delinquencies in the payment of property taxes rose from 4.2 percent in fiscal 1970 to 7.2 percent five years later. Between 1973 and 1975 the nation's economy experienced the ills of both inflation and recession, causing a sharp rise in the cost of city services and welfare expenditures and at the same time contributing to the deterioration of city revenues. New York was more vulnerable than other municipalities because it relied more heavily on sales and income taxes, not the property taxes found in most local governments. With sales and income taxes accounting for 24 percent of its total receipts in 1974, it was far more "susceptible to cyclical variations," according to a study conducted at the American Enterprise Institute in Washington.[11]

Eroding its financial base were pension obligations and extensive capitalization of operating expenses. Further, high unemployment and people on low, fixed incomes caused heavy increases of local public expenditures, cutting into the city's depleted funds. Family eligibility for the various welfare programs increased substantially, along with additional pressures on other city services, such as hospitals. Another severe economic downturn in 1973 cut even deeper into real estate and other tax revenues. The erosion stimulated by steadily rising wholesale and consumer prices contributed to the city's worsening fiscal condition. Sparked by the war in Vietnam, the spiraling inflation meant increasingly limited investments for the social needs of urban America. Among the most serious indications of the pressing requirements of cities in general and New York in particular were the destructive ghetto uprisings at the end of the 1960s. Black rage fell heaviest on the shoulders of local urban officials. Mayor Lindsay's strategies, ridiculed by Ken Auletta as "local socialism," caused further strains on depleted city coffers.

In the short run, inflation can impact severely on expenditure levels. For example, a time-consuming process is required to reassess property, which delays the city's response to the inflationary conditions affecting real estate. The time frame between fixing new property taxes and the dates on which collections are due constitutes another delay and further affects the city's intake. On the one hand, being more heavily dependent on sales and income taxes helps, somewhat, in a period of rising prices. But, on the other hand, inflation continued to undermine the city's budget as costs mounted steadily. Between 1960 and 1971, the price index for goods and services purchased by local governments rose twice as quickly as the rate for consumer purchases.

By the fall of 1974, awareness of the city's deep difficulties began to spread among financial experts. Karen Gerard, a Chase Manhattan Bank economist, prepared a number of studies which showed that the city's budgetary problems were not "political ploys to attract more aid." To maintain the rollover of mounting short-term debt, the city had to borrow $2.5 billion in a two-month period ending in November 1974. And it borrowed another $600 million in December. In total, the city secured in excess of $3 billion in loans in calendar year 1974, a fourfold increase in four years. Charles Morris noted, "The sheer volume of debt began to overshadow all the city's other problems."[11]

By late 1974 the city accounted for over 40 percent of short-term, tax-exempt borrowing in the nation, and with the redemption dates around the corner, danger signals began to flare. Exacerbating this condition was the fact that the market for tax-exempt securities was weakening everywhere. Insurance companies suffered substantial underwriting losses and had little need for tax shelters. The commercial banks were shifting their investments overseas and enjoying large foreign tax credits. In 1970 the commercial banks took up 95 percent of the net increase in municipal debt; five years later they assumed only about 20 percent. The Advisory Commission on Intergovernmental Relations described the essence of the problem:

> Large cities have been operating in an increasingly difficult environment. The sources of stress often include declining population, the impact of collective bargaining by city employees, the impact of inflation on the costs of many labor-intensive services that city residents desire, a lack of growth in the tax bases of many central cities, and the slow growth in many of the cities' traditional sources of revenue. These and similar factors combine to create a fiscal and political tightness in the financial affairs of cities that makes them increasingly susceptible to financial emergencies.[12]

Lindsay's Responses

Morris suggests that in his initial years as mayor, John Lindsay was helped by increased revenues and made "significant progress toward restoring the city's financial integrity." However, from the start of his second term, the fiscal picture grew increasingly dismal, and his difficulties intensified. The yearly struggles over the city budget, and the pleas for state and Federal support tended to dominate the activities of his last term. The economic recession that began in 1969 and inflation impacted on New York City more than most anywhere else in the nation. Spending pressures and union goals sent expenditures upwards while revenues declined precipitously.

The city's heralded facilities were, meanwhile, being seriously impaired. One of the most visible was the parks and playgrounds. Rubble-strewn areas with crumbling structures, rows of benches missing slats for seating, and shattered brick shelters that looked like bombed-out London during World War II, went unrepaired because of a personnel shortage. Despite extensive vandalism ravaging parks and playgrounds, there were fewer laborers, attendants, and custodians, and the budget cuts in parks maintenance and operations were aggravated by inflation. Park facilities had become unusable and unsafe. Former play areas for children were converted to settings for drug pushers, addicts, alcoholics, and muggers. Other equally important areas of concern included a sharp decline in public housing starts, a shortage of nurses and doctors, and a physical deterioration in the public hospitals and roads, bridges, and tunnels of the city.

In 1970 the Bureau of Labor Statistics (BLS) reported that a family of four living in the New York area needed a gross income of $12,134 to maintain a moderate living standard. This figure was 7.9 percent above the previous year and 14 percent more than the amount required in other metropolitan areas in the nation.[13]

Adding to the city's difficulties was increased tension between the mayor and Governor Rockefeller. The need for state aid to enable the city to survive compelled local officials to go begging at the state capitol. Meanwhile, Rockefeller introduced legislation empowering the state comptroller to audit City Hall's programs, created a state welfare inspector-general, and established the Scott Commission to investigate municipal operations. And the city's fiscal situation grew grimmer.

The mayor felt obliged to reject a record $2.4 billion Human Resources Administration expense budget for fiscal 1972, contending that the city could no longer afford to meet increasing welfare costs. He ordered a review of mandated programs and a study of the city's legal power to refuse to pay or accept new clients. He also warned that New York risked bankruptcy and elimination of essential services if it was obliged to continue welfare spending at the current rate.

Unemployment continued to rise, as did consumer prices, while interest rates climbed to record levels. Wages were also rising as working people sought to keep abreast of inflation. The response from Washington was unfounded optimism as the mayor underscored the budget crisis confronting the city, contending that the budget deficit for fiscal 1972 might approach $1 billion. He appealed to Washington for Federal revenue-sharing and assumption of welfare costs, to save New York and the nation's cities from bankruptcy. The mayor sought to dramatize the city's plight by offering four optional budgets, only one of which was reasonable and practical, given the circumstances.

Toward the end of April, some 10,000 city workers, most of them from DC 37, began a day-long vigil for increased state aid, first at a City Hall rally and then in Albany, to which they journeyed in a long caravan of chartered buses. It was in all likelihood the largest single outpouring of demonstrators in Albany in recent history, as buses crowded highways and streets. Chanting "Save our jobs, save our cities," and holding aloft hundreds of placards which urged lawmakers, "Don't take the service out of civil service," they rallied to save their positions. The *New York Times* characterized this outpouring of public employees as "unconvincing civic ambassadors," calling for "increased efficiency" in the performance of their jobs. Municipal unions, the editorial complained, had shown themselves expert at winning "more pay for less work," and did little to halt the deterioration in the quality of services—there continued to be dirty and unsafe streets, disruption in the schools, and equipment breakdowns.

The governor's original response to the mayor and to the public employee unions was negative but he eventually acceded to the pressures and undertook rather cool negotiations with the mayor. One factor that played an important role in his change of attitude was a sudden, marked decrease in his control over the state legislature. An agreement was finally reached whereby the city was authorized to borrow additional funds and adopt new taxes. The price for bipartisan support, however, was a pledge by Lindsay that the layoffs of city workers would be achieved through attrition. Despite this financial assist from Albany, the mayor warned that the city would have the tightest budget since the Great Depression, and still be faced with a $279 million budget gap. Apparently the mayor had played his cards well in securing aid from Albany. The crisis seemed over, but only momentarily.[14]

SUMMARY

The fiscal situation appeared to improve during the last year of Lindsay's administration (1973), perhaps an omen of the lull before the storm. In retrospect, however, his eight years as mayor were filled with dramatic change: welfare rolls soared as public dependency increased; racial divisions intensified with bitter denunciations from all sides and the costs of operating the city spiraled upward, requiring new taxes to meet expenditures. As far as improved wages and pension were concerned, public worker organizations had little to complain about. Others, however, criticized the mayor severely for his "giveaways" to unions. But these factors only partially explain the urban crisis. The recession, Federal austerity, the drying up of capital, and the changing structure of the nation's economy must be included among the major contributing factors.

Although it is difficult to pinpoint the time when the financial problems facing New York went out of control, it is clear that a critical state had been reached early in 1975 when the city's bonds and notes could no longer be sold at any reasonable price. In the next chapter, we review the city's response to the crisis under Mayor Abraham Beame and the role of the municipal unions led by Gotbaum.

NOTES

1. Jason Epstein, "The Last Days of New York," in Roger E. Alcaly and David Mermelstein, eds., *The Fiscal Crisis of American Cities,* New York: Vintage Books, 1977, p. 59.

2. *Ibid.,* pp. 60–62; George Sternlieb and James W. Hughes, "Metropolitan Decline and Inter-Regional Job Shifts," in Alcaly and Mermelstein, *The Fiscal Crisis,* p. 158; Richard Knight, "Growth Pole," in Eli Ginzberg, ed., *New York is Very Much Alive,* New York: McGraw-Hill, 1973, pp. 12–13, 15.

3. Charles L. Schultz, Edward R. Fried, Alice M. Rivlin, Nancy H. Teeters, and Robert D. Reischauer, "Fiscal Problems of Cities," in Alcaly and Mermelstein, *The Fiscal Crisis,* p. 190; James R. Dumpson and Paul Schreiber, "Welfare and Income," in Lyle C. Fitch and Annmarie Hauck Walsh, eds., *Agenda for a City, Issues Confronting New York,* Beverly Hills, CA: Sage Publications, 1970, pp. 87–88. Charles Morris, *The Cost of Good Intentions,* New York: Norton, 1980, pp. 34, 35, 37.

4. Dale Heistand, "Minorities," in Ginzberg, *New York,* pp. 110–111; Miriam Ostow and Charles Brecher, "Work and Welfare," *ibid.,* p. 167; Michael Harrington, *The Other America,* Baltimore: Penguin, 1963, Chapter 4; Raymond D. Horton, *Municipal Labor Relations in New York City, Lessons of the Lindsay-Wagner Years,* New York: Praeger, 1972, pp. 6, 11; Marcia Freedman, "Opportunity and Income," in Ginzberg, *New York,* p. 94; Sternlieb and Hughes, "Metropolitan Decline," p. 159; Wallace Sayre and Herbert Kaufman, *Governing New York City,* New York: Norton, 1965, pp. 75, 423–446.

5. Dick Netzer, "The Budget: Trends and Prospects," in Fitch and Walsh, *Agenda for a City,* p. 653; Attiat Ott and Jang Yoo, *New York City's Financial Crisis,* Washington, D.C.: American Enterprise Institute for Public Policy Research, 1975, pp. 24–25; Raymond Horton, *Municipal Labor Relations,* Chapter 6; Ken Auletta, *The Streets Were Paved With Gold,* New York: Random House, 1979, pp. 47–51; Maxwell Research Project in the Public Finances of New York City, *New York*

City: Economic Base and Fiscal Capacity, New York: State Study Commission for New York City, 1973, p. 37; Charles Brecher, *Where Have All the Dollars Gone? 1961-1971,* New York: Praeger, 1974, p. 3.

6. William K. Tabb, "The New York City Fiscal Crisis," in William K. Tabb and Larry Sawyers, eds., *Marxism and the Metropolis,* New York: Oxford University Press, 1978, p. 244; Congressional Budget Office, *New York City's Fiscal Problem: Its Origins, Potential Repercussions And Some Alternative Policy Responses,* background paper no. 1, October 10, 1975, Washington, D.C.: U.S. Government Printing Office, 1975, pp. 16-19. For a different interpretation of the fiscal crisis, see Ott and Yoo, *New York City's Financial Crisis,* pp. 24-28; and Ken Auletta, *The Streets,* Chapters 3, 4, and 5.

7. Damodar Gujarati, *Pensions and New York City's Fiscal Crisis,* Washington, D.C.: American Enterprise Institute for Public Policy Research, 1978, p. 8; Congressional Budget Office, *New York City's Fiscal Problem,* p. 16; Seymour Melman, "The Federal Rip-off of New York's Money," in Alcaly and Mermelstein, *The Fiscal Crisis,* pp. 181-188; Kirkpatrick Sale, "Six Pillars of the Southern Rim," *ibid.,* pp. 165-180; Julio Vitullo-Martin and Richard Nathan, "Intergovernmental Aid," in Charles Brecher and Raymond Horton, eds., *Setting Municipal Priorities 1981,* Montclair, NJ: Allanheld, Osmun, 1980, pp. 51-55; Jack Newfield and Paul DuBrul, *The Abuse of Power,* New York: Viking, 1977, pp. 71-73.

8. "The New Politics of Less," *New York Affairs* 3, no. 1 (1975):10. Morris, *The Cost of Good Intentions,* pp. 145, 191; Newfield and DuBrul, *The Abuse of Power* pp. 71-72; Melman, "The Federal Rip-Off," pp. 184-187; Dick Netzer, "The Budget," p. 660.

9. Auletta, *The Streets,* p. 166; Morris, *The Cost of Good Intentions,* p. 222; "The New Politics of Less," *New York Affairs* 3, no. 1 (1975):3-55. Lee Solomon, the magazine's publisher, was among the few who initially used this phrase.

10. Congressional Budget Office, *New York City's Fiscal Problem,* p. 7; Newfield and DuBrul, *The Abuse of Power,* pp. 28-36; Morris, *The Cost of Good Intentions,* p. 202. Note on that same page a chart showing the outstanding short-term debt of New York City during the years 1965-74.

11. Ott and Yoo, *New York City's Financial Crisis,* p. 14; Charles Schultze et al., *Setting National Priorities: The 1973 Budget.* Washington, D.C.: The Brookings Institution, 1972, Chapter 9; Morris, *The Cost of Good Intentions,* pp. 222, 223. For more on the uncontrollable impact of recessions on New York City's unemployment, number of welfare recipients, and the sales tax base during the years 1970-75, see Congressional Budget Office, *New York City's Fiscal Problem,* p. 10.

12. Advisory Commission on Intergovernmental Relations, *City Financial Emergencies: The Intergovernmental Dimensions,* Washington, D.C., July 1973, p. 56.

13. Morris, *The Cost of Good Intentions,* p. 126; *New York Times,* January 5, 1970, p. 1; May 1, 1970, p. 28; December 21, 1970, p. 41. This budget, allowing for few luxuries, provided for the use of public transportation or the purchase of a two-year-old used car every four years, a new television set every ten years, and one movie every four weeks. In examining the consumer price index, the BLS concluded that inflation had eroded workers' salaries sharply since 1968.

14. *New York Times,* April 28, 1971, pp. 1 and 46; April 29, 1971, p. 34; May 29, 1971, p. 27; June 9, 1971, p. 1; June 23, 1971, pp. 1, 49.

17
The Fiscal Crisis: Threat and Response

For over a decade, the city's expenditures exceeded revenues, but it was always possible to cover the deficit. The bond market had generally responded favorably, allowing states and cities throughout the country to finance their growing budgets through borrowing. In the fall of 1974, however, the first year of Abe Beame's tenure as mayor, he announced that a serious budget gap confronted the city, with still worse to come. The estimates varied, depending on which official one believed. But most agreed that the city's debt was fast approaching $3.3 billion, with its outstanding notes at $12.3 billion. It was then that New York began experiencing difficulty in selling a variety of short-term notes.

The initial reaction of many union leaders was total disbelief. For years the city government had played the game of crying crisis as a strategy for pressuring the state to increase its share of financial support. This time, however, some municipal unions were advised by their financial consultant, Jack Bigel, that Beame was not exaggerating and that the city was in dire straits. According to Barry Feinstein of Teamsters Local 237, the full dimensions of the difficulties would not be clearly known for several months.

The fiscal crisis presented a dramatic challenge and signaled a major turning point for municipal labor. In retrospect the events surrounding the city's fiscal emergency indicate that New York, and the nation as well, had entered a new era—"the politics of less." The U.S. labor movement was increasingly forced to confront a new, threatening situation. Intensifying problems had erupted in the textile and garment industries, steel, automobiles,

A member of DC 37 reveals anger and frustration at a delegates council meeting upon learning that Mayor Abraham Beame has just ordered thousands of layoffs and cutbacks of public workers as a result of the worsening fiscal crisis.

machine tools, and other industrial enterprises. These dramatic events profoundly altered labor's outlook and strategies, compelling a reexamination of their hard-won gains at the bargaining table. During the same period, Gotbaum and his union collaborators came under pressure to renegotiate past victories.

The fiscal emergency illustrates the importance of a subsystem comprising a relatively small number of actors who play key roles in shaping public policy, in which private power and public authority are joined. During the city's fiscal crisis of the 1930s, this subsystem was dominated by bankers, who held the key position in determining the decisions and shaping the role of government. By the 1970s, however, a vibrant and influential municipal labor movement helped make the subsystem less elitist and more visible by enlarging the circle of the decision-making process to include three sets of participants vital to the eventual outcome—the municipal unions; the private sector, represented by bankers and investors; and the state government, particularly Governor Hugh Carey. The investment and banking interests were now compelled to share their political power with unions and with government representatives. Forced into a coalition bargaining strategy, union leadership was confronted with the difficult task of maintaining control over rapidly developing events.

This chapter details many of the decisions and responses of DC 37 and its allies to the fiscal crisis, the motivations behind them, and the impact they had on the city, the union, and relationships between the three sets of participants comprising the subsystem. The only institution capable of challenging the power of investors and bankers and of shaping the course of events because of its size and potential influence, was the coalition of municipal unions. And Victor Gotbaum was accorded the command post of this alliance.

Under DC 37 leadership, a cohesive and influential partnership was forged from competing organizations. The five major strategies pursued by this labor coalition will be analyzed: the avoidance of default and bankruptcy, attrition preferred over layoffs, public appeals through the media, utilization of union pension funds, and coalition bargaining. Each of these major policies posed problems and difficult choices for the unions. The price they paid would be substantial—cuts in salaries and fringe benefits, layoffs, and a shattered morale. But as participants in the decision-making subsystem, they were able to exert significant influence over the strategies and soften the impact on their members.

BEAME AS MAYOR: THE CRISIS BEGINS

In the 1973 election campaign, Abraham Beame finally attained his long-held dream of becoming master at City Hall. With that achievement, however, he was immediately confronted with a weakened economic base, a heavy short-term debt, rising municipal costs and a series of critical spinoffs from one of the worst recessions since World War II. There was nothing new about these problems for Beame, for he had tried to deal with them previously at the Budget Bureau and as comptroller. But his strategies, or more accurately "gimmicks," had only helped conceal the city's budget gaps.

Soon after taking office, Beame's fiscal advisers discovered that the year's deficit reached somewhere between $200 and $300 million, with the next year's estimate projected at $1.5 billion. While suggesting that the city resort to attrition, Beame increased the police force at the same time, as he had promised during his campaign. Inflation continued to spiral upward, especially since the dramatic Arab oil price increase put additional pressure on the city's expenses and cut into the incomes of its residents. Private-sector job losses and increased unemployment meant further declines in tax receipts in constant dollar terms. But Beame carried on, not believing that the situation was any worse than in previous years. As he borrowed again, he continued to underestimate expenses, overestimate revenues, and invent the usual stopgaps to postpone the day of judgment. Meanwhile, Comptroller Harrison Goldin and his aides noted wider gaps and spotted additional distress signals. One indication that the mayor realized that the financial picture was deteriorating was the announcement in the fall of 1974 that he would have to cut back the number of civil servants, the first such move since the Great Depression. Gotbaum's immediate response was to denounce the proposed dismissals, insisting that not one permanent worker would get a "pink slip."

In Washington, meanwhile, President Gerald Ford cautioned that the national economy was in terrible shape. Unemployment stood officially at 7.1 percent, with 6.5 million out of work. Some economists contended that a more realistic figure was 9 million unemployed, but that did not include the wave of layoffs that occurred around Christmas time, those partially unemployed, and those who had been discouraged from looking further for the lack of jobs.

At meetings with Beame, Deputy Mayor James Cavanaugh, and others, Gotbaum insisted that permanent civil servants be protected, and sought ways to insure that laid-off provisionals be hired under funds provided by a new Federal program that President Ford had approved. Activity reached a frenetic pace as anxious labor leaders and municipal officials met frequently at City Hall, telephoning each other constantly between meetings. Agreement was soon reached on three key items. First, since no union leader could manage alone the complexities of the deepening crisis, they would have to work out answers together. The alliance eventually brought together all public unions, including the uniformed services, but excluding the United Federation of Teachers (UFT) and several small organizations. Second, Gotbaum, as chair of the MLC, would also act as their spokesperson. During the 1960s, many of these same union leaders had gone their independent ways. To give Gotbaum this assignment was no easy concession on their part. This was corroborated by labor lawyer Murray Gordon, who represented the Committee of Interns and Residents (CIR), as well as the Fire Officers. The latter group was conservative, and not particularly sympathetic about an alliance with hospital aides and clerical and blue-collar workers, whose status they viewed as beneath their own. The CIR, on the other hand, was comprised of a group of young, radical doctors who, as products of the 1960s, were generally suspicious of trade unions. They refused for a long time to join the Gotbaum-led coalition, despite the latter's reputation as a socially sensitive labor leader.[1]

The traditional rivalries among unions were well known. DC 37, for example, had won a representation election for thousands of school aides over the UFT in the mid-sixties. But in 1969 the UFT made some inroads into DC 37 territory when the battle for the paraprofessionals in the Board of Education resulted in a split in control: family assistants and family workers went to the Council, and education assistants and associates, teacher aides, and auxiliary trainers went to the UFT. Among the uniformed service unions, parity relationships served as a constant source of conflict, as each union sought more for its members in a seemingly endless escalation. Most of the unions simply did not trust each other. Among the examples of disruptive assertiveness was the UFT push for the Stavisky–Goodman bill, which proposed that 21 percent of the city's budget be set aside exclusively for the Board of Education. It was a strategy to rehire thousands of teachers at the cost of other municipal jobs. Finally, there were longstanding ideological and tactical differences among the unions.

A key objective of Gotbaum was to keep the collective bargaining process alive. The issuance of a reckless "Fear City" pamphlet by the police and fire unions was viewed as destructive and unsettling by other labor leaders. Not until the 1978 round of collective bargaining did the UFT under Shanker join the MLC, although they did participate reluctantly in one of the most crucial decisions emanating from the crisis, the use of union pension funds. It was inevitable that Gotbaum be accorded a central role, for he headed the largest municipal union, his organizational base was stable and disciplined, his skill as negotiator was well known, and he had become a popular media personality. The police and firefighters, on the other hand, were troubled by internal divisions, and John DeLury, head of the Sanitation Workers, was in failing health.

A third important aspect of their convergence was the presence of Jack Bigel, veteran trade unionist and expert in the city's financial affairs. Having served as consultant to the Sanitation Workers and DC 37, his reputation as a fiscal wizard grew, for he was often better informed than the city's fiscal officers. His command of the budget, the specifics of wages, pensions, and the costing-out of fringe benefits soon attracted the attention of other union leaders, and they came to rely on his projections. The Council's heavy dependence on Bigel was also due to the fact that in 1975 the Department of Negotiations and Research was staffed by only two people. Not until the following year was department head Alan Viani able to expand his professional support by appointing an economist, Dr. Carol O'Cleireacain, and a budget analyst. Viani saw himself as a negotiator, in close touch with rank-and-file feelings, rather than as a financial expert and counselor to Gotbaum during the fiscal crisis. Bigel's easygoing personality, warm relationships with union leaders, and willingness to share sources of information helped provide them with a common understanding of what the spreading fiscal crisis portended. His contacts within the city administration afforded him immediate access to vital data as well as a knowledgeable appraisal of the situation. Although Gotbaum and Beame were not friendly at this juncture, it was Bigel who helped smooth over this problem, always enjoying the role of broker. Albert Shanker underscored Bigel's negotiating activities as his major contribution, as he connected the key actors to each other and fashioned compromises. Viani saw Bigel's role as that of a broker rather than as fiscal expert.[2]

Another area of consensus among labor leaders was that the

city had to avoid default and bankruptcy. Given the gravity of the situation and the incredible pressures on them, these leaders were comforted by the knowledge that Bigel had the facts, and could be trusted implicitly during the many months of tense decision making that lay ahead. Bigel, in turn, thoroughly enjoyed his role as adviser. As Barry Feinstein recalled these developments, "We all decided New York simply could not go bankrupt, that it would be worse than the sacrifices we had to make." The fact of the matter, he suggested, was that "we were just scared to death of all the questions default and bankruptcy evoked. No one had the slightest idea what this would actually mean for our pensions, the possibility of large unchallenged layoffs, and the impact on our retirees."

Gotbaum concluded that putting the city under a Federal bankruptcy judge would mean an entirely new ball game, excluding union as well as city officials from traditional negotiations. Once the city defaulted on its indebtedness, subsequent financial, employment, and work decisions would be the result of rulings by a Federal bankruptcy referee, alien to, and divorced from, union leaders and the normal process of politics. The referee alone could decrease the number of workers; cut the city's contributions to the pension, health, and welfare funds and endanger pension benefits of retirees; increase the hours of labor at certain periods of the year; and take back many hard-won gains secured by municipal unions over the previous 30 years.

No one really knew how long it would take or how intricate the processes would be. Gotbaum's legal counsel warned that any fiscal plan adjustment "*must* have approval by a majority of each class of creditor," thus placing large creditors in a position to block any plan "that subordinates their interests to other claims upon the city's funds." Likewise, pension fund beneficiaries might well be vulnerable to great losses from a default under the new pension law. In the meantime, workers had to be paid and city services maintained. Gotbaum warned, "I won't roll the dice with some Federal appointee over the lives of our members—there are human beings who would suffer, not statistics." It was Felix Rohatyn, one of the key figures to emerge from the investment community during the crisis, who insisted that it was Gotbaum's role and leadership that saved 100,000 municipal jobs. Gotbaum argued and pleaded with the other labor leaders until they finally agreed that attrition, in many forms, rather than layoffs would be the acceptable way of shrinking the work force, for its consequences would be less severe for the unions.

Unable to secure the funds necessary to fill the budget gap, and with credit dried up, Mayor Beamer announced plans in mid-January to dismiss 2,000 permanent civil servants and an equal number of provisionals. Gotbaum responded heatedly that no worker would be sacrificed to "feed the buzzards of Wall Street." He pointed out that the layoffs were meaningless in economic terms, because there was simultaneous public service hiring, and the $8.3 million projected saving was minuscule when compared with the huge deficit facing the city.[3]

THE UNIONS RESPOND

The situation, however, continued to worsen, finally forcing those associated with the MLC to come forward with their own plan, which was largely the work of Bigel:

1. Cut the remaining 1,964 "pure" provisionals still on the city payroll, instead of permanent civil service workers. Estimated savings: $7.5 million.

2. Cut up to 20 percent of the $295 million the city spends every year in contracting-out. Estimated savings: $60 million.

3. Through use of city retirement systems funds provide incentive to employees age 63 and over to retire early. Estimated savings: $157 million over several years.

4. The municipal retirement systems would purchase up to $400 million in city bonds, at lower interest rates than the 9.4 percent rate now paid to banks by the city. Savings undetermined.

5. All MLC unions would participate in a meaningful productivity program with the city to produce "substantial" savings.

6. Union leaders would meet with Governor Hugh Carey and congressional leaders to press for additional state and federal aid to the city.

Items 4 and 6 indicated that the public unions were on new, dangerous grounds. The decision to offer funds from workers' pensions was not easily or readily reached, for it required great soul-searching and convincing on the part of the individuals involved. They knew that confidence in the city's ability to pull through the crisis had dropped perceptibly. And with bankers and municipal bond holders no longer willing to invest in New York's future, why should public worker unions endanger the hard-won gains of their members? Besides, was it legal?

It was an extremely difficult and wrenching period for Gotbaum. Pulled in different directions by conflicting professional advice as to the legitimacy of such a move, and constantly confronted with the turbulent background of an endangered city, the AFSCME leader spent at least one troubled weekend in a deep depression. He was finally convinced by Bigel that the city's fiscal status was so precarious that unless the municipal unions stepped in with a major transfusion of funds, default and bankruptcy were inevitable. Reaching a definitive decision, Gotbaum, with the aid of Bigel and Feinstein, struggled to convince the other labor leaders to go along with investing a considerable portion of their unions' pension funds in city bonds. Eventually, even a reluctant Shanker was pulled along, but at the very last moment.

Agreeing to item 6 meant that public employee organizations would join city representatives in a major lobbying effort to convince state and federal officials that more money was needed. This strategy meant that unionists were enlarging the circle of participants in the city's fiscal decisions and, eventually, in the collective bargaining process itself. Bailing out the city in such a critical situation would inevitably mean new regulations, new restraints, and new forms of supervision. Agreeing to put up pension funds as capital and inviting state and federal participation underscored the seriousness with which union leaders viewed the financial condition of the city. Acceptance of a modified plan, however, was delayed until later in the year, after pressure mounted for deeper cutbacks and more severe actions.

As the crisis worsened, an increasingly hostile climate began to envelop negotiations between the city and municipal unions. Civil servants were indiscriminately charged with selfishness, with pursing their own narrow, parochial interests, and with being unconcerned with the viability of the city. New York's plight was viewed by many "good government" voices and editorial writers as a consequence of high wages, fat pensions, and "unconscionable" fringe benefits. Union contracts, they maintained, had become "outrageously excessive and inflationary." Over and over again, public workers were depicted as "rip-off artists." The constant din against city employees constituted an almost daily barrage of attacks. Typical were the columns of A. H. Raskin of the *New York Times,* who often criticized civil servants for their inefficiency and poor productivity. For years, scholars like Wallace Sayre, Herbert Kaufman, and Raymond Horton warned of the dangers of the growing power of municipal unions, viewing them as a "force for evil." These attitudes were increasingly expressed through the media by the City Club, the Citizens Budget Commission, and an array of academics and journalists.[4]

A number of state and Federal officials repeated the charge that the city had lived beyond its means, allowing its unions to win exorbitant contracts. Bankers and investors also joined the chorus of critics. This growing antagonism toward public workers was particularly upsetting to Gotbaum, who was always sensitive to public opinion, and who was determined to take the plight of workers to the public. He sought to put their problems in the direct, simple, yet dramatic terms of economics. Typically, he struck out at the private interests, charging them with enjoying comfortable profits while workers suffered from inflation and recession. "Working people," he insisted, "were fed up with the recession and the inflation," as well as "the downright indecency of carrying the economic burden on their backs—while the oil interests and the sugar interests rack up profits at a record pace, the tax-dodging wealthy get off scot-free." Runaway inflation cut into paychecks as so-called pay raises daily lost significance. He persistently illustrated workers' difficulties in making ends meet, detailed deteriorating living conditions in the central city, where most of his members lived, and spotlighted their shrinking buying power. He offered the findings of members who, as price watchers, checked their neighborhood supermarkets comparing current prices with those three years previous. Based on a list of 20 commonly purchased items, they found that latest prices averaged 48 percent higher. Time and again Gotbaum repeated:

> We're sick and tired of the budget being put on the backs of workers who have already taken a cut in real wages. We're being asked to sacrifice when there's no sacrifice on the part of the banks, large corporations and utilities.

As the city's condition continued to worsen, an indecisive, ambiguous mayor characteristically waffled between threatening new layoffs and offering reassurances that the city was not doing too badly. Throughout the first half of 1975, the threats of city bankruptcy, immense layoffs and immediate wage freezes were heard constantly, moving fearful municipal unions to counter, at times, with strike warnings. Beame, meanwhile, continued to delay making any decisive decisions or taking unpopular actions, carrying on with his usual maneuvers. He admitted that he needed at least $1.29 billion in state and federal assistance to save the city. He sought federal guarantees for the city's securities, some Federal Reserve loans, outright interest-free loans, and urged the Treasury Department to purchase city notes. To add to his woes, the bankers cut off the city's cash flow in April. A number of individuals and groups urged default or bankruptcy, among these friends of the union movement like Herman Badillo. The federal government, under Ford's leadership, not only refused to help, but exacerbated tensions by reprimanding the city again and again, as did the heads of key congressional committees. This unfriendly climate and growing hostility toward public service workers further upset the municipal unions.

By this time, the mayor's prestige began to crumble as he was increasingly forced to defer to others for help in pleading the city's cause. Governor Carey became actively involved, joining with a number of prestigious city bankers to plead New York's case before Treasury Secretary William Simon and President Ford. Not only did Federal officials refuse support but they worsened the situation by lecturing the mayor on the city's profligacy and the need to mend its ways with more severe action. In Albany, Republican legislators showed little interest in the city's plight, urging that it tighten its belt. By May, city officials acknowledged that only 1,941 of the proposed 12,700 layoffs had actually occurred. Finally, in June, with substantial debts due and the city coffers empty, the mayor concluded that he could no longer postpone the inevitable. It was then that some 9,000 layoff slips were distributed to city workers, including at least 5,000 members of DC 37. Within a month, the numbers of dismissals passed the 13,000 mark.[5]

UNION CUTBACKS

It was in this context—the refusal of banks to buy city bonds, the rebuff of Federal and state governments to appeals for help, the increasingly negative climate of public opinion, along with the fear of imminent default—that Gotbaum and his colleagues reached their first difficult decision, to give back previous gains. DC 37 agreed to an immediate reduction of city payments into welfare and pension funds for new employees, the elimination of some reduced summer hours, and unlimited transfer of civil servants among departments.

The little by-play between Gotbaum and Beame over summer hours indicated the role the labor leader was determined to play, on behalf of his union's members, in the decision-making process revolving around the crisis. Before air conditioning was installed in city offices, workers were allowed to leave work an hour early during the summer months. In July 1975 the mayor decided that the city could no longer afford the program and unilaterally eliminated it. AFSCME immediately brought the issue to arbitration, claiming a willful violation of the contract. The Council won its case, but within a week, at the Americana Hotel meetings, where municipal unions agreed to give up one work rule each as a helpful concession to the beleagured city, the DC 37 executive director surrendered the shortened workday. He explained:

> We successfully defended summer hours against the mayor's attempt to unilaterally rule them out—and then we gave it up in negotiations (for those who work in air-conditioned offices). I don't think that's so strange—defending our contract is absolutely imperative; *voluntarily* surrendering an item may be tactically necessary when the overall situation requires it.

Sanitation workers gave up some overtime, and other unions followed, enabling the mayor to call this a "milestone in labor negotiations." In addition, the union alliance agreed to join city officials in their jaunts to Albany and Washington to plead for assistance. Putting their lobbying operations into full gear, top union leaders testified before legislative committees, their staffs prepared extensive, detailed reports, and they argued with administrative officials and legislative leaders on behalf of the city. These actions proved inadequate, for Beame soon warned that some 17,000 workers would have to go.

Union leaders were annoyed by the fact that the bankers remained quietly in the background, refusing to commit themselves. According to Feinstein of the Teamsters, they were hoping for an arrangement on their own terms, one that would mean "complete subservience of the city to the banking community; they would even name the accountants, tell the city how to operate its administration, and indeed, who would do what. There was no disguise in what they wanted—they would run the city as a banker's government."

Calls for more cuts in services and more layoffs came from the banking and business communities. Fed up with their behavior, Gotbaum decided that they simply had to be forced into the public arena. Having enjoyed the benefits of profit making from their city investments, it was time they shared in carrying some of its burdens. He also believed that the banks should be selling city bonds at far less than the "usurious" 9.5 or 10 percent they were demanding. A confrontation with the bankers was arranged for June 4 when Gotbaum and his colleagues led an estimated 10,000 city workers into Wall Street to picket the headquarters of the First National City Bank. Signs and chants focused on the huge profits amassed by bankers, while public workers took the brunt of cutbacks. Gotbaum's rhetoric echoed through the narrow canyons of the Wall Street area when he bellowed, "Jobs and services are a hell of a lot more important than profits." And then, rather dramatically, he announced the planned withdrawal of $15 million in union funds from First National.[6]

At the same time, the seesaw between the mayor's threat of layoffs and their postponement kept unions in dizzying rounds of defensive action. Thousands of public workers received pink slips, only to have them withdrawn within days. Half of these notices, for example, were rescinded for AFSCME locals in the Parks, Highways, and Social Services Departments.

CETA: A NO-WIN CONTROVERSY

Illustrative of the many serious difficulties confronting municipal unions, and of the constrained, no-win situations in which they found themselves, was the CETA controversy. By midyear 1975, Viani and Gotbaum realized that some of the recently fired union members could be rehired for the same jobs through provisions of the Comprehensive Employment and Training Act (CETA). The Federal government would pay up to $10,000 of workers' salaries and fringe benefits, while the city picked up the balance. Although CETA lines could not be used to displace permanent civil servants, some violations did occur.

Conflicts arose between civil servants who had been fired and then rehired under CETA, and more recently hired unemployed CETA workers, many of whom had worked previously in antipoverty programs. While both groups were members of DC 37, the union, guided by the principle of seniority, insisted that these laid-off public employees be assigned CETA jobs, even if it meant displacing some of the other group of workers. Negotiator Alan Viani insisted, "No one wants to bump existing CETA workers," but "on the other hand, we will not permit the city to lay off experienced workers who got their jobs through the merit system and replace them with inexperienced workers who got their jobs through a community clubhouse." A small group of these "inexperienced" CETA workers denounced the union, alleging racism. State Senator Carl McCall from Harlem quickly joined their cause by lashing out at the union, insisting that "It's ironic and revealing that the same union leaders fighting a wage freeze are perfectly willing to steal jobs from the poor and leave minorities completely out in the cold." Gotbaum immediately took McCall to task for his "cheap shot," contending that ". . . what is shameful is the fact that he knew that city workers laid off in these low-paying jobs are themselves mainly poor and minorities; he knew that no union could stand by and see its members laid off and replaced by other workers, however pitiable their condition."

It was, indeed, a "pitiable" situation. Over the years, the union and its leadership had displayed unyielding dedication to the city's poor and had worked diligently to strengthen its ties to minority populations. Suddenly, the fiscal crisis and job layoffs had placed the Council, in this instance, in an extremely difficult position. DC 37 was able to bring several thousands of its laid-off members onto CETA lines. At the same time, however, in the face of grumbling from those members who had been part of the civil service, Viani reminded them that "CETA employees are workers, too. They are entitled to union representation and coverage under the union contract." He insisted that they, too, were victims of the fiscal plight and were simply trying to support their families like everyone else. The Council sought to find placements for laid-off CETA workers, and in 1978 fought a federal ruling limiting employment to 18 months.[7]

STATE TAKEOVER

With financial markets closed to the city, and the Federal government under Republican Gerald Ford refusing to help, the state appeared as a last recourse. It was at this time that investment banker Felix Rohatyn, of Lazard Frères, emerged as fiscal consultant to Democratic Governor Hugh Carey. Known in the financial world as a bright, articulate, and successful investment expert, he soon began to enjoy a growing reputation in the world of politics. As Carey's emissary, he shuttled between his investment and banking associates and city and state officials. In the process, he helped forge a new link between the worlds of politics and finance. Within a remarkably short period, in June 1975, the Municipal Assistance Corporation (MAC) was established by the state, giving it a new influential role in city finances. This state authority was invested with the power to issue its own bonds on behalf of the city and was also authorized to segregate city revenues in order to guarantee its bonds, e.g., sales and stock transfer taxes were funneled directly to MAC for its cash reserve. While severely limiting the city's borrowing power, MAC was empowered to pre- and post-audit city expenses, redesign its accounting procedures, and oversee issuance of short-term notes. MAC could borrow $3 billion to tide over the city until October, anticipating that New York City would then be in a position to reenter the bond market on its own.

The central goal of MAC, to get the city back into the bond market, was expected by its board members to be attained before the end of the summer. "We didn't know at the time," recalled MAC treasurer Donna Shalala, "the actual size of the deficit or the accumulated debt." It was incredible that no one had reliable figures. While the board thought, originally, that the maximum loan needed to rescue the city was $4 billion, before long its members realized that double that figure was a more realistic estimate— $6 billion in short-term and $2 billion in long-term bonds. Beame complicated matters when he simply refused to do anything about another $1 billion needed for the city's cash flow for the year. With a budget of some $11 billion, the city's debt of $8 billion was incredible.

The key participants agreed that default was to be avoided at all costs, for they feared the possible role of the courts in allocating funds for city services. Important business and industry leaders worried about the impact of the chaos on the economy, while no one really knew what this meant for the poor, the elderly, and the large numbers of laid-off women, blacks, and Hispanics. In addition, Shalala and many others believed that default would block City Hall from borrowing for a long time. Finally, none of the bankers or investing houses were anxious for the city to go broke, for it would undermine their credibility. "Losing face," according to Shalala, "was not easily acceptable." Furthermore, while there were big bondholders, a number of ordinary citizens across the nation, especially retirees, held a considerable portion of the city's bonds and would be directly affected. The consequences for them were hard to imagine.[8]

By August, MAC announced that it was unable to raise the billion dollars that the city required for solvency, and its members insisted that the mayor take more dramatic steps to restore investor confidence in MAC bonds. In response, Beame threatened to lay off an additional 27,500 workers, institute a freeze on wages, impose tuition at City University, and increase subway fares. Gotbaum lamented that these actions were not set in a broader, more comprehensive, long-range plan which would have to include not only the city and state but the federal government and the banks.

When strike threats were heard from sanitation workers, Gotbaum discouraged such action, warning that it would be counterproductive, if not a tragic mistake. Job actions or strikes were not simple strategies, easily turned on or off. Recalling his Chicago and New York experiences, the Council Director knew that a number of critical factors had to be considered by union leadership, including conditions beyond their control. There must be clear support from other unions and the public, an awareness that the issues could be resolved at some point, and that the workers were sufficiently disciplined to return to work when that decision was reached. As AFSCME economist Carol O'Cleireacain noted, "Negotiating 'clout' depends on leadership skills in the unions— the ability to present a justifiable case to the public and the other unions to elicit their support, to effect and maintain worker and union discipline, and to deliver a settlement." Teacher-leader Albert Shanker put it succinctly when he stated, "A strike is a weapon you use against the boss who has money. This boss has no money." In addition, Gotbaum warned that the problem was not at City Hall but with state and Federal officials. "To strike the city would be to visit on the people of the city our anger and frustration—but it would not bring back jobs." But his counsel was ignored as some 10,000 Sanitation "wildcatters" took to picket lines in July to protest 3,000 layoffs; they were joined shortly thereafter by discharged and disgruntled policemen.

As soon as MAC announced that it was unable to sell the bonds required to improve the city's position, new layoffs appeared imminent. An emergency meeting of representatives from the city, the MLC, and MAC was convened at the Americana Hotel on July 24, followed by a series of all-night sessions lasting an entire week. Finally, MAC forced city officials and union leaders to accept a more stringent package, with the promise that money would then be forthcoming from bankers. The teachers and police unions refused to go along with the agreement, which provided for the deferment of wage increases won in the previous contract. The 6-percent increase due workers in July was deferred for one year, although Gotbaum managed to win agreement that deferral would be on a graduated scale. Those earning less than $10,000 would postpone one-third of the 6-percent hike; those between $10,000 and $15,000, two-thirds; and those over $15,000 would defer the entire increase. The full salary rate, however, would remain in effect for other purposes, such as pension computation. A cost of living adjustment (COLA) that had been agreed to in 1974 would go into effect, as promised, in 1976. Summer hours were surrendered by those in air-conditioned offices. The overall consensus prevented individual unions from competing with each other, inasmuch as it permitted them to negotiate separately only on those matters that did not impinge on the framework of the wage deferral agreement.

City administrators were told to eliminate or consolidate select agencies, delete certain expense items from the capital budget, increase transit fares, cut expenses for transit and higher education, and promise management and productivity reforms. All told, a $1 billion savings was anticipated. Finally, MAC agreed to lobby for transfer of certain city services to the state, such as courts and corrections.

While the unions finally endorsed this wage deferral arrangement, it seriously strained their unity. Gotbaum was convinced that in light of labor's decision to avoid layoffs (although some had already occurred) few other options were available. For police and firefighters union leaders, who were facing rank-and-file challenges, this was perhaps the worst time to accept a wage deferral. Although not a member of the MLC, Shanker did attend the Americana sessions, since they would affect his forthcoming collective bargaining negotiations. However, he spoke out against the agreement, reportedly having said, "Because Gotbaum accepted this you have to accept it or get something worse." After a heated shouting match with the DC 37 leader, which nearly came to blows, Shanker was invited to leave. On his way out, he was reported to have said, "Is that why they wanted me to leave, so they would have a majority?" In the end, the alliance held, although the agreement was a serious setback for labor.[9]

MORE STATE ACTION

As the summer wore on, neither this agreement nor other MAC activities proved adequate to insure banker confidence. The city was pressed by the governor, MAC, and other state officials for more cutbacks in personnel and services. Finally, the mayor was pushed out of the inner workings of the decision-making. With the advice and guidance of Rohatyn, the governor struck the final blow when he helped create a more powerful state authority, the Emergency Financial Control Board (EFCB). The essence of its objective was "to preserve the ability of city officials to determine programs and expenditure priorities within available financial resources." The EFCB was authorized to exercise detailed review over all contracts and expenditures by the city; review, with power to modify, the city's financial plan required under the act; insure consistency of contracts within the requirements of the plan; determine revenue estimates; approve any borrowings; issue orders binding on local officials; and prohibit local officials from issuing false or misleading information. The emergency act also required the development of a three-year financial plan, to produce a balanced budget in fiscal 1978. Thus, the city was mandated to move toward greater austerity and reduce local expenditures substantially. The board included the governor, state and city comptrollers, the mayor, and three public representatives. The "public" members all came from the banking and private sectors. Mayor Beame had one vote—his own.

The Gotbaum coalition maintained an uneasy watch as the EFCB evolved. Liberals in the city's delegation to the state legislature winced at the disappearance of local home rule, but were finally brought around by Gotbaum's urging that it was a necessary step. Why had the unions gone along with another substantial change in the bargaining process, and with what appeared as a threat to their influence? In the first place, the governor had indicated an awareness of their concerns. Carey had invited the key union leaders to sit in on the crucial meeting in his chambers, along with the mayor and his staff, when the outline creating the EFCB was initially presented. As Feinstein recalled it, "We were actually surprised to be at this high-level gathering. As we quietly looked around the room of state and city governmental officials, we realized that we were the only outsiders privileged to be present." Here was apparent evidence of the unions' partnership with the state. Consequently, the unions felt that Carey's recognition of their role was evidence enough that their position in forthcoming negotiations would be respected and their advice sought.

Second, there was growing confidence in Rohatyn. Gotbaum and Bigel had worked closely with him since the creation of MAC, and were impressed with his knowledge and talent in handling complex negotiations. Furthermore, Gotbaum found him sincere, sensitive to the social needs of the city and its workers. He was flexible and open, the least "institutionalized" among the private sector representatives they had met. Gotbaum also noted that Rohatyn showed a loyalty to "what he was doing, not only to an organization." As a result of this new working partnership, the businessman came to accept the labor leader's arguments for attrition, rather than layoffs, and succeeded in convincing the bankers to approve this strategy. Gradually, a warm personal friendship developed between the investment banker and the union leader, which eased their interplay with the governor and the bankers and investors. It was Rohatyn who provided clear and effective communication between these important sets of players, particularly in the case of the suspicious labor leaders.

Another factor that facilitated labor's support for the EFCB was gubernatorial and legislative acceptance of two provisions insisted on by the unions; one guaranteed the integrity of the collective bargaining process, and the other provided that attrition, not layoffs, would be the primary tactic for shrinking the city's work force.

These amendments, along with Gotbaum's confidence in his ability to negotiate effectively, brought the reluctant unions along. A final factor, though not of least importance, was that the public unions had given up on the mayor's maintaining the credibility of the city's finances. When Beame learned that Gotbaum, Bigel, and Feinstein had agreed to support the EFCB, "a hurt mayor turned to us outside the governor's office and accused us of having sold out the city. We were stunned at the mayor's short-sightedness that things weren't as bad as they really were."

Weakening of the mayor's role and the new set of actors dominating the state-created boards made for a decided shift away from the unions' traditional and more comfortable bargaining relationships. The banking and private interests now held a public place in the decision-making process. Not only did they continue to hold an important influence over the city's financial affairs as "private" bankers, but they had secured an input within governmental bodies as well. As one close observer put it, "The negotiations, far from being an exclusive city–union affair, became everybody's business when Ellinghaus and Rohatyn joined the talks." And for the coming months, indeed years, two major questions confronted union leaders: Could collective bargaining survive? Were the bankers in control of city government?[10]

The EFCB immediately set to work developing a new series of complex financial arrangements. A $2.3 billion plan evolved, utilizing bank loans, city and state pension funds, state borrowing on behalf of the city, prepayment of real estate taxes, and purchases of MAC bonds by the city's sinking fund and the State Insurance Fund, all of which, it was hoped, would carry the city through to the end of the year. Also recommended was a three-year plan to eliminate the $3 billion debt, an increase in MAC borrowing capacity from $3 billion to $5 billion, and segregation of state revenue-sharing funds to guarantee future issues. By the fall, the state had advanced the city more than $800 million in payments for education, welfare, and other revenue-sharing items. It had taken out loans on behalf of the city and invested state pension money in MAC bonds to subsidize its daily needs. So heavy was the state's investment that its note issues also became risky, forcing it to resort to a complicated transfer of money to prevent its housing finance agency from defaulting.

THE UNIONS' PENSION FUNDS

Despite all this help, however, the city's fiscal position worsened. Again, there was talk of imminent default. Convinced that the city was in a most precarious state, Gotbaum decided to push the use of union pension funds as a source for new city capital. This decision involved endless days of tense, very difficult negotiations with other union leaders who had to be assured that this was the only way possible. Actually, Gotbaum and Shanker, as well as the unions, could have been sued for using the pension funds of members for loans to New York City, which was in such serious financial straits. The sheer magnitude of its indebtedness was overwhelming. Recalling the reactions of board members of the various pension funds, Shalala noted that they were very nerous and, indeed, fearful of the high risk involved in their approval. All fell in line, except Shanker. The Teachers' leader had instructed his representatives on the retirement board to hold back support, hoping that he could wrest assurances from the EFCB that the recent UFT contract would not be substantially modified in any way.

"Admittedly," explained Shanker, "we resisted longest on putting in our pensions—but we bore the lion's share of the 1975 crisis." Some 15 to 20 thousand teachers had been laid off during the year, a cutback, he claimed, that was decidedly more painful than for other unions. Besides the disastrous impact on morale, and on the concept of tenure, working conditions were adversely affected by the introduction of larger classes and the loss of much-needed special services for foreign-speaking youngsters and others among a rapidly changing student population. After the initial budget cuts by the city, the UFT had to confront a second round of cutbacks by the Board of Education, "so we had two bites taken out of us. We had two employers." Shanker also complained that Governor Carey, whom his union had supported for election the year before, had been unreachable. With all their frustrations, and under attack from many sides, the teachers felt beseiged. The use of their hard-earned pensions was the last straw and, he contended, many members urged him not to support this move. However, with unyielding pressure from influential friends like former mayor Robert Wagner and Richard Ravitch, and after one long night of pleading, Shanker finally capitulated.[11]

The public unions proposed that the retirement systems use their $8.5 billion holdings to borrow $4 billion from the banks at prime rates. With this capital, they agreed to purchase MAC bonds, making it unnecessary for the city to "go to market" for the remainder of its three-year fiscal plan. Included in the complex negotiations, the city was afforded an opportunity to convert its short-term debt into longer-term bonds. It was Bigel who helped work out the details of this financial arrangement. In its defense, he argued that the unions would be borrowing at 8 percent, but since the bonds would mature at 11 percent they would make a profit without touching their principals. Eventually he was proven right. The unions did emerge with handsome returns, in fact, "a terrific investment," according to Rohatyn, although at the time it may have appeared risky. When completed, many viewed the municipal unions as "the city's major financiers." The bankers were involved in the intricacies to the extent that they agreed to put up the necessary currency, but the money was backed by the unions' funds. The extent of the bankers' "partnership" in this fiscal package was limited.

Rohatyn, however, looked at the emerging partnership differently. He viewed it as a more equal and balanced one, each party contributing its share to the solution of an exceedingly complex and serious situation. The investors converted their short-term notes into long-term notes, they reduced their interest rates as fiduciaries, and they contributed new credits. Further, he noted, "They couldn't contribute to closing a $1.7 billion budget gap on the expenditure side because they were not part of it. Compared to what they could do, the banks did quite reasonably. The only additional thing the banks could have possibly done was to lower their interest rates even more."

With this infusion of union funds, the Ford administration in Washington finally gave its approval to legislation guaranteeing $2.3 billion in seasonal loans to the city. To win this federal aid, Rohatyn resorted to unusual political and educational tactics. By skillful use of a printout containing a listing of investors in city bonds nationwide, he demonstrated that New York's default would impact on the entire country. Thousands of the city's creditors were located in cities, towns, and hamlets across the country. Some small localities were reported to have invested as much as half their assets in New York bonds, as had thousands of retirees in Florida and other sunbelt states. Facing up to a deep national hostility toward New York, which made it tough to sell its bonds during the crisis, Rohatyn subsequently recalled warning lawmakers and the White House, "what was bad for us was not good for them."[12]

By the end of 1975 the municipal unions in New York had gone along with a number of threatening concessions or givebacks: wage deferrals, a reduction in the work force by some 38,000, a loss of hard-won fringe benefits, changes in the setting for collective bargaining, and loans from their pension funds. The rigid economic conditions seriously constrained new wage and other demands of unions. Except for the wildcat strike of sanitation workers, a job action by police, and the teachers strike in September, the unions held together in a relatively disciplined coalition, enabling Gotbaum to speak with one voice for most of them. With Bigel verifying management's claims of a continued budget crisis, the municipal unions sought to accommodate themselves to the situation. Alan Viani suggested that it was not so much a question of having a handle on the facts and statistics as it was developing a process for negotiating arrangements by which the city would emerge from its critical situation.

Gotbaum played a central role throughout these developments, speaking forthrightly to his membership as well as to the coalition partners. He acknowledged that the crisis was real and that sacrifices had to be made by municipal workers. Of primary concern to the AFSCME leader, however, was that the unions be accepted as a partner in designing the various programs with which to meet the city's overriding difficulties. He struggled to protect the integrity of collective bargaining, holding firm to his contention that the coalition should participate in every important decision and that the sacrifices be shared. Viani saw the situation as a constant "behind-the-scenes struggle," for as each problem surfaced, various strategies were put forth in an endeavor to find the money to pay the creditors.

The high level of trust forged by Gotbaum and Rohatyn enabled the major parties concerned—the state, investment bankers, and the unions—to make the tough decisions necessary to avoid default. It was Rohatyn, with a broader perspective than most others, who cleverly wove the varied participants into a dependent network, making it difficult for any of them to leave the intricate web of negotiations without endangering the entire delicate arrangement. However, under the new EFC Act, it was difficult, at times, to identify the employer for collective bargaining purposes. It imposed another level of authority that influenced the character of labor–management negotiations, particularly through its detailed control over contracts and city expenditures. According to a member of the city's OCB staff, "In the beginning, the EFCB did not actively participate in negotiations with public employee unions, although all parties knew the board was waiting in the wings. . . ." In creating MAC and EFCB, state officials and private businessmen increased their political influence at the expense of the city. For public unions, the game had shifted to another ballpark. The concessions made by DC 37 and the other municipal unions in 1975 were substantial, but the crisis was not yet over.[13]

ON THE DEFENSIVE: 1976–77

Events in 1976 and 1977 continued to place the unions in a defensive posture. The continuing fiscal crisis forced municipal workers to take another round of cutbacks in their living standards, and these were compounded by inflation and a recession. For the staff of DC 37, the early months of 1976 were spent in an endless series of rearguard actions seeking to protect jobs, while revenue shortfalls plagued city officials with dismaying regularity. Adding to these difficulties, the United States Senate failed to override President Ford's veto of a bill that would have provided some $137.8 million in direct aid to New York. In his veto message, the president attacked the bill as "an election-year pork barrel," claiming it "would do little to create jobs for the unemployed." Angered by this action, Gotbaum responded that the country needed a Democratic president. He signaled his political action staff to go all out for Carter when he won the nomination.

In addition to the dismal fiscal picture, public workers found themselves under a persistent barrage of criticisms for their "big" wages and "fat" pensions. There were sharp attacks from Otto Kinzel's State Pension Commission, which recommended drastic reductions in retirement benefits for those who joined the pension system after 1973, and the Temporary Commission on City Finances threw its support behind severe cutbacks in fringe benefits. Written by Professor Raymond Horton of Columbia

University, the latter report called for elimination of union welfare funds, assumption by employees of 25 percent of the cost of health insurance, reduction in annual leave, increases in the work week, and elimination of welfare funds for retirees, as well as of health insurance coverage for retirees under 62.

Leading the assault of the press pack was muckraker Ken Auletta. His 16-page *Agenda to Save the City* attacked the civil service system, especially seniority, which he characterized as "dumb," because it did not recognize "superior skills, superior motivation" when it came to layoffs. Along similar lines were broadsides from "good government" groups like the Citizens Budget Commission and the City Club, decrying the excessive wages and luxurious pensions resulting from "union-dictated" contracts. Federal officials continued their barrage of criticism, exacerbating an already difficult situation. This was particularly true of Wisconsin's Senator William Proxmire, chair of the powerful Banking and Currency Committee, which had oversight authority of the federal emergency loan program, and Treasury Secretary William Simon, who had final say as to whether loans would be given. Discounting the sacrifices already made by New York's public workers, they demanded still deeper cutbacks in city expenditures.

Senator Proxmire's committee issued a report—based primarily on Simon's allegations that fringe benefits and city wages were exorbitant, and that New York's workers were incredibly privileged compared to other workers—and warned that "those who received inordinate fringe benefits should bear some of the costs of the city's forced financial retrenchment." The senate panel recommended sharp cuts in fringe benefits and a six-year wage freeze as a precondition for continuing the federal emergency loan program. The *Wall Street Journal* supported Proxmire and Simon, stating that "the biggest favor" Mr. Simon could do the city would be "to pull the plug on the loans. . . ." Jack Bigel replied to Raymond Horton's study, criticizing its "conceptual errors" and "shabby statistics." In a public debate on the issues raised by Horton's report, the regional director of the Bureau of Labor Statistics, Herbert Bienstock, called the professor's findings "polemical figures," concluding that there was no basis for judging his data, "because they do not exist; you are dealing in a factual vacuum."[14]

The essence of union responses to charges of "undeserving contracts" was to illustrate how the city's wages and pensions were not out of line compared with those of other municipalities. When consideration was given to the city's cost of living, New York ranked sixteenth in pay scale among 24 cities with populations over 500,000; skilled maintenance workers were sixth; public safety workers, first; and janitorial workers, seventh. Pension comparisons were reportedly difficult because, in contrast to New York, other cities often provided cost-of-living adjustments. While initial retirement benefits for New York retirees were higher, cities with COLAs eventually overtook them. Representing the worst paid among city workers, Gotbaum sought to publicize their inadequate pay and benefits. Typically, he would recount how the average Council member, who retired at age 63, was entitled to the "munificient" sum of $4,300 annually. "Dignified retirement" was still an unfulfilled dream for the membership. In regard to low-income workers in 1976, some 60,000 members of DC 37 earned less than $9,200 a year. Seventy-four percent were below the minimum family budget (defined by the Bureau of Labor Statistics) necessary to eat, dress, pay rent, and conduct a family's life.

At the bargaining table, Gotbaum sought the same cost-of-living settlement that had been won by the TWU earlier in the year. Transit Authority negotiations were the first, projecting the parameters for other municipal unions, including a cost-of-living increase in return for unspecified productivity arrangements. But Mayor Beame, still unable to commit himself to what appeared to be a costly settlement, left it up to the EFCB to reject it. The state agency, in turn, provided for a slightly higher cost-of-living adjustment than previously negotiated, but put a 6-percent cap on any other cost-of-living increases during 1977. Further, these payments would not be made unless tied to productivity savings to finance them. It was obvious, in this round of negotiations, that the EFCB was no passive onlooker.

In May, well after the transit settlement, EFCB decided to issue wage guidelines for the city which were to apply to all municipal workers for the duration of the fiscal emergency. In essence, this labor policy decreed that there would be no general wage or salary gains or increases in fringe benefits. Only when definite, measured savings could be determined, through productivity gains, reductions in fringe benefits, or other board-approved savings could wages be increased. And contracts were henceforth to provide for ways of cutting down pension costs. Union leaders were upset by the directives and alarmed that the EFCB had not consulted them beforehand. With the main contracts covering some 160,000 police officers, fire fighters, sanitation workers, and social service and clerical workers due to expire by the end of June, the state board had, in effect, not only decreed the terms that were negotiable, but barred any change in the wage scale. By expressing displeasure with the transit agreement, and threatening to withhold federal loans if wage freezes were not put in place for three years, Proxmire and Simon exacerbated an already difficult situation. According to Joan Weitzman, "Proxmire urged Simon to intervene in city labor relations and to demand substantial reductions in fringe benefits before renewing the loans which the city was to receive on July 1."

Above all else, Gotbaum was determined to protect the collective bargaining process under which municipal unions had achieved their great gains. He pushed the members of the state board to participate in negotiations, so that DC 37 would not be "yo-yoed back and forth between City Hall and the EFCB," as had been the case with the teachers and the transit workers. "We did not have these problems," explained Gotbaum, "because Stephen Berger, the director of the EFCB, and other representatives were right there at the table with us, and were a party to the agreement."

Convinced that the city was still tottering on the brink of default, and confronted with growing public hostility and resentment toward unions and civil servants, Gotbaum felt that the coalition had to show its good faith by helping the city narrow its budget gap. In addition, Washington simply would not budge, holding on to the city's cash-flow lifeline. The final agreement called for city workers to get a new COLA similar to that won by transit employees, a continuation of the productivity COLA based on worker productivity in salary rates, job security guarantees, no mandated loss of fringe benefits, and establishment of a labor–management council to recommend savings and to monitor use of new revenues coming to the city. In return, the unions agreed to defer part of the COLA increase and to negotiate on various means to reduce labor costs by $24 million over the next two years. Each union had the option to decide how it would bargain on these savings. DC 37 promised its members that no fringe benefits would be lost, that cuts would be made through savings, increased productivity, and reductions in fringe costs or new revenues.[15]

According to the AFSCME leader, the new contract that

emerged strengthened job security and established a joint labor–management productivity council, which accorded the union "a strong voice" to protect workers and preserve collective bargaining. In reality, it was a holding operation, warding off the more stringent demands made by Simon, Proxmire, Horton, "good government" groups, and the media. To offset the shock waves and low morale that swept the Council, Gotbaum sought ways of giving members a sense of some progress. New services were introduced, such as prepaid legal, medical, and dental plans. The legal program was initiated with support from the Ford Foundation and, for the first time, provided workers with help for their problems with small claims, family difficulties, and landlord–tenant relations.

In contrast to the immediate, negative reactions of Council members, who knew only that they had not received any overall wage increases, their executive director viewed the situation from an historical perspective. Fully aware that fiscal stringencies would confront the municipal government for some time to come, and that general wage increases, of a significant scope, would be difficult, if not impossible to attain, he sought to insure not only city acceptance of the legitimacy of legal, as well as other benefits, but expanded governmental subsidization of them in the future. He believed that with this approach, he could further enhance the union's position as provider of services as well as wage increases.

Despite this settlement, the nonprofessional hospital workers struck the HHC for four days in August, as a protest against the dismissal of some 1,350 workers. This action followed recommendations by a task force set up to adjudicate conflicts between Local 420 and management, over where cuts could be made. To aggravate the fiscal difficulties, the state set new, lower Medicaid reimbursement rates for the city's hospitals. HHC officials had pressed for more money in order to ease the number of layoffs, but because of this new cut in aid, between 2,500 and 3,000 hospital workers faced dismissal. Through the efforts of OCB and the appointment of an outside mediator, Basil Paterson, the strike quickly came to an end. Under the agreement, the union surrendered $10 million in cost-of-living raises for 1976, and a similar amount the following year, if necessary, to save the jobs of 1,350 workers. The city also agreed to restore some funds to HHC, which promised not to layoff employees, despite the reduction of Medicaid rates. Gotbaum was determined to save as many jobs as possible, despite the need to sacrifice wage increases. As he put it, "I wish to God the economic condition of the Health and Hospitals Corporation were better, but I am satisfied with the settlement. We couldn't face the reckless tragedy of 1,350 workers being laid off, facing a heartless future."

Compared to the internal turmoil at transit, police, and fire-fighter unions, where rank-and-file members challenged their leadership, the DC 37 director was able to maintain a firm position and keep the Council united for the next round of negotiations. According to Viani, Gotbaum's relationship with AFSCME members contrasted sharply with that of most of his labor colleagues. He operated openly and forthrightly, explaining the decisions to be made and the reasoning behind them. The threat of layoffs unnerved many at the Council, especially when exaggerated figures as high as 10,000 circulated during the summer months. Although morale had dropped sharply, and workers were nervous for their jobs, Gotbaum's constant communication with members had a calming effect. The loss of a job was painful for the individual involved, as well as for the union, which resorted to extraordinary efforts to save them. Viani and his staff spent endless hours reviewing contracts and personnel arrangements in search of any possible technique that might enable them to hold on to workers. This strategy sometimes caused unexpected internal difficulties. For example, to save the jobs of 500 caseworkers, Viani found that they could be shifted legitimately to another category, that of clerk supervisors. The leader of the clericals, however, opposed the transfer, arguing that these positions were set aside for promotional opportunities for his local's members. Finally, with Gotbaum's personal intervention, the conflict was momentarily resolved; the caseworkers were saved, but many clericals were unhappy. It was a painful, no-win game.

The AFSCME leader maintained publicly that the 1976 contract marked "the end of the long, negative road of abuse on which civil servants had been traveling for the last two years." In this sense, he was overly optimistic, for it was essentially a defensive contract and a far cry from the great victories of previous years. Fully aware of the constraints forced on them by the crisis, Gotbaum sought to remind the membership that they had, after all, been successful in "keeping the city afloat, keeping our jobs and our fringe benefits, and keeping our dignity. . . . "

Since the crisis erupted in its most threatening form, wage

freezes, layoffs, and attrition constituted the major responses of City Hall. Between January 1975 and May 1976, the total payroll declined by over 47,000 workers—from 294,522 to 247,110. Under pressure from the new state agency and key federal officials, Mayor Beame cut back and economized even more than projected in his financial recovery plan. Attrition was the primary policy adopted, except in the most urgent of situations. Overtime for employees was limited, a freeze on promotions instituted, and workers benefits reduced. The overall impact was an immediate, marked shrinkage in services to the city's population—a number of schools, hospitals, libraries, fire stations and police precincts around the city were closed, garbage collections were less frequent, and subway service seriously curtailed, especially between rush hours.

The state legislature banned pension bargaining for a time, and new legislation placed further restrictions on retirement benefits. Freezes and dismissals also insured the increasing loss of the city's middle management and the denial of wage increases for those who remained. The frozen pay structure served as a disincentive at a time when the city most required increased productivity. Finally, while layoffs cut labor costs, at the same time they caused higher expenditures for increased welfare cases and insured new social and economic problems. As Weitzman noted, "It is difficult to understand the logic of laying off employees who, instead of performing work for the public, instead collect unemployment insurance, welfare payments, food stamps, and Medicaid."

As part of the last leg of the city's three-year rescue plan, which would begin July 1, 1977, the municipal budget had to be balanced and the remaining deficit eliminated. Compounding the city's problem were the overall effects of economic recession and inflation. Recession meant, for example, that the city's welfare case load increased by some $64 million in one year, and inflation contributed to the spiral of Medicaid costs by $60 million. For those who had alleged that by contributing their pension funds to save the city, unions would thereafter dominate collective bargaining negotiations, the 1976 contract proved this charge false.[16]

THE ILLEGAL MORATORIUM AND NEW TENSIONS

The Court of Appeals permitted the city to avoid contractual obligations for the payment of wages, but in a series of cases brought by some municipal unions, the judges did not allow City

Hall to ignore its non-wage obligations. In 1976, the court struck down the New York State Emergency Moratorium Act, which had postponed enforcement of the municipality's short-term obligations for three years. New York's state constitution prohibits the city from contracting any indebtedness, unless it pledges its "faith and credit" for the payment of the principal and interest. This pledge, the court warned, was a commitment to pay and use in good faith the city's revenue powers. Thus, the recently developed bond moratorium was found illegal.

In March 1977, bankers dissatisfied with the system of controls put in place by Albany proposed the formation of a new state-controlled budget review board with additional sweeping powers over New York's budgets. Under their plan, the board would be empowered to approve all city budgets and borrowing, to seize control of its revenues, and seek criminal penalties if the municipality defied its directives. While Beame opposed the idea, and Viani labeled it as "horrible," the proposal indicated that cooperating bankers were still uncertain about the city's viability. It was then that Gotbaum launched a vigorous attack against the bankers, charging them with undue pressure to gain control of the city's finances and to constrain the collective bargaining process. Jack Bigel joined the chorus of critics when he reminded the bankers that for many months they had refused to make any loans—"not one red cent." He condemned them for seeking political control over the city's budgets and for attempting to make elected officials mere "store window dummies and ribbon-cutters at branch-bank openings." As far as he was concerned, the bankers had one overriding motive, and that was to run the city for their own selfish purposes.

As a result of the court's moratorium decision, the city was again on the brink of default, having to find another $1 billion with which to pay off notes that had become due. With the deadline only days away, and the banks refusing to help directly, the labor coalition and Mayor Beame met in emergency, around-the-clock sessions. They finally came up with a proposal in which the unions agreed to: a "stretch-out"* of the city's bond obligations to the workers' pension systems; continuation of the investment of $38 million of pension funds in city bonds; the sale of a new security by MAC to savings banks; and a new offer by MAC to exchange its bonds for outstanding notes held by institutions and individuals.

---

*Postponement of payment to a later date.

The bankers and investors also played a part in strengthening the city's financial condition by agreeing to stretch out payment of a debt, and to a partial moratorium amounting to a substantial sum of money.

After this last-minute proposal was quickly ratified by the EFCB, Treasury Secretary Michael Blumenthal of the new Carter Administration approved a $255 million federal loan, enabling the city to get through the next few months. The threat of "payless paydays" was set aside for the moment. Gotbaum took delight in informing a relieved public that "perhaps for the first time, the people of this city and the country could clearly see that the unions care about keeping this great city alive—while the bankers seem more concerned with their billions in the Bahamas." Ever since the financial crisis brought the city to the precipice of default and bankruptcy, Gotbaum had been denouncing the role of the huge banking institutions. They were attacked regularly in the DC 37 newspaper for precipitating the fiscal crisis and for having done little to resolve it. Optimistic that the budget would be balanced without further layoffs, and that the city's financial situation would be improved by an increase in Federal "counter-cyclical" aid, the AFSCME leader predicted that the banks would eventually come around to accepting "their share of responsibility in the crisis they helped to create." Even the hostile *Daily News* recognized the role of municipal unions in its headline: "Unions Offer to Bail Out City."[17]

In mid-June, a successful sale of $250 million in MAC bonds at the relatively low interest rate of 7.5 percent encouraged Bigel and Gotbaum. While warmly praising the investors of the city, the *New York Times* neglected to mention a single contribution of labor. "That's where investor confidence comes from," Bigel maintained, "from the EFCB and the First National City Bank quoting the figures on the attrition in the city's work force." He then spotlighted the fact that since June of 1975, city workers had lost $180 million to inflation and $330 million in wage deferrals.

LABOR AND BANKERS COOPERATE

This enmity and heated exchange between unions and bankers suddenly took a new direction. For some time representatives of the MLC and the bankers had been meeting intermittently in an endeavor to evolve some type of short-range solutions to the fiscal difficulties. These meetings, however, were usually held in a tense, adversarial atmosphere. Conservative and quiet in demeanor, and frustratingly cautious in their exchange of viewpoints, the bankers contrasted sharply with the outspoken and direct style of labor leaders. Two groups could not possibly have been at greater variance in social background and public behavior—predominantly Anglo-Saxon Protestantism pitted against ethnic Jewish, and a smattering of Catholic, union leaders. Viani and Donna Shalala observed that most of the bankers were "incredibly naive...ivory tower" types who had never had direct relationships with unions before and, indeed, feared the labor leaders. They were bright individuals who, with a few exceptions, felt uncomfortable in the presence of this new crowd of participants. Felix Rohatyn, of European-Jewish origin, and Walter Wriston, who was from an academic background, shared far broader perspectives based on experiences unique to the world of banking.

Pushed to the breaking point at one meeting by the bankers' persistent refusal to respond frankly or directly to the overwhelming pressures facing them, Gotbaum finally lashed out in a thundering voice. After accusing them of neither understanding nor caring about the critical impact of the fiscal crisis on working men and women, the AFSCME director rose roughly from his chair, looked angrily at the group on the other side of the table, and stalked out of the room, followed by the rest of the labor contingent.

Aware of more foreboding complications facing the city, Bigel decided on a new tack. Within days after Gotbaum's outburst, the union consultant telephoned Walter Wriston, head of the First National City Bank, who spoke for the financial leaders. When Wriston's secretary stated that the banker was away from the office but would call back on his return, Bigel's secretary bet her employer one week's wages that Wriston would never respond. Within the hour, Wriston returned the call. Bigel suggested that the time had come for bankers and labor leaders to sit down in a calm setting to discuss the city's problems and evolve some long-range solutions. Wriston agreed immediately, but asked one favor of Bigel—that he stop calling him a "fascist." Bigel replied that it was not he who had, but that he could assure him it would not happen again, at least in his presence. Bigel, in turn, advised Wriston that he would not take exception, personal or otherwise, if the banker continued to call him an "unregenerate socialist."

Shortly thereafter, the bankers and the labor leaders began meeting more regularly. Eventually, out of these gatherings evolved the MUFL Group—the Municipal Union/Financial Leaders—cochaired by Bigel and Wriston. There had been a good deal of mistrust on both sides, making it difficult, according to Rohatyn, for the two sides to have a frank exchange. "There was a lot of suspicion," he explained, "but there were bankers like Pat Patterson of Morgan Guaranty and Wriston of Citibank with whom Victor had no problem," on an intellectual level. In the course of many meetings, there were some tense moments and heated exchanges, but both sides eventually learned much about the other. Rohatyn further noted, "Wriston and Patterson learned a lot about Victor's side of the world. The labor leaders learned about our side of the world. And I learned a lot about both worlds." Before the end of 1977, a joint settlement on a major public policy was issued in the form of a response to President Jimmy Carter's disappointing announcement that the welfare reforms he had promised during the 1976 campaign would be postponed at least until 1980. Both the bankers and union leaders agreed that social service programs were a national responsibility, and urged that state and local governments should not be forced to contract needed public programs or to raise their taxes to uncompetitive levels because of these national problems. They suggested that if the Federal government assumed one-half of the cost of the programs of aid to families with dependent children and Medicaid, the city's tax burden would be cut from $786 million to $394 million. And the state's budget would benefit by a reduction in costs from $1.2 billion to $600 million.

While the banker–union meetings did not produce any dramatic results, they did help create a calmer atmosphere for exchanging views, and both groups did modify their positions on several concrete matters. For example, the bankers came to appreciate the rationale behind the unions' demands for an agency shop and withdrew their long-standing public opposition. Also, after discussions concerning comparative wage levels and fringe benefits of public workers in the nation, the bankers no longer attacked those in New York as "astronomical." For their part, union leaders reappraised the bankers' claims for an increase in interest rates on mortgages. Learning that the threat from interstate competition could easily mean investing banking money elsewhere in the nation, the unions no longer opposed their requests for increased rates. They also issued several joint resolutions: supporting construction of a West Side Convention Center and the hiring of additional ethnic minority workers in the private sector. Occasionally they complimented the city for working to weather the fiscal crisis.[18]

Murray Gordon, independent labor attorney and influential representative of the Fire Officers in many decisions involving the fiscal crisis, discounted rumors that the DC 37 leader had been coopted by the banking interests, as a result of his developing friendship with Rohatyn. Gordon insisted that Gotbaum was bright enough to recognize that these "big business types" were a powerful component in city affairs and that it was far better to deal with them directly and forcefully. "Vic is the same man," the labor lawyer said, "and the crisis matured him. He was able to see, up close, real power at work and learned quickly how far labor could press its demands. No question, he maintained his integrity throughout. No doubt, he had grown a great deal and stayed honest."[19]

SUMMARY

The city's fiscal emergency constituted a severe political and organizational crisis for municipal unions in New York as they struggled to preserve, among other gains, one of the most advanced collective bargaining systems in the nation. Its continuation was constantly challenged as the city's critical situation unfolded. The responses of municipal unions was funneled primarily through Gotbaum and those closely associated with him in DC 37, and the MLC. With consummate skill he created an influential working alliance out of competing union organizations. Assisting him throughout in mastering the financial complexities and in projecting the city's fiscal future was labor consultant Jack Bigel.

From the outset, the public union leaders agreed on three important strategies: they would do everything possible to protect their collective bargaining rights and maintain their influence in decisions affecting their workers, they would protect the city from default and bankruptcy, and they would recommend attrition rather than layoffs. In unequivocal terms, Felix Rohatyn maintains that it was Gotbaum's overriding leadership and strategy that saved the jobs of 100,000 public workers. Admittedly, on a number of matters there were sharp disagreements, so that holding the group together was no easy task.

Influenced by Bigel's data, Gotbaum quickly concluded that state and Federal assistance were absolutely essential to save the city. Thereafter, the unions joined in strenuous, eventually successful, lobbying efforts in Washington and Albany. Inherent in this search for outside funding, however, was the danger of additional constraints on city autonomy. New York's mayor, meanwhile, lost substantial control to new participants, who assumed increasing power over the city's financial affairs. The creation of MAC and EFCB gave the state control over the city's budget and borrowing. Among the new actors were the governor and representatives of the banking and investing communities. At the same time, another set of particpants emerged on the national level, including the president and key legislative and administrative officials. Each of these officials became partners in New York's financial affairs, eventually forcing the city to alter its spending patterns by cutting back severely on its work force and services. As a consequence, Gotbaum and his colleagues were compelled to scrutinize every statement, project, and action taken by these new players, and to insure union involvement at critical stages to protect the collective bargaining process.

Adding to union burdens was pervasive public hostility and sharp criticism from civic groups, media newsmakers, academics, and a variety of muckrakers. Public unions came under a steady barrage of attacks for their "big" wages, "fat" pensions and "lazy" workers, and were held responsible for the city's deteriorating condition. Pressed to defend municipal workers against this unceasing public assault, Gotbaum assumed a heavy schedule of interviews, academic seminars, and appearances before a variety of groups and civic organizations. He sought to explain the economic difficulties facing city workers with rising inflation, and the psychological tensions evoked by constant threats of layoffs. It had to be demonstrated that civil servants were people too, with the same anxieties, aspirations, and commitments as the rest of the city.

When the city was again on the verge of collapse in 1976, Gotbaum was among the first to be convinced that the accumulated capital in workers' pension systems had to be tapped in order to save New York, and he gradually convinced his MLC colleagues of this. Nevertheless, even this signal contribution by public unions proved inadequate in winning over public support and confidence. Many now feared that public employee unions would henceforth write their own contracts with the city. In this instance, they paid little attention to Rohatyn, who concluded that the unions had been "pretty good" in keeping their commitments separate from labor negotiations.

With the investment of their pension funds, municipal unions emerged as a vital and sustaining element in the city's solvency. By 1980 the five major union pension systems, with assets of more than $7 billion, held about 40 percent of all city bonds and 18 percent of all MAC bonds. As a consequence, the unions were able to assure their participation in innumerable decisions, extending their access to new individuals and groups, including the once isolated banking community. In addition, the unions developed stronger ties with city officials, as they jointly negotiated the terms of the city's fiscal rescue with Federal and state officials.

Each of these strategies posed problems and difficult choices for the municipal unions. The price they paid was substantial— cuts in salaries and fringe benefits, and thousands of layoffs which shattered the historical sense of security for civil servants. Sustaining public employees and their organizations was the role of Gotbaum. His personality, knowledge, and skills afforded public worker unions the cohesion and strength necessary to preserve the collective bargaining process. And while the city lost substantial autonomy over finances, and new players entered the decision-making process, the unions maintained the core of their influence for future days, and helped save their city from bankruptcy. In the context of the larger scene, New York's municipal workers emerged from their most threatening crisis of the twentieth century far healthier than many workers in textiles, auto, steel, and other private industries. By the 1980s, it was the public unions in New York that retained their viability and negotiated from a position of comparative strength.

NOTES

1. *New York Times*, November 23, 1974, pp. 1, 62; January 5, 1975, p. 32; *Daily News*, December 7, 1974, p. 3. Evelyn Seinfeld, "Chronology of the New York City Fiscal Crisis: July 18, 1974 to April 4, 1977, xerox" Department of Research and Negotiations, DC 37.

2. *Public Employee Press*, April 23, 1976, p. 4; May 7, 1976, p. 11; Joan Weitzman, *City Workers and the Fiscal Crisis*, New Brunswick, NJ: Rutgers University, Institute of Management and Labor Relations, 1979, p. 77; interviews with Murray Gordon, April 28, 1980; and Alan Viani, March 10, 1981.

3. Memo, Julie (Topol) to Vic (Gotbaum), April 15, 1976; the *Village Voice*, May 26, 1975, p. 4; *Public Employee Press*, September 26, 1975, p. 11; Seymour Mann and Edward Handman, "The Role of Municipal Unions," *City Almanac* 12, no. 1 (June 1977):11. Also, interviews with Gotbaum, September 16, 1980 and January 10, 1984; Jack Bigel, February 24, 1981; Alan Viani, March 10, 1981; Carol O'Cleireacain, February 24, 1981; Albert Shanker, December 13, 1982; and Felix Rohatyn, January 10, 1984.

4. "Program Planners," untitled report prepared by Jack Bigel and his staff for the MLC, undated; *New York Times*, January 31, 1975, p. 30; Lee Dembart, "The Public Disdain of Public Employees," *New York Times*, June 27, 1976, section 4, p. 3; Walter Mossberg, "Public Employee Unions Hit Tough Going as Strikes, New York's Ills Stir Opposition," *Wall Street Journal*, December 12, 1975, p. 34; A.H. Raskin, "Public Employee Unions Are No Longer Riding High," *New York Times*, December 21, 1975, Section 4, p. 6; Attiat Ott and Jang Yoo, *New York City's Financial Crisis*, Washington, D.C.: American Enterprise Institute for Public Policy Research, 1975.

5. DC 37 news release, February 27, 1975; *Public Employee Press*, May 9, 1975, p. 6; *New York Times*, January 31, 1975, p. 30; April 11, 1975, p. 69; April 17, 1975, p. 50; April 23, 1975, p. 1; May 21, 1975, p. 1. United States Congressional Budget Office, *New York City's Fiscal Problem: Its Origins, Potential Repercussions, and Alternative Policy Responses*. Washington, D.C.; U.S. Printing Office, October 10, 1975, hereafter cited as Congressional Budget Office, *New York City's Fiscal Problem*.

6. *New York Times*, June 5, 1975, p. 31; July 9, 1975, p. 48; *Public Employee Press*, August 8, 1975, p. 2; Jack Bigel, "A Perspective on the Fiscal History of NYC FY 1976 Through FY 1979." An unpublished report issued by Bigel's consultant firm, Program Planners. Also, interview with Barry Feinstein, May 6, 1981.

7. *Public Employee Press*, July 11, 1975, p. 4; September 12, 1975, p. 2; memorandum to Victor Gotbaum from Alan Viani, re: summary of meetings and proposals on CETA, July 11, 1975; *Public Employee Press*, March 25, 1977, p. 4; memorandum to Victor Gotbaum from Marcia Lamel, re: outline for field review on net employment effects of public service employment, October 13, 1977; interview with Marcia Lamel, January 17, 1984.

8. Interview with Donna Shalala, treasurer of MAC and presently president, Hunter College, New York City, February 16, 1982.

9. Carol O'Cleireacain, "The Union's Economic Demands—The Case for Labor," *City Almanac* 16, no. 2 (August 1981):5; Fred Ferretti, *The Year the Big Apple Went Bust*, New York: G.P. Putnam's Sons, 1976, p. 271.

10. Interviews with Victor Gotbaum, September 16, 1980; Julius Topol, formerly general counsel and then director, MELS, DC 37, March 17, 1981; Barry Feinstein, May 6, 1981; Jack Bigel, February 18, 1982. See also, David Lewin and Mary McCormick, "Coalition Bargaining in Municipal Government: New York City in the 1970s," research working paper no. 327A, Graduate School of Busi-

ness, Columbia University, May 1980, p. 9; Feretti, *The Year the Big Apple Went Bust*, p. 267.

11. Interviews with Donna Shalala, February 16, 1982; Richard Ravitch, former head of the Urban Development Corporation and then of the Metropolitan Transportation Authority, December 8, 1982; and Albert Shanker, December 13, 1982. There were actually five different retirement systems governed by separate boards of trustees—teachers, police, fire, sanitation, and those for members in DC 37.

12. Interview with Felix Rohatyn, January 10, 1984.

13. Joan Weitzman, "The Effect of Economic Restraints on Public-Sector Collective Bargaining: The Lessons of New York City," in Hugh Jascourt, ed., *Government Labor Relations*, vol. 1 (1975–78), Oak Park, Ill.; Public Employment Relations Research Institute and Moore Publishing Co., 1979, p. 336; interviews with Alan Viani, March 10, 1981; and Albert Shanker, December 13, 1982.

14. Ken Auletta, "How the Lies of New York's Political Midgets Are Destroying the City," *New York Magazine*, March 22, 1976, pp. 40, 41, 42, 43; *Village Voice*, May 26, 1975, pp. 5–8; *Public Employee Press*, February 27, 1976, p. 3; April 9, 1976, p. 3; April 23, 1976, p. 5; *Wall Street Journal*, June 14, 1976, p. 8; *New York Times*, June 15, 1976, p. 31; Mann and Handman, "Role of Municipal Unions," p. 11; *Public Employee Press*, July 9, 1976, p. 7.

15. DC 37, Department of Research and Negotiations, "Beyond the Rhetoric," 1976, mimeographed, p. 2; Congressional Budget Office, *New York City's Fiscal Problem*, pp. 671–673; Alan Viani, "New York Revisited—A Year of Crisis," *Oklahoma City University Law Review* 1, no. 1 (Spring 1976):74–80; Weitzman, *City Workers*, p. 337; *Public Employee Press*, July 9, 1976, pp. 2–5; Lewin and McCormick, "Coalition Bargaining," p. 17.

16. *Public Employee Press*, July 9, 1976, p. 2; Weitzman, *City Workers*, pp. 339, 341; interviews with Gotbaum, September 16, 1980; Bernard Stephens, February 2, 1981; Alan Viani, March 10, 1981; Bart Cohen, September 22, 1981.

17. *Daily News*, March 8, 1977, pp. 1, 3; *Public Employee Press*, March 11, 1977, p. 3. Also interviews with Alan Viani, March 10, 1981; and Jack Bigel, February 18, 1982. In addition to $1.2 billion in city and MAC paper bought before November 1975 through city employee pension funds, $4.8 billion more was committed between fiscal 1976 and fiscal 1980.

18. Minutes of the Municipal Union/Financial Leaders (MUFL) Group, between June 20, 1977 and November 22, 1978. Walter B. Wriston to Victor Gotbaum, December 7, 1978; George Roniger to Victor Gotbaum, December 13, 1978. Also, interviews with Victor Gotbaum, September 16, 1980; Jack Bigel, February 18, 1982; and Felix Rohatyn, January 10, 1984. Participating frequently for the banking community were Walter Wriston of Citibank, David Rockefeller of Chase Manhattan, John Hannon of Bankers Trust, Ellmore Patterson of Morgan Guaranty, John McGillicuddy of Manufacturers Hanover, Felix Rohatyn of Lazard Frères and chairman of MAC, and George Champion of the New York City Economic Development Council. For the municipal unions were Victor Gotbaum, Barry Feinstein, Albert Shanker, Michael Maye of the firefighters, John Lawe of the Transport Workers, and Jack Bigel.

19. Interview with Murray Gordon, April 28, 1980.

18
The Contest for Power

The challenge of the fiscal crisis proved the value of collective action and skilled union leadership. Gotbaum's talents and persistence kept labor an intimate and vital participant in many of the major decisions confronting the city and the state. Elsewhere in the nation, union power was being eroded as the economy fell into a precipitous decline. Despite highly publicized attacks against public service workers by a new mayor, Edward Koch, the coalition strategy proved successful in stemming the anti-union tide and in winning important wage adjustments and benefit extensions. As the 1970s ended, some dramatic events erupted within the Council, catalyzed and exacerbated by tensions between Jerry Wurf and Victor Gotbaum, which came to a head in the latter's short-lived attempt to capture the International presidency.

DOWNHILL FOR LABOR

In 1954 just under 35 percent of the nonfarm workers in the nation belonged to unions, but within 20 years this skidded to 21.9 percent. Facilitating this erosion in union organization and influence was a long-term structural shift in the U.S. economy. Employment growth flattened out in traditional union strongholds, like manufacturing, mining, construction, and transportation, but soared in the hard-to-organize service, trade, and finance industries. The rise of multinational corporations undercut labor's economic leverage, and hundreds of thousands of union jobs in the shoe,

One of the last photos of Gotbaum and Wurf together before the latter's death in 1981, and after Gotbaum's abortive attempt to unseat Wurf as International president of AFSCME.

clothing, steel and electronics industries were lost to imports from nations with cheap labor in southeast Asia and Latin America. White-collar workers, who now dominated the labor force, tended to spurn unionism, and management introduced a variety of new techniques to avoid unions or crush them. By November 1980, when joblessness stood at 8 percent of the nation's work force, unemployment further weakened union ranks. About 25 percent of UAW members were out of work because of a two-year depression in Detroit. Anti-union sentiment was widespread. Illustrative of this was the general support given President Ronald Reagan when, without much public protest, he fired 11,500 air-traffic controllers for their illegal strike in August 1981.

In Congress, labor's much-vaunted political influence continued to wane. Under the banner of deregulation, championed by the Republican leadership, conservatives in the Senate mounted an attack on Federal labor laws. Anti-union decisions were handed down by administrative agencies like the National Labor Relations Board, which was packed with Reagan appointees. Throughout the nation, unions continued to lose support, even among workers. Polls showed that one-fifth of the families with one or more members belonging to unions disapproved of them. By 1981, only 55 percent of the American people favored unions, down from 76 percent in 1957. In a recent poll, the general public rated union leaders as not much better than used-car dealers. Labor's generally poor image, made worse by the rise of potent political movements on the right, caused humiliating defeats for union-sponsored legislation in Congress. While the labor force grew, the enrollment in unions remained essentially the same. Workers employed in manufacturing dropped from 23 percent to a new low of 16 percent over a 20 year period. In sharp contrast, almost half the U.S. work force was in services. McDonald's hamburger chain, for example, hired more than three times as many workers as United States Steel. Labor unions quickly learned that it was far more difficult to organize service workers who were spread out in many places, than employees on an assembly line in a single plant. Service workers lacked the spirit for collective action.

At the same time, workers became more aware of the fact that they might strike themselves out of jobs, and used the strategy far more selectively. In many negotiations, unions surrendered previous gains in exchange for more job security. Workers at Chrysler conceded $1.1 billion in an attempt to help the company stay afloat. Employees at a new Goodyear plant near Akron, Ohio, agreed to a base pay of $8.62 an hour, while fellow unionists received more than $10 at a comparable older factory.

Success in organizing drives declined throughout the nation. One bright spot, however, was in the expansion of public employment. One of every four jobs created was in government. And within the public sector, the largest growth was in state and local government. Union membership among public sector employees rose dramatically. AFSCME became the sixth largest union in the nation, from 234,000 in 1964, when Jerry Wurf took over the presidency, to a claimed 1 million in 1978.[1]

NEW PERSONAL INFLUENCES

The 1970s brought dramatic changes to unionized workers in New York as the fiscal crisis forced a realistic understanding of the city's condition on its leaders. Gotbaum's intense involvement with union and city negotiations created extraordinary personal pressures for him. Even his closest associate, Lillian Roberts, lamented that she found it difficult to meet in the same close fashion of pre-crisis days. During this period, Victor divorced his wife, Sarah, and subsequently married Elisabeth (Betsy) Flower. He moved easily in the social circle and network of her younger friends. As one of the more renowned leaders in the city, he had no difficulty in associating with her among New York's elite. His closest friend became Felix Rohatyn, who helped sustain him with new economic ideas.

On weekends, Betsy Gotbaum consciously prodded her husband out of the city to a small, unpretentious retreat in Bellport, Long Island, where they would be close to Rohatyn and other new friends, and where Victor could unwind. The Gotbaums' new acquaintances included influential people in business and politics. At these gatherings, Gotbaum spoke bluntly on behalf of the union point of view, sought to alter certain misconceptions, and forcefully present his reaction to contemporary issues. At weeknight dinners and socials, it was not unusual for the Council director to argue with the head of the New York Federal Reserve Board, Walter Wriston of Citicorp, and other influential bankers. According to Rohatyn, Gotbaum presented his point of view forcefully and skillfully, playing the role of educator to those with an anti-union perspective. He generally responded to caustic remarks about labor by referring to the shortsighted role of industrial management at Chrysler, General Motors, and Ford in refusing to plan, in advance, to counter the competition of foreign cars, to educate the U.S. public to buy smaller vehicles, and to involve workers in plant management. And yet, with full awareness of the poor performance of its management, Gotbaum defended the government's moves to save Chrysler from imminent bankruptcy and collapse, and had personally telephoned Congressmen to urge support of Federal loan guarantees to the beleaguered auto corporation. He could not forget that, like the city's fiscal crisis, thousands of jobs were at stake. He had also urged labor, industry, and government to cooperate in long-range industrial planning.[2]

The DC 37 organization had emerged as one of the more effective forces in a highly fragmented political scene, with evidence of its national reputation revealed in a *Time* magazine article commemorating the centenary of the American Federation of Labor.

From the many top union leaders available to be interviewed, only three were quoted and their photographs prominently displayed— President Lane Kirkland of the AFL–CIO, President Douglas Fraser of the UAW, and Victor Gotbaum from New York City. It was not the AFSCME international president who was accorded the spotlight, but a regional leader.

In DC 37, bread-and-butter unionism was closely linked to reform and ,social advocacy. Council members demonstrated and marched frequently with their green and white overseas caps and banners in national demonstrations for civil rights and against the regressive economic and social policies of Republican and Democratic administrations. At times, this militant Council found the national leadership of AFSCME and of the AFL–CIO not active enough in giving direction and inspiration against growing conservatism in Washington.

As the intensity of the city's fiscal crisis lessened somewhat, the organizational base of DC 37 appeared to be in a comparatively healthy state. The Council's structure remained intact, and its influence unimpaired at the bargaining table and in political lobbying. With the membership still filled with anxiety because of the dangerous economic situation, most local leaders tended to mute their differences and accept Council direction.[3]

LOCAL INDEPENDENCE REASSERTED

The independent tendencies of certain locals, which had been dormant during the prolonged fiscal crisis, surfaced again. The Technical Guild Leadership, spearheaded by Richard Izzo, sought to distance its professional membership from the large numbers of lower-paid, unskilled members of the Council. In fact, Izzo initiated independent collective bargaining negotiations with the city, mistakenly concluding that he could do better for his members than with coalition bargaining under Gotbaum's leadership. He also turned to the courts in an unsuccessful endeavor to break his local's affiliation with the Council.

Traditionally independent, with its own headquarters, newspaper, and assigned negotiator, and usually expounding a more radical outlook on issues, the Social Service Employees (Local 371) were headed by serious, unsmiling Joe Sperling. Taking advantage of a bitter internecine conflict between Wurf and Gotbaum, Sperling and many of his local's officers showed little concern for the sensitivities of the DC 37 leadership, or for the need of a cohesive Council. But it was James Butler and his supporters in Hospital Local 420 who would soon plague the Council and its director. During these years, rising numbers of black workers filled the ranks of DC 37, enabling a number of them to move steadily into prominent positions of leadership in locals and on Council staff. In the process, they replaced many of the Italian-American blue-collar workers who, under Wurf, had helped found and build the Council. Al Diop, a young black unionist who had succeeded Tom Hagan as president of Local 1549, joined Gotbaum as one of the two elected vice-presidents to the International executive board from New York City. The membership of Schools Local 372 rose dramatically by 1975, and its president, Charles Hughes, became head of the Council's PAC, winning recognition as one of the key leaders of the Council. He was courted by Edward Koch, during mayoral elections, by the president and secretary-treasurer of national AFSCME, and by President Jimmy Carter.

With the support of Wurf and secretary-treasurer William Lucy, Hughes shocked the Council's delegation at the 1980 convention in Anaheim, California, when on the eve of elections, he unexpectedly announced his candidacy for one of the two International vice-presidencies from New York City. With evident support from the International office, campaign banners, hats, ribbons, and leaflets for Hughes suddenly appeared on the convention floor. This secretly planned move against the two incumbent candidates, Gotbaum and Diop, seemed to throw down the gauntlet to the Council leadership. Hughes's subsequent endorsement of Koch's campaign for reelection as mayor in 1981, against the overwhelming sentiment in DC 37 for neutrality, particularly among blacks, was another of a series of moves that appeared to challenge the Council. Hughes insisted that he had remained throughout a committed ally of the Council's leadership. By cooperating with the International president and Lucy at Anaheim, he had hoped to lessen the hostilities raging between Wurf and Gotbaum and eventually create a rapprochement between the two.[4]

The modest role played by Al Diop has been in sharp contrast to the rhetorical skill and often surprising behavior of Hughes. As president of the Clerical–Administrative employees since 1970, he was intimately involved in tripling his local's membership. Comprising close to one-fourth of the Council's strength, Diop and his staff serviced their members, strengthened the Council as an integrating force, and endorsed Gotbaum's leadership.

VIETNAM—A UNION ISSUE

Gotbaum had been an intimate member of the COUR caucus which planned and executed the Wurf challenge to Arnold Zander. In a sense, it was inevitable for them to confront each other over the leadership of the International union. They were strong, independent, skillful, and dynamic leaders and neither was prepared to take orders from the other.

While Wurf included Gotbaum in the early months of his kitchen cabinet, the new International president had a most difficult time disengaging himself from DC 37 organizational and policy developments. He took over complete direction of New York's welfare strike in January 1965, and sought to do the same during the hospitals election campaign later that same year. Only when Gotbaum threatened to resign did the president leave. Subsequently, Wurf objected strenuously to the new executive director's creation of the divisional structure for DC 37, but through will and determination, Gotbaum won. Antagonism was always just below the surface in this tense relationship. An issue of importance to both, which brought them into open conflict, was the war in Vietnam.

Gotbaum and Lillian Roberts were early opponents of U.S. invasion of Vietnam. In 1966 the Council leader spoke out against the war and permitted use of his name for marches and protest rallies. At the same time, Wurf, who personally opposed the war, was anxious to be elected to the AFL–CIO executive council. Wurf was aware that President George Meany was a cold warrior who strongly supported U.S. policy in Vietnam, and according to Wurf's biographer, Joseph C. Goulden, "assiduously avoided taking any positions that would unnecessarily offend Meany." He goes on: "An issue on which Wurf particularly suffered, in those years of self-imposed silence, was the Vietnam War. He knew Meany's strong pro-war feelings. To Meany Vietnam was a litmus issue—cross him here, and you were blacklisted forever."

Wurf, however, did not remain silent on the issue. As a delegate to the AFL–CIO convention, he supported George Meany's endorsement of President Lyndon Johnson's escalation of the war. When a Boston leader offered an anti-Vietnam resolution at the biennial AFSCME convention in 1966, it was Wurf who took the floor to urge its defeat. Since communist nations had no free trade unions, he insisted that there was no freedom in Vietnam and that there was, therefore, no war of liberation. The antiwar proposal was rejected by voice vote. Wurf now had reason to expect election to an AFL–CIO vice-presidency.

The International president went even further to prove his loyalty by silencing any AFSCME leader who dared criticize the war publicly. And this brought him into conflict with Gotbaum. The day after the executive council of the AFL–CIO reaffirmed its support of U.S. involvement in Vietnam, an ad in the *New York Times,* sponsored by the Trade Union Council of SANE, attacked the president's position. One of the individuals endorsing the statement was the DC 37 executive director. Wurf immediately telephoned Gotbaum and angrily demanded that he refuse, thereafter, to publicly support this antiwar position, for he was too closely identified as DC 37 executive director. Gotbaum responded that since DC 37 had not taken a stand for or against the war in Vietnam, he felt free to follow the dictates of his conscience. He advised Wurf that should the delegates council vote to support the latter's position, he would then discontinue his activities with SANE.

Insisting that this was a matter of vital concern to the "welfare of the union," Wurf appeared at the next meeting of the delegates council in New York. Recalling that AFSCME delegates to the last AFL–CIO convention had voted to support the U.S. war in Vietnam, he went on to denounce SANE and the antiwar movement as communist-led, and insisted that the Council's director immediately withdraw from further SANE activities. Deciding not to exacerbate the situation any further, for he did not want to split the Council on a nonunion issue, Gotbaum advised the delegates that should they support the International president, he would discontinue his activities with SANE. The motion to endorse the AFL–CIO position was carried by a majority. At this juncture, Gotbaum stated that as a veteran who hated war, his position on Vietnam remained the same, but as executive director he would abide by the Council's decision.

Since local autonomy was respected by the Council, the Social

Workers and Librarians adopted their own antiwar resolutions, while the Technical Guild, Laborers, and Motor Vehicle Operators warmly supported the war. Within days after Meany finally acquiesced to Wurf's election to labor's "inner club," in October 1969, the delegates council of DC 37 voted to reverse its policy, declaring that, with responsible organizations, it would "help bring about a meaningful withdrawal of American forces and help speed up the establishment of peace in Vietnam."[5]

AN IRASCIBLE LEADER

Seeking to avoid meetings with Wurf, and what he felt would be further confrontations, Gotbaum declined election to the IEB until 1974. Only when the two incumbents from New York City were characterized by Wurf as errand boys for Gotbaum did the latter permit himself and Al Diop to be elected as regional representatives. Gotbaum became increasingly upset as he observed the dictatorial tactics of Wurf at IEB meetings. Soon the Council director emerged as a lone voice to challenge Wurf's actions and antics. The president's abusive treatment of IEB members and his so-called parliamentary style appalled him. But equally disturbing was the realization that few, if any, vice-presidents were prepared to take on Wurf, for they had concluded that his power and resources were overwhelming. Only in private would a number of them approach the New York leader and applaud his questioning and challenging.

Alienated by the complete capitulation of IEB members to Wurf's domination, Gotbaum soon grew disenchanted with his colleagues and appeared distant from them. Several close observers concluded, as a result, that the New Yorker missed opportunities to strengthen his national standing by fostering friendships and meeting informally with colleagues. Except for brief moments spent with Gerald McEntee from Pennsylvania, and tennis matches with another board member, Gotbaum did not socialize with other vice-presidents. At a crucial moment in AFSCME history he would have no enduring support from them.

Wurf's irascible temperament and stinging criticisms facilitated a disruptive impact on IEB meetings, as well as on those in the field among numerous AFSCME locals and councils. Although a brilliant organizer and strategist, and with an ability to select outstanding staff, his personal behavior insured that Washington headquarters became a revolving door for many skilled professionals and, according to his biographer, a site for "his personal thunderstorms."

Sensitive to Wurf's indignities toward the Council and others in AFSCME, Saki Miyashiro, Gotbaum's executive secretary, began to urge him to consider a race for the presidency. She was aware that many of the loudly advertised AFSCME organizational and educational programs were inadequate, ineffective, or with little substance. She knew that the International president was reestablishing some of the repressive organizational patterns that had inspired the original COUR insurgency, for Wurf had created a variety of "Special Arrangements" under new forms of pseudo-trusteeships of Councils around the country. Staff members on the International payroll were running statewide operations in Rhode Island, Iowa, Illinois, Colorado, Louisiana, and Massachusetts.[6]

There were enough reappearances of old Zander tactics to oblige Wurf's former COUR colleagues to leave Washington. Joe Ames, however, continued on as head of the pioneering Judicial Panel. When the panel ruled, in July 1977, that Wurf's administratorship over the Rhode Island Council had to be lifted, the first time in 12 years that he had been overruled, the AFSCME president lost all sense of responsible behavior. Wurf ordered headquarters staff and IEB members to isolate and harass Ames from that moment until he was hounded from the organization he had served for more than 25 years. Even Goulden's sympathetic study of Wurf's leadership concedes that this dispute with Ames "did cause many persons in AFSCME to take a hard look at Wurf's performance." At the same time, the International president pushed through the IEB a Judicial Panel Study Committee that insured subsequent repeal of the independence of this unique democratic experiment in American trade union history.[7]

In April 1978, Gotbaum learned that secret negotiations between Wurf, President William McGowan, and attorney-lobbyists James Featherstonhaugh and James Roemer, of upstate New York's Civil Service Employees Association (CSEA), had resulted in a merger. A cornerstone of this agreement was a kickback clause that meant a return of some $8 million of International dues to CSEA's treasury. Traditionally a company union, CSEA began resembling a labor organization during the Rockefeller years in Albany. A solidly Republican, conservative organization, the direction behind the McGowan presidency was supplied by its two powerful attorneys, Featherstonhaugh and Roemer.

Having lost a considerable portion of its membership to raids from upstate AFL–CIO unions, and in an endeavor to protect the remaining membership of more than 200,000, CSEA lawyers initiated negotiations with Wurf. By affiliating with AFSCME, upstate CSEA would theoretically gain the protection of the AFL–CIO constitution against jurisdictional raiding by affiliate organizations. For Wurf, merger with CSEA would offset organizing failures and losses elsewhere in the nation, and bring the inflated AFSCME membership to over 1 million. There was no commitment then, or subsequently, by CSEA attorneys to the historic trade union traditions or social welfare goals of AFSCME. It was simply, from their point of view, a marriage of convenience and protection.

LIFELINE TO THE PRESIDENCY

CSEA became the largest single bloc in AFSCME, with more than 20 percent of the vote at International conventions. If united, Gotbaum with DC 37, McEntee with Pennsylvania, and McGowan with upstate New York could become a trio of key political brokers within a stone's throw of a majority. With the help of an embittered David Trask in Hawaii and a sprinkling of votes elsewhere in the nation, the next president of AFSCME could be selected by them. In May, after conversations with McGowan and the lawyers of CSEA, Gotbaum concluded that he had their support in a race against Wurf. Shortly thereafter, he arranged to meet with Joe Ames and Gerald McEntee in Washington. Gotbaum explained the evolving situation, as he saw it, underscoring Wurf's increasingly negative impact. By the end of the evening, according to Ames and Gotbaum, McEntee agreed to support Gotbaum for the presidency in 1980, in return for which Gotbaum would step down in four years for the Pennsylvania leader. Gotbaum promised to rid AFSCME of Wurf's administratorships, revitalize the organization, and bring stable, democratic leadership to the union.[8]

DC 37's leader began to speak out publicly against Wurf. From activists across the country, Gotbaum learned that the International president was not intent on helping to coordinate and assist the work of councils and locals but rather was imposing his complete control from Washington headquarters. Not until well along into 1979, however, did Gotbaum begin an insurgent campaign by bringing Al Bilik into DC 37 headquarters; but it was too late. Bilik had considerable organizing talents, and he knew the union and members throughout the country. But he could not undo the negative impressions of Gotbaum's aloofness among IEB members, the divisiveness within the Council, or the tremendous power of Wurf.

Gotbaum's approach to his campaign contrasted sharply with the COUR insurgency on behalf of Wurf. One of the appeals of the original COUR battle had been that Wurf was the candidate of the "little guys" against powerful incumbents. However, significant structural changes had occurred since the 1964 challenge to Zander. Over the years, Wurf had created a very different organization, establishing sizable statewide Councils that were beholden to him. By 1979, not only was AFSCME much larger, but a few individual units could determine the outcome of an election. As a result, Gotbaum perceived his best chance for the presidency was to win support of a handful of units—CSEA, Pennsylvania, Hawaii, and, of course, DC 37—along with whatever local assistance he could muster around the country. For some who had been in the original COUR campaign, and a few close supporters, this strategy was viewed with dismay, but they remained silent. Despite the growing centralization of power in Washington, they continued to believe that Gotbaum should, at the very least, base his campaign on broader support, rather than depend on the big three.

At a strategy planning meeting, Gotbaum and key staff members agreed to raise funds to hire a campaign staff. Gotbaum asked the Council's political director, Norman Adler, to assist in the campaign. Adler believed that CSEA was in their camp, but as subsequent events demonstrated, he had badly misread McGowan and his powerful, opportunistic lawyers. Most important, however, he underestimated the dominance of the Wurf organization. The president knew every facet of the International's power structure. Bitter and angry that Gotbaum had dared to challenge his incumbency, he labored to undermine the insurgent's efforts in New York and to suppress dissidence wherever it appeared. Adler and the Council director had misjudged the awesomeness of the president's office and its boundless resources with which to threaten and buy off potential Gotbaum supporters.[9]

THE BUTLER AFFAIR

Within days of public noises about Gotbaum's possible candidacy, Wurf began calling on vice-presidents, councils, and locals across the country to endorse his reelection. In New York City, he jumped into the developing conflict between the Council leadership and the Local 420 president, James Butler, over the latter's unsubstantiated disposition of some union funds. Wurf found no difficulty whatsoever in allying himself with leader of the Hospitals local, despite the fact that he had bitterly denounced Butler in the past.

Since 1973, the auditing reports of the local indicated that Butler was not adhering to proper accounting procedures concerning the disposition of certain union funds, was not maintaining adequate records, or submitting monthly operating statements in accordance with the financial standards code of International AFSCME. Although alerted to these shortcomings by Roberts, and then by Gotbaum, Butler seemed unable to remedy the situation. When the auditor advised Roberts, in October 1978, that there was poorer adherence than usual to the code, with undocumented disbursements by Butler of at least $15,000 in one year alone, and responding to advice given her by close informants in the local, she pressured Gotbaum to meet again with the hospital leader and suggest that he resign.

Unfortunately, Gotbaum did not weigh carefully the wisdom or the possible motive of this recommendation, or project its ramifications at this strategic moment. Nor did he consult with other respected and knowledgeable local leaders who might have been more objective, in their appraisal of the situation, and wiser in their suggested tactics. Knowing Wurf as few others did, Gotbaum should have realized that if he were to respond to Robert's recommendation, and if Butler did not resign, the International president might take advantage of just such an opportunity to intervene on behalf of Butler to divide the Council and frustrate Gotbaum's insurgent candidacy. However, feeling that he had no alternative but to respect the advice of his closest associate, and listen to her claimed intelligence of the rank-and-file situation in her home base, Local 420, the Council director implemented her recommendation and soon found himself cornered.[10]

At first, a defensive, angered Butler seemed to accept the suggestion that he resign, but after consulting Lucy and Wurf in

Washington, he quickly altered his posture and initiated a type of civil war unfamiliar to the DC 37 leadership. Insisting that he was fighting for his union career, supported by his local's executive board, and sustained throughout by the fiscal resources of the International office, Butler resorted to destructive and debilitating warfare. The battle escalated, with lawsuits in the Federal and New York courts, and charges in the hallways and offices of hospitals and at union headquarters in New York and Washington. Innocent unionists, as well as involved participants, were soon drained by periodic guerrilla raiding activities by some of Butler's husky colleagues who disrupted delegates council meetings, and traumatized staff and Council members with physical abuse and threatening rhetoric in union offices. A hospital worker lost her sight in one eye during one of these skirmishes.

The months and years of legal actions, physical threats, confrontations, and disputed local elections that followed ruptured the Council and upset its leader. It was not unusual for Butler to address the executive director as "Massa Gotbaum," and portray him as a racist and a bigot. Despite a subsequent legal "settlement" between the warring parties, Wurf was strengthened by this internecine conflict. It also meant the loss of some 12,000 hospital votes for Gotbaum in the midst of his presidential campaign. Butler's ability to sustain his challenge to Gotbaum, with the financial and legal assistance of Wurf, and his continued hold on a majority of those of his members who came to vote at disputed local elections, destroyed Lillian Robert's base of power and shattered any expectations she might have had to succeed Gotbaum. It was only a matter of time before she would seek her future elsewhere.[11]

100 CHURCH STREET

As part of his campaign to destroy Gotbaum's candidacy, Wurf announced at the December 1978 meeting of the IEB that he had opened a special International office at 100 Church Street, in New York, near DC 37 headquarters. Contending that the Council's Education Department was in a state of continual flux as a result of Gotbaum's firing a succession of directors, he insisted that the International had to step in to help the Council and other AFSCME units in the metropolitan area. This intrusion into local jurisdictional affairs sparked a heated debate between Gotbaum and Wurf, while IEB members sat listening quietly.

This move enabled Wurf, through his "Church Street" appointees—Nat Lindenthal and Vince Scovazzo—to harass the New York leader on his home grounds, to sow seeds of discord, and to worsen existing tensions. Both Lindenthal and Scovazzo had been discharged previously from DC 37, purportedly for ineffective leadership, demeaning behavior, and personality conflicts with the Council's associate director. Embittered by their removal, they spent the next few years as Wurf's surrogates in a war of attrition against DC 37 and its leader. They encouraged disaffection from Gotbaum's presidential race, pressured Charles Hughes to challenge Al Diop for his seat on the IEB, and sought to defeat Gotbaum's allies through an opposition slate at Council elections in January 1981. Lindenthal sought to undermine the director through the executive board, the delegates council, and James Butler, until Gotbaum would be forced to resign. It was contemplated that Wurf could then influence the Council to install Lindenthal as the new executive director. These warring tactics from Church Street did not cease until Jerry Wurf died and Gerald McEntee succeeded him as president.[12]

WURF STOPS GOTBAUM

At the same time, Wurf carefully nurtured the presidential aspirations of a number of IEB vice-presidents, including McEntee, assuring them individually that he would not stand in the way of their succession upon his retirement from office. By September 1979, virtually every vice-president fell into Wurf's fold. And when McEntee succumbed to his pressure, the game was really over for Gotbaum.

The final blow came in late October 1979, at the upstate convention of the CSEA. Months earlier, President William McGowan and attorneys Featherstonhaugh and Roemer had pledged their huge voting bloc to Gotbaum's presidential candidacy, making it a credible venture. Despite a tremendously warm, boisterous welcome by the assembled convention delegates, and McGowan's introduction of Betsy Gotbaum as the wife of the next president of AFSCME, the two CSEA lawyers had made their private deal with

Wurf. Not only did they arrange for some $8 million of dues kick-backs from International AFSCME, but they made clear their abhorrence of Gotbaum's militance by dumping him unceremoniously, and without warning, shortly after his arrival. A bare majority of CSEA's leadership on its executive board dutifully voted to reject Gotbaum's nomination and shelved plans for an insurgent campaign in 1980.

At this point, Gotbaum should have withdrawn his candidacy. Without any organized support within AFSCME, his insurgency was stillborn. But he mistakenly believed that his continued presence as a potential candidate might act as a stabilizing factor and facilitate a compromise with Wurf. In the face of threatening regional hearings by the IEB Judicial Panel Study Committee, he sought assurance that the independence of this unique labor experiment would be preserved. He also hoped for some settlement of the Butler affair, to insure the continued affiliation of Local 420 with DC 37. But Wurf would not respond to peace overtures sent through McEntee.[13]

After weeks of rumors in Council headquarters, division directors Gary Foster and John Toto were dismissed in mid-November 1979. Gotbaum's rationale for the discharges included their personality clashes with Roberts, lack of trust in them because of their close relationship with Lindenthal at 100 Church Street, and because they allegedly served as conduits to Wurf. In addition, they had been publicly critical of Council leadership, which the executive director viewed as an act of disloyalty. Under extraordinary pressure from within the Council, and upset by the heavy handedness of Wurf, Gotbaum momentarily lost his coolness and usual good timing. Reportedly urged by Roberts that both division directors had to go, the action sent a wave of rumors through Council headquarters, and the executive director found himself defending his actions before the delegates council, a special headquarters staff meeting, and an executive board that sustained him by a divided vote. A hovering Wurf worsened the situation by immediately placing the dismissals on the agenda of an IEB meeting for debate and investigation. When they did not regain their Council positions, Wurf added Foster to his staff at 100 Church Street and Toto returned to the presidency of his local. These dismissals temporarily intensified internal hostilities and weakened Gotbaum.

Not until March 1980, when faced with an incipient revolt in support of the International president by Charles Hughes, did Gotbaum put a halt to further internal setbacks by officially taking himself out of the presidential race. Within days, he received a conciliatory phone call from Wurf. Although Gotbaum may have created his own setbacks through an ill-conceived political campaign, the bad timing of the Butler affair, and the dismissals of Toto and Foster, neither he nor DC 37 suffered any fatal wounds. In fact, he was about to secure one of his better collective bargaining agreements, and the Council would soon reward him with an uncontested reelection.[14]

In 1977, DC 37 achieved two major victories. Early in the year, the union won a long struggle to keep city employees in the social security system, ending the pullout threatened by Mayor Beame. Gotbaum had warned the mayor that such action would precipitate a strike, because social security was a ''basic, crucial, and irreplaceable benefit for city workers.'' If the move had gone through, half the city work force would have lost all social security benefits, since they did not have the 10 years' coverage required for eligibility.

One of the more remarkable legislative victories for public employee unions was achieved in Albany on the eve of adjournment in mid-July. After one of the longest and most chaotic sessions in history, and despite assurances by knowledgeable observers that the proposal didn't stand a chance, the agency shop bill passed. For almost seven months Norman Adler, delegations from Council locals, thousands of members in a letter-writing campaign, and representatives of the state's Public Employee Conference had been lobbying strenuously for its enactment. The Council's electoral alliance with key Democratic and Republican lawmakers paid off handsomely, assisted by a recent decision of the U.S. Supreme Court which ruled the agency shop constitutional. This long-time goal of DC 37 provided that nonmembers pay a fee, equivalent to dues, to officially recognized unions which represent them.

As for the city itself, there was the start of a recovery, for not only was the new budget for fiscal 1978 balanced but it provided for an increase in hiring and promotions. Additional Federal aid to the city amounting to $342 million enabled it to appoint 9,400 to CETA jobs, while sustaining a decrease of 2,940 employees through attrition. For the first time since the city was faced with bankruptcy, it veered away from the edge of the precipice.[15]

KOCH CONFRONTS COALITION BARGAINING

The renewal of contractual negotiations in 1978 was accompanied by some new developments. The collective bargaining process remained intact, although constrained by serious fiscal and economic conditions. For the duration of the crisis, however, the style of bargaining underwent an important change, shifting from the typical adversarial negotiations to a more "integrative" style. While under the strain of possible fiscal collapse, the unions displayed a more cooperative behavior and a problem-solving approach. It was not the win-or-lose pattern that had exemplified the process in more normal times.

The Carter administration made clear that it would not help New York until the state agreed to safeguard the city's financial arrangements, and the next round of collective bargaining was concluded. A new, irascible player entered the scene in the person of Mayor-elect Edward Koch. In the course of the mayoralty campaign of 1977, Koch had indicated new directions he hoped to pursue. Shifting away from a traditional, liberal reputation as a member of Congress, he warned that retrenchment and cutbacks had to be continued. Specifically, he called for across-the-board layoffs and the closing of select municipal hospitals. For the first time in recent history, a leading Democratic candidate in the city projected an anti-union image, promising that he would not duplicate Lindsay's "giveaways" to municipal labor. DC 37 maintained a neutral posture in the initial primary battle, but backed Mario Cuomo in the runoff with Edward Koch. Gotbaum found Koch's stance as "labor tough guy" distasteful, and his attacks on the public service workers and their pensions demeaning.

At a post-election seminar for newly elected mayors at Harvard University, lecturer Gotbaum urged the new crop of city executives, including Koch, to get to know their community's labor leaders, to keep lines of communication open, not to "drop bombs in the press" without first alerting union heads, and to stay away from the bargaining table during actual negotiations. Koch soon disregarded virtually all of these suggestions, which contributed to a series of confrontations. The new mayor deliberately nurtured an image as a "hard-liner" toward city employees, upsetting municipal labor leaders by his lack of sensitivity or appreciation of their efforts to secure the city's fiscal viability. Although disliked by organized labor, Koch's independence and confrontational style endeared him to the general public. His sharpness, verve, and quotable expressions won him access to the channels of communication. Responsive to public discontent, he voiced growing dissatisfaction with city services, even if it meant attacking his own bureaucracy. Public workers often served as the target, criticized as "underworked," "overpaid" and retiring with "big pensions." Koch skillfully converted angry protesters into amused listeners. With a sense of symbolic gesture, he cheered the public as he lashed out against the common foes—"the special interests," particularly labor unions.[16]

With the approach of another round of negotiations in 1978, the AFSCME director made a strong appeal to municipal labor leaders to join together in coalition bargaining. This new pattern differed from previous cooperative endeavors, which set the bargaining goals more explicitly. In coalition bargaining, the actual dimensions of setting wage scales and major benefits would be left to a few key negotiators led by Gotbaum. A second round or tier was provided that would allow for some organizational and local autonomy, but on less crucial, noneconomic issues. It was the DC 37 executive who pointed out to his municipal labor colleagues that the city was "being scrutinized by Washington, and the financial market will benefit tremendously if we can avoid the headlines and hassles that are usually involved when negotiations stretch out for month after month with each union bargaining separately."

Apparently Gotbaum was convincing, for all civilian as well as some uniformed employee unions joined the coalition bargaining. He was aided in his appeal by the continuing fiscal crisis, the relative stability of union relationships, and the codification of bargaining procedures that mandated formal union coordination through the MLC. Plagued by internal dissension, the patrolmen, the firefighters, and some other uniformed employee unions felt that they could do better on their own. In the end, they came out with the same basic results. The MLC was further strengthened by the decision of the United Federation of Teachers under Shanker to join the coalition. This meant that the MLC represented some 50 unions with over 200,000 city workers. While reluctant at first to deal with this group, the mayor eventually went along.

New York's newspapers strengthened Koch's resolve to put the public unions in their proper place. The *Daily News* advised Koch to "Hang Tough on Union Demands," while the *Post* trumpeted a survey purporting to show that New Yorkers wanted Koch to take a stand that "required no sacrifices on their part but placed the burden on city workers." It was clear that public opinion continued to run strong against city employees, and the mayor was determined to ride the crest of that wave to success in the forthcoming negotiations.[17] The city's fiscal condition, meanwhile, continued to be in a precarious state. Further aggravating negotiations was the renewed uncertainty of Federal and state input. Key senators like Proxmire of Wisconsin and Edward Brooke of Massachusetts persisted in opposing continuation of the seasonal loan programs. Both warned that the city and state would have to develop more imaginative approaches. The White House refused to help unless assured that the state, the labor unions and the city's financial community were making maximum efforts at cooperation.

KOCH DEMANDS SIXTY GIVEBACKS

Koch's new budget in 1978 had been made considerably more feasible by some tough decisions made during the Beame administration. With renewal of collective bargaining imminent, Koch instructed Deputy Mayor Basil Paterson to take charge of negotiations rather than the Office of Labor Relations, which he did not trust. The new mayor sought to insure control through his own appointee. Paterson was instructed to place on the table a list of some 60 giveback demands, among the most important of which were a termination of all current COLAS, and a halt to night-shift differentials, legal services, education funds, rest periods, and coffee breaks. Public employees were asked to return to a 40-hour workweek during the summer, to pay 50 percent of the cost of health and hospital coverage, and agree to end all restrictions on layoffs.

A shocked Feinstein retorted to Paterson, "The only demand you didn't make was for the elimination of the employees. If these demands are serious, then you are not serious about negotiating a contract." Koch's confrontational style was not unlike that of Lindsay's when the latter first assumed office, denouncing the "labor czars" and refusing to be their "captive." Announcing that the city was broke, and that no money was available for wage increases, Koch stood firm. Again and again, Paterson found himself mopping up after the mayor, whose aggressive style worsened difficulties around the negotiating table. Far more conciliatory in tone, Paterson tried to keep the rhetoric cool, but was constantly undercut by the mayor.

With the help of Jack Bigel, augmented by the work of the DC 37 staff and Murray Gordon, some $800 million of surplus cash was identified in the city's coffers. Coalition leaders felt that this sum could be applied to wage increases. While not overjoyed by the earlier transit settlement, which offered a bargaining pattern for other municipal workers, Gotbaum and his colleagues pushed the mayor for a similar accord. A temporary diversion delaying negotiations was repayment of the wage increases that had been voluntarily deferred in 1975. That agreement provided for payment of the postponed raises by the end of June 1978 if the city had regained financial stability. While both sides agreed that this condition had not yet been met, the unions contended that the increases had to be repaid when it was financially feasible, while Koch insisted that the raises had simply lapsed. After submitting the dispute to arbitration, three impartial members of the Board of Collective Bargaining held that the city's obligation continued. This was the first of a series of setbacks for the mayor.

The agreement reached provided for a 4 percent raise in pay for each of the two years of the contract, which constituted the first increase in four years. While Gotbaum viewed the contract as inadequate, since it did not keep up with inflation, he felt it was a turnaround from the no-cost contract of 1976 and givebacks by public employee unions. Not a single giveback demanded by the mayor was conceded. In retrospect, Council negotiator Viani felt the union had done fairly well and that "workers who were terribly upset, if not unnerved by events, the threats of lay-offs, and the serious erosion of their paychecks, appeared calmer, and the unrest lessened."

The results should have demonstrated to the mayor the limitations of his defiant, confrontationist strategy. Koch had not won a single giveback he had originally placed on the negotiating table, and he had to repudiate virtually every hard-nosed goal he had set for himself. Murray Kempton put it baldly when he concluded, "The mayor arrived at Victor Gotbaum's tent...to accept this compact with the municipal unions, bravely bearing aloft his own scalp." In light of what he wanted to achieve—to hold unions in check—the mayor had not succeeded. Nevertheless, his continuing media coverage and wide popularity still promoted the feeling that he was doing well.

Union leaders did not expect their members to be dancing in the streets, for they had settled for considerably less than what others in the private sector were getting. But in light of the fiscal crisis still plaguing the city, the municipal unions were at least emerging from negotiations with dignity and some gains. The era of no-cost agreements had come to an end. Ratification of the contract reached an all-time high for DC 37 when 93 percent voted in its favor.

After more than three months of additional bargaining, city and union negotiators reached agreement on a new citywide contract covering "noneconomic" matters. The welfare, education, and legal services funds were reorganized into a single benefits fund that would be the recipient of all contributions previously made separately by the city, permitting greater economy and flexibility in the disbursement of benefits.[18]

After much lobbying of Congress and the White House by Mayor Koch and MLC representatives for fiscal assistance, and shortly following the newly negotiated wage contract, Congress voted loan guarantees to the city. As President Carter signed this congressional enactment in front of New York's historic City Hall, he was surrounded by a prominent cast of beaming labor leaders and key Federal and city officials.

A LOSS WITH SOME GAINS

With the expiration date of the EFCB set for mid-1978, Gotbaum denounced the board, warning that labor would not tolerate its extension. "We accept our responsibilities," he insisted, "and we have no quarrel with an audit or review board, or a balanced budget. But we will not see this city anchored to a board that destroys the autonomy of the city." On this issue, however, he and his labor colleagues lost, for not only was the board's life extended, it reached into the twenty-first century, and "emergency" was dropped from its title. The board was given a more permanent role in city affairs. The amendments imposed a new criterion to which impasse panels had to accord substantial weight in rendering rewards in the future—the city's "financial ability... to pay the cost of any increase in wages or fringe benefits without requiring an increase in the level of city taxes...."

By the end of the year, the city's economy showed improvement, including an increase in the number of jobs for the first time in nine years. New York also experienced the lowest seasonal borrowing in 20 years. Coalition bargaining had also insured a cohesive labor group and a disciplined and accommodating work force. Over the four-year period of crisis, city employment had fallen as much as 24 percent, offset somewhat by CETA funds from Washington which helped create jobs in the parks and human services.

In the November 1978 elections, 113 of the 120 candidates endorsed by the union, led by Governor Hugh Carey and Lieutenant Governor-elect Mario Cuomo, swept to victory. Although supporting primarily liberal Democrats, the Council also played a vital role in the reelection of at least six Republican state senators—John Calandra and Christopher Mega won by less than 2,000-vote pluralities, while John Marchi beat out his Democratic opponent by just over 3,000 votes. Leaders in both major parties were aware that DC 37 political operations had developed into one of the most formidable political forces in the city. They knew that in three special elections in the Bronx, Council members had helped the victories of three independent candidates, setting back the vaunted political machine of Democratic boss Patrick Cunningham. In each of these contests, DC 37 threw in a hundred or more of its political activists, replacing many of the old Democratic clubhouse canvassers.[19]

By the end of 1978, Council members again supported the Gotbaum slate, for all of the top officers were reelected without opposition. Three long-time local leaders did not seek reelection as vice-presidents on the eve of their retirement from public service: Fannie Fine of Finance Employees Local 1113, Helen Smith of Health and Hospital Employees Local 768, and John Crumedy of Custodial Employees Local 1597. The three, representing different ethnic groups, personified the best of the early pioneers of DC 37. A different generation of leaders was about to step forward, with Gotbaum as the link between the old and the new.

THE NEXT ROUND, 1979-80

Mayor Koch continued to maintain his broad-based popularity. Despite the fact that citizens expressed growing dissatisfaction with deteriorating services, the blame did not fall on him. With consummate skill before public audiences and reporters, he distanced himself from serious problems in ways other mayors envied. "How am I doing?" became a classic phrase, often provoking laughter from the very people suffering discomforts. Unlike his predecessors, he kept an independent posture, refusing to court the city's public unions. Koch felt confident that his base was secure, built by his own appeal to the general public. He continued to confront municipal labor, particularly Gotbaum, with attacks on the city's hospital system, urging the closing of a number of its units.

Another source of ongoing irritation was the mayor's civil service reform package sent annually to Albany. In an attempt to expand his managerial prerogative, he asked for cutbacks in civil service workers; that managers be permitted to select, for appointment, one out of ten persons on the civil service list, instead of the limits of one in three; that citywide transfers be permitted without union or individual consent; that layoffs be based not only on seniority but on quality of performance; that the number of challenges to civil service examination questions be limited; and that 10 percent of the city's managers be selected without examination. Adding to his strained relations with Gotbaum, Koch continued to speak out against the agency shop and public unions.

By March the news had improved, with talk of a possible treasury surplus. Koch promised to rehire 4,000 CETA workers who were slated by Federal law to lose their jobs as well as 2,000 new employees. Saving some of the funds for the next round of negotiations, he hinted at a 2 percent hike in wages. The state's key negotiator, Felix Rohatyn, warned the city not to talk of a "surplus," since this would be misunderstood in light of the fact that New York still owed about half a billion dollars in payroll items in the capital budget. "The city," he admonished, "just has a little less of a deficit than was expected in terms of the world that we all live in." Further, in the next two years New York would have to get itself back into the financial markets, not only with short-term notes, but with "long-term financing on which it is going to have to get investment grade ratings." He warned of the possibility of another recession up the road, which, combined with inflation, offered little room for a "surplus." Finally, he was not optimistic about Federal help.

Rohatyn's predictions proved to be correct. The mayor had to change course when the Federal government not only refused additional support, but warned of plans to cut back counter-cyclical aid and CETA. The city was also directed to phase out any normal operating expenses from the capital budget within three years, instead of the ten allowed under state law. Again, pessimism and anxiety spread among city workers. Concerned with the vital need for Federal input, the labor coalition established its own lobbying office in Washington and collaborated with city lobbyists to pressure for more CETA money, oppose cuts in social security, and urge urban aid and continuance of Federal assistance.[20]

In the meantime, seeking to implement his campaign pledges to close down wasteful, unnecessary municipal hospitals, the mayor issued his "Plan for Improving the Effectiveness of Hospital Services in New York City." The cornerstone of this proposal was the closing of the huge Metropolitan Hospital in Hispanic East Harlem and Sydenham in Harlem proper, service reductions, and a $30 million decrease in the budget for hospitals.

For years, Lillian Roberts had been battling a succession of presidents of the HHC who sought to curtail or limit hospital services. When confronted with this latest and most serious threat, Roberts transferred part of her campaign to the streets and spurred unionists and community residents to action. Meanwhile, anger grew in the black community, which perceived Koch as insensitive and hostile.

A dedicated corps of Council members at most hospitals took their campaigns into the communities with marches, rallies, and lobbies of city council members and state legislators. This grassroots initiative generated the pressure to compel Koch's retreat. On May Day 1979, 10,000 unionists from across the labor spectrum and community activists circled City Hall to protest the mayor's plan. Responding to Harlem congressman Charles Rangel, the NAACP, and DC 37, Secretary Joseph Califano of Health, Education and Welfare ordered a federal investigation into possible civil rights violations in the city's proposals to shut down hospitals in ghetto districts. Shortly thereafter, city and state health officials agreed to keep Metropolitan Hospital open, while HHC president

Hoffman announced that the proposed $30 million in cuts had been reduced to $13 million, and the projected layoff of 1,000 hospital aides had been revoked. Not until a year later did the city finally abandon Sydenham. Again, the mayor was blocked by DC 37 and its community allies.

After months of fruitless endeavors, and finally recognizing that he would not be permitted to obtain in Albany what he could not achieve around the bargaining table, Koch formally withdrew his civil service reform package from consideration. Norman Adler hailed this as a "most successful" legislative session, despite highly organized opposition from conservative groups like the National Right to Work Committee and the School Boards Association.

Frustrated by this series of defeats, and by constant criticism and attacks from DC 37 headquarters, Koch finally blasted the Council's director. He insisted that Gotbaum used "the most vicious language and it's not right and I'm tired of taking it." He then denounced the state legislature for "knuckling under" to the municipal union leader.

Angry exchanges between the two continued uninterrupted, poisoning the environment for the 1980 negotiations. Talk of more layoffs exacerbated the situation, causing increased anxiety among civil servants. Worker frustration mounted as inflation ate away at their standards of living. In the five-year period since 1975, the Consumer Price Index had risen some 40 percent causing, according to union data, wage losses for Council members that ranged from 11 to 23 percent. *Business Week* insisted that, "This year's soaring inflation is causing major problems for cities across the country, and New York City may become the next casualty." The journal noted that labor's contract concessions, over the previous five years, had helped finance the city's "painfully slow rescue from bankruptcy."[21]

ACROSS BROOKLYN BRIDGE

When the mayor firmly turned down a set of union proposals, at a critical stage in transit negotiations, the TWU closed down the subway and bus systems for 11 days in April. What followed on television was a major coup for Koch. With thousands of city residents streaming across Brooklyn Bridge, commuting to and from work in a colorful assortment of dress, the mayor was seen on most television screens warmly greeting puffing citizens, urging them on like a cheerleader at a football game. "Never give in to intimidation," he shouted at them, "never give in to political or physical threats." When one passerby suggested that Koch halt these divisive remarks, the mayor called the critic a "wacko," a term he enjoyed using. Instead of facilitating sound labor relations, the mayor seemed to be spotlighting public workers as pariahs.

Immediately after the transit workers secured a new contract from the MTA, providing for a 9 percent increase the first year and 8 percent the second year, the mayor lashed out that it was "too much," warning that its equivalent for municipal workers would bankrupt the city. Koch insisted that "the city won the battle in the streets; the Metropolitan Transit Authority lost it at the bargaining table." MTA Chairman Richard Ravitch had betrayed him, the mayor insisted, for the contract was an "outrage."

Upon returning from the AFSCME international convention at Anaheim in June, where Wurf was reelected without opposition, Gotbaum set to work to avoid another destructive city strike. Bruce McIver, Koch's director of labor relations, recognized that Gotbaum was still in control of the coalition, and that he "was the one you had to move." After being alerted to the city's bottom line of the proposed wage settlement, Gotbaum urged its negotiators to proceed without delay, and alerted his labor colleagues as to the ultimate possibilities.

Although Koch had hoped to conclude contracts with the uniformed workers first, and then confront the Shanker–Feinstein–Gotbaum coalition with a tough posture, he found that serious dissensions among the police, firefighters, and other uniformed unions made that impossible. In sharp contrast was the comparative stability of DC 37 and the overall unifying leadership of Gotbaum within the MLC. Despite his deep personal dislike for the coalition leader, Koch found that he had nowhere else to turn. Fortunately, labor lawyer Edward Silver had been asked by the city to help McIver negotiate the 1980 contracts. Believing in informal, personal dialogue, Silver spent many hours in quiet discussion with Gotbaum, hammering out the terms of a settlement.

The coalition finally presented two alternatives as a final offer. The first called for a 9 percent salary increase the first year and 8 percent the second, with the equivalent of a 1 percent giveback. The other provided for an 8 and 8 percent increase, with no givebacks. Three hours later, after speaking with the mayor, McIver informed more than 100 sleepy members of the coalition's negotiating committee, "I'm accepting your proposal of 8 and 8 with no givebacks." Gotbaum had been advised by Viani and union economist Carol O'Cleireacain that the city could not afford more money.[22]

VICTORIES AT THE STATE HOUSE AND IN-HOUSE

Earlier that same month, after a four-year campaign by DC 37 that included lobbyists, busloads of Council members, and thousands of letters, both houses of the state legislature enacted a bill extending to all public employees in the state the standards of the Federal Occupational Safety and Health Act (OSHA). Its passage, which would have a constructive impact on working conditions throughout the state, was also facilitated by maturing relationship of DC 37 with Republican lawmakers and the endeavors of the Public Employees Conference. OSHA passed the Republican-controlled Senate at a time when the Federal program was under heavy attack from conservatives and management groups. New York became the first state in the nation to provide money for safety-related repairs.

Toward the end of 1980, following major successes at the negotiating table and in Albany, Gotbaum was reelected for another two-year term without opposition, and his slate won handsomely over the one proposed by Wurf's surrogates. In the race for treasurer, Arthur Tibaldi was reelected for a seventh term by an almost two-to-one vote over John Toto. For secretary, Elaine Espeut (Local 957) defeated Louise DeBow of Local 420 by a 20,000-vote margin. The tide was finally turning decisively against the International president, who had sought to destroy Gotbaum in New York. Cautious supporters became less cautious, the friendly ones more vocal, and the overwhelming numbers of local leaders merged ranks to stop Wurf. At about the same time, Richard Izzo and his supporters in Local 375, who had been hostile to the Gotbaum regime and sought to disaffiliate from DC 37, were overwhelmingly defeated by an insurgent rank-and-file slate headed by activist Louis Albano. Not long afterward, Joe Sperling and his allies were retired decisively by members of Local 371. Only James Butler and Local 420 continued to sound a discordant note within DC 37.[23]

It was during this period that a number of major changes occurred in the top management of the Council and its newspaper. In December 1980, associate director Ed Maher retired, and after 14 years as *PEP* editor, Bernie Stephens relinquished his post to his long-time associate, Walter Balcerak. In July 1981, after 16 years in the Council, Lillian Roberts accepted an appointment by Governor Carey as New York State industrial commissioner. She was the first black woman to hold such a high state post in New York. Soon after, the first general counsel and the founder-director of the MEL program, Julius Topol, retired.

Assigned to replace Roberts and Maher as acting associate director was youthful, tireless Stanley Hill, who had come up the ranks from caseworker to shop steward and president of Local 371. Appointed Council representative in 1972, he was promoted to assistant director and then director of the Clerical–Administrative Division. A new prince consort began to serve who was generally perceived as being easy-going and unifying. New to these imposing responsibilities, Hill, like his predecessors, had to earn the respect of city management and the confidence and admiration of the membership.

UPBEAT AND DOWNBEAT, 1981

An obstacle to the city's recovery was the 1980 recession. Surprisingly, however, the impact was not as severe as in previous years. An economic survey by Morgan Guaranty Trust found New York in comparatively good condition, which impressed municipal experts around the country "and confounded those critics who had written off the city as moribund." In February, the city successfully sold $75 million of long-term bonds, the first disposed of in the public market without the help of a state agency or a federal guarantee since the onset of the fiscal crisis. After having initially urged bankruptcy, the *Wall Street Journal* admitted that it had pursued the wrong policy. But the city had suffered severely. As a result of layoffs, resignations, and retirements between 1975 and 1980, the number of civil servants was reduced by some 65,000.

From 253,677 city employees, in 1975, there remained, five years later, 189,882. No service, not even the so-called "essentials," was left untouched.[24]

In Washington, the economic program that President Ronald Reagan steamrolled through Congress in early 1981 turned out to be a declaration of war against cities, working people, and the poor. It bristled with new spending for armaments, while slashing funds for social programs. Greeted by Republican lawmakers and much of the public as the solution to the nation's ills, many Democratic congressmen waved the flag of surrender and voted for the president's economic program. As unionists began to understand the meaning of the president's budget cuts, the first signs of a movement to fight back began to appear in some urban centers. In May, before several thousands in New York's Foley Square, Gotbaum lashed out at Reagan's economic policies. They had been tried in the 1920s and didn't work then, unless "Washington thinks that what this country needs is another depression." The nation soon got one.

At the DC 37 Leadership Conference in June, AFL–CIO secretary-treasurer Thomas Donohue gave the first hints of a national protest. Soon, preparations were under way for a Solidarity Day March in September, to protest the Reagan administration's attack on vital social programs, and to reaffirm grass-roots, rank-and-file support for social justice. In only six months Reagan had turned Congress into a rubber stamp, undermined social programs that took some 50 years to build, surrendered the battle against hunger and malnutrition, and announced the largest, most expensive peacetime military build-up in the nation's history. The AFL–CIO Solidarity Day turned out to be one of the largest demonstrations in U.S. labor history as some 400,000 unionists and others journeyed to Washington from all parts of the country. The largest contingent was some 20,000 DC 37 members.

A gaunt, sickly Wurf, showing visible signs of his battle against imminent death, wearily climbed the high podium to address the massed assemblage. With a voice that no longer carried his former deep bombastic blasts, he warned against over-optimism. In spite of the "monumental turnout" there was no guarantee that these endeavors against the Reagan administration would prove successful. As if summing up the decades of his own struggles as a labor leader, he reminded the rally that it was only the beginning of a long, difficult, frustrating process to turn the country around. In less than three months, Jerry Wurf was dead at the age of 62. Wurf and Gotbaum had once fought together to make AFSCME a representative, viable, and potent voice for social and economic progress. Their last joint endeavor was to merge forces against the Reagan administration on Solidarity Day.

SUMMARY

With the approach of contractual negotiations in 1978, municipal unions moved into a new, substantively different relationship through coalition bargaining. In this two-tier system, negotiations involving wages, pensions, and other economic considerations became highly centralized, and were carried on by the MLC under Gotbaum's leadership of a small coterie. A separate tier focused essentially on noneconomic issues, and was carried on by individual bargaining units. Although the movement toward coalition bargaining had actually begun in the late 1960s, when municipal unions sought to coordinate their activities, it was the fiscal crisis that energized this tendency and brought it to a new level of development.

Coalition bargaining enabled weaker unions to increase their leverage and to deliver to their members as much as was gained by the strongest ones. It reduced, for both the city and the unions, the uncertainty concerning pay parity relationships inherent in unit bargaining. For the city, coalition bargaining meant dealing with far fewer public employee organizations and units. City Hall was now able to negotiate with a more cohesive and disciplined work force which, through its leadership, was constrained in wage demands and requests for fringe benefits, for these union negotiators understood and appreciated the serious fiscal condition of the city. Finally, coalition bargaining helped put a halt to the escalation involved in normal, inter-union rivalry for better contracts.

While coalition bargaining secured material gains, it also invited less participation of individual unions, and of their membership, overall, in the making of crucial decisions. Whether the MLC affiliates will hold to this process in the future is open to conjecture. Despite abatement of the city's fiscal crisis, a threatening, more conservative climate has been sweeping the nation. Increasingly effective attacks on unions in private industry, on wage levels and health plans, and on social welfare gains made in the past half century have become a source of constant pressure on all levels of government, including the city. And these disturbing developments may force municipal employee organizations, who have already been through it in New York City, to keep the coalition process alive as a defensive measure. If so, the price may entail surrendering some of each union's autonomy and the limited participation within their ranks.

The city's fiscal crisis, the economic downturn of the nation, the general shift to the right, and the increasingly negative attitudes toward public workers and their contractual gains created a more pessimistic and constrained environment for DC 37 and its coalition partners. But the Council has made important economic and political strides, and its members continue to enjoy an expanding array of vital services. Elsewhere in the nation, union colleagues are not faring well.

Proud of his achievements in New York City, and confident in his ability to give national AFSCME a more imaginative and stabilizing leadership, Gotbaum believed he had an excellent opportunity to supplant the administration he had once helped create.

For much of the labor movement, the transition of power has rarely been resolved successfully, to insure, at the same time, the integrity of the challenge and the internal strength of the organization. Known for his insight and timing, Gotbaum sadly misjudged Wurf's determination and ability to frustrate his organizational ambitions. Wurf knew he was ill and that his time was short, and yet he used every power and resource of his office to block Gotbaum's aspirations. The membership was never canvassed, nor indeed considered, in this critical decision.

Gotbaum's determination to challenge Wurf involved errors in judgment and strategy that contributed to dissension within the Council. As a masterful tactician, Wurf devoted himself to exacerbating these tensions, facilitating turmoil, and undermining the DC 37 director in his own backyard. Church Street was a constant reminder that the International president would do anything to stop Gotbaum, even if it meant seriously weakening the Council. There were some local leaders, protected by the Council's autonomy, who were prepared to take advantage of these internal divisions. For a while there were ominous signs of dissension within the organization, but Gotbaum was soon able to reassert his influence, which was strengthened by newly elected officers in several traditionally independent locals. One of the tests of his continuing authority and leadership was demonstrated in the favorable contracts he delivered to members in 1978, and again in 1980, despite the determination of a new, aggressive mayor to clip the wings of Gotbaum and the municipal labor movement.

Despite his constant involvement with the fiscal emergency, Gotbaum pushed his political action operation into full gear at the state capitol. With the cooperation of Republican senate leader Warren Anderson, who was won over by the union's GOP strategy, the legislature and governor approved the agency shop. This enactment provided the union with additional funds and a stable source of income, enabling it to institute and maintain a highly professional level of services and projects. At the same time, Gotbaum recognized that, along with the rest of the nation, public employees were confronted with a new era in which raises of a size that would materially improve the living standards of union members no longer seemed possible. And so he turned to servicing members through new ways to improve their daily lives, by means of Council-sponsored medical, dental, mental health, and alcohol addiction plans, along with pioneering legal assistance.

Although there was a meanness in Wurf's strategy to prevent Gotbaum from becoming his successor, he unwittingly did DC 37 a great service. From the vantage point of New York City, Gotbaum continues to be in an excellent position to give imaginative and dynamic leadership to many facets of the labor movement. He heads not only one of the largest public service unions in the country, but is a pacesetter for others to emulate. And with its fabulous media network, New York City provides him with invaluable opportunities to disseminate his progressive ideas for social justice, peace, and equity among a wider and more diverse audience.

THE COUNCIL'S LEGACY

Philosophically, Gotbaum gave the Council an independent, progressive orientation on a wide range of issues. DC 37 has defended the rights of the poor and the aged, supported the ecological movement, and spoken out forcefully in the struggle for civil rights and human dignity. While a critic of Soviet communism and aggression, it has rejected the cold war strategy and supported detente and negotiation in building toward peaceful relations. It lent its name to liberation movements around the world, encouraged independence from colonial rule, furthered the development of individual rights and democratic institutions everywhere, advocated responsible control of the military buildup, and endorsed the nuclear freeze movement.

Although Gotbaum led the Council in the progressive tradition of Walter and Victor Reuther of the UAW, he always remembered that his diverse membership was not cohesive or united in its political or social outlook. How was he able, then, to bring about increasing support for his kind of reform unionism and social advocacy? Overall there appeared to emerge some carefully designed strategies. In the first place, he knew that he had to fulfill his major function as a union leader, which was to negotiate good contracts on the fundamental day-by-day concerns of the members. As he noted, on a number of occasions, "If a union leader doesn't bring bread and butter home to his people he can't bring about social ideology. A leader has to first and foremost protect his people."

Having achieved concrete, material gains, he moved on to the broader scene, dealing with issues of less immediate concern to members. Aware of the Council's wide range of philosophical and political viewpoints, he consistently supported the policy of local autonomy, which permitted each unit to pursue its own ideology. In contrast to social workers and librarians, who tended toward a more militant posture on social issues, the Technical Guild and blue-collar locals were far more conservative, while the hospital and clerical workers were warm adherents of his principles.

Gotbaum accepted the role of educator as a major responsibility. Union leaders, he insisted, had to educate their members, to inform them so that complex issues could be more readily understood and evaluated. At meetings, conferences, workshops, and in his PEP columns, he patiently explained the motives and reasoning behind his controversial stands. He sought to link personal and more narrow concerns of members to the larger scene of societal problems. He reminded members:

> We have to challenge the establishment not only when it fails
> to deliver for our members, but when it fails to deliver for the

community. The beating we took in the passage of the Rockefeller–Travia bill was spearheaded by the same forces who insist on maintaining an establishment that is completely oblivious not only to the needs of the labor movement, but to the needs of the lower-economic citizens of our community.

On other occasions, he urged unionists to become involved in environmental issues, warning that rotten ecology and rotten social problems "go hand-in-hand." A society unconcerned about the needs of its poorer citizens, which spent its riches on military hardware instead of eliminating hunger and poverty, could hardly concern itself with the nation's polluted environment. But, he insisted, "If you're serious you'll fight both problems or else the poor and the rich will go down the drain together."[25]

Both Wurf and Gotbaum helped build union power in New York City with their creative leadership and unbounded energy. They were extraordinary sons of immigrants who had a vision of an America in which workers of hand and brain would share its abundance, and all minorities its social justice. The union they and its members created in New York City was not only a monument to their dreams, but afforded reality to the hopes and aspirations of working men and women everywhere. The cultural diversity of the DC 37 membership sometimes created a delicate problem for its leaders, but it also provided a vital legacy for the city and the nation. It demonstrated that in the struggle for economic and social justice for all, diversity and imaginative, responsible leadership can be an effective partnership for achieving great dreams.

NOTES

1. U.S. Department of Labor, Bureau of Labor Statistics, *Handbook of Labor Statistics,* December 1980, Bulletin 2070, p. 412; *Business Week,* December 4, 1978, pp. 55–63; *Time,* November 16, 1981, pp. 124–125. The growth rate of public sector unions was illustrated by the fact that 33.6 percent of all local government employees were represented in bargaining units in 1976, as compared to some 25 percent of private sector employees.

2. Report of Victor Gotbaum to DC 37 group leaders meeting, December 10, 1980. Also, interviews with Gotbaum, May 11, 1981; and Felix Rohatyn, January 10, 1984.

3. Authors' notes, DC 37 group leaders meeting, April 10, 1981; *Time,* November 16, 1981, p. 124. The union's paying membership, which topped 106,000 in 1975, fell slightly to 101,000 by 1981. However, as a result of recent

state enactment of the agency shop, over 24,000 unaffiliated city employees were now paying fees, equivalent to union dues, for DC 37 services. This brought the official membership to over 125,000. Of the five major locals, the greatest advance was made by the Clericals (1549), jumping from some 24,000 to just under 30,000, including over 5,000 agency fee contributors.

4. Interview with Charles Hughes, March 15, 1984.

5. District Council 37 meeting minutes, November 22, 1966; *Public Employee Press*, October 31, 1969, p. 4; November 21, 1969, p. 4; interview with Sumner Rosen, September 22, 1981; Joseph C. Goulden, *Jerry Wurf: Labor's Last Angry Man.* New York Atheneum, 1982, p. 187.

6. Solomon Bendet, regional president, CSEA, to Victor Gotbaum, October 31, 1978; Bill Kemsley, Vermont State Relations Board, to Victor Gotbaum, December 26, 1978; Victor Gotbaum to Kemsley, March 5, 1979; James Hemphill, Arcadia, Louisiana, to Victor Gotbaum, June 15, 1979; interviews with Bert Rose, September 16, 1981; Joe Ames, October 26, 1981 and January 13, 1984; Al Bilik, November 30, 1981; Bertram Perkel, December 27, 1982; Al Diop, March 2, 1984. Also, Goulden, *Jerry Wurf*, pp. 227–230.

7. Joe Ames's memoranda of International executive staff meetings and of daily events at Washington headquarters, from May 21, 1977 to July 3, 1979. Also A. L. Zwerdling, general counsel of AFSCME, to Jerry Wurf, September 14, 1977; Jerry Wurf to Joe Ames, October 11, 14 and November 2, 1977; Ames to Wurf, October 13, 25, 27, 28 and November 3, 1977; Bill Hamilton, of AFSCME headquarters, to executive staff, all department heads, October 28, 1976; Lloyd J. Simpson, president/director of Council 77, to Wurf, October 31, 1977; Bill Hamilton to Ames, November 1, 1977; August 24, 28, 31 and September 20, 1978; Don Wasserman to Ames, October 31, 1977; Zwerdling to Ames, march 7, 1978; Larry Rubin, editor, *Public Employee*, to Marguerite Blanch, April 14, 1978; Ames to International secretary-treasurer William Lucy, September 14, 1978; Goulden, *Jerry Wurf*, pp. 275–280.

8. Interviews with Joe Ames, January 13, 1984; and Victor Gotbaum, December 27, 1980 and March 6, 1984. Fifty-one percent of all AFSCME members were located in New York, Pennsylvania, and Hawaii. Of the 965,000 paid-up AFSCME members in June 1979, CSEA and DC 37 represented virtually all of the 356,000 in New York, McEntee and his Council 13 encompassed 64,000 of the 82,000 in Pennsylvania, and David Trask's Local 152 contained 17,000 of the 31,000 members in Hawaii. If Gotbaum could rely on all of the votes in CSEA, DC 37, and Council 13 alone, he would start with a nucleus of 43 percent of AFSCME's membership. But he would require an additional 63,500 votes to attain 50 percent of the overall total.

9. *New York Times*, May 20, 1979, p. 52; Joe Mueller, Milwaukee, Wisconsin, to Victor Gotbaum, August 22, 1979; *Des Moines Sunday Register*, September 9, 1979; Al Bilik to Bernard Stephens, September 24, 1979; *Labor Notes*, October 23, 1979, p. 3; Tom Jennings to Al Bilik, November 20, 1979. Also, interview with Al Bilik, November 30, 1981.

10. Buchbinder, Stein and Co., Certified Public Accountants, to NYC Department of Hospital Employees, Local 420 of AFSCME, July 11, 1973; July 25, 1974; May 20, 1975; June 15, 1976. Harvey J. Nuland to Mitchell Craner, February 20, 1979. Interviews with Beverly Gross, November 30, 1982; Bertram Perkel, De-

cember 27, 1982; Joe Ames, January 13, 1984; James Butler, March 1, 1984; Victor Gotbaum, March 6, 1984; and Elisabeth Gotbaum, March 13, 1984.

11. William Lucy to James Butler, February 2, 1979; Kipnis and Karchmer, Certified Public Accountants, to the executive board, NYC Department of Hospital Employees, Local 420 of AFSCME, July 17 and August 31, 1979, containing detailed review of the disbursements report for Local 420; pending litigation involving DC 37, AFSCME, and/or Local 420, prepared by Sipser, Weinstock, Harper, Dorm and Liebowitz, legal firm for Local 420 in dispute with DC 37; personal observations of Bernard Bellush at meetings of DC 37 executive board, delegates council, and of Council representatives at a caucus meeting in Washington, D.C. Also, interviews with Murray Gordon, April 28, 1980; Beverly Gross, general counsel of DC 37, November 30, 1982; Bertram Perkel, legal consultant to DC 37, December 27, 1982; and James Butler, March 1, 1984. The authors have also examined extensive legal briefs related to this controversy.

12. Authors' notes of Victor Gotbaum's report to group leaders' meeting, December 20, 1978; Joseph T. Lynaugh to Victor Gotbaum, August 8, 1980; DC 37 delegates council minutes, October 29, 1980; "The Day of Decision is Here," opposition slate leaflet distributed at January 27, 1981 delegates council meeting. Also, interviews with Bernard Stephens and Walter Balcerak, December 20, 1978; John Toto, May 28, 1979; Edward Handman, November 18, 1980; Nat Lindenthal, April 2, 1982; Al Diop, March 2, 1984; Victor Gotbaum, March 6, 1984; and Charles Hughes, March 15, 1984.

13. Norman Adler to James Featherstonhaugh, February 1, 1979; undated memorandum to Gotbaum showing endorsement of Wurf by Gerald McEntee, David Trask and others, for a total of 18 of 21 vice-presidents, excluding the four from CSEA and DC 37. Also, interviews with Norman Adler, October 27, 1979; Victor Gotbaum, November 9, 1979 and March 6, 1984; Al Bilik, November 30, 1981; and Elisabeth Gotbaum, March 13, 1984.

14. Notes taken by author at group leaders meeting, November 21, 1979; at DC 37 staff meeting, November 21, 1979; and at delegates council meeting, November 27, 1979; Joseph A Yablonski, Washington lawyer for Toto and Foster, to Jerry Wurf and William Lucy, December 4, 1979; Lucy to Yablonski, December 5, 1979; Gotbaum to Wurf, December 6, 1979. Also, interviews with Al Bilik, December 19, 1979; Bertram Perkel, December 27, 1982; and Charles Hughes, March 15, 1984.

15. *Public Employee Press,* January 14, 1977, p. 3; January 28, 1977, p. 5; July 15, 1977, p. 3; August 26, 1977, p. 3.

16. Richard Walton and Robert McKersie, *A Behavioral Theory of Labor Negotiations,* New York: McGraw-Hill, 1965. See especially Chapters 1 and 10; *Public Employee Press,* September 16, 1977, p. 2; October 21, 1977, p. 3; December 9, 1977, p. 3; Edward Koch, *Mayor, An Autobiography,* New York: Simon and Schuster, 1984, Chapters 10 and 14.

17. Jack Bigel, "A Perspective on the Fiscal History of NYC FY 1976 Through FY 1979," pp. 49, 53–55; issued by Program Planners; David Lewin and Mary McCormick, "Coalition Bargaining in Municipal Government: New York City in the 1970s," research working paper no 327A, Graduate School of Business, Columbia University, May 1980," pp. 18–23; David Lewin, Raymond D. Horton, and James W. Kuhn, *Collective Bargaining and Manpower Utilization in Big City*

Governments, Montclair, NJ: Alanheld, Osmun 1979, Chapters 2 and 3; *Daily News*, December 30, 1977, p. 5; May 10, 1978, p. 24; *New York Post*, January 16, 1978; January 27, 1978, p. 3; February 10, 1978, p. 3.

18. *Public Employee Press*, March 10, 1978, p. 3; October 6, 1978, pp. 3,4; *New York Times*, June 6, 1978; p. 1; Murray Kempton, "To Victor Belong the Spoils," *New York Post*, June 6, 1978; p. 19. Arvid Anderson and Marjorie London, "Collective Bargaining and the Fiscal Crisis in New York City," *Fordham Urban Law Journal* 10, no. 3 (1981–82):380; Koch, *Mayor*, pp. 99–100, 101–103, 118, 122, 125. Also part of the noneconomic agreement was: the extension of combined confinement and infant care; retirees gained the right to change their health plans every two years; the disability benefit was raised from 50 to 66²/₃ percent, while the death benefit was increased from $3,000 to $5,000. Optical benefits were expanded, while those of the education fund and legal services were extended to include 20,000 additional public workers.

19. *Public Employee Press*, January 28, 1977, p. 3; March 25, 1977, p. 14; November 17, 1978, p. 8.

20. *New Yorker*, September 10, 1975, p. 55; Felix Rohatyn address, April 25, 1979, Annual Institute of New York City Council on Economic Education, Pace University.

21. *Public Employee Press*, June 24, 1979, p. 4; August 31, 1979, p. 3; September 14, 1979, p. 3; September 28, 1979, pp. 4, 5; September 19, 1980, p. 3; *Business Week*, March 31, 1980, p. 92; Koch, *Mayor*, pp. 206ff. The Legislature extended the agency shop for another two years; increased protection was afforded ambulance drivers and MVOs; indemnification was extended to many city employees who might be found liable for acts of negligence; full funding was provided the City University of New York upon takeover by the state, and CUNY's collective bargaining rights were now to be protected by the State Public Employment Relations Board; funds were made available to retain 200 instructors of addiction in the New York City schools; and salary increases were provided court employees throughout the state. Equally important were the bills that Adler was able to kill in committee.

22. *Public Employee Press*, April 25, 1980, pp. 2,3; June 27, 1980, p. 3; July 11, 1980, p. 3; Michael Oreskes, "To Victor Belongs the Spoils," *Daily News*, June 22, 1980, p. 5; The mayor kept a diary of these events and he tells it from his perspective in Koch, *Mayor*, pp. 169–205.

23. *Public Employee Press*, June 27, 1980, p. 5; July 11, 1980, p. 7. In addition, there was a long list of legislative victories including pension system improvements, establishing special medical review boards, increased financial incentives for school breakfasts, and improved outpatient reimbursement for the HHC. Adler, Richard Winsten, and their college interns were again able to kill Koch's civil service reform proposals and other hostile measures. Defeated on the Toto slate for reelection as council vice-presidents were Oscar Honig, Michael Gentile, who had served longer than any other incumbent, and Joan Reed.

24. Morgan Guaranty Trust, "An Economic Survey," Report 1981. An in-house document. See Charles Brecher and Raymond Horton, *Setting Municipal Priorities, 1980 and 1981*. Montclair, N.J.: Alanhead, Osmun 1980 and 1981.

25. *Public Employee Press*, June 21, 1967, p. 2; May 8, 1970, p. 7; Victor Gotbaum, xeroxed notes for a group of young people, March 12, 1974.

Appendix: Local Unions of DC 37

Local	154	N.Y.C. Miscellaneous Employees
Local	299	N.Y.C. Recreational Employees
Local	371	Social Services Employees Union
Local	372	N.Y.C. Board of Education Employees
Local	374	Quasi-Public Employees
Local	375	Civil Service Technical Guild
Local	376	N.Y.C. Laborers & Highway Repairers
Local	384	Board of Higher Education
Local	420	Hospital Employees
Local	436	United Federation of Nurses
Local	461	N.Y.C. Lifeguards
Local	508	N.Y.C. Lifeguard Supervisors
Local	768	Health & Hospital Employees
Local	924	N.Y.C. Laborers
Local	957	N.Y.C. Housing Authority Clerical Employees
Local	983	Motor Vehicle Operators
Local	1062	Supervisors of Automotive Plant & Equipment
Local	1070	Judicial Conference & County Employees
Local	1087	Prevailing Rate Employees
Local	1113	Finance Employees
Local	1157	Highway & Sewer Foremen
Local	1189	N.Y.C. Psychologists
Local	1212	Seasonal Employees
Local	1219	Real Estate Employees
Local	1251	Board of Education Clerical-Administrative Employees
Local	1306	Museum of Natural History
Local	1320	Sewage Treatment Workers & Seniors
Local	1321	Queensborough Public Library
Local	1322	Department of Water Resources
Local	1359	Rent & Rehabilitation Employees
Local	1407	N.Y.C. Accountants, Actuaries & Statisticians
Local	1414	Upstate Water Supply
Local	1455	N.Y.C. Traffic Employees
Local	1457	Youth House Employees
Local	1482	Brooklyn Public Library
Local	1501	Zoological Employees

Local 1502   Brooklyn Museum
Local 1503   Metropolitan Museum
Local 1505   N.Y.C. Attendants, Park Service Workers &
              Debris Removers
Local 1506   Parks Climbers & Pruners
Local 1507   N.Y.C. Gardeners
Local 1508   Uniformed Park Officers
Local 1549   Clerical-Administrative Employees
Local 1559   Museum of Natural History
Local 1597   N.Y.C. Custodial Employees
Local 1655   Transit Authority Employees
Local 1665   Museum of the City of New York
Local 1757   Real Property Assessment
Local 1759   Consumer Affairs
Local 1795   N.Y.C. Stationary Firemen
Local 1797   Custodial Foremen
Local 1930   New York Public Library
Local 1931   TBTA Maintainers
Local 2021   N.Y.C. Off-Track Betting Corporation
              Employees
Local 2054   N.Y.C. College Assistants
Local 2507   Emergency Medical Service Employees
Local 2627   Electronic Data Processing Employees
Local 2906   N.Y.C. Marine Workers

              Retirees Association of DC 37

Index

About the Authors

Jewel Bellush is emeritus professor of political science, Hunter College, City University of New York and was guest professor, University of Utrecht, The Netherlands, and Fulbright Professor, University of Haifa, Israel. She has served as associate staff director of California governor Edmund Brown's Commission on Metropolitan Area Problems, staff director of Mayor John D. Lindsay's New York City Commission on the Study of State-City Relations, and director of the Women's Center for Community Leadership at Hunter College. Besides numerous articles, she is coauthor of *Urban Renewal: People, Politics and Planning* and *Race and Politics in New York City*.

Bernard Bellush, a native New Yorker, is a product of its public schools and City College, of the City University of New York. After World War II, he returned to his alma mater as an involved faculty member and was an activist-officer with the American Veterans Commission, the Academic Freedom Committee of the American Civil Liberties Union, and Americans for Democratic Action. Twice Fulbright Professor of American History at the University of Utrecht, the Netherlands, he has lectured extensively, worked with labor unions and adult education, and written on Franklin D. Roosevelt, the New Deal, and John G. Winant. This work culminates 37 years of collaborative endeavors of this husband and wife duo of teachers, writers, and activists.